THE MAN WHO WOULD DAM THE AMAZON

THE MAN
WHO WOULD DAM
THE AMAZON

&

Other Accounts
from Afield

John G. Mitchell

University of Nebraska Press

Lincoln and London

Library of Congress Cataloging in Publication Data
Mitchell, John G.
The man who would dam the Amazon, and other
accounts from afield / John G. Mitchell.
p. cm.
"Ten of the twelve pieces gathered here first appeared
in Audubon . . . the other two, in Wilderness" – P.
Contents:
The man who would dam the Amazon – Traps –
The mountains, the miners, and Mister Caudill –
Brushpoppin' the Slickrock –
Alaska 1977: where have all the tuttu gone? –
Alaska 1987: legends from an Eskimo garden –
A man called Bird – One golden isle –
Refuges – The needle of the eye –
Back to the Beaverkill – Notes on COSP 118.
ISBN 0-8032-3147-4 (alk. paper)
1. Natural history – Outdoor books.
2. Nature study
3. Man – Influence on nature.
[1. Natural history.
2. Man – Influence on nature.]
I. Title.
QH81.M73   1990   333.7'2 – dc20
89-78517   CIP   AC

For Steven Ledyard,
The MitchCoop

CONTENTS

ACKNOWLEDGMENTS

The following pieces are reprinted courtesy of *Audubon* from the issues indicated:

"The Man Who Would Dam the Amazon," March 1979. Copyright © 1979 by John G. Mitchell.

"Traps," originally published as "Soft Skins and Sprung Steel," July 1982. Copyright © 1982 by John G. Mitchell.

"The Mountains, the Miners, and Mister Caudill," November 1988. Copyright © 1988 by John G. Mitchell.

"Where Have All the Tuttu Gone?" March 1977. Copyright © 1977 by John G. Mitchell.

"Legends from an Eskimo Garden," May 1988. Copyright © 1988 by John G. Mitchell.

"A Man Called Bird," March 1987. Copyright © 1987 by John G. Mitchell.

"One Golden Isle," originally published as "Cumberland, Floating Free," July 1984. Copyright © 1984 by John G. Mitchell.

"The Needle of the Eye," originally published as "Thirty Years on Ike's Autobahns," November 1986. Copyright © 1986 by John G. Mitchell.

The author gratefully acknowledges the considerable help of Kathleen Fitzpatrick, Jennifer Reek Gilliland, and Schellie Hagan of *Audubon* magazine; the enduring confidence of *Wilderness* editor T. H. Watkins; the daring imagination of *Audubon* editor Les Line.

NOTICE:

COLOR THEM GRAY

For one curious reason or another, the craft of journalism is regarded with a measure of contempt nowadays by those who presume to know where to draw the line between art and information. If the reader is so inclined, stop before it's too late. Turn back. Do not pass Go. I am a journalist. I write for magazines. Ten of the twelve pieces gathered here first appeared in *Audubon,* the magazine of the National Audubon Society; the other two, in *Wilderness,* the quarterly journal of the Wilderness Society. On the masthead of *Audubon,* I am listed as a field editor. A good, flat, open word, *field.* It covers a multitude of topics and sins. People unfamiliar with my work assume, because I write mostly for *Audubon,* that I must write about birds. Mostly I do not. There is "A Man Called Bird" in this book, but only a few critters with feathers on them. There are natural settings depicted here, but precious little that might qualify as nature writing. These accounts concern conflicts in the out-of-doors. There is some history, some travel, some biography, too. But for the most part what we have here are renderings of special places—the wilder, the better—where certain people have stirred things up in a big way.

Some of these pieces are on the long side—longer, at least, than you are likely to find in most periodicals of general interest (and in every last periodical of conservation interest but *Audubon* and *Wilderness*). The prevailing notion appears to be that readers of periodicals have short attention spans; therefore, those who write for the periodicals should suck in their cheeks. I have heard more than one editor opine that three thousand words is the outside limit beyond which journalists (and presumably their readers) fall off the edge of the earth. In view of the fact that it is virtually impossible to explore a special place literately in three thousand words or less and also explain how certain people have stirred things up, I am grateful to the editors of *Audubon* and *Wilderness* magazines for their tolerance of longer expeditions.

Of course, even some of my best friends have short attention spans, some of the time. I mean, for books, give them their *War and Peace* and a long vacation in the rocking chair. That's okay. But for magazines, give them captions and No-Doz. I just hope that folks who found some of these stories too long to be countenanced in a journal won't now find them too short to be tolerated in a book.

The pieces are spread over quite a lot of territory, topics, and time. They range from the upper Amazon to the Arctic Slope of Alaska, from brush popping in Utah to strip-mining in Kentucky and trout fishing in New York. The time frame in which they originally appeared spans a dozen years. Rather than attempting to update some of the senior accounts, I have left them pretty much as they were written. Besides, though some of the players in these pieces may have been replaced over the years, the plots, even after a decade, remain essentially the same. Human subsistence, for example, is still a highly controversial wildlife-management issue in Alaska, as it was in 1977. Nearly ten years after I wrote the story called "Traps," men and women still debate the manner in which furbearing animals are converted into coats. And about the only difference between Brazil's deforestation policies in the Amazon Basin in 1978 and now is that now they are unimaginably more sinister and destructive.

What many of these stories may have in common, I hope, is a sense of history. On the whole, environmental journalists have given short shrift to the past, possibly because so many of them are so busy reinventing the ecocatastrophes of the future. And yet the most important lesson of history seems to have been framed especially for those who care most about the natural world and the future of its resources. The economist Paul Taylor best articulated the lesson (and I will invoke his words again before we're finished here) when he asked: "Is it true that what we learn from history is that we learn nothing from history?"

Now, there's a question brooking no ambiguity whatsoever. It deserves a simple affirmative answer, and it shall get that in this book. But I hope you won't find any *other* simple answers in the book. Journalists are often forced into simple answers by the constraints of space and attention spans. And that is unfortunate because, apart from Taylor's question, I can't think of too many other ideas that deserve the quick-and-easy fix. If I have learned anything after thirty-five years of reporting and writing for newspapers and magazines, it is how to eschew the easy fix. The people you speak with—your subjects, your sources—almost always see things in black and white because black and white are the surest path to the easy fix. They presume to know where to draw the line between the two, and invariably they try to position themselves on the "right" side, whichever color that may happen to be. And what you must try to do, as a journalist, is to resist seeing things exactly as they see them, and then draw your line across the colors instead of between them. And by doing that, you will often discover that the truest color of all is gray. That, at least, has been my own experience and my conscious intent.

By the same token, I stake no claim to objectivity. Show me an objective journalist and I will show you a charlatan. Objectivity as a conceptual function exists only in the deluded minds of a few professors of journalism and some editors of certain newspapers-of-record. It is a myth. For a journalist to be truly objective in reporting a situation, he or she would have to compile every known fact and detail relevant to the subject and then lay it all out end-to-end, nonstop. Forget attention spans. Every last bit of the tale has to be there. Select out one fact, drop it to the cutting-room floor to make the piece fit or to stroke an attention span, and there goes your objectivity. But profess a particular bias, as I do, and there goes your objectivity truly.

My bias runs toward natural things. I try to make the grays I see favor them. I am favorably disposed toward rainforests, beavers, razorback ridges, slickrock canyons, tundra plains, barrier beaches, live oaks, and dead snags. And—without even a trace element of good faith, hope, or charity—I have nothing but the greatest measure of contempt for the bureaucrats and bottomliners who would spoil these things. At the same time, I have much admiration for a few of the players in these pieces who, at first glance from my own perspective, would appear to be positioned on the "wrong" side of the line. You will meet these people along the way, the trapper Giroux and the Eskimos, who would have their cake and eat it too—yes, and the man who would dam the Amazon. And I think you will get to like these people almost as much as I did. So long as you color them gray.

THE MAN

WHO WOULD DAM

THE AMAZON

A great cloud like an anvil rises over the llanos. It is cumulonimbus, streaked with gray across its base, dense and pearly on the vertical column, ice-white around its flat fibrous crown. Above the plains, the cloud appears as tall as the Cordillera Oriental of the Andes, two miles high and now some 200 miles behind us. We are airborne. Our course is to the southeast; our destination, the Amazon. It is Easter Sunday. With the cloud's permission, since it happens to be in our way, we shall arrive at the river while bells are ringing in the churches of Leticia. *Con su permiso, la nube grande.* With your permission, of course.

The cloud possibly first rose somewhere over the South Atlantic earlier in the week. Then, it would have been a young cloud made of molecules skimmed from the surface of the sea, drawn to the sky by the heat of the sun, fused in the cradle of the trade winds. Perhaps it drifted lazily past the Cabo de São Roque on Brazil's east coast, crossed that coast near the equator, then scudded west up the broad basin of the Amazon River. On its overland journey, the cloud grew taller and denser, for the river below it in places was not unlike a sea itself, the sun was hot, and vapors of water peeled easily from the flooded *varzea*, the riverine forest, at the edge of the passing cloud's shadow. And now, heavy with water, the anvil-cloud is already across the Colombian border on its way to the mountains, to be wrung with finality on the high green slopes where the rivers begin.

The plane is an ancient C-46, fitted for cargo. It is carrying potatoes and gasoline to Leticia. On the return flight to Bogotá, it will carry dried fish. The pilot is Colombian. In English, for my benefit, he identifies the tributary rivers over which we are flying. The Guaviare first, feeding to the Orinoco. The Vaupés and the Apaporis, feeding to the Amazon. And beyond the cloud, where llanos scrub rolls down into Amazon rainforest, the Caquetá, the churlish source of Robert Panero's obsession.

"This Panero," the pilot said earlier on the airstrip at Villavicencio. "He is Colombian?"

No, I replied, he is North American; which explained nothing, so I added, "Irish-Italian-New York, mostly, and in general a citizen of the world."

"And he wants to build dams?"

"Not exactly," I replied. "He wants Colombians and Brazilians to build dams. He is only the man with the idea."

"It is a good idea," said the pilot. "At least, better than most."

"There are those who would call it a bad idea."

The pilot turned his face to the sky. "Always it rains on the way to Leticia," he said, sadly. "I think it would be a good idea if this Panero of yours could build us a dam to hold back the clouds."

Nothing can hold back this cloud. It is too high to climb over, too wide to fly around. So we are going through it. The pilot draws himself close to the controls, wraps both hands tightly around the wheel. His knuckles are like pearls in the sunlight. Then the sunlight is gone. The C-46 enters the anvil at an altitude of 4,000 feet. In the edge of the cloud is a soft wan yellow twilight that fades in a second to colorless dusk. Rivulets of water stream suddenly across the cockpit windows. There is a leak in a seam above the control panel. Water rolls over the edge of the panel, finds a channel around the altimeter, and pools on the floor between the pilot's feet. In the pool I see a Robert Panero reservoir, miniformed.

It is easy enough to understand why we must fly through this cloud, but it is not easy to accept the reason when the cloud seems so determined to scramble our flying whole into its many parts. We must fly straight through to conserve fuel. Energy is precious. There must always be a little fuel in the tank for the unexpected turn of events. Clouds such as this have torn planes apart, yet planes such as this, flying off course to avoid air turbulence, have squandered their fuel-tank reserves and gone down in the forest. Given the nature of the country, search and rescue operations are mere formalities. Bush and cargo pilots therefore generally prefer to take their chances in the clouds, concluding, no doubt, that it is better to ascend into heaven after thirty seconds of thunderstruck falling than after thirty days of crazed wandering, alone and lost in the Amazon wilderness.

Heaven is deferred. With a final slap of wet air, the cloud expels us into sunlight. Ahead, the sky is filled with high cirrus and low cumulus and smaller thunderheads trailing rain veils across the roof of the forest. The forest is everywhere below us now. It is the greatest forest I have seen, the greatest I will ever see. We have somehow missed heaven and come instead to the green hell. Or have we missed the hell and come instead to the green heaven? It is beyond reckoning. We are more than 1,500 miles from the Atlantic. If this were North America and our position were somewhere in the sky over Kansas City, the forest below would cover everything from Louisiana to North Dakota and would stretch eastward to the Atlantic shore at Portland, Maine. A forest half the size of the contiguous United States. I'd call that heaven.

"This Panero," the pilot says later at the airstrip at Leticia. "How much do you know of him?"

I want to tell the pilot that I probably know as much or as little of Panero as he, the pilot, knows of the Amazon. But instead I only tell him that Panero is a remarkable man who believes that in damming the Amazon is the preservation of South America.

"And where would the big dam be?" the pilot asks.

"Near Santarém," I reply, "downstream from Manaus. It would create a reservoir more than twice the size of Lake Superior. And that's the biggest lake in the world."

"It is a good idea," the pilot says.

I explain that the reservoir would be visible from the moon.

"*Bueno*," says the pilot. "As it is, from the moon one can see only the oceans."

And I reply, since he is Colombian and it is Easter Sunday: "Yes, but the oceans were constructed by God."

The early Spanish called it *La Mar Dulce,* the freshwater sea, and it must have been a terrible thing to behold at flood through eyes accustomed to the parched gullies of Castile and Aragon. They had come to it from the west, over the mountains, bearing the flags of Gonzalo Pizarro. They were looking for gold in the kingdom of El Dorado, but they found only misery in the forest of the freshwater sea. Desperate for food, Pizarro dispatched his lieutenant, Francisco de Orellana, down the Coca River in a forest-built brigantine. "Be back in twelve days," said Pizarro. Orellana was not back in twelve days. The Coca was swollen. It carried the brig to the Napo, and the Napo carried it to the great central river flowing east to the saltwater sea. Months passed. It seemed to Orellana that the river might be without end. Along the way there was trouble with some of the savages who lived at the river's edge. In the jungle were strange women warriors, fierce and tall. Orellana called them the Amazons. It was a grave error on the Spaniard's part. If, having found his way at last to the Atlantic, Orellana had only kept quiet about these Amazons, it is likely the river today would bear his name.

By whatever name, it is a river of superlative proportions. It drains the entire heartland of a continent—2.5 million square miles embracing portions of Venezuela and Guyana; half of Brazil and Peru, two-thirds of Bolivia and Colombia, with a fair slice of Ecuador added to complete the basin's political catholicity. Measured from its mouth, the farthest source is the head of the Rio Apurímac at 17,000 feet in the southern Peruvian

Andes. The distance between is 4,000 miles. On its way to the sea, the river is joined by more than 1,000 tributaries, of which seventeen exceed 1,000 miles in length and at least two surpass the Mississippi in volume.

From the north flow the sand-laden Branco and the dark, humus-stained Negro; from the west, the Japurá, Putumayo, Napo, Tigre, Marañón, Ucayali, Juruá, Purus, and Madeira, all the color of cream-laced coffee, rich with the silt of the Andes; and from the south, the clear-watered Tapajós, Xingu, and To-cantins. The estuary is 200 miles wide. In its middle sits an island, Marajó, that is nearly as large as Switzerland. Into this estuary pours one-fifth of the entire planet's freshwater flow. Estimates vary, but generally fall into the range of six to seven million cubic feet per second at floodstage—or eight trillion gallons a day, more than twenty times the volume needed daily in the United States for industry, agriculture, and electrical power generation. The flow is sixty times greater than the Nile's, 350 times greater than the Hudson's. A hundred miles off Marajó, a sailor can dip a cup into the Atlantic and, drinking, taste no salt.

It is said that a fifth of the Amazon Basin at one time of year or another is underwater. Annual rainfall averages five to ten feet. More rain can fall on Leticia in a day than on Paris in a year. The rivers overrun their banks. They cut across their own oxbows. They flow sideways toward each other as well as forward toward the sea. A riverine village raised on stilts over mudflats in August can become a flotilla of shacks adrift on the river by March. Or the river can suddenly change its course, in which case the mud-flats revert to the forest. Subsistence crops of cassava, corn, beans, and bananas must be harvested in haste. From his frugal garden clearing beside the river, the native of Amazonia keeps one eye fixed on the level of the water while the other appraises the size and shape and drift of the pearl-columned clouds.

For a variety of reasons—including those having to do with climate, access, opportunity, and the cultural predilections of twentieth-century men and women—people in the Amazon Basin are relatively few. Like the volume of the river's flow, they do not lend themselves to easy and precise quantification; and if the numbers one hears from time to time seem to differ greatly, it is only because one census taker's geographic perception of the region is not often another's. In any event, the number I accept is seven million. To replicate such a density in the United States, one would have to depopulate the entire nation but for the residents of New York City and Philadelphia, then sprinkle those survivors lightly across the contiguous republic, from border to border and coast to coast. This is a human density lower even than that of the Sahara Desert. And it suits this tropical country. It suits the country especially since Amazonians are not sprinkled, but rather concentrated in such cities as Belém and Obidos and Manaus and Leticia and Iquitos, and in smaller towns and villages along the mainstream river and some of its tributaries.

Over the years, as best they could, the rivers tied the region together; and today they are still the main "highways" of Amazonia, however devoutly certain politicians and engineers in Brasília might wish to alter that reality with overland asphalt. Since the Emperor Dom Pedro II of Brazil opened the Amazon to international shipping more than a century ago, ocean-going vessels have plied the freshwater sea as far as Iquitos, Peru, 2,300 miles inland. Yet commerce has not always been brisk. The only significant boom occurred at the turn of the century, in the export of rubber. It put Manaus on the map. Unfortunately for the boosters of that city and for the economic development of Brazil, the ships hauling Amazon rubber had already hauled seed stock of the Amazon rubber tree, which was soon found to sprout more profitably from the plantation soils of Southeast Asia. End of boom.

Still, brave men from the bows of their riverboats would scour the Amazon shores for a new El Dorado. There had to be *something* exploitable in this vast basin—and there was, but no one could see it. They could see only iron ore and tin and manganese and diamonds and coal and sulfur and beryl and rock salt and potassium. They could see only fish and bananas. They looked for petroleum but found little. And that was a pity, for the Amazon nations—and Brazil in particular—were beginning to rely most heavily on petroleum. They needed it not only to move their automobiles around the streets of São Paulo and Bogotá but also to automate their factories, air-condition their offices, and light their homes; and Brazil needed it to fuel the long-haul trucks that would soon be rattling over the Transamazonian highways—the ones paved with asphalt—to the frontier outposts in the forest at the river's edge. And because they always seemed to be looking for something else, neither prospector nor politician took special note of the passing clouds and the fallen rain roiling a thousand and one powerful rivers. They looked for the new El Dorado, and all the while it was slipping unseen under their keels.

There was a time when the big river flowed the other way. Or so it is said. The time was Paleozoic, a quarter-billion years ago. The place was Gondwanaland, and South America was only a part of it. Then, the Andes had not yet emerged. Yet there were mountains to the east, where today one beholds their eroded stumps in the Guyana and Brazilian highlands. The rain falling on those ancient heights streamed down to a central river, and the river flowed west to the Pacific Ocean. Epochs later, in Mesozoic times, Gondwanaland began to break apart. South America, drifting west, collided with the Pacific plate. The collision blocked the mouth of the river. The river turned into a landlocked sea, a sea no doubt so vast it would have been visible from the moon. Further tectonic heaving and shoving uplifted the Andes, so that presently the inland sea began to drain eastward to the Atlantic through a gap in the eroded highlands of Brazil. Thus, full reverse—and with it an Amazon River and forest that have remained virtually unchanged over the course of the past fifty million years. Nevertheless, some South Americans say of the Amazon that it is a place where God has not quite finished His work of creation. The statement implies a desire for improvement, a modification of perceived imperfections. Possibly some people are hoping for a dramatic event—a shifting of the earth, a closing of the gap in the highlands near Santarém, a return to the inland sea. But there is at least one individual who is extremely reluctant to leave such a great work to heaven. He is this North American, Robert Panero.

From beyond the Andes, Panero had come to the Caquetá River in a Martin A20 attack bomber fitted for reconnaissance, courtesy of the Colombian Air Force. The bomber was not quite as ancient as I was to find my Leticia-bound C-46, for the year then was 1964, and time had not yet retarded the plane's capacity to shed rain. Panero himself was in his prime. He was thirty-six. Though not a large man, he had the appearance of possessing a strength that might shed anything, the look of a good fast breakaway halfback. Later, the football connection would strike him in a different way. He would think of himself as a quarterback of ideas. He would think of his ideas for the Amazon, yielding scant yardage against the decision-makers; and, with a faint smile for the joke on himself, would say, "The trouble with playing quarterback is that sometimes you find yourself stuck with the ball, and no running backs, and no one downfield to throw it to."

Panero sat in the co-pilot's seat. The pilot was Colombian. Behind them sat Daniel Fernandez of the Inter-American Development Bank. Up front in the glass nose of the plane, in the bombardier's greenhouse, crouched William McGuigan of the Stanford Research Institute. McGuigan felt uneasy. The Martin A20 was flying low across the roof of the forest. McGuigan had every reason to believe that the pilot knew what he was doing, and every reason to suspect that the pilot would do it differently if only he would crouch with McGuigan for a moment in the nose of the plane. Then they were out of the treetops, and the pilot rolled the bomber into a sharp turn over the Caquetá.

They had come to the river to see where it might be dammed. It was Panero's idea. Panero was head of the economic development section at the Hudson Institute, the think tank operated by Herman Kahn in Croton-on-Hudson, New York. Kahn had told Panero: Go fix South America. And Panero was eager to try, for his heart was already south of the border, he loved to travel, and he liked flying low among treetops in small planes; or at least better than McGuigan liked it. At Croton, in the placid sanitorium-environment of the institute, amid green lawns and trim Tudor cottages, Panero was edgy and bored. He would sit at his desk insulated with maps and data sheets, dreaming of places where he had been or would be to test ideas against the topography of undeveloped country. In time—for Kahn or for himself as freelance entrepreneur—he would be to Angola (with ideas for a dam on the Congo), to the Mekong Delta (with ideas for development unacceptable to the U.S. military), to Corsica and Yucatán and Algeria and Sweden and the Caroline Islands (where his ideas for a supertanker port at Palau would raise the hackles of environmentalists who view Palau as an Eden). But now Panero's charter was to fix South America, and after consultations in Bogotá, he had decided to start with the Caquetá.

The river flows from the Andes more than 700 miles to its confluence with the Apaporis, which together roll as the Japurá to the Amazon at Tefé. The bomber came over the Caquetá about halfway between the mountains and the confluence, then followed it upstream. From the cockpit, Panero could see the marks of high water on the forest trees and guessed that the floodplain was as wide as ten kilometers in some places and wider yet in others. The Caquetá, in fact, was said to spill its waters on occasion into the Putumayo drainage a hundred miles to the south. It was not a good place for a dam. The plane flew on.

Presently, at a place called Araracuara, Panero noticed a change in the pattern of the water marks. The floodplain seemed to have narrowed, and the river itself was pinched to a mere fifty meters. He signaled the pilot to circle. On the second pass, Panero called to McGuigan over the intercom. "Here it is," he said. "Here's our leverage." And there it was—a low limestone ridge intercepting the river, a natural damsite one would never have noticed from a higher-flying plane or even from a boat. From high, variations in ground elevation are invisible to the eye under the thick forest canopy; and on the river, at boat level, one can hardly see into the forest for all the riverbank trees.

Topographical levers, Panero was to call what he had found at Araracuara on the Caquetá. Later he would fly in search of more of them on the Putumayo, the Napo, the Marañón, the Tigre, the Madre de Dios. He would fly to the main river at Santarém. Even now, in the bomber, he must have known that he would be spending much time at the level of the treetops, for suddenly he shouted to McGuigan on the intercom: "My God, what if every river in the whole damn basin has a narrows like this?"

We of the Sieve-46 have landed at Leticia. The tarmac, washed by rain a few minutes before our arrival, is steaming in the afternoon sun. I find shade against the wall of the airport terminal and watch the freight handlers unloading the plane. The barefoot ones are Indians; Tukunas, probably. They are short and sinewy, with arms like knotted vines; and their eyes, when they pass nearby, are of another time and another place.

Once, I suspect, before gasoline and potatoes, before Colombian airplanes and Brazilian trucks, the Tukuna eye beheld a different world in which everything had its place—the river and the floodplain, the jacarandas and the massaranduba tree, the bird-eating spider and the monkey-eating bird, the ocelot and anaconda, the piranha and pirarucu, the day and the night. Downstream in the country of the Tirio tribe, it was told that since each day begins where the river goes away, there is the source of all life; and where the day ends, in the mountains of the river's source, there is the land of darkness and the dead. How old the legend may be, no one can say. Perhaps it was first told in the forest after Orellana's conquistadors appeared from the West in their rusting armor. And perhaps it is still being told, for blue-eyed scouts still come over the Andes searching for El Dorado—even if El Dorado is only an idea, or a river pinched by a limestone ridge.

Robert Panero's idea keeps growing. It is like a tadpole in the process of succession from larva to frog. At each stage of development something new is added. The appendages change configuration, the body swells. But the essential blood and guts of the creature remain the same. The blood is the river, flowing, and the guts are a series of low earthen dams.

The first stage of the idea surfaced in 1965 in a fifteen-page report by Panero and Herman Kahn. They called it "New Focus on the Amazon," but it carried only a hint of how that focus might be sharpened in later reports. The document referred to Panero's discovery of the narrows on the Caquetá. It suggested similar opportunities on other tributaries. It spoke of the development of the Amazon Basin as a "unifying factor" on which several Latin American countries might focus their "attention, enthusiasm, and hope." It advocated the application of "sidewise" technology (the technocrat's answer to the "less-is-more" principle), as in the use of inexpensive shaped-charge explosives rather than imported bulldozers for jungle clearing and tree removal. And finally it suggested, in the barest outline, an opportunity to create a vast inland waterway network linking Brazil with Venezuela and the Andean nations. This would be accomplished through "elimination of natural barriers" to navigation on some tributaries of the Amazon, or by design of "new generations of river craft which would be able to surmount natural obstacles in an efficient and economic manner." Brazilian automobiles, the authors postulated could then be sold in Colombia in return for Colombian coal. Moreover, "if by some economical combination of man-made lakes, river diversion projects, and/or control of the Amazonian sources, the flood stage of the main stem of the Amazon could be significantly reduced, hundreds of thousands of square miles of dewatered, heavily silted, new land would become available [for colonization] where now only leached, lateritic soils exist above the current flood stage."

The second stage of the idea surfaced in 1967. Bearing the imprimatur of the Hudson Institute, it was entitled "A South American 'Great Lakes' System," and Robert Panero was listed as sole author. Now, instead of a vaguely defined waterway, the new scenario called for something resembling "the U.S.–Canadian Great Lakes system and the St. Lawrence Seaway." With simple earth dams raised ten to thirty meters above mean river elevation, the geography of the interior of the continent would be changed, wrote Panero, "in a most dramatic way." The Orinoco would be connected to the Amazon, and the Amazon would be connected to the Paraguay. A dam at Araracuara, on the Caquetá, would form a lake stretching 200 miles to the foot-hills of the Andes. A similar dam on the Ucayali in Peru, at the narrows near Orellana, would flood an area even larger. To make the Orinoco-Amazon connection, Panero would bypass the Casiquiare—the fabled natural "canal" between those rivers, traced by the German explorer, Baron Alexander von Humboldt—and instead, with dams on the Orinoco and the Negro, flood the Pimichin Basin "where an overland trail, presumably used by smugglers, has existed for centuries at a level considerably lower than the Casiquiare-Orinoco junction." To make the connection to the Paraguay River—which flows south between Bolivia and Brazil and through Paraguay to the Paraná, which flows to Buenos Aires—Panero would dam the Guaporé-Mamoré system (tributary to the Madeira) and force its waters backward to the Paraguay, thereby creating a lake to facilitate trade between landlocked Bolivia and seaboard Argentina. And for the Amazon proper, there would be the greatest of lakes, a two-fold Superior rising behind a thirty-meter dam at Monte Alegre, near Santarém. The lake would stretch 500 miles upstream, beyond Manaus, almost to Tefé, flooding an area one-third the size of France. Downstream, it would dewater 40,000 square miles of potentially "fertile" land. And alone among all things artifacted by human design, this greatest of lakes, this born-again Amazon sea, would be visible from the moon. From the moon, it would look like a bird with a large head and a sad eye—the eye being an island of Puerto Rican proportions.

"Amazon Dams," the third stage, emerged from Panero's desk at the Hudson Institute the following year, 1968. He was selling hard now, pushing for his lakes and the big dam near Santarém. He said they would have the effect of "pulling the continent together from the inside." But there were no buyers, inside or out, and some of his critics were getting strident.

Among other things, the theoretical costs of the project had been rising. A kind of conceptual inflation was at work. What was to have cost $250 million in 1967, for the main dam, was now $800 million, with another $50 million tossed in for the locks. Still, as Panero pointed out, "damming 20 percent of the total world's river flow at a single site is unique. Whatever dams do, this one should do more of." It could be, he said, "the biggest bang-for-a-buck dam in the world."

He would build it where the river has two branches—or, rather, an island in the middle. Construction would begin on the island and the low ground on either bank. The work would be "in the dry" and would proceed in the dry for all but six to seven miles of the dam's entire forty-mile length. Then, for the wet, each branch would be diverted by canal, so that that work also could proceed in the dry.

The big bang would come from the benefits. Manaus, partially surrounded by mudflats in the dry season, would now have an effective year-round deepwater harbor, though Obidos would need levees, like Baton Rouge. Navigation would be possible on a twenty-four-hour basis. Sediments would deposit uniformly in the shallows, and new land for farming would slowly be built along the shore of the inland sea. Though portions of this sea would not be usable because of protruding treetops, it might be possible to launch floating timber dredges to exploit the industrial potential of billions of board feet of drowned wood.

In his discussion paper, Panero looked upon these things and saw that they were good; but none was quite so good as the prospect of producing hydroelectric power. The Amazon dam would be the largest and cheapest source of such power in the world. With a powerplant of 60-to-80-million-kilowatt capacity, installed, and taking full advantage of the river's flow, one could achieve an annual generating capacity of 500 to 700 billion kilowatt-hours—more than fifty times the capacity of Egypt's mighty Aswan Dam on the river Nile. "In effect," wrote Panero, "this production level is the equivalent of about one-third of the total [hydroelectric] power generated in the United States."

The cost of such a powerplant, he noted, might run as high as $6.5 billion; yet reduced to a kilowatt-hour, the cost would factor out at only one-quarter of the investment associated with conventional hydroelectric projects elsewhere in South America. Moreover, inasmuch as the full capacity would not be needed at once, "as demand developed, turbines could be installed one by one over a twenty-to-thirty-year period." And reverting to sidewise technology, Panero further suggested that in lieu of installing classical North American or Russian turbines, "some version of waterwheels would suffice to produce a great deal of electricity and not require any foreign exchange." In fact, a similar sidewise solution might be applied to the other proposed lakes of Amazonia. There had been four such lakes mentioned in the 1967 report. Now Panero was referring to forty.

The distractions were growing as well. In Brazil, the earlier drafts had raised some official eyebrows, and the press, for the most part, was hostile. The Hudson Institute, it was speculated, was a front for the Central Intelligence Agency. Panero was a spy. His associates, flying around in Brazilian treetops, were collaborators in a sinister plot to internationalize the Amazon for imperialistic purposes. One had only to read of the summer riots in twenty North American cities to guess what Panero was *really* promoting: resettlement in the Amazon of millions of dissident U.S. blacks. Either that, or worse; for it also was said that Panero's mission was to develop the Amazon *pronto* as a place of refuge for survivors of the inevitable thermonuclear exchange between gringos and Soviets. So it was said.

Panero could laugh at some of the newspaper charges, but not at the international engineering and banking communities, which continued to ignore him. He could shrug off the reaction of Brazil's minister of the interior, who thought that Panero was crazy. But he could not shrug off Brazil's growing determination to favor highways over rivers in developing its last great frontier. "The highway," wrote Panero, "is a western transport solution and is not the answer in South America, at least in the interior." He warned that roads across floodplains would be washed out (and indeed, they would be).

At least one of Panero's colleagues at the Hudson Institute urged him to back off a little. "Stop scaring everybody," said Basil Candela, the systems analyst. "Don't get the Brazilians mad at you. Don't fight their road system. Complement it."

But Panero would not back off. He was fighting for yardage,

and he was angry—or at least as angry as one can be in a discussion paper issued by the Hudson Institute. How could the Brazilians not see the wisdom of his logic? Could not the Amazon, with dams, finally resolve the problem of Brazil's "clear lack of a national purpose?" Or was it true, as General Charles DeGaulle of France had once said, that "Brazil is not a serious country"? He had talked of the Amazon to the bankers, yet the bankers had replied, "People and money go in, nothing comes out." He had talked to the young engineers, and they had replied, "You have to be crazy to leave Rio for Manaus."

Still, Panero pushed for yardage. And the idea kept growing.

On Wednesday of Holy Week everything stops at noon in Bogotá, and those who can, head for the country. Panero, on holiday, was heading for Altamira, the ranch he rents for such occasions from his friend Mario Laserna, the Colombian ambassador to France. The ranch is situated in the foothills of the Cordillera Central, near Ibagué. At Altamira there are great fields of rice, a fine herd of Brahman cattle, fighting bulls, and a white horse named Vandeval, which means windstorm in English. Panero was now going to Altamira to ride Vandeval across the fields and spend a few days away from the telephone. And he was going there also to think about the Amazon.

Panero sat in the front seat of the car beside his wife, Victoria, who was driving. She is Colombian. They married in Paris in 1956. They have four children and two homes: a mountainside house overlooking Bogotá and an apartment in New York. Panero is in neither place much of the time. Bellhops and engineers in Tokyo, Paris, Stockholm, and Algiers have seen more of Robert Panero in a year than have most of his kith and kin in the Western Hemisphere. It is the occupational hazard of the business of selling ideas.

The road to Altamira took us through the southwestern *barrio* of Bogotá, a place of housing projects and slums. I was struck by the number of children. They seemed to be everywhere—in doorways and windows, in the street, in the littered lots between the hovels. Victoria Panero said, "There are twenty-five million people in this country, and half of them are under fifteen." Her husband watched the children from the window of the car and said, "There are one hundred and twenty million people in Brazil, and half of *them* are under fifteen. Unless things change, there will be nothing for them to do when they grow up."

Almost always, there had been something for Robert Panero to do—an occupational hazard of being North American and son of the successful Guy B. Panero, international consulting engineer. One thing he could do as a boy was to watch the steel girders rising over Rockefeller Center. Guy Panero engineered much of that, then went to Europe on other jobs with Robert in tow. Later, there was work for the father in Ohio and Tennessee, and high school for the son at the Kentucky Military Institute. As for college, Panero allows that he was "more or less kicked out" of every one he attended, including Harvard and Columbia. "I never did get a degree," he says. As if it mattered.

After a hitch in the army, engineering the nation's first nerve-gas manufacturing plant in Maryland, Panero went to work on projects in Detroit and Paris, married Victoria, and became acquainted, separately, with South America and Herman Kahn, who was then with the Rand Corporation. Kahn liked Panero's way with ideas and assigned him to help with a Rand design concept for an underground air-defense control center at Colorado's Cheyenne Mountain. Panero's solution was to disperse the center throughout a number of simple tunnels. It was clearly an application of sidewise technology, and the Air Force rejected it, opting instead for what Panero would later describe as "a monument calculated to impress the Daughters of the American Revolution." Panero did not care much for monuments. Yet that was what every client seemed to want. On one of the last projects with his father, before joining Kahn full time at the Hudson Institute, Panero was obliged to implement the engineering details of a Walter Gropius design for the new University of Baghdad. "They weren't building a university," he would recall on the way to Altamira. "They were building a monument. For the architect's fee, they could have put up Quonset huts and accommodated 10,000 more students."

It was a three-hour drive to Altamira that afternoon. We arrived at dusk. The ranch house sits on a hill overlooking the rice fields in one direction and a deep gorge of the Coello River in the other. Helen Panero, the oldest daughter, was riding with friends from the university of Bogotá. They had taken the horses into the gorge to swim in the river. The distance was not great; only the descent, about 700 vertical feet. To ascend the steep trail on horseback in the darkness would be folly. Panero and I stood for a moment behind the ranch house, looking down at the faint white ribbon of the Coello's rapids. We did not know then that Helen had decided, wisely, to ride out by a longer and safer route. "It's a helluva good place to swim," said Panero. "But getting down to it, and getting up from it, can kill you." Suddenly he leaned toward the abyss. In the half-light, it occurred to me that he was searching the slope not so much for the overdue riders as for something that his eyes only might discern. I had to stop myself from asking if what he was looking for might be the solution to the problem, a topographical lever, perhaps, to clobber convenience from the derelictions of that unfriendly gorge.

"The first element of progress," Panero was saying, "is that you don't give up what you already have." He had risen early at Altamira to drink his Colombian coffee while the sunrise colored the hills across the river; and now, before riding, he was telling me how all of South America is divided into three parts. And how, given a South American tendency to ignore the distinctions, progress would keep falling heavily between the cracks. It was, he said, a simple "c-a-t spells cat" briefing, and it would help me to understand better his plan for damming the greatest river system in the world.

According to Panero, within each nation of South America (and most of Africa and Asia as well) are three distinct "countries." There is A-Country, which is urban and twentieth-century. There is B-Country, which is rural and seventeenth-century-modernized. And there is C-Country, the unexploited frontier. In Colombian terms, A-Country is Bogotá; B-Country is Altamira, though somewhat on the plus side, and C-Country is—since there are few other towns to speak of in the Colombian Amazon—the wild outliers of Leticia. The dominant class struggle in A-Country is the technician versus the politician; in B-Country, the landowner versus the peasant, and in C-Country, the soldier versus the fugitive and the bush pilot versus the clouds. There is little difference between the A-Country of Colombia and those of its neighboring nations. Bogotá can hear clearly what Caracas has to say, and Quito listens to Lima. The B-countries have their own wavelengths as well. But neither Bogotá nor Altamira can tune in the drumbeat from Colombia's Amazon frontier. It is a country apart.

According to Panero, most politicians and investors attempt to promote development by concentrating their efforts in A- or B-Country. For the A-Country there are housing projects which, in the process of becoming new slums, attract the disaffected B-Country peasants to the cities, where their misery is only enlarged. For the B-Country there is agrarian reform, the unskilled management of which often results in a loss of productivity and a shortage of food for the A-Country. Then along comes a person such as Panero, saying, "Let us go instead to the C-Country and see what can be done there." But the bankers reply that C-Country has no "infrastructure," few exploitable resources (otherwise, would they not have been exploited?), hardly any population, and a notorious capacity for scuttling the best laid plans in highly visible and costly ways.

"All right," Panero said, as if I were the banker. "But three-quarters of South America is C-Country. And half of that is in the Amazon Basin. It's a clean slate. You start from scratch. There are no vested interests to upset. There is no local opposition." A large map of South America was spread out on a table between us. Along the coasts of the continent, the cities of A-Country were shown in black. Broad belts of gray ran between and away from them. Gray was for B-Country. As he talked, his hands moved back and forth quickly over the map. Now both fell heavily on the Amazon. "The white on this map is empty," he said. "Why focus on reform by chopping the gray?" End of briefing.

We rode later that morning across the fields of Altamira, this *caballero* Panero astride the cow pony Vandeval, storming the wind. It seemed a dry sort of country, though rice grows surprisingly well with hillside springs yielding water for the crop. From the springs, the water is diverted to shallow canals, and from canals into ditches. The flow of the water is controlled by weirs. Some are as large as a bed board, some as small as a book. They are made of wood, and by hand. By peasant hand, they are opened or closed depending on the needs of the fields. "This is B-Country," Panero said as we rested the horses. "And this is a Sumerian solution to the problem of growing rice where it never grew before. After all, why not? It works."

"Listen," I said. "Since you are going to fix up all that C-Country with dams like these weirs, wouldn't it be nice to know there is also a D-Country, a place to be left alone?"

"But there *is* a D-Country," said Panero. "It is the sea, and I'm saving that for my old age."

One wonders what business Leticia has being here. Not for myself, since I am only a tourist, and a brief one at that. The C-46 is being loaded with fish for the flight back to Bogotá—leaving shortly, the pilot says—and there is no other plane until Tuesday. I cannot wait until Tuesday, so I must go with the fish.

Leticia is an accident. One can guess as much from the maps. It is Colombia's fallen arch jammed between the right ear of Peru and the left shoulder of the state of Amazonas, Brazil. The accident happened like this. There was trouble on the border. In the 1930s there was always trouble on the border. Colombia did not want to lose its foothold on the Amazon. So it sent in the colonists, the brave ones who would keep the flag waving over the marketplace. They tried raising cattle, but the cattle died, and the brave ones ate fish. They tried growing crops, but the soil played out, and the brave ones ate bananas. Only one thing saved Leticia, as a community, from going the way of its cattle and crops; and saves it yet. The airplane. The boat and the barge help a little. The barge brings oil. The barge, chugging more than 2,000 miles upstream against the powerful current of the river, delivers oil to light the incandescent lamps of Leticia. The oil is from Algeria. After a month at sea and going upriver, a bargeload of oil delivered at dockside is about as full of energy as a minute's flow of the Amazon River past Leticia, or an hour's flow of the Caquetá through the narrows of Araracuara.

The airplane brings potatoes and gasoline. But it is the saviour because it also brings tourists. Three, four times a week now, the gleaming jets of Avianca swoop into this little airport with their A-Country cargoes of Swedes and Germans and Arabs and Argentineans and Japanese and North Americans come to tread lightly at the edge of the wilderness; come to the Amazon Safari, the boat ride to Iquitos, the visit to Monkey Island, the Indian villages, the drink at the bar of the *Parador Ticuna*, the tall tales of the leather-faced guides, and at the end of each day, with a flick of the thumb at a wall switch, the sudden illumination of one's hotel room with Algerian oil as the silent river sweeps by, lighting nothing, on its way to the sea.

Leticia, good-bye. The C-46 is boarded, cleared for takeoff, and rising now on its tired rivets, making the turn over the river, north. The coffee color of the water reminds me of the river of my youth, the Ohio at Cincinnati. I wondered then why that water was not blue, and asking, was told by my father that the Ohio favored a duller hue because too many people in Pittsburgh, upstream, had toilets. Which is not the case here. At least, not yet.

I sit in a bucket seat on the port side of the plane. The fish, in sacks, are stacked starboard. There are other passengers: a young North American couple with backpacks, from Colorado; some Colombian students returning to school after holiday, and an Indian woman with an infant in her arms and a cheap parish rosary around her neck. When the plane hits a pocket of turbulent air over the river, the Indian woman takes one arm from the child, makes the sign of the cross, then presses to her lips the rosary's tinsel crucifix. The students smile, as if they know better.

Through the Plexiglas windows, I can see the forest of Brazil sliding under clouds toward the place where the river goes away.

According to Robert Panero, the Brazilians do not like his dams or his great lakes because they are strictly NIH, which in think-tank talk means Not Invented Here. One supposes it is a matter of pride. Given the country's size and its cultural heritage, Brazilians have every reason to be proud, except when it comes to inventing their own ideas for doing something about all that empty white space on the national map.

Fifty years ago there were no ideas for the Amazon. The great experiment in reviving rubber at Fordlandia had failed. There were only words. At Manaus in 1940, President Getulio Vargas declared: "To see Amazonia is the heart's desire of the youth of this country. To conquer the land, tame the waters, and subjugate the jungle, these have been our tasks. And in this centuries-old battle, we have won victory upon victory." The people of Manaus looked around them and saw mostly defeats. Not one in ten of the youth of the country would ever see the Amazon. But one in three would see the hardscrabble hills of Recife and Natal and Fortaleza in the drought-plagued northeast, where overcrowding would soon prevail despite the bumper crop of white crosses over the graves of infants who perish of disease or starvation in the first year of life.

Thirty-five years ago, the idea was Brasília, a new capital city in the interior (though not in the Amazon Basin), and SPVEA, the Superintendency for the Economic Evaluation of Amazonia. SPVEA was to have received three percent of the federal budget to get things cracking. But, as one contemporary Brazilian history explains it, "the truth is that SPVEA never received the funds allotted to it by constitutional law . . . Its first five-year plan, sent to Congress in 1955, was never approved." In 1958, construction began on a highway from Brasília to Belém. It was passable six years later. Thousands of pioneers staked claims along the highway, cleared the land, and planted crops. But for the most part, their pursuit of agriculture was a disaster. There was joy only in Brasília, for at last there seemed to be a way to lure some of the crowded poor of the northeast closer to the trough of the Amazon frontier.

And it seems like only yesteryear that an idea popped into the head of Emilio Médici, then president of Brazil. He had flown to the northeast to observe the ravages of the worst drought in thirty years. He was appalled. The northeast was a desert. Dust rose over the hardscrabble hills in clouds, and falling, it powdered the caskets of babies awaiting interment in hallowed ground. Médici promised he would find a solution. He brushed his hand across the empty white spaces on the national map. There would be a new program of regional integration. There would be a new highway from Cuiabá on the Mato Grosso to Santarém. There would be another highway, Transamazonica, running more than 3,500 miles from Recife and João Pessoa, on the coast, clear across the Amazon Basin to the village of Benjamin Constant, where the fallen arch of Colombia is jammed between Brazil and the ear of Peru. There would be resettlement. A half-million people, at government expense, would be moved from the wretched northeast to the wonderful Amazon. And the word went out through the hovels of Recife and Fortaleza: "To occupy is to integrate." Or so it was said.

The bulldozers moved into the forest, clearing a 200-foot swath for each road. There were more than two now, for Médici's hand had passed many times over the maps, and each pass decreed yet another highway—from Pôrto Velho to Boa Vista, from Macapá to Caracaraí, from Alto Parnaíba to Cachimbo. But the big push was along the Transamazonica, west toward Peru. There was no time for surveys or soil tests. Damn the mosquitoes and full speed ahead. Bridge the small rivers, ferry the large ones, and fill in the swamps. And stampede the Indians. Head 'em up and move 'em out, rawhide. Or kill them, though not officially. Unofficially, this was C-Country. Local opposition was not allowed. To occupy was to integrate. Had not the same been done a century before in North America? Surely there was much to be learned from that earlier crossing, yet somehow the Brazilians got the historical sequences turned around: Forgetting about the covered wagons, they thought that the railroads had come first, before the people. So the highways of northern Brazil came first, with sixty-mile zones on either side reserved for agricultural colonization. A Homestead Act for Amazonia. But no covered wagons.

Once upon a time in Brazil, there was another Altamira. It could be found at a certain bend of the Xingu River, about 150 miles southeast of Santarém. This Altamira offered a special view of Transamazonica, for here one could see not only the people coming to conquer the Amazon forest but also the ones who had already tried and were fleeing in defeat.

Once, this Altamira was the shining example of successful re-settlement. At its peak, in 1973, it could claim a population that had soared in little more than a year from 4,000 to nearly 20,000. It could boast of its housing, its schools, its 130 bars and luncheonettes. There was much conviviality after dark. But every night at the stroke of twelve the lights went out in Altamira. The bars closed. The revelers undressed for bed by candlelight. And the great diesel generators of the city's powerplant rested until dawn. Why? Because the trucks of the Transamazonica could not, in the press of such rapid growth, deliver enough fuel to keep the generators turning around the clock, even as the mighty Xingu nearby rolled on to the Amazon, turning nothing.

Yet it was not the midnight darkness of Altamira that dashed the city's spirits. It was the forest, and the clouds like mountains, bringing rain, and the soil that turned to hardpan after the second harvest. It was mud and insects and long humid days in ragged fields of failing crops. No one in advance had explained these things to the settlers from the arid northeast. No one had said, "Look, it is going to be very different in the Amazon." And no one had even remotely anticipated that by 1975 more than 10,000 of Altamira's finest citizens would be heading back over the Transamazonica toward the sere hills of their homeland. "Transmiseriana," one Brazilian scholar would call it. Yet the misery was not only with the people. It was also with the land that the people had cleared and left behind—a hundred, perhaps a thousand square miles shorn in a few years of all the natural equilibrium that had been building since the time when the rivers were born.

Though many of the settlers had fled east, still the builders of the various highways pushed west. In five years, they extended 1,000 miles of mostly rough road into 5,000. But there were problems. Progress on some roads, just for the clearing, was measured in increments of five miles a month. Supervisors no longer spoke optimistically of deadlines. Cost estimates doubled. Entire sections of highway washed away in the floods. Directions were changed. The final section of Transamazonica, originally traced from Humaitá to Benjamin Constant, was shifted south toward Cruzeiro do Sul to make use of a roadway already existing. Then, from Cruzeiro do Sul, the highway was to plunge 100 miles through the forest to the Peruvian border at Boqueirão da Esperanca. But work on this last leg was suddenly stopped. There were no explanations. Was it because the Peruvians were no longer working on their own connecting highway from Pucallpa? Perhaps; or possibly it was because the Brazilian engineers did not like the sound of their new destination. Boqueirão da Esperanca. The Abyss of Hope.

The fourth stage of the idea, "Some Aspects of the Amazon Basin," emerged in 1972. Now, the villain of the piece was no longer Brazil. It was the river. There had been bad flooding the previous year—flood crests fifteen feet higher than normal, villages destroyed and wildlife drowned. In Panero's view, the river was insanely out of control. It was in a state of "disequilibrium." It brought life but also took it away. It scrubbed the topsoil from the face of the continent and squandered it at sea. Now, the first objective of dams was not navigation, not was it the harnessing of energy (for the Arabs had not yet forced the Western Hemisphere to think much of energy). The first objective was flood control. Without control, Panero reasoned, the Amazon was a "major liability." But if the waters could somehow be tamed, the basin "would in all probability be the largest asset of its kind in the world."

Panero also saw a way to complement the Brazilian highways.

As he explained it: "Any one of these dams would be a usable bridge for vehicles. In fact, they would be cheaper than bridges constructed without any flood control provisions. Perhaps of more interest is the fact that roads protected from flood (by such dams) could traverse the floodplain below dams without danger or high cost and with some assurance of never being 'washed away.'"

And finally Panero saw that he must deal with the environmental implications of his plan in general and of the big dam on the Amazon in particular. "We have really done almost no work on the ecological aspects of such a dam," he confessed in the 1972 report, "but at first glance it appears that the downstream effects are so enormously beneficial to such a large area that most ecological problems could be solved by judicious use of those benefits." For example, he suggested, one might use the mechanical energy "inherent in the mainstream dam to move sediment across from the upstream to the downstream zone." And nutrients might be added to the river downstream to replace those "banked" upstream behind the dam. A "bank of the topsoil of Brazil," he would call this greatest of great lakes. It was Panero's style. One did not dwell on the liabilities.

Robert Panero Associates is described as a study group in the fields of strategic development and management consulting. The company was formed in 1974, after Panero resigned from the Hudson Institute. The only product for sale is the idea. Most of the company's assets, therefore, are banked between the ears of the founder, Robert Panero.

In Panero's approach to the marketplace of ideas, there are a number of ways to earn a dollar. First is the base contract for consultation with a client on a long-range project, such as Panero's association with Nissho-Iwai of Japan in developing plans for a supertanker port at Palau. Second is what Panero calls "the license to hunt for ideas," a sort of open-ended arrangement in which, in exchange for an annual retainer, the consultant shares with his client his own general knowledge of international affairs and economic strategies. Panero has held two such licenses:

one from the Volvo auto-making firm in Sweden, the other from Saviem of France, the Renault truck-making subsidiary. There is also the one-shot entrepreneurial effort in the venture-capital field, in which Panero attempts to wed the cash of one nation with the labor skills or resources of another. "The idea," he explains, "is to make love, not war." And then there is the way *not* to earn a dollar. This is what truly challenges Panero. The trick is to come up with an idea that is so tainted with NIH, so ambitiously vaulted, so daring and bizarre—and so obvious—that no client or country will touch it with a ten-foot pole. The trick is to come up with something as untouchable as the biggest bang-for-a-buck dam in the world.

Panero confesses to a certain obsession with his Amazon idea, but it is by no means the only one with untouchable credentials. Among other grand schemes he is willing to discuss are Central Park North, the New Channel Crossing, the Isthmus of Tehuantepec, and the Chocó Connection—each of which more or less demonstrates his principle of topographical leverage and his addiction to thinking big.

For New York City's Central Park, Panero in the early 1970s proposed a plan so outrageously unconventional that the City Planning Commission felt obliged to handle it with tongs. Panero proposed a Manhattan heresy. He advocated selling off several "islands" of parkland south of 66th Street, at the beloved heart of the midtown greensward. With a portion of the revenues derived from the sale of this valuable real estate and its air rights ("billions of dollars," according to Panero), the city would build new housing for thousands on Randall's Island and at Hunt's Point in the Bronx. Then, by the right of eminent domain if necessary, the city would acquire all of Central Harlem from 110th Street north to the Harlem River, raze its squalid buildings, relocate its people to the new housing provided for them on Randall's Island and in the Bronx, and extend Central Park north to the river, where air rights for the raising of luxury towers would again be sold to the highest bidder. "Acting like a Rockefeller," Panero called it. And presto—a broader tax base, a bigger park, and a happier body politic. The tongs of the Planning Commission clasped Panero's plan firmly, then promptly dropped it into the nearest wastebasket. After all, Panero wasn't a Rockefeller.

The New Channel Crossing idea is of a more recent vintage. In fact, it may still be maturing in the cellar of Panero's mind. It goes like this. The old dream of tunneling the English Channel between Dover and Calais will never come true. It would be too expensive. Bridges and causeway? Not here, for the channel is deep and the currents too swift. But look there, to the north, and run the eye across the channel from Ramsgate to Oostende, Belgium. What do you see? You see topographical levers. You see shoals reaching toward each other from both shores. You see the way for bridges and causeway. It is only sixty-five miles. And you build islands over the shoals along the way. Then you recoup your investment by selling the real estate. Why not? It might work. According to Panero.

And now to the Isthmus of Tehuantepec, where Mexico narrows to a mere 150 miles separating the Gulf of Mexico and the Pacific Ocean. Here the levers are lagoons, two of them, each but a few miles from either sea. You dredge the lagoons so they are deep enough to berth superships of the 500,000-ton class. And you dump the spoil into inland swamps to make solid footing for industrial sites. Then you tie both ports together with a railroad. "This one," says Panero, "will drive the environmentalists straight up the wall." But he is not yet thinking much of the environmentalists. He is thinking of a handful of investors whose eyes grow large when he tells them that, if only they will touch it, Tehuantepec could by the year 2000 be the busiest port in the world. He is thinking: With Tehuantepec, who needs a Panama Canal?

And who needs the Panama Canal with a Chocó Connection? The Chocó is a rainforest valley running north–south along the Colombian side of the Panama border. Until Panero saw it in the 1960s, flying at treetop level in a small plane, the Chocó was regarded by Columbians much as they view their Amazon frontier. It was Siberia. But Panero saw some levers in the Chocó Valley. He saw the Rio Atrato flowing north to the Caribbean at the Gulf of Urabá, and the Rio San Juan flowing south to the Pacific, northwest of Cali. He saw damsites on both rivers, great lakes rising behind each dam, a navigational canal between the lakes, and approach canals connecting each lake to its ocean. He saw 3.3 million kilowatts of hydroelectric power, an interoceanic seaport two hours from Medellín (Colombia's chief manufacturing center), development of a mixed lode of copper, lead, zinc, gold, platinum, and bauxite, and new industrialized programs in fish and timber products. The Columbians saw all of it, too, and created a Corporación Nacional de Desarrollo del Chocó to implement the project in stages. Such is the nature of Colombia's changing governments that after more than a decade only the most tentative start had been made on a dam for the Rio San Juan. The Chocó, alone among Panero's grandest ideas, had finally been touched. But barely.

Over the years, Panero has perfected a system for manufacturing ideas. He calls it "the flying crap game," and it starts with the premise that the primacy of the cost-benefit ratio no longer applies. "In fact," says Panero, "it never did. In a cost-benefit situation, the American West would never have been developed. So what you have to do is mix analysis with intuition. Since you can't really trust your intuition, you have to trick it. You have to expose it to as many people as possible. You have to play off the experts. You have to create an ambiance in which everyone can be creative beyond his credentials."

The flying crap game is played under a set of stringent rules, and the first roll is Panero's. He follows a hunch. He aims for the Caquetá or the Chocó because intuition and some analysis inform him that he will find a lever there. A small plane is essential; or two, depending on the number of players he has assembled. He prefers the team motley: a consultant or two with pertinent specialties, a perceptive "international" from another country, a local decision-maker, an emissary from A-Country. He looks for people who are willing to concentrate for a week of twenty-hour days, eager to share impressions, too proud to quit, unafraid of the physical danger of treetop flying and the mental danger of articulating the unthinkable. And for ambiance, he attempts to foster an atmosphere of "amicable antagonism," in the belief that personal tension is the wellspring of productive thought.

The final roll of the game is a debriefing session. The players construct a "trial balance," a checklist of demographic and physiographic factors to which they assign plus or minus values. Out of that balance comes one of four possible scenarios for the landscape the players have traveled—a call to retrench, to do nothing; a signal to proceed with "business as usual," which in most undeveloped countries is synonymous with doing nothing; an imperative for some modest development; or (and here a fierce light glimmers in the flying crapshooter's eye) a rousing consensus to "go for broke." Panero regards all but the last as unlucky rolls.

The C-46 is north of the Putumayo now, and the Caquetá comes next. This is no flying crap game. We are so high the treetops have no individuality. They are a custard spilled across the saucer of our vision. The mind wanders down through the sky, into the filtered light of the overstory, through the hanging lianas and epiphytes to the world of the bird-eating spider and the monkey-eating bird. Remember always to follow the nearest stream. If it flows north, perhaps it will lead to the Caquetá. Or perhaps it leads nowhere. Be cautious. One must be careful crossing the stream, not knowing what swims there. It is said that while there are 2,500 species of Amazon fish known to science, for all science knows there might be 5,000. With the fish, the spiders, the birds, and the monkeys, one is never alone. There is so much of everything. Except for the fish, how did Noah ever fit all the others aboard? Perhaps there was a second ark, just for the Amazon. Or perhaps there was no need for an ark at the Amazon, where it has rained for forty days and nights every year since the rivers began. The mind wanders on.

Last night, Easter eve, I stood at the window of my hotel room in Bogotá and looked up the mountain called Monserrate at the Virgin of Guadalupe. Spotlighted, she appeared at the brow of the escarpment, all in white marble, her arms extended in the classic set of mountaintop statues throughout the Latin world. Pilgrims at Eastertime climb the mountain to beseech the Virgin for miracles. The path is very steep. It is even steeper in places than the trail that infuriates Panero, the one from the bottom of the Coello gorge to the ranch house called Altamira. Some of the pilgrims make the ascent on their knees, others on crutches. To call on the Virgin in such a fashion is a high price to pay of oneself. But, for miracles?

Last night, with a wandering mind at the hotel window, I imagined the Virgin had just climbed the east slope of the Andes, up from the llanos and the forest beyond, to beckon the people of Bogotá to follow. Come with me to the Amazon, she seemed to be saying. You'll find miracles there. But today, in the C-46, having seen the Amazon briefly and in passing, I am not so sure that I heard her correctly. I mean, about where it is that the people should follow. About the miracles, I have no doubt, for the Virgin spoke truly.

"There is a need," Panero had written across the top of a fresh page of legal paper one morning in Bogotá, "to restate and review the premises as a result of basic changes in the international environment for economic development." It was the beginning of a new manifesto on the Amazon. A great deal had happened in South America since 1972, and in the world. People were speaking of an energy crisis. People were complaining about the price and availability of gasoline and heating oil. Governments were tripping over their imbalance of payments. There was mild panic in Brazil. Energy consumption was growing at such a rate that it would double in ten years. Nearly half of the energy came from oil, and 80 percent of that had to be imported at a cost of $3 billion a year.

Even as Panero sat in Bogotá reviewing his premises, scientists from throughout Latin America were gathering at Guarujá, Brazil, to assess the future of a society grown too dependent on imported oil. There was talk of alternatives. The scientists spoke of nuclear power and of the reactor program under way in Brazil. The atom, yes; but it was not easy to join the Nuclear Club. And in the long run would it not be too costly? Was there not controversy already, as in North America, about the safety of nuclear reactors? Had there not been a fire at Brazil's Angra dos Reis reactor site, with subsequent coverups, investigations, and scandal? Were there not alternatives to the atom as well as to the fossil hydrocarbon? There was biomass, yes; sugarcane bagasse and charcoal, from trees. Brazil was experimenting with ethyl alcohol extracted from sugarcane and blended with gasoline for automotive fuel, and charcoal was already favored over imported coke for the production of iron. But, for electricity?

There was hydropower. And there was not hydropower. Though the potential for South America was very large, some 300,000 megawatts, the installed capacity was but a tenth of that. Without a single dam projected for the mainstream of the Amazon, Brazil's hydropower potential was more than 140,000 megawatts, yet only 17,000 were in use. This would increase by 1985 to some 35,000 megawatts with completion of the huge Itaipu dam on the Paraná River, among other projects south of the Amazon Basin. But that would be the end of it for the populous southeast, for Rio de Janeiro and São Paulo. Then there would be no other choice but north to the Amazon tributaries, to the Xingu and the Araguaia, which flows to the Tocantins. The great rivers of the north had hardly been tapped. Less than one percent of their potential was in use (mainly for local industrial consumption). The planners from Brasília had always said that the northern rivers were too far, that there was no way to transmit the volts from the jungle 1,000 miles or more to the coastal cities where the volts would be needed. But the planners were wrong, for now there was this new technology called high-voltage direct-current transmission, which did, in fact, permit delivery of large blocks of power over long distances. The energy of the Amazon was at last within reach. According to the scientists. And, as before, to Panero.

With elements of a new statement accumulating on his legal pad in Bogotá and at El Rancho Altamira, Panero was beginning to regain some confidence about the Amazon. Now he was looking at it as a "synergistic" concept, the parts of it working together to make the greater whole. It was a *system*, he said. No one part of it was indispensable. If you wished, you could forget the interbasin connections to the Orinoco and the Paraguay. You could even forget the big dam on the main river at Santerém (though he would rather you did not). Forget the big dam, he said, and you would still have 80 percent of the total benefits just by concentrating on the tributaries. He had started with four great lakes on as many tributaries, then upped them to forty. Now he was thinking of smaller lakes on "100 to 150 of the tributaries." Sumerian, synergistic, and serendipitous. Yes, there was serendipity in the concept as well, for he was beginning to discover things about the Amazon Basin that he had never expected. He had expected, with a breakthrough in development of direct-current transmission technology, that the basin, prodigiously dammed, could probably supply more electricity than all of South America could use in the foreseeable future. But he had not expected to find a way for South America to transform the surplus Amazon hydropower into exportable energy. And now he had the solution: hydrogen fuel.

Hydrogen is the lightest of the elements, and possibly the most elusive. It is forever hanging out in chemical reaction with carbon or with oxygen, and is not found free in nature. Where hydrogen hangs out with oxygen, there is water. The trick is to disassociate the two. A number of methods have been explored, including disassociation by solar and laser technologies, but these remain experimental. The only proven method for large-scale hydrogen production is electrolysis. In electrolysis, water is passed between two electrodes and an electrical current is passed through the water. Pfft. The two gases go their separate ways. The oxygen returns to the air, and the hydrogen is available for storage or pipeline transmission. It is said to be splendid stuff, hydrogen. Clean-burning on combustion, it gives off water vapor and a little carbon dioxide only. Scientists say it could be the fuel of the future. It is already a basic building block for most synthetics. It is essential in the manufacture of ammonia for fertilizer, of methanol, and of edible fats made from animal and vegetable oils. And it could probably come in handy in the gasification of coal and oil shales and the production of high-grade steel. There is only one catch in taking hydrogen from water.

The catch is that you can go broke on the cost of the electricity—unless, of course, you happen to have your electrodes astride the biggest hydroelectric bang-for-a-buck in the world.

Panero's discovery was not altogether serendipitous. He is a voracious reader of the literature of technology, and he had been reading about the magic of hydrogen for a long time. Among other documents, he had read a discussion paper on the subject by the Mitre Corporation in McLean, Virginia, issued under the sponsorship of the U.S. Environmental Protection Agency. "Hydrogen," according to the document, "appears to be able to replace all hydrocarbon fuels and, in addition, provide a material for synthetic manufacture of other hydrocarbons or materials. The use of hydrogen on a large scale and hence the hydrogen economy, becomes practical, however, only when one has an infinite inexpensive source of energy available for the manufacture of the hydrogen. Although some hydrogen might be produced using hydroelectric power, at present a very cheap source of electricity, this source is not large enough to spur development of the hydrogen economy." Panero's eyes paused over the last sentence. Not *large* enough? The hydrogen experts at Mitre were thinking like Brazilians. They were ignoring the Amazon.

"The hydrogen economy could begin in the Amazon," Panero was saying at Altamira. "For a very little dam you get a great deal of electricity—essentially unlimited quantities of electricity. You have a fifth of the planet's riverflow. It goes out every day whether you use it or not. It is reliable. It's renewable. And it's cheap. It is the cheapest, largest single renewable energy source in the world. It could satisfy the needs of the entire continent and provide energy for export through the foreseeable future. And the fascinating thing about it is that nature would be doing most of the work."

Of course, there would have to be conceptual studies. They would cost $10 million. They would demonstrate the concept's feasibility or lack of feasibility, and at the same time identify all appropriate sites for tapping the source. There would have to be a working international agreement among the Amazon nations, and a pooling of information. And in South America, that would be asking a lot. But what worried Panero was not so much politics as the price of oil. "It keeps going up," he said. "When the price gets high enough, then the countries here will be in serious trouble. Then there won't be time for serious studies, and they'll start damming the rivers like mad. That's the danger of it. In the lead time."

"What about the environmental impacts?" I asked.

"Study it," said Panero. "Study it now. But the environmentalists will say, 'Kill it now.' They won't want the studies because the studies might prove its feasibility."

I told Panero that at least he had confidence.

"Beautiful ideas are rare," he said. "You know it is beautiful if it is an idea you don't have to defend. It defends itself. It seeks its own time and constituency. No matter where you attack this idea, it should make sense. And the more you attack, the stronger it gets. If I'm wrong, and there is an environmental way to shoot it down, then it should be shot down. Then it would unravel like a sweater. But I'll tell you one thing. If you're going to unravel it, you're going to have to put in as much time as I did knitting it together."

Among certain North Americans of the environmental persuasion, there is a tendency to perceive the world's wilder places as parcels of a kind of international trust territory best left inviolate forever; or, if not forever, since that is a very long time, at least for a time sufficient to put the choice to some needier generation. Kenya, therefore, is perceived not as a nation but as a game preserve. Lake Baikal is to be entrusted not to the Soviets but to the International Society of Limnologists. The Amazon Basin is neither Brazil's nor Colombia's nor Peru's. With its green abundance, the Amazon is "the lungs of the world." It is the commons of the tropics. It belongs to itself and to every man. So goes the pattern of thinking among U.S. environmentalists, the kind of thought developing nations find hard to accept. Where the generators shut down at midnight, one does not find many candlelight fans of Henry Thoreau.

According to Panero (and to the record), environmentalists

have not looked kindly on his Amazon dams. For a decade, he says, they were "hopping around on one leg" trying to unravel his sweater. Yet none succeeded in finding a loose thread.

The early alarms, to be sure, were grandiose and insubstantial. It was said, for example, that the weight of the water in the greatest of Panero's great lakes would inevitably result in an earthquake of major proportions. Then it was said that the inland sea would somehow slow or alter the turning of the Earth, with consequent and grave climatic changes affecting all hemispheres. There would be a disruption of the carbon dioxide cycle. Temperatures would rise worldwide, the icecaps would begin to melt, and residents of Manhattan's Murray Hill would be sitting on their rooftops wearing life preservers. After all, if Panero was going to think big, shouldn't the environmentalists?

Then some people began to suspect that Panero's dams would take their breath away. In the destruction of the Amazon forest, the Earth would lose a source of oxygen second only to the sea. It was said by one scientist that the forests of Amazonia were responsible for 50 percent of the world's annual production of oxygen through photosynthesis. What was not said in most press accounts of this finding was that annual photosynthetic production is only about one-half of one percent of the world's pool of dissolved and atmospheric oxygen. In any event, the shortness-of-breath theory is still cited by many critics of Amazon development. And since Panero's idea is incapable of defending itself on this count, Panero himself rushes to its defense. He simply explains that if it is oxygen that worries you, then you should start thinking hydrogen. Remember those electrodes and how they could disassociate the two gases of water passing over a dam? All right. By isolating hydrogen, you replenish the atmospheric oxygen supply. You take a little from the photosynthesis, flooding forest, but give it back by electrolysis, making hydrogen. According to Panero.

Through all the yarn pulling, Panero has maintained a curious and sometimes ambivalent attitude toward issues of ecological concern. In general, his style has been to dismiss the issues in the process of acknowledging them. "Among the risks to be considered," he wrote in his 1968 report on Amazon dams, "are significant disruptions of the ecological balance with some surprise results—'surprise' in the sense that, usually, ecological problems are not significant in terms of a country the size of Brazil . . . We would expect none of these risks, though, to prevent construction of the dam. Such risks are present in all dams and reservoirs and have never really prevented any from being built."

Since 1968, ecological problems have indeed prevented some dams and reservoirs from being built, and Panero has tempered the cavalier outlook accordingly. Now, still acknowledging the unknown risks, he speaks of doing nothing in the Amazon that is irrevocable. "That's why we're talking Sumerian technology," he says. "That's why we'd build dams like the beavers make. If something goes wrong, you rip them out."

The way Panero sees it, the river is at fault, not the idea. It is his fundamental article of faith that the river is "out of control." The river shifts, fish die in cutoff lagoons. The river floods, man and beast drown. "When nature is so destructive," he says, "then something is out of whack. That's *nature* out of balance." Panero's thumbs close down now over the knuckles of his index fingers and he begins to twist them back and forth, slowly, like a man turning knobs on a shortwave receiver. "There is no way you can affront that river," he says to me over his moving hands. "But you can certainly tune it." Watching him, I wonder why it is he cannot receive the river's message. If only he would twist the knobs a little longer, then he might hear the melody of water as I do. Then he would know why the rivers have been singing since the morning the clouds declared war on the mountains.

The Andes are among the youngest mountains of the Earth, and under rain they erode easily. The caprock melts into sediment suspended in the streams. People look at the streams and say they are muddy, but only because the eye cannot see what is really in them. It is the stuff of life that flows by. It is nitrogen and phosphorous and calcium and sulfur. It is the food of the Earth. Downstream, the rivers swell, gathering an organic litter of pollen and seeds and humus and the corpses of insects and drowned beasts. In the flooded *varzea*, the rivers give and take from the forest, depleting and replenishing the storehouse of nutrients there. Then the rivers flow as one past Santarém to the island of Marajó, and across the great estuary to the sea. The Atlantic currents run to the north. Each day they receive from the river thousands of tons of highland sediment and lowland litter. And no one knows exactly where it all goes, or what it might do for life-forms encountered along the way. How does one trace a microgram of calcium shorn from the limestone of Araracuara? Does it flow to the jaw of a Caquetá catfish, to the tooth of a Caribbean shark, or to the shell of a Maine lobster? Or does it bequeath itself to no littoral creature at all, so that the calcium might better be banked on deposit for the future farmers of Amazonia, somewhere upstream behind a low earth dam conceived by Robert Panero?

Panero harbors an uncommon reverence for soil. He believes it to be the capital of the planet, a kind of currency not easily minted once it is spent. He does not like to think of the clouds pounding the mountains and the silt running thick in rivers to the sea. He does not like to hear Brazilians say, with their fine flair for hyperbole, that "a continent a day flows away." According to Panero, the sea does not need topsoil. The sea is so mammoth and has so much dirt already. Panero has a theory that even if suspended sediment does enrich the sea in some measure, the bottom line nonetheless shows a net loss. "I don't think we should let the rivers carry our capital away," he says, speaking globally. "Someday we're going to need that soil. We should begin to think now about locking the rivers up."

Though Panero would lock up the rivers, he would not throw away the key. Most dam-builders, lacking affinity for soil, do that. They build a classic dam, a monument of concrete and steel, a dam to impress posterity's children. And that is the end of it for the soil. The upstream silt is sentenced to life at the bottom of the reservoir, and no time off for good behavior. The soil is rendered useless; except that, in time, it builds up behind the dam and eventually fills the reservoir. By the time the reservoir is a marsh, the dam-builder is either long dead or on the pardonable side of the statute of limitations. No large dam is yet old enough to have wrought the miracle of the marsh. Dam-builders say it will never happen. If you like marshes, stick around.

Panero is different. He says it *will* happen. In fact, to a certain point, he wants it to happen. He wants the sediment to settle across the bottoms of his reservoirs, building mineral-rich layers of Andean silt. Because in twenty years, or twenty-five or thirty, so great is the load that the rivers carry, the deposits will have come to term. At which point you simply pull out the beaver dam, drain the reservoir, and cash in the account by putting the accumulated sediments to work growing crops. Meanwhile, somewhere upstream or down, you find a new place of topographical leverage, relock the river with a second earth dam, and open another twenty-year-term savings account. And when it is time to cash in on the second reservoir, you pull out the dam there and recycle it back to the place you began. This is rotation farming of a kind and scale never dreamed of, except by Robert Panero.

For all its serendipity, Panero's agricultural scenario raises more doubts among critics than any other phase of his Amazon plan short of the big dam itself—more than the little dams, the interbasin connections, the waterwheels making volts, and the electrodes making hydrogen. Colonial agriculture has accumulated such a disastrous record in the basin, and visited such visible destruction on the land it has already touched, that most scientists and some South American politicians tend to wince nowadays at the mention of any new large-scale farming venture.

Illusions of fertility, or the lack of it, have persisted for years. It was a basic assumption of Brazil's resettlement plan, for example, that since the forest biomass was so demonstrably rich, the soils could hardly be otherwise. Dissenters said the opposite. They said that the soils were too lateritic, that the basin was overall hardpan. On-site experience and the irrefutable testimony of radar scanning devices have since proved that the truth falls somewhere in between. While the basin soils are indeed largely lateritic (about 85 percent of the total area), there are also some sizable pockets of fairly fertile eutrophic soils, and the rich alluvia of the cyclically flooded *varzea*. However rich or poor the soil may be, the forest attends to its nutritional needs. With the aid of fungi, it feeds on its own organic litter. For the most part, writes Howard S. Irwin, the veteran tropical plant taxonomist and president of the New York Botanical Garden, "Amazonia is a desert covered with trees. Its ancient soils have released most of their nutrients . . . and have little more to contribute. The glorious rainforest has evolved its own strategies to take up, use, return, and take up again in a closed cycle the precious nutrient minerals that remain." But, he adds: "The breaking of that cycle can bring catastrophe."

Catastrophe came to the laterite soils along Transamazonica when the forest canopy was peeled away. Deprived of shade, the soil crusted over. Weeds sprang up, and pests proliferated in the absence of their natural enemies. But Panero's farming scheme would test a somewhat different set of conditions. The soil would be alluvial and, at least on the Andean tributaries, nutrient-rich. Exposed to direct sunlight, how long would that soil hold up? Could it last for twenty years without erosional depletion? Could the old *varzea* sustain a generation of harvests to tide the farmers over until the river had made its deposits behind Dam No. 2? Panero thinks, yes. Researchers cited by Howard Irwin, and others, think, maybe. But not in agribusiness-style south forties a third the size of France; in relatively small patches interspersed with forest, subsistence-style. Rice might do well, and beans and maize. And possibly jute for cash income. But on a grand scale? Most experts think not.

Panero asks only that it be studied. The unanswered questions disturb him. Everyone asks questions, yet hardly anyone has answers. The public-health people ask about schistosomiasis and the dread host snail that thrives in tropical reservoirs. The anthropologists ask about the survival of the Indians. The agronomists ask about the extirpation of weeds. And the limnologists ask: What will happen to Amazonia's greatest available source of protein, the fish of the rivers, if the rivers are impounded, aeration is reduced, and the *varzea* cannot precipitate its nutrients to the water because the *varzea* is no longer there, because now it is all beans and chemical fertilizer. Aside from beans, and the occasional cut-rate tourist, what will the cargo planes carry from Leticia? If there are no fish.

The fish on the starboard side of the C-46 impart an odor that will be with me for days. I will wear it like a cloak, for it is a good smell. It is the lusty stink of life and death in the river. It traces the spoor of a food chain. Tomorrow in Bogotá, a pilgrim blessed today by the Virgin of Guadalupe will dine on Amazon pirarucu. So deceptive is the alchemy of the river, the pilgrim will never guess he is partaking of the curd of mountain and forest, and will assume he is eating a fish.

We are beyond the mountains, approaching the airport at Bogotá. The cloud that tried to kill us over the Caquetá tried once again over the eastern slope of the Cordillera. The ancient rivets rattled like gunfire. The Indian woman shut her eyes and tightened her clasp on both infant and crucifix. The couple from Colorado stared straight ahead, across the aisle at the students sprawled on the sacks of dried fish. Then the C-46 broke into sunlight and everyone smiled.

We are safe on the ground now. The pilot is standing under one of the wings, saying good-bye to the passengers. "So. You are going to see your friend Panero?" he asks.

"In the morning," I reply. "Not tonight. Panero is a man of rules. He has rules for everything. Even for progress. So perhaps there is a rule for Easter as well."

"What is the rule for progress?" asks the pilot.

Suddenly I picture Robert Panero as he was at Altamira, with his hands going back and forth quickly over the white spaces on the map, over the C-Country, over the great forceful rivers and the forest that would stretch from Kansas City to Portland, Maine. And I explain to the pilot, "According to Panero, the first rule of progress is that one never gives up what he already has."

"That is a good rule for progress," says the pilot. "At least, better than most. And what is the second rule?"

"I don't know," I reply. "For progress, maybe the first is enough."

TRAPS

Nothing is absolute about the trapping of furbearing animals in North America—not the numbers, either of trappers or pelts; nor its contribution to the gross national products of Canada and the United States; and certainly not insofar as one might seek to measure all the hours and days of pain and stress inflicted on the living raw material of hats and coats and capes desired by folks who clock success by units of fashion. It is such an awfully long way from the trapline to Fifth Avenue.

Still, by calculations made imperfect as much by the nature of trapping itself as by the unsynchronized efforts of state and provincial statisticians to count the score, perhaps it is absolute enough to guess that a million Americans, and one-tenth as many Canadians, go into the woods with traps each winter season, and come out with the hides of twenty million animals. Muskrat, mostly from anywhere, and nutria from the bayou country. Wolf from the Yukon and lynx from Quebec. Beaver from Minnesota and coyote from Kansas. Raccoon from Ohio, red fox from New York. Twenty million skins moving up the fur chain, from trapper to buyer, through tanner and manufacturer, out of the warehouse to the salons of Montreal and New York and Paris and Milan, to the shoulders of the ultimate consumer who, for the most part, derives from fur less warmth than a certain icy touch of class.

Over the years, the commercial harvest of wild furs in North America has generated what is probably the most persistent—and virulent—debate in the history of wildlife management (or mismanagement, as some contenders would have it). The central issue is not whether the slaughter of wild animals for fashion constitutes moral behavior, though that is a good part of it, and perhaps a bit more than those of an animal-welfare persuasion are willing to admit. The central issue right now is the manner of the furbearer's entrapment and death, and whether it is humane—whatever *that* means—to employ devices of steel with jaws that snap shut on an animal's foot or leg; not killing it, just holding it live until such time as the trapper arrives with pistol or bludgeon or, for that matter, his boot. These are little deaths in the scheme of things, but, counted in millions, they do add up.

And ultimately the central issue must lean toward whether or not, in this age of high technology and of moon-shot solutions to almost anything that is wanted badly enough, alternatives can be found to supplant the steel leghold trap, at least in sets on land for non-aquatic species. I mean alternatives that will be acceptable not only to the trapper, whose logistical problems defy the simplest solutions, but acceptable as well to those whose concern for the furbearing species may preclude a like concern for human life-styles beyond their understanding. There are more than a few Americans, and vocal ones at that, who believe that the best alternative to the leghold trap is no trapping at all.

So here is the story I have to tell. In November 1981, I went into the woods of Ontario with Alcide Giroux, a Canadian trapper. I chose Canada because, though the United States produces ten times as many furs, trapping plays a larger role in the social and economic lives of our northern neighbors; and possibly, too, because the noise level of the debate is much less shrill in Canada—the heckling, softer. I chose Alcide Giroux because, given the central geography of his trapline, it seemed to me he might somehow represent a median between the two extremes of trapping as we know it on both sides of the border—a middle ground between the suburban hobbyist and the full-time subsistence bushwhacker of the North Woods. And with Giroux, in his own country, I hoped to test some of my own impressions and ratiocinations gleaned from contenders on both sides of the issue in the United States. Nothing in this story is absolute, except, for certain, the deaths of the creatures caught in Giroux's traps. And that is all of it. Absolutely.

I

It is as good a country for fur as any, north of Nipissing. There are fox tracks in the fresh snow, and poplars like whittled pencil stubs where beaver have been hustling dams. Along the streams and rivers running south to the big lake are signs of mink and otter; among the paper birch trees on the hillsides, the spoor of wolves; and lynx scat under spruce and pine, down in the valley. And this is just the tamest edge of it, for you can almost feel the breath of Toronto upon your back. It is a far piece yet to the boreal woods beyond Timmins, and farther still along the historic stocking-cap way past Lac La Ronge to the Great Slave Lake.

Not that I could see or sense these things when I arrived at Giroux's camp. It was dark already, though the moon peeked now and then through a scrim of clouds. I parked my car beside the railroad tracks—the Canadian National follows the Sturgeon River here—and crossed that river on a creaking, swinging footbridge that seemed anchored to a tumbledown farmhouse on the other side. The place was empty, locked up tight. A trail swung off to the left through open fields along the river. There was a light down that way, and the shape of a roof, and a wisp of woodsmoke in the peekaboo moonlight. Voices came from a shed out back. I knocked at the door and went in. Alcide Giroux and two other men were pegging a beaver pelt to a plywood board. "Hey, there," said Giroux, waving his hammer. "Where have you been? We were saving this one for *you*."

I had met Giroux the previous spring in North Bay. He was then president of the Ontario Trappers Association, which is based there and, for Canada, is second only to the Hudson's Bay Company in volume of raw furs purchased from trappers for marketplace auction. Giroux has a home in Lively, west of Sudbury, where at the time he was supervisor of surface operations at the Creighton Mines. He was edging into his late thirties then, married, with two sons who were eager to learn what their father knew of the woods. What he knew was considerable. He had been trapping for twenty-one years, right here on the Sturgeon River, in the sixty square miles of Registered Trapline NB-12.

The system in Ontario works like this. Down south, in suburban precincts and farm country, much of the land is private, and trapping is catch-as-catch-can. But up here, where the North begins, and on to the taiga shores of Hudson Bay, the turf for the most part is Crown land, government-owned. It is divided into some 2,800 registered areas, and an individual is granted the exclusive right to manage a trapline in each one. Most cases, the right is passed on, father to son. Phillipe Giroux, who died in 1964, passed NB-12 on to Alcide.

There are harvest quotas for certain species as well. The Ontario Ministry of Natural Resources informed Giroux, for example, that during the 1981–82 season his quotas would be fixed at one hundred and fifty-five beaver, four lynx, and two fisher. No more. And not many fewer, either; for to guard against what the Ministry calls "underharvesting," it is required that the trapper deliver at least three-quarters of each quota. Miss that mark a couple of years in a row, without valid reason, and—Bingo!— you lose your registered trapline. Giroux puts in long hours to make sure that never happens. Each fall, October turning November, he leaves his job and home in Lively and comes here to his camp on the Sturgeon River to spend four full weeks on the line, and no time off for early success. Then he returns on weekends in December and January to fill out the quotas.

In the skinning shed that first night, I asked him how he had made out the previous season.

"Good," he said. "We got the quotas. We also got ninety-nine mink, twenty-seven fox, twelve otter, and five 'coon. And five hundred and fifty 'rats." Meaning: muskrats. "It wasn't the best year, though. In '79 I got six hundred and two 'rats." He wiped his forehead with the back of his hand and walked around the plywood board, away from the stove. "Hey, John!" he said. "It takes crazy people to go in and get 'em, eh?"

It is not as crazy as it used to be, at least logistically. NB-12 is laced with old logging roads, and Giroux explained that he uses them in the fall to good advantage in his four-wheel-drive truck. (Weekends, later on, he pulls the trapline closer to camp and forsakes four wheels for a snowmobile.) Open water permitting, he travels with a canoe lashed to the top of the truck, for river work and business about the larger ponds. And there are three small boats, with motors, stashed at strategic big-water points along the line. "You weren't expecting dogsleds, were you?" he said. "It's still hard work. You'll see."

"Tomorrow?"

"Tomorrow we go here," he said, and tapped a map on the wall with his forefinger. "And here." The finger moved west from the Sturgeon, hooked north, and circled home. "Maybe forty, fifty miles. You see this?" It was a pencil mark, just off the dotted line of a woods road, indicating the location of one of Giroux's sets. Giroux said, "We'll be going there in the morning. I think, maybe, we find a fox waiting there for me."

The clock was pushing eleven when the men finished their chores in the shed. David Van Exan of the Trappers Association said a round of goodnights and headed for home in the nearby village of River Valley. The other man was Langis Tremblay, who normally works out of Pointe Bleue, on Lac St. Jean in Quebec, for the federal Department of Indian Affairs; but who now had been remanded into the custody of Alcide Giroux, in Ontario, for a couple of weeks of intensive training. The idea seemed to be that Tremblay, working with Giroux here, and for a time with another Ontario trapper up at Emerald Lake, might pick up some trapping savvy worth sharing with the Indians of Lac St. Jean. Another Indian Affairs visitor from Quebec, one Daniel Guérin, was said to be long zonked in his sleeping bag in Giroux's cabin—proof-of-the-pudding, as Alcide had said, that it is still hard work out there in the woods, General Motors and Evinrude notwithstanding.

Before turning in himself, Giroux showed me the accommodations of his cabin: a barrel stove in the basement, a Franklin upstairs in the main room, plumbing with running water from the well, electricity by wire from the highway, and, for me, a hideabed sofa with a mattress as big as the Ritz. I told Giroux that this was some kind of velvet life for a big woods trapper, and he said, "You weren't expecting a lean-to, were you?"

"What about that other place, the farmhouse at the bridge?"

"That was my grandparents' home," he said. "My father lived there, too. This place, I built myself in '71."

"Your grandfather, was he a trapper?"

"A farmer," said Giroux. "He raised cows and vegetables in these fields here. But my grandmother, she trapped. She taught my dad. A Paquette, she was, from Otter Lake, Quebec. Those people were trappers to the beginning, all the way back."

"So you carry on. Why? You've got a good job at the mines."

"Yes, but the mine is not what is in the blood."

The Sturgeon drains one whale of a watershed north of Nipissing: two thousand square miles or more. By the time it rushes under the swinging bridge at Giroux's camp, the river is swollen with the waters of the Pilgrim, the Yorston, the Obabika, the Grassy, and the Temagami, and its color under clear skies has the reddish tinge of tea—the tannin imprint imparted by the chemistry of softwood trees. We crossed the bridge at dawn and got into the truck and drove up along the river checking sets for mink and beaver, and then Giroux and Tremblay put into the river in the red canoe and I drove the truck upstream to the place where they would be taking out. It was cold. I was glad to be in the truck instead of on my knees in the cedar-rib bow, bucking the wind and the current on open water. After a while the canoe came around a bend on the far side of the river. Tremblay grabbed an alder branch to anchor the craft to the shore. Giroux leaned down over the inshore gunwale. When he came up again, he was pulling a wire out of the water. At the end of the wire was a trap. The trap held a beaver. Drowned in the Sturgeon, first catch of the day.

Like most professionals, Giroux relies on a variety of trapping techniques and devices, each suited to the microgeography of the beat he is covering and the habits of the species he seeks. At any one time, at least on the fall line, he may have as many as 250 sets to visit—a hundred of these for beaver, the rest for muskrat and mink. In two out of three of these sets, Giroux uses long-spring leghold traps, generally placed in shallow water with the chain attached to a slide wire anchored by rock or railroad tie-plate to where the water runs deep. The foot of the furbearer comes down on the trap pan, the trap's jaws snap shut, and the animal instinctively dives for deep water. The trap chain slides along the wire in only one direction, and, given the weight of the trap, what goes down does not readily come up again. For beaver, death is by submersion asphyxia. It takes about nine minutes; somewhat less for a muskrat. A mink will take water into its lungs and drown in less than three minutes. Giroux does not claim these time frames as absolute. They are stopwatch averages, determined by researchers at the University of Guelph, and elsewhere.

The other traps on Giroux's line—about a third of the total inventory—are Conibears. Killer traps, so-called because, when triggered, two rotating steel bars are designed to strike an animal's head, neck, or thorax area with sufficient crushing force to kill it, ideally within seconds. Though the Conibear has been modified to achieve greater effectiveness in recent years, it is still far from ideal as a dryland killer. Giroux is not reluctant to concede the imperfections of the Conibear. Neither are the stopwatch researchers in university labs. Consequently, Giroux employs this trap predominantly in underwater sets, so that it drowns the animal should it fail to crush it; and only sparingly on dry land, in sets constructed specifically for fisher. For the rest of his dryland trapping—for fox and lynx, and for wolf—he uses necksnares, homemade from aviation cable, with a special slip knot that moves in one direction only. The animal lunges to escape the restraint. And thereby chokes itself to death in the tightening noose.

I saw the result of a well-placed necksnare—twice, as a matter of fact—later that morning at the spot that Giroux had pointed out on the map, the spot where he said a fox would be waiting for him. We walked up a hillside to an aspen grove with hemlock understory, and there was the fox, a red one, dead in one of Giroux's snares.

"A day's pay, that one," said Giroux.

"What will it bring you?"

"A hundred and twenty-five dollars, maybe."

"Yahyah!" yelled Langis Tremblay, and clapped his mittens together. "We catch the fox."

There was not much sign of a struggle. The snare, which had been placed about eight inches above the ground, was securely fastened to an aspen tree, and soil disturbance in the area seemed insignificant to that which generally prevails (so I am told) around a fox caught in a leghold trap.

"How long did it take to die?" I asked.

Giroux ran his hand over the thick red fur. "It's hard to tell," he said. "Ten minutes, maybe fifteen. But unconscious, sooner. It's the most humane way. You cannot do well with a fox in a Conibear. And to leave it caught by the paw for a couple of days, even for twenty-four hours, is not a very nice thing to do."

While Giroux and Tremblay unfastened the fox from the snare, and replaced the wire with a new one, and touched up the set with broken-off branches of hemlock planted like saplings on either side of the snare, I moseyed around the hillside, looking for sign. There were rabbit tracks in the snow. I followed one pair into a shrub-hemlock thicket, started to lift one foot through the brush, and tripped flat on my face. Something tight was holding my shoe-pac. A wire. An Alcide Giroux airplane-cable necksnare. Footsnared. *Damn.*

"Yahyah!" yelled Tremblay. "We catch the American."

I was up on my knees by the time Giroux got over to turn me loose. "Hey, partner," he said. "For red fox, you look a little too gray."

"I'm sorry. I didn't see it."

"That's good," he said. "Next time, fox won't either."

It was a long day. We worked west from the Sturgeon, checking traps and snares, stopped for tea at mid-morning, lunched in the cab of the truck, took one of the stashed motorboats up a tributary into beaver-dam country, came back to the truck, and drove on. By late afternoon, Tremblay had lost his edge of heady exuberance, and my own head was nodding in the cab of the truck. The sun had set, dusk rolling down into darkness, when at last we parked at the railroad tracks and unloaded the catch into a wheelbarrow for the last leg home, across the bridge and down through the fields to Giroux's camp. Four beaver, seven 'rats, two fox, one mink, one napping tenderfoot, one winding-down visitor from Quebec, and the honcho himself, still bright-eyed and bushy-tailed. Crossing the bridge, I looked at the water, black as ink now, swirling toward Nipissing. I asked Giroux if the Sturgeon had ever played any major role in the fur trade of olden days.

"Not much," he said. "Indians probably came down this way, and some traders may have come up. But the big traffic was west. Nipissing to the Great Lakes. The Grand Portage. That was something, eh?"

"They discovered North America," I said. "Not the saltwater sailors. The *coureurs de bois* and the *voyageurs*."

Giroux turned left with the wheelbarrow at the end of the bridge, past the fallow stubble of his ancestral fields. "Ah, Radisson!" he said behind a frosted plume of breath. "Vérendrye! They did it. Ah, yes."

They did it for fur. More than for anything else—more than souls or conquest or settlement, more than a Northwest Passage to the silks and spices of Cathay—they unpuzzled the shape and texture of the continent in their overreaching quest for fur. They saw it all, from Montreal to the Mackenzie, from Michilimackinac to Rocky Mountain House, from Moosonee to Coronation Gulf. It was a time when kings wore ermine collars and commoners shed rain under beaver hats. Canadian fur. It kept Europe's bankers hopping for a hundred years. The cartographers, too. Those paleskin adventurers in birchbark canoes were halfway to Siberia before tidewater folk south of the St. Lawrence had dusted their boots with Appalachian grit. While Puritans looked for God and their own way home in the forests of New England, Scotsmen stood on the barren grounds of northern Saskatchewan, looking at musk-ox and grizzly bears. Four years before Daniel Boone blazed his wilderness "road" two hundred miles from the Yadkin Valley of Carolina northwest to the Kentucky River, Samuel Hearne had found his own way, overland, from Hudson Bay to the mouth of the Coppermine River, 2,700 miles northwest of Montreal.

A Frenchman broke the first ice. His name was Etienne Brulé, and he wasn't yet eighteen years old when Samuel de Champlain sent him scouting up the Ottawa River, first paleskin ever. Brulé turned west on the Mattawa, carried over a height of land later to be known as the La Vase Portages, dipped into Nipissing, and crossed it to the French, which brought him presently to Georgian Bay on Lake Huron. Thus did Brulé open the Great Lakes to the fur trade. This was in 1610. The Pilgrims hadn't even opened their first turkey.

Of all the early rovers, perhaps none loomed so large as Pierre Esprit Radisson and his partner in trade, the sieur de Groseilliers. Historians have not been especially generous to this freebooting pair, for Radisson's journals were riddled with ambiguities and he was too often given to bloat. "We were Caesars," wrote Radisson of his far-flung travels, noting that in the wilderness there was "nobody to contradict us." Though scholars since have tried, there is still some speculation that Radisson may have been the first white man to reach the Upper Mississippi (in 1659, more than a decade ahead of Marquette and Jolliet), the first to reach James Bay by canoe from Lake Superior, and surely one of the first to haul furs from the interior over Brulé's portages, east of Nipissing. And in 1668, Groseilliers sailed from London into Hudson Bay to build and secure a trading post, Rupert's House, at the edge of the richest lode of beaver in North America.

The accomplishments of Radisson and Groseilliers, as well as their access to the English court of King Charles II, presently led to the granting of a royal charter. It authorized Prince Rupert, Duke of Cumberland and Earl of Holderness, to incorporate into one body politic a "Company of Adventurers of England trading into Hudson's Bay"—the Hudson's Bay Company. A fur monopoly would be extended across the breadth of Rupert's Land. It would embrace, in modern geographic terms, all of Quebec and Ontario north of the Laurentian watershed, all of Manitoba, much of Saskatchewan and Alberta, and a portion of the Northwest Territories. The trading posts, the "factories" as they were called, would soon reach out from Rupert's House, north by northwest, to the Arctic Circle.

In the St. Lawrence Valley, the French were not much impressed by Rupert's royal charter. They were building their own forts for trade with the Indians, pushing their canoe routes into the Nipigon country, to Rainy Lake and Lake of the Woods, to the Assiniboine and the Red River of the North. The principal pathfinder was Pierre Gaultier de Varennes, sieur de la Vérendrye. With one or another of his four sons, Vérendrye kept chipping at the far edge of sundown, seeking a path to the western sea. No one knows just how far he got; to the Mandan villages on the wide Missouri, for certain; and, more than likely, beyond that. Some scholars say a Vérendrye was standing in Wyoming, looking up at the Shining Mountains, thirty years before Meriwether Lewis was a glimmer in his papa's eye.

When the English took possession of Canada after the treaty of 1763, trade along the old Brulé and Vérendrye canoe routes passed from the French to a group of adventuresome Scots based in Montreal. They formed the North West Company to compete with the men from Hudson's Bay, and no more colorful a gang of rousters ever tumped fur in North America before or since. The Nor'westers, they came to be known. And for the long haul out that way, they employed men, mostly of French descent, who were one-third galley slave, one-third stevedore, and one-third pure grit. The *voyageurs*. Ah, yes.

They came at it from both ends. From Lachine, at the head of the Montreal rapids, the brigades set out Brulé's way, to Nipissing and Huron, and around the rapids at Sault Ste. Marie, and across 450 miles of Lake Superior water to the Grand Portage near Isle Royale. Eight, maybe ten men to each *canot de maitre*, the thirty-six-foot canoe of birchbark stretched on a cedar frame. Two, maybe three tons of trade goods stashed in each canoe—tobacco and cookpots and grease and axes and lead and powder and rum. All of it packed in ninety-pound bales, and each *voyageur* required to carry two at a time over a portage, and sometimes three. And, sometimes running. Then back to the start of the portage for another load. They walked and ran almost as far as they paddled.

At the Grand Portage, a thousand miles from Montreal and two thousand from Fort Chipewyan on Lake Athabasca, the brigades from Montreal rendezvoused with the *hommes du nord*, the men of the North, for a tradeoff of cargoes. Into the *canots de maitre* went the furs for Montreal. Into the lighter canoes of the North went the trade goods, and *au revoir*. Back across the Grand Portage went the men of the North, back to the Pigeon River, back to Lac la Croix and Rainy, back to the Winnipeg, the Pas, the Churchill, La Ronge, Ile à la Crosse, Fort McMurray, Athabasca. Some went farther, to the Great Slave Lake.

In 1821, the Nor'westers merged with the Hudson's Bay Company. In 1822, the Americans William Ashley and Jedediah Smith poled the Upper Missouri past the graves of long-gone Frenchmen. Astor's men stood at the mouth of the Columbia River. Furs piled up outside the stockades. Indians sat in their wickiups, braiding sinew into snares. Mountain men spent more time building deadfalls than walking their traplines. In Upstate New York, a farmer named Sewell Newhouse sat at a blacksmith's anvil, fooling with pieces of iron. "What'cha got there, Sewell?" someone probably asked. Newhouse may have answered, "I got me a leghold trap." This was about 1823. *Snap*. If you didn't know any better, you'd think that was only yesterday. Judging by how little trap technology has evolved since then, maybe it *was* only yesterday. I mean, in the same century and a half, the trapper's rifle evolved from a black-powder muzzle loader into a clip-fed semiautomatic repeater. The *canot de maitre* catapulted into the sky, a Cessna with floats. The snowshoe mushed on to the snowmobile. But traps? Whatever happened, or didn't happen, that, for the most part, after 150 years we should still be hitched to the hardware of Old Sewell's anvil?

During the night, north of Nipissing, the temperature fell sharply and ice like Lucite closed down on the ponds and pools of Registered Trapline NB-12. We went over the swinging bridge at sunrise. Giroux said, "Today we change some of the sets, from fall to winter. This is the dormant time. The animals don't move so much. Things slow down between the open water and freezeup." We drove north and parked at the head of a trail. At the end of the trail was a beaver dam. Giroux slipped his hands into a pair of black rubber gloves that came above his elbows and snapped together over the back of his neck. He chopped a hole in the ice with a hatchet, then rigged a drowning set with the trap just under the surface of the water. Behind the trap, he pushed a poplar branch into the mud on the underlip of the dam.

"What's that for? To mark the place?"

"For bait," said Giroux. "Good fresh poplar is hard to beat. It is candy to the beaver." He straightened up and looked across the ice at a house made of sticks—the wickiup of *Castor canadensis*. "I'll tell you this," he said. "In one week I'll have that beaver for sure. Just one or two. We leave the rest here for next year."

By mid-morning, we had three big beaver, from other ponds, in the back of the truck. "How many is that altogether?" asked Daniel Guérin, one of the two young men from Quebec.

Giroux said, "For the season so far, that makes eighty-five. I would like to get fifteen more by the end of the week. That will leave fifty-five for the weekends, to fill out the quota. Then I put my feet up, eh? Then I have earned a good rest."

"Maybe we rest tonight," said Langis Tremblay. "Tonight we let the American skin out the *castors*. Why not?"

There were plenty of reasons why not, and I said so. Let the pros do it. Besides, Giroux's brother, Maurice, who has a sawmill nearby and runs his own registered trapline up toward Red Cedar Lake, was one of the best skinners in all of Canada. In 1965, Maurice Giroux ran away with the top honors in the timed beaver-skinning contest at the annual convention of the Ontario Trappers Association. Seventeen minutes by the stopwatch—skinned, scraped, and then stretched on a plywood board. A real surgeon, that one.

The convention at North Bay was where I had met Alcide Giroux the first time around. It is held in the association's building on Bond Street, not far from where the old Nor'westers swaggered under their tumplines down the Trout Lake carry to Nipissing. It is a building of cavemous rooms where furs are sorted and graded and displayed, and then auctioned. At convention time, two floors are given over to exhibits. Regional trappers' councils come in from Georgian Bay and Temagami and Hearst, and set up their booths. There are visitors from afar as well, for the association claims members—some 23,000 in all—from every province and many of the United States; and there is a certain eclectic look to the crowd, as though buffalo plaids were no more in fashion than blue serge. Eclectic, too, in the sense that differing points of view seem to be represented—say, as to the manner of a furbearer's entrapment and death. For here is a display by the Woodstream Corporation of Lititz, Pennsylvania, manufacturer and distributor of the Victor and Oneida leghold traps, while over there is the booth of the Canadian Association for Humane Trapping, whose members believe, as Alcide Giroux does, that to leave an animal caught by the paw for a couple of days is not a very nice thing to do.

The executive secretary of the Canadian Association for Humane Trapping (CAHT, acronymically) was a lively young woman from Toronto named Marietta Lash. I found her that day at her booth, between a thick stack of pamphlets and a video screen. A tape was running visuals across the screen, and the voice-over was saying that a professional trapper is a humane trapper. I turned from the screen and listened to Lash. "Most of the humane organizations, especially in the United States, are against trapping," she said. "We're not. We want to work with the trapper. We want to help find new methods, new devices—and encourage their use—that will make death a lot easier for the furbearing animal."

A number of years ago, Lash explained, CAHT encouraged the use of the Conibear killer trap. With a fund of $40,000, it exchanged Conibears for steel-jaw legholds—one Conibear for each trapper willing to make the swap. Then field and laboratory tests began to show that Conibears do not always kill quickly. CAHT promptly canceled its exchange program. And now, she said, it was crossing its fingers with high hopes for Milan Novak's new footsnare.

The snare was on display at the other end of the exhibit room, so we walked up that way together and talked with the inventor himself, who was also the supervisor of fur management for the Ontario Ministry of Natural Resources. Novak's spring-operated footsnare is a holding device rather than a killer. "There are places," said Novak, "where you cannot use a killing trap. Because of domestic animals. So we must come up with something that holds the furbearer with as little discomfort as possible."

The footsnare may do that. Tom Bradley, an Ontario trapper who field-tested Novak's device, said: "I'll stand behind it all the way. Okay. When I first looked at that snare two years ago, I said, 'I don't like it.' I sure like it now. The first year, I got a hundred and fifty fox, and you couldn't tell which leg was caught on any of them. It holds. There's nothing wrong with it, if you check it every day. And if you don't, you're not a trapper."

In the minds of some fur people, however, there is doubt that Novak's snare can ever replace the leghold trap for dryland captures. Some skeptics say it will not work in sets that are covered with crusted snow. "Listen," said a man who called himself Peter Askins, and presented his card from the Woodstream Corporation. "I'm telling you: American trappers will not buy it."

"But they'll buy the status quo," I said.

It occurred to me then that challenging Askins in North Bay was a bit too typically hot-head American. I mentioned this later to Marietta Lash, saying that down below, in the States, it was one great big shouting match, the pros and the antis, trappers and humaniacs, fangs at each other's throats. No dialogue, no working together. All snarls and froth at the mouth. And she said, "I know. It's a shame. It's a waste. How can you possibly get someone around to your way of thinking if you're forever telling him he's the scum of the Earth?"

11

On the morning of my third day with Giroux at his camp on the Sturgeon River, we went across the fields and into the woods to brush out his skidoo trail for the winter trapline. Giroux and Tremblay broke trail through the snow in an old tractor. Guérin and I followed on foot. Today was to be our "rest" day, Giroux had said. Just enough exercise to keep us from getting stiff in the joints. Besides, he didn't want these French Canadians going home to Quebec and giving him bad marks for hospitality; or the American, either, for that matter. Giroux needn't have worried, for he had already co-opted us cunningly: partridges for supper one night, moose steaks the next. On that kind of fare, one could hardly begrudge the provider's zeal for hard work.

"It is easier here than at Emerald Lake," Guérin was saying. "You work for it *there*, I can tell you."

Guérin and Tremblay had just spent two weeks in training at Emerald Lake with the Ontario trapper Lyle Hurst. Emerald lies up north near Lake Temagami, in country that seems to prefer canoes to pickup trucks.

"With Lyle, there is so much more walking and paddling," Guérin said. "There are only two roads, one on either side of his territory. To get one beaver, we had to walk in a mile to the canoe, paddle it across a lake, carry it a half-mile, maybe, and paddle some more to the beaver house. Then we had to come out the same way, and that beaver was heavy. I suppose you do what you have to do. It depends on the country." We heard the tractor stop in the woods ahead of us, and the sound of an axe clearing brush. Guérin said, "How is it done in your country?"

I told him it is done every which way, that there are men still in the mountains of the West and in Alaska who do it Lyle Hurst's way, and some who do it Alcide Giroux's way, and others who, lacking space and distance, practically do it with a hand reaching down into highway culverts from the cabs of their trucks.

"How do they fill up their time," said Guérin, "when it is so easy?"

"They worry a lot," I said. "About the ones who would like to take away their traps."

There was a time, and not so long ago at that, when the leghold wars seemed far removed from the drift of most Canadian trappers' lives. The news from the Front was erratic, but they followed it as best they could, if only for confirmation of how crazy in matters of wildlife these neighboring North Americans could sometimes be. They had heard, for example, about this fellow named Cleveland Amory who was making big sounds about banning the leghold trap. They had heard, too, of Amory's colleague, the actress Mary Tyler Moore, and of how, before a subcommittee of the U.S. House of Representatives in 1975, she had testified that "behind every beautiful wild fur there is an ugly story," and then, with much emotion, recited a bit of verse:

> 'Tis strange how women kneel in church
>   and pray to God above,
> Confess small sins and chant a praise,
>   and sing that He is loved,
> While coats of soft furred things upon
>   their shoulders lie,
> Of timid things, of tortured things
>   that take so long to die.

And perhaps they had heard as well of the astonishing naiveté with which some U.S. congressmen then addressed the issue of the leghold trap—one Glenn Anderson of California saying that painless capture of a furbearer could be achieved "simply by wrapping weather stripping across the jaws of the steel trap." Or Clarence Long of Maryland, laboring under the impression that most leghold traps have teeth. Or Ronald Sarasin of Connecticut, offering the box trap as a humane alternative in that it "does not instill panic or fear in the animal," a common misconception—indeed, a cherished bromide—among the have-a-heart folks.

All of it seemed remote. Yet even by 1975, only the most isolated North Woods bushwhacker could fail to see that public attitudes toward traps and trapping were beginning to change in Canada, too. All those new and sallow faces on the sidewalks of Vancouver and Toronto, faces of people without roots in the country. People growing up in the cities and never knowing the woods and the animals in their own right, but rather as they might be if woods were cities and animals could somehow be invested with *human* rights. People more akin to Americans in Buffalo or Boston than to their own compatriots in Bella Coola or North Bay. And not unlike some of the Americans, though often without the Americans' penchant for the strident insult and the theatrical pose, increasing numbers of urban Canadians were speaking at last on behalf of the voiceless—those soft furred things, out there in the woods, that take so long to die.

"Hey, partner!"

It was Giroux, stepping out of an evergreen thicket with axe in hand. Tremblay had gone ahead in the tractor. We stood in the snow, resting and talking, and I asked Giroux if, in the course of official business for the Trappers Association, he had ever run into this trap-hating man named Cleveland Amory.

Giroux smiled and shook his head—negative. "Now who's that other one down there?" he said. "The lady."

"Alice Herrington? Friends of Animals. Christine Stevens? Animal Welfare Institute. They're the big ones."

"Alice," he said. "She's something, eh?"

"You ought to meet her lieutenant for New England—Priscilla Feral. She's something, too."

Giroux then expounded at length on the prevalence of women in the humane movement, and on the prevailing scent of expensive perfume at humane rallies. "You know what goes into making a lot of perfume?" he said. "Beaver castors. That's right. Once, at a rally, I said to this perfumed lady, 'You smell good. It's the beaver castors.' "

"And what did *she* say?"

"She said it was a cheap shot."

"You got off easy," I said. "That could only have happened in Canada."

Priscilla Feral, a Connecticut friend of mine likes to say, is the Jane Fonda of leghold disarmament. I do not know whether that is a slur or a compliment, for my friend is a person of ambiguous politics. For my own part, I confess to admiration. For Jane Fonda. For Priscilla Feral, I must reserve judgment. Objectivity is so elusive in any event.

I thought about Priscilla Feral when I was in the woods of Ontario with Alcide Giroux. I thought how leavening it might be for her, and for her Friends of Animals, if she could be here just to see him working, and talk with him a while to discover what he feels for animals, and maybe get over to Lively to meet Giroux's wife and learn what *she* feels for animals, too. And then I thought how salutary it might be if Priscilla Feral would go back to Westport, Connecticut, and open the window of her office overlooking U.S. Route 1, the Boston Post Road, where it doglegs off toward Norwalk, and listen to the sound of all the trucks going by. Big trucks bearing particle boards from Georgia and phosphate products from Florida; trucks heaped high with reconstituted things upon their shoulders, vegetable and mineral things from the plundered landscapes that take so little time to die. Sure, there are plenty of guns and traps and snares where the trucks come from. But I imagine that there are chainsaws and draglines and bulldozers, too. It is sad to report that there are several things in America more elusive than objectivity. One of them is the wild country that most furry animals need, just to live.

Priscilla Feral's crusade for leghold disarmament was in its third or fourth year when I caught up with her one blustering March night at a legislative hearing in Meriden, Connecticut. The hearing had been called by the lawmakers to examine public sentiment for and against a state senate bill that would ban the use of leghold traps in Connecticut. Most of the lawmakers, and

Feral, too, had been through all of this before. A year earlier, a similar bill had been drafted, heard, and then killed in a senate deadlock, short by a single vote. And a year or so before that, leghold prohibition was likewise dispatched on a rules technicality. So it did not look too promising for Feral and her allies in Meriden this particular evening. Among other things, in an audience of well over six hundred people, these friends of animals were roughly outnumbered—and therefore outcheered and outheckled—by a margin of three to one.

Strangers to Connecticut—I am thinking now of my friend Alcide Giroux—are greatly puzzled by the news that men still trap, and fight with rancor to protect their opportunities to do so, in this tiny nutmeg colony that is noted not for fur but for its bustling production of aircraft engines and nuclear submarines, its silverware and ball bearings, its insurance emporiums and multinational corporate headquarters nestled in manicured country-club settings. Yet strangers do not see the woods between the mill towns, or the garbage-can 'coons; or, for that matter, the faded blue collars of folks who work at dull jobs all day in the factories and look to the woods for some space to vent steam. They are not in great numbers proportionately. Of those that be, most pack shotguns and squirrel rifles and fishing rods, not traps. Still, those few who do trap manage to turn over several million dollars in fur every year. I know of one man in New Haven, and that's quite a city, who in a season takes upwards of one thousand muskrat from the Quinnipiac Marsh, the periphery of which is spangled with factories and warehouses. That's how he makes his living. Trapping 'rats. But there aren't many like him. In Connecticut, you could count them on the digits of two hands, with fingers to spare.

So who, then, were all these men in windbreakers and buffalo plaid shirts (but only one in a coonskin cap), sitting with their wives or children, filling the center rows in the auditorium at Meriden, scowling at the strangers from the white-collar seacoast and at this slim blonde woman who moved back and forth along the perimeter of her troops like some cocksure battalion commander? These men in the center could not all be trappers.

And indeed, they were not. For the most part they were hook 'n' bullet men, hunters and fishers come to pack the hall at the behest of the Connecticut Sportsmen's Alliance. During part of the hearing, I stood with a man from the Alliance at the rear of the hall. He said, "Look. It's as simple as this. They want human rights for animals. If we let them take away our traps, the next thing you know they'll be taking our guns. And then our fishing rods. We won't sit still for it. That's why we're here tonight to support the trappers." The dominoes theory, neat and simple. It may not be valid. But it does turn heads.

To borrow a phrase: If you've seen one leghold hearing, you've seen 'em all. And they are nasty. First you have the game managers. They say that the proposed legislation will outlaw *all* metal traps, not just the leghold. They speak of this "surplus" of animals that is going to die from starvation and winter-kill—as though, if animals could talk, they would eagerly opt for death in a leghold trap. (An audible sneer from the disbelievers.) And sometimes the managers speak of the scourge of rabies—as though trappers stood alone at the public-health barricades, defending us all against slavering plague. Though this, too, is a largely invalid theory, why not? In the war of ideas, one must turn heads.

Now the folks in the audience are warming up, hooting and jeering as each side sends a new speaker to the microphone. State Senator Amelia Mustone, the sponsor of this measure, reports that the leghold trap is banned in fifty-one nations throughout the world. "Yeah?" hoots a plaid in the row behind me. "You know why? Most of those countries don't have fur-bearers. It's too damn hot."

It is now the turn of Priscilla Feral of Friends of Animals. She moves to the microphone and begins her statement in a clear, strong, controlled voice. Still, there is an edge of anger in it, and of hurt, too. The plaids are taunting her. On the stage, a gavel raps for quiet. Feral holds a pencil in her left hand, gestures with it, waves it back and forth over a table beside the microphone. In the middle of the table is a #2 Victor leghold trap. The trap is set; the jaws, open. No device is crueler, she says. It is a "monstrosity." It is "sadistic, immoral, and unnecessary." The pencil hovers, circles over the trip-pan in the center of the open jaws, then stabs downward. *Snap*. (An audible sneer from the center aisle.) Feral takes her hand away from the trapped pencil. She looks along the row of lawmakers on the stage above her. "What are you afraid of?" she demands, almost in a whisper. "Let this bill *fly*."

Feral is followed to the mike by a man from the other side. His name is Kramer. He, too, has set a #2 Victor, with open jaws, on the table. He says he has come to demonstrate—and now his sarcasm begins to drip—the "excruciating pain" of being caught in this devilish device. But he will not use a pencil. He will use his hand. *Snap*. The hand comes up, fingers clamped in the sprung jaws of the trap. Kramer smiles bravely at the lawmakers. Look, Ma, he seems to be saying, it doesn't hurt. The plaids leap to their feet, cheering. The gavel falls. State Representative Mary Mushinsky addresses the man with his hand in the leghold trap. "Mr. Kramer," she says, "I'm glad that you didn't go into Phase Two of the demonstration—and that is to chew off your hand." Guffaws from the seacoast. So it goes.

About six weeks later I called on Priscilla Feral at her office in Westport, and we talked while the trucks rolled by on the Boston Post Road, bearing to market their cargoes of ossified habitat. She had lost again, she said. The state senate had just shot down Amelia Mustone's bill, 21 to 15. Too many politicians had folded under pressure. Those fish and game clubs, she said. They whipped up a lot of action.

I told her what the man from the Sportsmen's Alliance had said, about people like her not wanting to stop at the leghold trap—the dominoes theory.

"That's a lie," she said. "The leghold trap is the issue."

But how did she feel about trapping, in general?

"Personally? Leghold, Conibear, Havahart—if the idea is to turn an animal skin into a coat—it's all the same. I don't like it."

And how did she feel about hunting?

"I wouldn't mind seeing that banned, too."

"Then we're into the dominoes, aren't we?"

"You asked me how I felt," she said. "Not what I'm prepared to do about it."

Among some of the things that Feral *is* prepared to do is to play a little game she calls "Trapping Trappers." The idea is to get yourself a pair of hip boots and a metal detector and to tramp through the swamps searching for leghold traps. When you find one, you take a stick and spring the trap. *Snap*. And if the trap has been set illegally—out of season, for example, or too close to a muskrat lodge—why, then you impound it. You take it away. The year before last, Feral claims, she walked away with thirty leghold traps in Connecticut. And now she is distributing a new membership flyer: "Join Friends of Animals," it reads. "Trap trappers for fun and profit . . . Despite the appearance the trapped trapper presents of writhing and screaming, there is no evidence to support the claim that he actually feels pain."

I hear an echo here. It sounds to me like a Cleveland Amory put-on. "Hunt the Hunters"—remember that one? Fun and games in the war of ideas. And yet, when you take the tongue out of this kind of cheek, you find that it is not such a small game after all, for it tastes too much of antipathy. It smells too much of cultural bile.

The bile flows in both directions, like the traffic out there on the Old Boston Post Road. There is a yellow stripe down the center of the road, and what you have to do is stay to the right. Always, be *right*. Because the other side is always wrong, for being *different*. This isn't just a matter of politics, or issues. It can also involve such matters as the color of your collar, and where you live, and how; and whether you're high on *Archie Bunker* or *Masterpiece Theatre*, buffalo plaids or designer jeans, James Watt or Jane Fonda. It may also have a lot to do with which way you read the cosmic bottom line: *Man*kind, or, as Cleveland Amory would have it, man *kind*.

In Priscilla Feral's office is an envelope filled with mail. Her "hate file," she calls it. Letters from her adversaries, though mostly anonymous. Letters of physical threat and of lewd innuendo. Old boiler-plate stuff, actually, unless you happen to be the recipient; and not so terribly surprising either, considering the intellectual deficiencies of the "sportsmen" who penned the notes. Priscilla Feral, so far as I know, does not reply in kind by return mail. She just sits in her office, alternately seething at, or covertly relishing, the meanness and scorn that her enemies heap upon her. When she speaks of them, her selection of modifiers begins with "macho" and runs on to "nuts." And her eyes flash like skinning knives fresh off the strop when she says, as she did that time in Westport: "I'm going to beat those good ol' boys. One of these days."

Management is the important thing, Giroux was saying in the evening of my third day with him on the Sturgeon River. Now we were in the truck, going up the road to his brother's place on the hill, to watch Maurice skin an otter. We had been talking about the leghold wars in the States, and Giroux said he could not understand why these people in the humane organizations had so little regard for the principles of wildlife management. "Look up here," he said. "This is a nation of resources. Managed right, they could last forever."

I wanted to say, but didn't, that nothing lasts as long as forever, and that what is right for one may be wrong for another.

We turned into Maurice's driveway and parked the truck in front of the skinning shed. Maurice came out to greet us. "From Connecticut?" he asked me.

"From Ohio, originally," I said.

"There are many trappers in Ohio. A lot of raccoon, eh?"

I said it was my understanding that, among the states, Ohio was second only to Louisiana in the production of wild furs.

"Are you a trapper?" he asked.

"A long time ago," I said, "I trapped Norway rats out of my father's vegetable garden."

And Maurice smiled, and winked at his brother, and said: "These rats of yours—are they still in fashion?"

The common rat—the city species, *Rattus norvegicus*—looms large in the folklore of Ohio's trapping fraternity. I didn't know how large at the time of my visit in Ontario. All I had to go by were these old stories of how the Norway rat had been recruited, in a manner of speaking, to help the wildlife managers and the country folk of Ohio convince their city cousins that they should not, by constitutional amendment, outlaw the use of the leghold trap. That was back in 1977; and so, knowing how stories have this way of growing like Topsy over the years, I decided that after I got home from Ontario I should go out to Columbus, Ohio, and have a chat with the people from the Wildlife Legislative Fund of America, which is headquartered there, serving the same function in defense of the leghold trap as, let us say, the National Rifle Association of America serves in defense of the snub-nosed revolver.

This much I knew when I arrived at the door of the Wildlife Legislative Fund in Columbus:

In November 1977, Ohioans had been asked to vote on a proposed constitutional amendment, the key provision stipulating that "no person shall use in any manner in the trapping of wild birds or wild quadrupeds any leghold trap in this state." The issue had been placed on the ballot by petitions obtained by the Ohio Committee for Humane Trapping, an ad hoc group with ties to Cleveland Amory's Fund for Animals. Opposing the proposition were Ohioans for Wildlife Conservation, a spinoff group of the Wildlife Legislative Fund, which had already defeated an attempted leghold ban at the statehouse, and whose president, James H. Glass, was the man I was now about to see.

For their own part, the pro-amendment forces waged a shabby campaign. They spoke of cruelty. Their television spots showed a Teddy Bear caught in a leghold trap. They squabbled among themselves over strategy. Amory himself, less than a week before the election, felt compelled to hop a jet into Dayton to condemn his Buckeye cohorts for poor planning and management, then added that the amendment's only chance for passage would be public reaction against media "overkill" by the other side. For its part, the other side had recruited the Norway rat.

"It will be against the law," said the other side, "even to trap rats." (The amendment included a provision prohibiting the use of *any* trap that might cause "continued prolonged suffering," and Glass's folks figured, rather artfully, that rats are sometimes caught in a rat trap by a leg, and must, when so caught, experience prolonged suffering.) One writer who monitored the media blitz cited similar alarms broadcast by Ohioans for Wildlife Conservation: "I'm concerned that rats bite people"—"Animals sick with rabies are going to invade our parks and playgrounds"—"Your family may face a nightmare"—"Crops will suffer tremendous damage, and food prices will rise." And then there was this television spot: Rats (from a laboratory, no doubt) scurrying out of a drawer when a housewife opened it to get food for her youngsters.

On November 8, 1977, voters in Ohio went to the polls and defeated the proposed amendment by a margin of two to one. Soon after that, the Wildlife Legislative Fund—and its tactics—went national.

A total ban on the use of leghold traps prevails in only one of these fifty United States, and that is Rhode Island where, if you were to set one off in a cloister in Newport, the snap of the jaws would likely be heard in the pews of Pawtucket. Elsewhere, partial bans of one kind or another are imposed in Florida, South Carolina, and a number of counties in North Carolina and New Jersey. Massachusetts, for the most part, prohibits use of the leghold on land, but permits drowning sets in water. Tennessee proscribes dryland use of the leghold except in burrows, as does Connecticut, all of the furies of Meriden and of Priscilla Feral notwithstanding. And this, according to James H. Glass of the Wildlife Legislative Fund of America, is just about as far as it will go.

Glass and I talked for several hours at his office in Columbus. He is an expansive sort of man, full of enthusiasm and a certain confidence that comes from having propped one's chin on the cutting edge of the corporate world. All this and Ohio State ag-school, too. And a cool, detached, dispassionate view of his adversaries on the other side. If anything, he seems to pity them for their inability to see the true light. "We shed light on issues, not heat," he said. And then, "Are animals animals? Or are they people? I think they're animals."

He told me about his organization. In fact, there are two. The Legislative Fund is the political action force. It lobbies. Then there is the Wildlife Conservation Fund, which traffics in litigation, research, and education—no one like to use the word *propaganda*. The directors and staff are more or less the same for both entities. In 1980, the Funds took in and spent about $800,000. Among the directors and trustees that year, in addition to Glass, were Daniel M. Galbreath, president of the Pittsburgh Pirates; Henry Foner, president of the Joint Board of the Fur, Leather, and Machine Workers Union (AFL-CIO); Joseph J. Foss, former governor of South Dakota, World War II air ace, and winner of the Congressional Medal of Honor; Dale L. Haney, chief of the Ohio Division of Wildlife during the media battles of 1977, and president of the Victor Division of the Woodstream Corporation; and David B. Meltzer, chairman of Evans, Inc., reputedly the world's largest furrier. And until President Ronald Reagan summoned him to Washington to serve as Assistant Secretary of the Interior for Fish, Wildlife, and Parks, the list also included G. Ray Arnett, past president of the National Wildlife Federation and first chairman of the Wildlife Legislative Fund of America.

The Fund, according to Glass, monitors about six hundred legislative bills each year, at all levels of government and in matters involving all aspects of hunting, fishing, and trapping. More than half of these bills are related to trapping issues. Glass said he figured the animal-rights people weren't having much luck at the statehouses. The Fund beat them hands-down in Oregon and California, as well as in Ohio. So now, he said, the other side was aiming for trapping restrictions by counties and municipalities, and the Fund was going to beat them there, too. "Besides," he said, "nobody traps in downtown Columbus anyway."

I asked him about the 1977 referendum. He said, "We wanted to set up committees to fight it in every one of Ohio's eighty-eight counties. The experts said it couldn't be done. We didn't *know* it couldn't be done—so we did it. We ran it like we were building an airplane from the ground up. It took us a year to get organized, but in six weeks we raised $680,000 in nickels and dimes."

I asked him about the television ads. And the Norway rats. "Look," he said. "You can't give someone a wildlife management course in a thirty-second TV commercial. You have to go for the people issues. The way that proposition was worded, it *would* have banned rat traps."

When I left Jim Glass at his office in Columbus, I went away with a heavy briefcase stuffed with Fund reports and pamphlets and papers of one kind or another. Sorting through them now, I find two that are highly instructive. The first is a paper written for the 44th North American Wildlife and Natural Resources Conference in Toronto in 1979 by James W. Goodrich, a director and vice-president of the two Columbus-based wildlife funds, and an expert public relations man in his own right. In this script, Goodrich assails the opposition for consistently parading "on the edge of truth" and creating "mammoth hoaxes in their propaganda program." Then he explains how the Fund won the media war in Ohio in 1977. There was a survey. The survey showed that while two-thirds of the people of Ohio believed trapping is cruel to animals, they really didn't know very much about trapping, and less about wildlife. Thus, Goodrich and his colleagues fell upon a "piece of strategic information"— "When people understand the need to control wildlife populations . . . they will support trapping." The facts, writes Goodrich, "are on our side, and do not be intimidated by the antis' shrill outbursts. Believe that the American people and the American press are educable about the necessity for wildlife management. They will understand, if we tell them, that uncontrolled wildlife populations are bad for people and bad for wildlife."

All of which turns me now to the second illuminating document from Columbus, a sixteen-page pamphlet entitled "Trapping Benefits People and Wild Animals." This one is clearly aimed at an urban audience—the folks who know nothing of wildlife—for here, under the cover photograph of a menacing-looking raccoon, is a caption noting that 'coons "can live in city sewers, emerging only at night." Hot stuff, for openers; but tepid compared to the headlines inside:

Wildlife Rabies Is Prevalent in Most of the U.S.
Coyote Trapping Aids Bubonic Plague Control
Wild Furbearers Damage Multi-Billion $ Crops
Beavers Threaten Timber Crops
Muskrats Devil Golf Course Managers
Bobcats—Killers of Sheep, Goats, Calves
Disease-Prone Animals Are Too Abundant

And I hear the voice of James H. Glass, saying: "We shed light on issues, not heat."

Or is it the voice of inconsistency? Have not wildlife management publicists such as Glass and Goodrich been telling us all along that there is this surplus of animals destined to die by nature's cruel ways, out there in the woods? Have they not said that much of this surplus can be harvested by trappers without any harm to the furbearer population? Well, if there is to be no harm to the muskrat population, then won't muskrats go right on deviling golf course managers? And didn't I see somewhere in the literature of the Victor Division of the Woodstream Corporation that "scientific management ensures that only surplus animals are taken, thus preventing inroads into the breeding populations and helping ensure that the survivors are more healthy and efficient breeders"? But, breeders of what? Of their kind? Of fur pelts? Or of rabies and the bubonic plague?

In 1975, the President's Council on Environmental Quality sent the following advisory to a congressional committee considering legislation (later rejected) to restrict use of the leghold trap: "The Council has examined the possible relationship between discontinuation of the steel leghold trap and rabies and can find no reliable data anywhere that suggests such a relationship. The incidence of rabies does not appear to increase or decrease with changes in trapping methods. The contention that rabies increases dramatically when steel leghold traps are banned seems entirely without merit." Not that the Council, with what was then a sizable scientific staff, should be considered the last word on the subject of rabies; though I suspect it comes a lot closer to the last word than the Wildlife Legislative Fund of America. With *its* staff.

And in 1977, even as that ill-worded constitutional amendment was going down the tube in Ohio, the Institute for the Study of Animal Problems published a research monograph on traps and trapping prepared by the consultant Martha Scott. Though the Institute is a division of the Humane Society of the United States, and would therefore seem to have a particular axe to grind, Scott eschewed the traditional fonts of humaniac wisdom. Instead, she ferreted her sources out of the scientific literature of the wildlife management profession itself, drawing heavily, for her discussion of diseases, on the *Journal of Wildlife Management, Wildlife Review, Biological Abstracts, Bulletin of the Wildlife Disease Association,* and—now here she was raiding the good ol' boys' own library shelf—the *New York Fish & Game Journal.* Among her findings, based on the literature:

"Small carnivore populations are able to withstand a high level of control without being affected numerically beyond one generation."

"Reproduction may actually be stimulated by control practices."

"It is only when trapping reaches an intensity which, if continued, may threaten the exploited population, that effects on wildlife disease are probable."

"The rationale behind commercial trapping," Scott writes, "has absolutely nothing to do with 'management' of animals. Commercial trapping exists, by definition, because of the existence of a market for furs. Demand for furs, and hence the fur market, varies in complete independence of 'management' considerations. Those who market furs have not, and probably could not, influence demand to serve such considerations. There is no effort to develop a market for skunks, although skunks are the major vectors of rabies."

"And what happens," I was asking Alcide Giroux that night

we went to his brother's skinning shed, "when you catch a skunk by mistake?"

"I feel sorry for it," said Giroux. "And I hold my nose."

The otter hung by its paws from a chain attached to a rafter in Maurice's skinning shed. Maurice worked from the top down, first slicing a bit with his knife, then peeling the fur with his thumb. Bared, the forelegs looked like a pair of frail and very sunburnt human arms, though I do not think that anyone else saw them that way. It was a fine pelt, and Maurice took his time with it for the benefit of his observers in general, and of the trainees, Tremblay and Guérin, in particular. Alcide sat on the edge of the skinning table, making a figure-eight lock-knot for a noose at the end of one of his necksnares. Earlier, Tremblay had voiced some doubts that the Indians of Lac St. Jean could be persuaded to use the necksnare for fox and wolf and lynx, after so many years of using the leghold trap.

"We must save the snare," Giroux said as he slipped the open noose around his forearm. "But the question is—which one? There has not been enough research. The trapper finds the dead fox, but he doesn't know how long it took the fox to die." Suddenly, with a sharp pull, he closed the noose around his arm. The cable dug in and held fast. "See," he said. "The neck of the fox—" and twice jerked his captured arm against the unrelenting tension of the cable. The wire dug deeper, and a bloodless white line popped to the surface of his skin. "There should be no such thing as tying a fox or a lynx by is paw," he said. "You kill it. Like *this*. It works."

To a varying degree, they all work; the Mohawk and the modified Conibear, the Compensator and the Canada, the Bigelow and the Gabry Challenger, the long-spring leghold and the coil-spring leghold, the Victor Stop Loss and the Oneida Jump, the necksnare and the footsnare, the Havahart and the Sure Strike. There is this old saying about building a better mousetrap. And the tinkerers keep trying. The U.S. Patent Office is flooded with patent applications for new trap designs. In recent years, more than 350 different kinds of traps have been tested in Canada alone. Yet for all the tinkering and testing, not one single trap—by any reasonable definition of what might constitute a *humane* capture or kill—can be said to "work" efficiently 100 percent of the time. Perhaps no trap ever will. So little else does.

In 1975, the general manager of the Ontario Humane Society, one Thomas Hughes, appeared in Washington at a congressional hearing on the leghold trap. It was his conclusion then that the "futile search" for an acceptable alternative might prove one thing, if nothing else—"that the humane trap, as such, may never be found." Still, there was one last shred of hope, and Hughes constructed it like this: "I believe very firmly, Mr. Chairman, that if government would say to industry, which takes millions of dollars out of these animals—if government would say, 'Five years from now you will have to stop trapping if, in the meantime, you have not come up with an alternative,' then I think you will see a frantic search by industry to find the alternative." Of course no government, neither U.S. nor Canadian, has issued such an ultimatum. The search goes on. In the United States, it has been anything but frantic.

It might be said that the search got off to a bad start. Sometime in the 1870s, so the story goes, a dying trapper, penitent for all the blood and gore on his conscience, bequeathed to the humanitarian Henry Bergh a sum of $40,000. Bergh accepted the money and proceeded to offer prizes for the invention of humane traps. The record does not indicate what improvements issued from this contest; though one might guess, given the toothy bite of leghold traps in those days, that the Bergh Awards probably resulted in some minor advance—equivalent, let us say, to the medieval dentist's discovery that pliars are more humane than chisel and hammer when extracting a tooth. No matter. Bergh distinguished himself by preaching against cruelty across the length and breadth of America. In the winter, it is said, he attired himself in fur, head to toe.

The Anti-Steel-Trap League, based in Washington, D.C., entered the fray in the 1920s. One of its most colorful crusades was an effort to cast shame upon the Association of Audubon Societies—from whence, the National Audubon Society—for using steel to trap muskrats at the Paul J. Rainey Wildlife Sanctuary in Louisiana. In an article entitled "Blood Money for the Audubon Association," Mrs. Edward Breck, the League president, charged that between 1927 and 1932, nearly a quarter-million animals were taken in steel traps on the sanctuary; and that, over an eight-year period, the Audubon Association had realized more than $100,000 in revenue "from this nefarious business." Audubon President T. Gilbert Pearson explained that the trapping of muskrats was necessary at Rainey in order to prevent them from over-grazing the three-cornered grass that dominates the sanctuary marshes and is a staple for geese. Mrs. Breck did not buy that argument. In her article, she quoted a Rainey neighbor as saying that the Audubon traps were catching not only muskrat but, in fact, "large numbers of ducks and geese" as well. The League in its time stirred up much heat, and some light, too. It did not, however, have much success either in banning steel from the Rainey Sanctuary or in bringing about any significant change in the design of American traps.

In the 1950s, the trapper Frank Conibear came out of the woods of British Columbia with an idea for a quick-kill trap. He sold the patent to an American manufacturer. The new device was widely hailed as a humane alternative to the leghold. It worked. But not every time. Sometimes, it *didn't* kill; it crippled. Frank Conibear returned to the manufacturer with modifications for improving the trigger mechanism, the striking bars. After some foot-dragging, the changes were introduced in the late 1970s. Still, for the Conibear and other so-called killer-traps, there remained one inherent flaw: since they have this potential to kill, their use on land is prohibited in some of our more domesticated jurisdictions. Catch-22. To placate the humaniacs, and maybe your own conscience, you build a better "mouse-trap"—and then government says you can't use it because it might kill a dog or a cat. And since many, if not most, U.S. trappers operate in Tabby 'n' Rover country rather than in wilderness, this means back to square one—the leghold trap. But the leghold is deemed to be inhumane, especially if it is going to result, as the humaniacs say it often does, in a three-legged pet. Catch?

Which brings me to the cage, or box, trap. The tender trap. The Havahart, for example. Many people in the humane movement believe this to be the only acceptable trap, in that it takes an animal alive and presumably unharmed. Havaharts are hot backyard items among the gentry of suburban America. Good for pesky garbage-can 'coons, and for the woodchuck savaging bulbs in the daffodil beds. But for the trapper? A single Havahart suitable for raccoon costs upwards of forty dollars and weighs nearly twenty pounds. For the same price, and less weight, a trapper could buy and put into place a dozen coil-spring leghold traps, or more than a half-dozen Conibears. I think of Alcide Giroux and of Registered Trapline NB-12. To work it with Havaharts exclusively, I figure Giroux would need a Mack truck, twelve stout *voyageurs* with strong backs, and a *canot de maître* to replace his skimpy canoe.

Much of the heat in the continuing debate over the leghold trap centers on the question of whether or not an animal so caught actually suffers extreme pain and stress, and to what extent steel jaws inflict damage to flesh and bone. Some leghold apologists like to start with the premise that animals, being animals, do *not* experience pain, much less such emotions as fear and anxiety. Others say that after an initial struggle, the animal simply lies down and goes to sleep with a numb foot. Such are the traps of the human mind. For their part, the anti-legholders go to the other extreme and trot out their photographic dossiers that are calculated to hit you like a scream in the night. So if that is the heat of it, where is the light?

Possibly the best light comes now from Canada, where government researchers recently completed a review of field studies conducted on both sides of the border by biologists, wildlife managers, and trappers. Among findings cited were these:

— Of 87 animals taken in coil-spring leghold traps, 35 showed no signs of injury, 28 showed minor to moderate skin lacerations, 15 had sustained fractures, and 17 had chewed their feet or toes. (Animals with multiple injuries were apparently counted more than once.) This from L. T. Berchielli and B. F. Tullar, Jr., in the *New York Fish & Game Journal*, 1981.

– From Quebec, three trappers reported catch records for muskrats in terrestrial (nondrowning) leghold sets. With #1 Victors on short chains, they captured 12 muskrats, two of which were already missing a front leg. Seven other 'rats had "wrung off"—the trapper's euphemism for a situation in which an animal escapes by leaving a part of itself behind in the trap. With #1 Victors on long chains, the trappers took 17 muskrats, three of which had almost wrung off.

– From Ontario, Milan Novak reported in 1980 that of 26 raccoons taken in #2 legholds modified to prevent full closure of the jaws, eight had cut tendons or broken bones, two had extensive swelling, but none had chewed a foot.

– From an earlier study, Novak reported that 25 of 84 animals caught in terrestrial leghold sets showed signs of struggle and "prolonged death." But only nine of 336 animals taken in leghold drowning sets showed evidence of a struggle.

– In a research paper on coyotes in Upper Michigan in 1979, K. R. Morris reported that while trapped limbs often seem to sustain only minor injuries, X-ray examination will prove later that sometimes these limbs have broken bones or badly torn tendons.

As for the nonselectivity of the terrestrial leghold set (for some critics, an issue in its own right), a report from Texas in 1974 found that in a predator-control program aimed at bobcats and coyotes, nontarget species taken exceeded the captured predators by a ratio of 1.3 to 1. The nontarget animals included peccary, rabbit, deer, wild turkey, quail, vulture, and owl. But to be fair, one can hardly extrapolate Texan tragedies throughout the rest of North America.

While the incidence of wring-offs and fractured bones can be measured, however uncertainly, what remains elusive is the measure of suffering experienced by the animal in a leghold trap. Laboratory tests are not altogether conclusive, for the simple reason that the animal is already under stress from being there.

And in the field, what can one possibly do? At the *snap*, leap from behind the nearest tree with a dry-cell battery in one hand and an electroencephalograph in the other?

Still, this much is known. All mammals have sensory systems hitched to their brains. Biologists call it the paleospinothalamic system. It conducts pain from its source to the regions of the brain controlling emotional feeling, and therefore, behavior. Every vertebrate species ever examined has such a mechanism, in one form or another. It is a fact of life denied only by intellectual troglodytes and the sort of biblical fundamentalist who believes that Eve was manufactured out of Adam's rib in a place called the Garden of Eden, about four thousand years ago.

At the Humane Society of the United States in Washington, D.C., is a veterinarian-author and ethologist named Michael W. Fox. A few months before joining Giroux on his trapline, I called on Fox, and we sat in his office talking about what science has deduced about thresholds of suffering out there in the woods. Fox said: "We can't use objective tools to measure the subjective. There is always going to be an element of doubt. The gap can be bridged only by ethics, in the sense that we should give the animal the benefit of that doubt."

He spoke of the earthworm. He said that the worm, when disturbed, secretes a chemical to communicate its alarm. He spoke of fish. Under stress, some fish change color. He spoke of the pain reflex, of panting by canids, of pupil dilation and increased pulse. I asked him what it meant when a captured coyote, for example, lies down and curls up beside the leghold trap. He said: "The absence of behavior is behavior itself. In humans, it is called catatonia, or tonic immobility. But, you see, pain is not the primary issue. It is fear and anxiety. There are the real stresses. These are *wild* animals we speak of. When they cannot escape from restraint—regardless of pain, there is anxiety."

In laboratories, Fox said, researchers have confined rats, without painful stimuli, at close quarters. The rats cannot move around. It is that tight in the cage. Within twelve hours, he said, gastric ulceration sets in. Within twenty-four hours, some of the rats are dead.

"If that's the case," I said, "then, short of a quick kill, there is nothing to minimize the suffering. The Havahart, then, is no better than the leghold."

"What I'm arguing," said Fox, "is that even the so-called humane trap is unacceptable."

I relayed some of this to Alcide Giroux when we returned to his camp from Maurice's. Giroux was spreading a couple of lynx skins to dry in front of the Franklin stove, and he said, "Fox, eh? That's a good name. I like it."

"It's his real name, too," I said. "Some people used to wonder, though. Here was this Mike Fox, author of *The Soul of the Wolf*."

"Wolf is also a good name," Giroux said. "Now your friend in Connecticut—the one who traps pencils?"

"Priscilla Feral."

"For real? How did she get a name like *that*?"

"She chose it," I said. "And since most of the trappers down there don't know what it means, they figure she's got to be French Canadian."

For bedtime reading at Alcide Giroux's camp on the Sturgeon River, I had brought along the *Report of the Federal Provincial Committee for Humane Trapping*. It was hot off the press, the valedictory of a team of Canadians who had spent the better part of seven years trying to set some standards to make death a lot easier, or at least faster, for those furry critters out there in the woods. I can hardly call the *Report* a good bedtime story. In fact, for an American it can be downright depressing. It makes you wonder what is so wrong in your own country that nothing—*absolutely* nothing—comparable has even been undertaken by the States, and why Canadians of differing perspectives can communicate with one another while we still shriek from the dark of our ideological caves. Sometimes I think one of the best things about being American is the Canadian connection. There are so few truly civilized nations left in the world, it's nice to have one for a neighbor. Who knows? One of these days, something good might rub off on old Uncle Sam. Like what? For openers, like the Canadian effort to set standards for humane trapping.

The Federal Provincial Committee for Humane Trapping was established in 1973 in response to a growing concern among Canadians about the hardware and methods used in the harvest of furbearing animals. It brought together representatives of the federal and provincial governments, the fur industry, the humane establishment, and the trapping fraternity. (A scientific and technical advisory subcommittee was also appointed, and among its members was the trail boss of Registered Trapline NB-12, Giroux himself.) The committee's mandate was broad: "Within a maximum of five years [later extended to seven], to recommend to the provinces, traps and trapping techniques for all furbearers which will, insofar as the state of the science or the art will allow, provide the greatest 'humaneness' in holding or killing furbearers . . ." The committee defined the concept of a humane death as being one in which an animal suffers minimal distress—death or unconsciousness leading to death within three minutes. Humane capture was defined as one during which an animal is held not only with minimal distress but with minimal physical damage.

In its seven years, the committee received more than $1.3 million in grants from the federal and provincial governments and from the private sector. Among the private contributors: the Canadian Association for Humane Trapping, the Ontario Trappers Association, and the Hudson's Bay Company. Research participants included the University of Guelph, McMaster University, the universities of Alberta and Saskatchewan, and the Ontario Research Foundation. More than three hundred trap inventions were submitted to the committee for consideration. More than one hundred were mechanically evaluated for impact and clamping forces. Of those classified as killer-traps, sixteen were found to have some humane potential for specific animals under certain conditions.

Regarding the use of steel-jaw leghold traps in terrestrial sets, the committee had this to say in its final report: "In summary, research and field studies have demonstrated that [this trap] is nonspecific, causes injuries in all species studied, and results in observable distress and probably pain in many individuals . . . Trappers recognize the limitations of leghold traps for [marten, mink, and fisher], and the recommendation for using quick-kill traps for only certain animals is enshrined in the Canadian Trappers Federation Code of Conduct and other similar codes. FPCHT files contain letters from trappers whose motivation for working on new traps was dissatisfaction with legholds or even remorse for having caused suffering to animals they had trapped with inadequate devices in the past."

Still, the committee found that in Canada, as in the United States, legholds are used more commonly than any other kind of trap. A survey in Alberta showed the ratio of legholds to Conibears to be about four to one. Another survey, by the committee itself, sought to determine the number and kinds of all traps used by a random sample of members of the Ontario Trappers Association. The overall response indicated that legholds accounted for 43 percent of the trappers' hardware; Conibears, 31 percent; killing snares, 25 percent; and such other devices as footsnares and submarine box traps, scarcely one percent. Given the leghold's continuing preeminence, the committee was moved to conclude that "discontinuance" of unmodified versions of this trap "will have an impact on the trapping activities of many Canadian trappers; but the impact need not be severe if made under phase-out conditions, and can in the long run be expected to benefit the industry. Implementation of the recommendations outlined in this report would in the long term allow some 98.5 percent of all furbearers trapped in Canada to be taken in methods with the potential for allowing rapid unconsciousness or submersion asphyxia."

In its recommendations to the provinces, the committee all but swept the leghold trap into the waste bin. Among the recommended trapping methods, by species, were these:

— For mink and muskrat—on land, killing traps only; underwater, killing traps or leghold drowning sets ensuring rapid submergence of the animal in at least twelve inches of water.

— For raccoon and fisher—killing traps only (though evidence is cited for suggesting "an excellent potential for specialized footsnares for raccoon").

– For beaver and otter—killing traps only, both on land and in water. The committee notes the need for further research on holding devices designed to take beaver when they are long underwater and short on oxygen. On the basis of laboratory tests, the use of slide-wire drowning sets is *not* recommended. The tests showed beaver conscious and struggling up to nine and a half minutes after entrapment.

– For lynx, bobcat, badger, and wolverine—killing traps only (though for lynx and bobcat, the committee sees some potential for footsnares and necksnares).

– For fox, coyote, and wolf—killing traps "should not be used." The behavioral characteristics of wild canids, the committee says, are such that "the effectiveness of killer traps is limited." What's more, the striking and clamping energy levels required to kill canids are so high as to render the traps "very dangerous" to their owners. Therefore, the committee recommends the use of modified leghold traps, while citing a "potential" for footsnares. A modified leghold is defined as one in which "the force or action of the restraining mechanism is diffused by the materials and/or conformation of the restraining parts."

And how do the various constituencies in Canada feel about the committee's final report? For its part, the moderate Canadian Association for Humane Trapping is rather pleased—or will be, when and if the provincial wildlife ministries get around to implementing the recommendations through regulatory reform and trapper education. CAHT believes there is still much research to be done, especially in the area of underwater trapping and in establishing kill-threshold criteria for a number of understudied species. It is *not* pleased with the factor of three minutes as the time frame for a humane death, and hopes for some shortening up there.

The Canadian Trappers Federation has "serious reservations" about the three-minute limit as well, but its perspective, of course, is from the other side of the stopwatch. And for the most part, the Federation finds "not aceptable" the repetitious restrictions to killing traps only, especially in the case of lynx and bobcat, and the restriction to modified legholds for the wild canids. "By the very nature of their neck structure," the Federation observes in its critique of the committee report, "lynx and bobcat are particularly suited for quick, humane death in a proper cable and lock combination-type killer snare." As for the canids: "There is a consensus among trappers that a proper cable and lock combination on a killing-type snare is an effective and humane device for use on fox, wolf, and coyote. It is therefore a necessary tool for fur harvest and trapline management."

And how did Alcide Giroux, the technical advisor, feel about the report that night north of Nipissing when he spread the lynx skins to dry in front of the Franklin stove?

He said, "I told them: 'Listen, I'm only a trapper, but what the hell have you done to research the *snare*?'"

Apparently they had not done as much as they might have, and certainly not as much as Giroux would have liked. They had interviewed trappers who were expert with snares, as Giroux was. They had gone with a few into the field to see what the necksnare had done to coyotes. In a laboratory, they had monitored the snaring by neck of a lynx and a fox. The lynx jumped into the air and died in five minutes. The fox, according to the committee report, "fought the snare deliberately and consistently, and was subjected to euthanasia after five minutes."

"That fox wasn't wild," said Giroux. "It was from a fur farm. The whole thing was done wrong. There has to be more research to determine which wire and which lock work best."

Giroux threw a log into the Franklin and went to bed in the other room. I slipped into my sleeping bag on that mattress as big as the Ritz and watched the fire backlighting the tufts on the ears of the lynx on the floor. And I thought to myself, and of the lynx:

If I were in your paws and had the choice, Mister Lynx, I would prefer to take it as you did, with Alcide's aircraft cable around my neck, jumping in the air like your friend at the laboratory, choking, dead in five minutes or even fifteen; rather than caught by the foot in a modified leghold, then waiting and waiting, the sun coming up and the sun going down—for the blow to the head and the boot on the chest, still waiting.

The fourth day was to be my last as the tenderfoot of Registered Trapline NB-12. In the evening, I would split for North Bay and beyond and leave this big woods trapper with a bit more room in the cab of his truck, and no more stumbling into fox snares, and no more questions. Giroux said that I should stick around another day to be on hand when his hundredth beaver came out of the water. "But first we must get the ninety-first," he said. "So let's go." And we did that.

We crossed the swinging bridge with a wheelbarrow full of carcasses from the last night's skinning. Giroux had told me earlier that, in a season, he returns more than three tons of "meat" to the woods, recycles it to the bellies of such scavengers as the fox and the fisher and the whiskey jack, and ultimately, reduced to nutrients, to the soil itself. Of course, Giroux's generosity is not without a measure of enlightened self-interest, for what might be food in the belly of one animal can also be bait to the snare for another. Still, Giroux is satisfied to know that nothing is wasted. "You go back in the woods in the spring," he said, "and nothing is left, not even a bone." But the scavengers do not get all of it. Sometimes Giroux saves the hindquarters of a young beaver for his own use, or for friends. Beaver is good meat, and some Canadians are partial to it. I know at least one American who likes to eat beaver, too. We had had some for supper the night before—cut into stew chunks, boiled to skim off the fat, then fast-fried on the stove in an iron skillet by our capable chef, Dave Van Exan of River Valley. A fine texture, beaver; with a taste just about where calf's liver might be if a calf could eat poplar, swim underwater, and live free.

Watching Giroux work his trapline that morning, I began to think that maybe it would be a good idea if I trapped *him*—snared him by the foot when he wasn't looking, trussed him up, took him south across the border (declaring him at Customs on the way), and then turned him loose in Ohio or Connecticut, say, just to see how many good things might rub off on some of the trappers down there. I mean good things like not wasting meat, and not settling for the status quo, and actually caring a great deal about reducing the time frame of an animal's death. Not that such qualities are totally lacking among trappers in the United States. I suppose if a lot of them would stop yelling back at the humaniacs long enough, you'd find a good number with the same fine sensibilities that I admire in Giroux. In any event, a recent study of American trappers would seem to indicate as much.

The research, sponsored by the U.S. Fish and Wildlife Service, was conducted by Professor Stephen R. Kellert of the Yale School of Forestry and Environmental Studies. Kellert is probably the nation's most knowledgeable investigator of American attitudes toward wildlife and natural habitats. For this particular project, he examined a random sample of members of the National Trappers Association, and then compared the results with findings from a larger survey of three thousand Americans representing a broad cross-section of demographic and animal-related activity groups, such as hunters, fishermen, birdwatchers, environmentalists, livestock producers, humane types. "Trapper attitude scale results were often outstanding and unusual," Kellert reports in his summary of the investigation. The trappers were characterized by "exceptional knowledge of animals and a strong appreciation and concern for protecting wildlife and natural habitats even at the expense of various human benefits." Among twenty activity groups, for example, trappers showed a higher degree of knowledge about animals than any other group, except for birdwatchers—higher than members of environmental and humane organizations, and a great deal higher than backpackers and anti-hunters. On the naturalistic scale (described as a "primary interest in and affection for wildlife and the outdoors") and the ecologistic scale ("concern for interrelationships between wildlife species and natural habitats"), trappers again scored near the top, in both instances beating out birdwatchers and backpackers, not to mention the humaniacs. And as an indicator of the trapper's attitude toward habitat protection—even where an issue might not be directly related to fur-bearers—Kellert posed the following premise:

"A large coastal city has an unemployment problem. A major manufacturer wants to build a new plant on a marsh it owns which could employ one thousand people, but conservationists claim this will destroy land needed by a rare bird. Do you agree that this plant should be built, even if it endangers the bird species?"

Eighty percent of the trapper-respondents did *not* agree that the plant should be built. And an even higher percentage did not agree with the statement: "Natural resources must be developed even if the loss of wilderness results in much smaller wildlife populations." Among the general public queried in the larger survey, only 51 percent of the respondents disagreed with that statement.

But for all their concern for protecting habitat, Kellert notes, the trappers surveyed "were strongly oriented toward the consumptive use of animals, and expressed strong antipathy for moralistic objections" to "human dominance over animals and nature." On the issue of the leghold trap, for example, the trappers were almost unanimous. Ninety-six percent said they saw nothing wrong with using steel leghold traps to capture wild animals. Only 18 percent of the general public in the larger survey agreed with them. And 57 percent of the general public said they did not think it was right to kill an animal to make a fur coat.

I was mulling around the edges of that last figure—a U.S. majority opposed to killing animals for fur coats—later that morning when Giroux and Guérin returned to the truck from the Sturgeon River with a big fat beaver between the gunwales of the red canoe. It was a "blanket," Giroux said, explaining the beaver grader's quantitative pecking order for the species: small, medium, large-medium, large, extra large, blanket (like the one here), and super blanket. A top-quality blanket such as this could go for eighty dollars at the auction in North Bay. Five, maybe six, pelts of like size and you have the raw material for a coat that might hang in a shop in New York with a tag asking five, maybe six, thousand dollars. Or more, much more, if the beaver are sheared for the designer Viola Sylbert, then dyed in swaths of flame, green, and copper; or embroidered with metallic gold by Oscar de la Renta. As I was saying: It is such an awfully long way from the trapline to Fifth Avenue.

From Giroux's trapline, the first stop for fur is the receiving department at the Ontario Trappers Association warehouse in North Bay. Each pelt received there is tagged with a computerized ticket bearing the trapper's identification number, and is then graded by size, quality, and color, and remanded to a pile of similar skins that will be sold as a lot, or a string of lots, at an upcoming auction. Samples of each lot are racked for display to the buyers; the rest of the skins—the "bulks"—are stored under refrigeration at temperatures hovering just above freezing. On each skin sold, the trapper pays a four percent commission to the association and a royalty averaging five percent to the provincial government. Prices vary from auction to auction and from year to year, depending on the whims of the arbiters of fashion and on the economic condition of the western world. In 1981, beaver averaged $34.57 per pelt, down from $47.74 in 1980. Muskrat brought $7.51, down from $8.19. Lynx was up, from $214.38 to $282.00; red fox, up from $65.43 to $67.93; and wolf, up from $72.74 to $94.20. The trouble with beaver and muskrat seemed to be linked in part to an unfavorable Eurodollar exchange. The mark and the lira were off. Besides, beaver and muskrat can tie up the investor's money for a long time. It is the penalty one pays for dipping a skin in a vat of dye. How those Germans and Italians do love the colors of the rainbow garnishing the guard hairs of imported wild fur. If only God could go back to square one and make over the muskrat—magenta, perhaps. The Italians would be eternally grateful.

I had gone to the auction at North Bay in April. Most of the fall and winter pelts had already been sold; so that, as auctions go, this was by no means a large one. There were only 290,000 muskrat skins to choose from, and various thousands or hundreds of other pelts. Still, the warehouse was crowded with brokers and manufacturers' representatives from London, Paris, Frankfurt, Milan, Montreal, and New York; and their pinstripe suits stood in contrast to the long white butcher jackets of the sales staff, and the buffalo plaids of the trappers come to observe firsthand how well or poorly the world condition would now reward them.

They were bidding on beaver when I walked into the auction room. Alex Shieff, the association's sales manager, sat behind a high wood-paneled podium at the end of the room, saying: "We'll start these at thirty-five dollars." A hand flicked up from one of the long tables below the podium. "Thirty-six I have in the center," snapped Shieff. "Forty now on the right. Forty-four I have, going to forty-five. Are you all through? Forty-five dollars all done!" I sat through the sale until one particularly fine lot of Ontario beaver went for eighty-one dollars a skin, and then walked out through the display rooms past long rows of cross fox and gray fox and red fox to a rack where lynx skins hung in lots of four on pieces of twine looped through their eye sockets. The top lot here was Number 7,000. Each of the lynx was about five feet long, from the snout down to the tips of the slack hind paws. Superb skins, these. Soft to the touch. A rich, light brown fuzz under the silver tips of the guard hairs. They were to go for four hundred dollars apiece in the afternoon, to Gillick Fur Trading, Inc., of Montreal. I wondered, then, who would be wearing these skins a year from now, and whether or not the wearer would ever pause to wonder herself where the lynx had come from, and by what instinct or notion it had padded to the snare or the trap, and whether it had jumped in the air and died in five minutes or, caught by a paw, awaited the longer ending? Or would the owner of these skins wonder not at all? There are still folks in the cities who think—if they stop to think at all—that food is manufactured in the back rooms of the supermarket. Perhaps one can wear a lynx coat under the same impression: a lynx doesn't live and die—it springs fully tailored from the plate of a Singer sewing machine.

At 7:30 that evening, the 290,000 muskrat pelts came up for bid, by lots of a thousand or more. They lasted until two in the morning. There are six levels of quality for muskrat, and eight of size (from XXL down to "mice"), making a total of forty-eight possible grades, and demanding of a sharp pair of eyes on the skins in the grading process. In the morning, I watched Terry Demers, an association grader, going over some bulks that had come in too late for the auction. Demers trained for this job for six years. When she started, she was the only female fur grader in North America—a puzzlement to me, for I'd guess that women probably have a better eye than men for color and texture. Now she is also qualified to grade otter, and has become proficient with marten as well. Demers stood at a table in her white coat that morning, quickly turning each skin in her hand ('rats are stretched and dried leather-side out), reaching inside to check the fur, then flexing each skin and tossing it into the appropriate pile for size and quality. On a good day, she said, she can repeat this process five thousand times.

The secret of grading 'rats is in the look of the leather, not the feel of the fur. The leather, in effect, speaks for the fur. Dark, the leather says that this is a 'rat taken in the fall, and not yet in prime. Going lighter, the leather speaks of winter and longer hair. Papery, and here is a 'rat from the spring. Blotched around the kidney area, and you have a "shedder." Ticked here and there with tiny half-moon cuts that would be invisible from the fur side, you have a 'rat bitten by a competitor during the mating season. The bites will become holes in the fur in the tanning process. Demers held up a skin peppered with half-moon cuts. "See how they behave themselves?" she said. "Now what would the humane society have to say about this?"

It was a very long day, that last one with Giroux, north of Nipissing. By lunchtime, we had checked nearly two dozen sets, had taken two each of beaver and muskrat, a fox and a mink, and retrieved a large timber wolf, dead, from one of the necksnares. Giroux takes great pains preparing and setting his necksnares. New from the store, the wire is cut to a certain length, then boiled in a pot with twigs from a silver maple, to take off the oil. In the woods, he carries the snares coiled in a white plastic shopping bag, and before taking one out, washes the human scent from his hands by rubbing and crushing a spruce bough. And at the end of each season, he unfastens the noose of a snare and leaves the wire hanging on a branch in the forest, to acquire a further measure of natural flavor for the year ahead.

Over lunch beside a warming jackpine fire, Giroux said that he was growing concerned for the scarcity of mink. "They're not here," he said, "at least not the way they used to be. Plenty of mink around here over the past ten years. But now—" and he shook his head. We had talked about mink earlier in the week with his uncle Pierre Giroux, who lives nearby and traps for the bulk of his income. Pierre had said, "Yes, the mink are going down. Maybe it is the white-spot disease, tularemia." Muskrats seemed to be down, too, he said. There was always a reason for things like this. The trouble would just have to run its course. Then Alcide, as though it were imperative to change the conversation to a pleasanter topic, told his uncle about how he had trapped an American journalist in one of his fox snares. "That's good," said Pierre. "I never caught an American myself, but once I caught a Czech. In a snare, too. The Czech was afraid of wolves. One night in the bush, he heard the wolves howling, and he started to run. He ran the wrong way. For a while, he thought that a wolf had come up and caught him by the foot."

Along the streambeds we checked that afternoon, Giroux's traps yielded muskrat and beaver, but no more mink. Giroux, of course, would survive without more mink, and so would the marketplace. Most commercially utilized mink nowadays—indeed, most furs overall—are "ranch" animals, raised in pens like so many chickens. Such mink, if you can call them that, represent about 55 percent of the North American traffic in raw furs. Mink ranches number in the thousands. Among the states, this is big business in Wisconsin and Minnesota, in Washington and Oregon. Mutation is the name of the game, for color. You can breed Autumn Haze or Emba Pastel, Lunaraine or Azurene, Pearl or Palomino. And then there is black mink. "Black mink for the lady, tuxedo for the gent," they like to say on New York's Seventh Avenue, in the fur garment district. "They go together."

Fashions in fur, as in almost everything else, have oscillated wildly over the years since the end of World War I. When the doughboys came marching home from France, they found their ladies wrapped in coats of cloth with simple fur collars. The cloth soon gave way to full-length fox and raccoon. In the first three post-war years, one hundred million pelts were sold in the United States. The fur industry, for the first time since the heyday of the beaver trade, was off and running again. Henry Fairfield Osborn, the mammalogist, expressed grave concern for the target species. "Furs are now a fashion, just as feathers were forty years ago," he wrote. "Furs are worn in midsummer purely for personal adornment, or to make a display of wealth and luxury."

Though wealth and luxury did not universally prevail through the Great Depression, the trade in furs did. Fashion designers began to toy with new ideas. Out went the long-hair furs, and in came the short. Black mink for the lady, tuxedo for the gent. If diamonds were a girl's best friend, what was her second-best friend? "Make mine mink," the girls responded, and the ranchers obliged. But the daughters of the girls in mink found mink *boring*, so the tastemakers trotted out a line they would advertise as "Fun Furs"—rabbit and lamb, mostly. And spotted cats, too. In 1962, Jacqueline Kennedy, the First Lady of the land, appeared before the eyes of the world in a splash of spots. She was wearing a leopard coat. Six years later, the United States imported 150,000 spotted skins—leopard and cheetah and jaguar and ocelot. A year after that, Congress passed the Endangered Species Act. And that, sartorially, put an end to the spots. No matter. The industry could survive a slump. Besides, now there were all these international designers adding furs to their collections—Yves St. Laurent and Oleg Cassini and Diane Von Furstenberg, among others. The labels helped. By 1973, retail fur sales in the United States were approaching a half-billion dollars. Suddenly, the long-hair furs were in again. Lynx coats were going for $15,000; Russian lynx coats, using the belly fur only, for $150,000. On the avenues, they had a new phrase for it. They called it "Savage Chic."

One day in New York, I turned off Seventh Avenue into West

30th Street and called at the office of Gary Kugler, who is an executive with the American Fur Merchants Association and the Fur Conservation Institute of America, the latter serving more or less as the industry's primary public relations arm. Kugler presented me with a fact sheet on the state of the industry in 1979—the most recent year for which figures were then available. The sheet listed U.S. retail sales at $858.4 million, exports of garments and pelts of $395 million, 600 manufacturers, 7,400 retail establishments, and 250,000 workers "employed directly or indirectly in the United States."

I told Kugler that I could understand these figures in the abstract, but that I was puzzled nonetheless. What was this special fascination for fur, I wanted to know, that could motivate an individual to lay out big bucks for a single garment?

Kugler said, "It's three things, really. First, fur *lasts*. Second, it's *warm*."

"And third," I said, "it's sexy."

"It's more than that," he said. "It's a symbol of—" and he paused, searching for the words, and then, finding them, said, "—of having *made* it."

Eight beaver, three 'rats, a wolf, a fox, and a mink. All in a day's work. And now Giroux was in striking distance of his *Castor* quota. Tomorrow, for sure, he would take his hundredth beaver out of the water, and the rest he would save for the winter weekends. "Yahyah," said Langis Tremblay as we crossed the Sturgeon on the swinging bridge. "Eight beaver is good. But—ohoho—we have only one fox."

Moose steaks for supper, and then, *au revoir*. We stood in the moonlight outside Giroux's cabin. Giroux said, to the two from Quebec: "John asked yesterday what I will do when I retire from the mine at forty-nine. I told him there will be trails and traps and fishing and hunting and cutting the firewood, and before you know it, there goes the year."

"It sounds like a good year to me," I said. "Maybe I'll come back for it if I can."

"Be careful where you put your feet," said Tremblay.

"Good luck," said Guérin.

"Good-bye," said Giroux.

I wished them the same and went up the trail along the fallow fields to the tumbledown farmhouse, and across the river to the railroad siding, and into the car, and down the highway at last to North Bay. In the morning there was a flight to Toronto. I sat by a window in the plane. When I fastened my seatbelt, the lock went *snap*.

We took off and circled over the big lake, and then headed due south over the forest. Looking down, I imagined all the men out there, riding the woods roads in their pickup trucks, checking their lines, poking holes in the ice at the edges of beaver dams, rigging their slide wires and their snares. Just like Giroux. And I thought of his bloodline running back through Paquettes to the very beginning, maybe all the way back to the stocking-cap time of Etienne Brulé, and how difficult it must be to have so much of oneself from the past, when so much of the present is moving so rapidly into the future. Except for the traps. The traps didn't seem to be moving at all. Where were all these new killer traps favored by the Federal Provincial Committee for Humane Trapping? And where was Milan Novak's new foot-snare? Bogged down at the factories, probably. Production problems, no doubt. Marketing difficulties, I daresay. There is a reason for everything. And an excuse, too. Meanwhile, there was this other factory down in Lititz, Pennsylvania, where the Woodstream Corporation was investing heavily in modern manufacturing equipment. For what reason? To make its Victor leghold traps more humane? Hardly. To compete in the leghold market with its Asian imitators. So much for progress.

And finally, I wondered that morning about my own bias and my ambiguity of feeling about this matter of fur. How could I empathize with the life-style of Alcide Giroux in particular, and of woods-savvy trappers in general, and at the same time scorn the wearing of the skins of the animals they kill in their traps? For if you could strip away all this cultural malarkey about having *made* it in fur, and that icy touch of class, and the designer labels that often account for the unaccountable priciness of fur, and if you could be sure that the wildlife managers who set the limits and quotas knew what they were doing (which may well be too much to ask), then—why not? It sure beats warming up to polyester. Besides, the animal is going to die one way or another, sooner or later. Come to think of it, so are we.

Then I saw again in my mind's eye the skin of the lynx on the floor of Giroux's cabin, drying in front of the Franklin stove. Only now it was hanging from a rack in North Bay, a rope through its eye sockets. There was a voice from another room, saying *we'll start these at three hundred and fifty dollars three hundred and eighty I have in the center now four hundred on the right now four hundred and twenty I have going to four hundred thirty now you have four hundred fifty on the left on the left on the left are you through four hundred and fifty all done.*

THE MOUNTAINS,

THE MINERS,

AND MISTER CAUDILL

The mountains rise southeastward of Eden, or what used to be Eden in some people's eyes. *Ken-ta-ke*, the Indians had called it, meaning "among the meadows." Yet when the first paleskin rovers climbed at last to the mountain gaps, they could see no meadows, only a great forest swathed in blue haze on a turbulent ocean of razorback hills. On closer inspection, the hills were found to be laced with coal. But the scouts had no use for coal, so they pressed straight on, north by west, toward the promised land.

Next through the gaps came the cornpatch folks to the coves and hollows of the Kentucky razorbacks. Determined to give some account of the hardships they were forced to endure in this unforgiving but picturesque land, the cornplanters bestowed on their creeks and crossroads such descriptive names as Quicksand and Thousandsticks, Beefhide and Poor Fork, Rowdy and Cutshin, Frozen and Defeated, Hell-Fer-Sartain (For-Certain, that is), and Kingdom Come. For several generations, the residents of these places lived in lean isolation. Then, about the time that newfangled applications of electricity were being introduced elsewhere into almost every phase of American life, a use was discovered at last for Cumberland coal. Whereupon the corn-planters were transformed into miners; their mountains, into a colony for the coal barons.

The miners came out of their hollows to the company towns—towns named to honor such corporate moguls as Fleming and Jenkins and Lynch and McRoberts; or a corporation itself, as in Seco, for the South East Coal Company; or possibly a feature or by-product generic to the industry, as in Carbon Glow, Coalgood, Neon, Drift, Talcum, or, for that matter, Lost Creek. For about two generations, through boom and bust, the residents of the towns lived and worked in bondage to the companies that housed and employed them. Then, about the time that petroleum began to flow into almost every phase of American life, though hardly enough to supplant coal, the moguls proceeded to replace most of their miners with mining machines. Whereupon, there being no other work for the laid-off miners, and no turning back to the corn-patch, not a few were consigned to absolute poverty; their hamlets, to trash heaps.

Rarely if ever before in the annals of industrial colonialism had so little been left to so many. Here, in a region from which the companies had extracted great wealth (and would soon extract even more), were several of the poorest counties in the United States. Welfare and food stamps replaced company scrip. Schools produced illiterates. Roads and bridges collapsed as the hauling of coal shifted from rail cars to Mack trucks. Creeks ran opaque with effluent from privies. Hepatitis spread like the worst kind of plague. So did intestinal worms. Men with the black lung were old—or dead—before their time.

At last, having stripped the mountaineers of their dignity, the coal barons turned their attention to stripping the mountains of their verdant good looks. Instead of boring a tunnel into a coal seam, and mining there, underground, the idea now was to peel away a strip of the mountainside, the trees and the soil and the rock, and proceed to mine the coal in horizontal cuts, on the newly exposed surface. The resultant spoil was simply pushed from the edge of the cut and allowed, over time, to gully and erode into the nearest hollow, much to the detriment of the creek therein, not to mention an occasional cornpatch or cabin. Above the cuts loomed the vertical highwalls of shale or sandstone, oozing water in sinuous rills. At certain times of a sunny day, seeps glistened like tears on the shaven cheeks of the ravaged mountains.

On an unsunny, rainslick morning in the spring of 1960, a lawyer named Harry Caudill went out from his home at Mayking, near Whitesburg in Letcher County, to deliver the commencement address at an eighth-grade graduation in some tumbledown, two-room, coal-town schoolhouse. Caudill would never forget it. There were seven graduates. One had been orphaned by an accident in the mines. The father of another sat wheezing with silicosis. Only one of the parents had steady work. A leak in the roof spattered rain on a scarred desk. Gusts of wind rattled the windows in their flimsy frames. Outside, he could see a muddy playground pooling the rain, a cluster of empty houses, an ancient pile of mining slag. Then everyone stood for the singing. The song they sang was "America the Beautiful."

Harry Caudill would think of that schoolhouse sometimes when he looked up from his place at Mayking to the purpled majesty of Pine Mountain, yonder across the valley of the North Fork of the Kentucky River. There was such a great and awful distance between the bitter reality of this valley and the bright promise he perceived on those still unspoiled slopes. One day, not long after, Caudill turned from the mountain view and, since he was given to an oratorical style, began to dictate to his wife, Anne, the first fine fragments of an angry book.

Night Comes to the Cumberlands, published by Atlantic-Little, Brown in 1963, delivered a scathing indictment of strip-mine abuses, a mind-boggling revelation of a regional people at peril—"an anchor," he called them, "dragging behind the rest of America." Caudill's polemic made a lot of folks mad, but it turned heads. And in the long run it would sharpen America's distaste for the excesses of strip-mining just as surely as Rachel Carson's *Silent Spring*, that other great classic of the early sixties, would poison the nation's appetite for DDT.

Though *Cumberlands* would have a profound effect on the molding of public policy—for example, the Kennedy-Johnson efforts to bandage the wounds of Appalachian poverty, the enactment of federal strip-mine legislation a decade later—books and policies and laws would prove no match for the entrenched and intertwined interests of King Coal and Kentucky politics.

More than a quarter-century and a dozen Caudill books later, night still shrouds the razorback hills and hollows of the Cumberland Plateau. And Harry Caudill, though not as lonely for allies as before, continues his long fight to bring, as he once put it, "the sad reality and the splendid dream a littler closer together, for my friends, my kinsmen, my fellow mountaineers."

I

The best way to Caudill country, if you are coming in from the north, is to aim for Lexington on Interstate 75, exit onto the Bert T. Combs Mountain Parkway, and then mosey along to the razorbacks on State Route 15 through Vortex and Ned, past turnoffs to Viper and Sassafras. That way you go through the looking glass. That way, on the outskirts of Lexington, you see where some of the Cumberlands' bituminous profits get laundered as real estate. You pass the velvet bluegrass downs of the horse farms, mile after mile of pasture and manse, the long driveways sweeping back from pillared gates. Old money? Sure, money that has known wood-panel station wagons and mint juleps in silver cups. But there is something else here, too, a kind of glitzy prime-time architectural panache that suggests fresher coin—money dating, say, from about the time that the Arab oil embargo, in the seventies, brought on the second coronation of King Coal and made overnight millionaires of a handful of opportunistic Kentuckians.

The Mountain Parkway puts that away fast. This is one of those four-lane Appalachian Development Highways built in the sixties to bring the mountains closer to the meadows, the mines to the markets. Before you know it, you are into the limestone knobs of Daniel Boone National Forest, which can only mean that the fabulous Red River Gorge is somewhere nearby—"the little Grand Canyon of eastern America," Harry Caudill (pronounced CAW-dle) once called it.

After the turnoff for Hazard, at Campton, you begin to sense what really makes Kentucky tick. And it isn't bluegrass. It's coal. Coal piled high in the big Mack trucks that are roaring by out of the southeast, tarps fluttering in the airstream (or, more commonly, in open defiance of laws designed to keep coal dust out of the ambient air, no tarps at all). And the empty trucks going your way, deadheading back to the mines for another load and another run to the market. Where does it all come from, this stuff that keeps the lights of America burning, that bulks so big in the Kentucky dollars derby that all other homegrown products—bourbon, burley tobacco, fried chicken, you name it— are left at the gate? I mean, those highwalls you see now and then around a bend of the road, giving some faraway hill the look of a Shawnee scalplock. Those are the old cuts, the cruel cuts that saddened Harry Caudill and led him to write that first angry book. But where does it come from *now?* The trucks turn on, the trucks turn off these little side roads as you get on toward Breathitt and Perry counties, but where are the mines? And where is this poverty, hand-in-glove with the riches of coal, that Caudill speaks of? It's not to be seen from the highway at Jackson; nor at Hazard, either. But then appearances are always deceptive, when perceived through the looking glass.

The glass—the windshield, if you prefer—does not tell who owns the land beside the road here, or beyond the ridge where the Macks turn off up the gravel roads. But if these Kentucky coal counties are anything like their counterparts in the rest of Appalachia, then you can bet that most of the land on the surface and nearly all of the rights to the minerals beneath are owned by boardroom folks who hang their hats not in Jackson or Hazard but in Houston or New York City. At a conference on the land and economy of Appalachia not long ago, someone trotted out a study showing that, in an eighty-county region, absentee landlords controlled three-quarters of the land. Forty-six of the top fifty landlords were corporations.

And the glass does not tell how, in order to extract coal from southeastern Kentucky, some of these same corporations now use a process that Caudill himself could hardly have imagined in those long-ago days of the first book. The process is called "mountaintop removal." Huge machines, some with high-lift scoops as long as a football field, take it *all* off now, no fooling around with scalplocks and highwalls. Just put the machines in place and start leveling the whole top of the mountain until an entire seam of coal lies exposed. Then scoop it up and truck it away and fill the adjacent hollows with the leftover spoil and—*voilà!*—you have a capital investment, a flat piece of real estate in an up-and-down country where flatness commands the topmost dollar.

And of course the glass cannot begin to reveal the hard facts of the human condition on the Cumberland Plateau. Facts that show unemployment rates today to be among the highest in the nation; two out of three adults without work in some counties, the jobless caught between a lack of diversified opportunities and the concentration of coal production into fewer and fewer hands. And over it all hovers a lingering stench of political corruption and lax enforcement of health and environmental regulations, such that southeastern Kentucky may well stand topmost in America for the impurity of its water and—this you *can* see, up the side roads—the ubiquity of its wastes. Land and people are inseparable, Harry Caudill had been saying over and over all these years. If the one becomes poor, the other "will sink with it into dusty oblivion."

Mayking is a hop and a skip past Whitesburg on the way to Pound Gap, and here we are. The Caudill place sits on an open slope above the valley, with a pine plantation on the hillside behind, some hemlock in front, a beech or two, a big tulip tree. The house is brick. Spring flowers are in bloom beside the walk. Once upon a time, about forty years ago, nothing but broom sedge and hardrock sprouted here, the legacy of a century of cornpatch cultivation. The hoe and plow, according to Caudill, had posted "the last of the fertile soil to the Mississippi Delta." The lawyer and his bride, moving in, put the land together again with conifer plantings and brush piles to catch the annual fall of needle and bark scale. Go and do likewise, Caudill would tell his readers later on: "Find some jaded land and buy it . . . Plant it in trees . . . It is a wonderful way to grow in wisdom, while enriching a nation that cannot grow by a single inch though its people multiply ceaselessly. A healing land can be therapeutic in the treatment of many human ills."

And there he is at the open door, tall, angular, the long slope of the forehead running back from those hooded, almost oriental eyes. He speaks—an anecdote, an allusion, a quote from some lion of literature—and right away you recognize the rhetorical delivery as *New York Times*man Ben A. Franklin once described it: the voice of one "who orates even the most routine utterances, with frequent rolling recitals . . . in a sonorous mountain drawl." We plan the visit. There will be a drive in the white Mercury in the afternoon, to some of the old company towns, Seco and McRoberts possibly. Anne Caudill used to call these courtesies to visiting firemen "Harry's Horror Tours" but doesn't anymore; there have been so many. And later, tomorrow perhaps, or next time down this way, we will take a happier drive to a wondrous place called Bad Branch, other side of the mountain.

What mountain might that be, I'm asking.

"Pine Mountain," he says, pointing at the great ridge across the valley. "Isn't it wonderful? It broods over us and pities us, and it would weep for us, too, if it had tears."

Pine Mountain dominates southeastern Kentucky. It is the Commonwealth's front range, its cornerstake in the true, honest-to-hardrock Appalachians. In form, the mountain resembles an extruded spine rather than a peak, and it stretches 125 miles almost from Jellico, Tennessee, to Elkhorn City, Kentucky. The northwest face of Pine Mountain—that brooding face into which Harry Caudill stares every day—rises almost 2,000 feet in places above the creeks and rivers that course at its feet. The highest point is fixed at 3,273 feet above sea level, and Caudill can see that from his place, too. In all of its linear miles and vertical feet, the ridge is cut by flowing water in only one place, at

Pineville, where the mighty Cumberland River has carved its way through the rock, hellbent for the Ohio. Yet here and there is evidence that ancient waters tried elsewhere to breach the mountain barrier, for notches appear some two to five hundred feet below the crest of the ridge—Bear Wallow Gap is one of them, Salt Trace Gap another, and, not far from Caudill's, the notch known as Scuttlehole, up near the head of Cowan Creek, and Ran Polly Gap, head of Bad Branch.

Pine Mountain, like much of the high country roundabout that has not yet been flayed by the strip-miners, supports one of the most superb forests on the face of the earth—"Appalachia's glory," Caudill has called it, a woodland "tenacious of life and deeply rooted in the vicissitudes and triumphs of antiquity." Foresters hold it by a different handle. They call it a mixed mesophytic forest, meaning it is distinguished by a complex diversity of tree species, numbering more than one hundred and thriving under the moderately wet conditions one would expect of an area averaging fifty inches of rain a year. The scholar-of-the-house in such botanical matters, one E. Lucy Braun, described the mixed mesophytic as the oldest of all the deciduous associations, the seedbed, if you will, of all other types of hardwood forest throughout eastern North America. Here are towering pencil-straight tulip poplars, sugar maples and sourgums, white oaks and black walnuts, hickories and cherries and ashes and redbuds and magnolias, persimmons and sycamores and willows, hollies and rhododendrons, hemlocks, cedars, and pines.

Once there was a different sort of forest growing here, and a different roll and pitch to the land. By the geologist's clock, the time was Pennsylvanian, 300 million years ago. There were no mountains. The Father of Waters hadn't even been born yet; it lay under a vast and shallow sea. This Kentucky country here was low swampy coastal plain. It was hot. Out of the limestones and shales laid down in earlier times sprouted a strange, steaming forest of giant horsetail calamites and towering mosslike lepidodendrons and ferns. For millions of years, through all of Pennsylvanian time and then some, these flowerless but prodigiously reproductive green things thrived under a tropical sun, storing up its radiant energy, topping out, begetting yet another generation of green things, then toppling to the floor of the swamp, one rotting layer upon another. By and by the accumulated weight of all this litter caused a subsidence of the earth and the sea rolled in from the west, depositing new layers of limes and shales above the fern-forest peats. As the weight of the overburden increased, so did the temperature of the petrified litter. Thus did the earth's own pressure cooker begin the process that would turn the peat into coal.

Meanwhile, the lay of the land was getting complex. The Appalachian Revolution was under way, with much folding and faulting, drifting and uplifting. Caught in the pinch, a great block of the earth's crust thrust itself to the northwest along a hundred-mile fault line. The front edge of this troughlike block would become known as Pine Mountain. West of the fault, a high peneplain stretched where once only seas and swamps had prevailed. Now it was time for erosion to go to work on the plain's softer rocks. Thus did Appalachian water begin the process that would sculpt the sinuous valleys and dissected hills of the Cumberland Plateau.

And ultimately the water would expose those long-buried seams of bituminous coal. On a fine spring day in 1751—too recent a time to show even on the second-hand of the geologist's clock—a buckskin rover, name of Christopher Gist, was working his way up the North Fork of the Kentucky River. He had just trekked a full circle through the Ohio Valley, sniffing things out for some speculators back Virginia way, and now he was heading for Pound Gap and home. There probably were a handful of paleskins this side of the fault-block mountain before Gist, but none kept a journal. Gist did. He had already noted the "almost impassable" ledges and steep banks along the "Little Cuttaway" (his name for the North Fork), had cursed the laurel thickets that one could hardly creep through without cutting the way. Now he was just a cut short of the Gap, maybe right down here in this valley below Caudill's place. "On all the branches of the Little Cuttaway River," Gist would write in his entry for March 27th, "was great plenty of fine coal."

Since 1973, the year of the Arab oil panic, the Commonwealth of Kentucky has led the United States in the production of coal, distancing itself from such old-time front-runners as Pennsylvania and West Virginia, and such up-'n'-comers as Wyoming. Last year alone the industry extracted 177 million tons from Kentucky's two principal coalfields—the western, in the rolling country called Pennyrile, and the eastern, in the razorbacks of the Cumberland Plateau. The western Kentucky coal, which accounts for about a third of total statewide production, tends to have a higher sulfur content and has been used over the years by public and private utilities to generate electricity. The cleaner, hotter-burning eastern coal was long-prized for coking before Big Steel hit the skids; now it is in demand throughout the Ohio Valley as "compliance" coal—that is, as the utilities' fuel-of-choice in complying with federal standards for sulfur dioxide emissions. As those standards get tighter in the years ahead, and they must if there is ever to be any end to the dreadful effects of acid rain, the demand for low-sulfur eastern Kentucky coal will become even greater. About half of the annual production in the eastern fields is extracted by surface mining; but this portion, too, is likely to rise, especially as the big corporations, with their big machines, find it increasingly practical to secure the coal not just by shaving the mountains but by cutting their heads off as well.

The eastern Kentucky coalfield, part of the larger Appalachian Coal Province that runs from New York and Pennsylvania down into Alabama, covers some 10,500 square miles. It is believed to contain accessible reserves of about 50 billion tons, or enough coal, in round numbers and without any change in the rate of production, to last well into the 24th Century (by which time, one hopes, the survivors of acid rain and the greenhouse effect will have found some better way to make the dark light enough). Geologists further parse the territory by dividing the eastern coalfield into six parts. One of those parts is the Hazard

District, which embraces Breathitt, Harlan, Knott, Leslie, Letcher, and Perry counties, the very heart and soul of Caudill country. That's for horizontal definition. For vertical, the geologists take a slab of the earth almost a mile thick, and parse *that* into four or five formations, and rummage around in the one they call Breathitt, after the county, and find about forty-five different layers of coal interbedded with various strata of siltstones, sandstones, shales, and nodular limestones. The coal seams get names, too: Hamlin and Fire Clay and Amburgy and Upper Elkhorn, among many others. In the Hazard District, the seams of all the accessible formations are thought to contain about 17 billion tons, or 90 percent of what was there when people first started plucking the stuff two centuries ago.

And that is a truly frightening thought, for if extraction of only ten percent of the coal can leave the Hazard District looking like *this*, with all of its tumbledown company towns and its tearful highwalls, what will the district look like if or when the remaining 90 percent has been plucked from beneath the nodular limestones and reamed from the flats of the topless mountains?

To appreciate just how vulnerable these mountains may be, consider Kentucky's curious and sorry failure over the years to guarantee what is elsewhere in America generally taken for granted—namely, that a man's home, or mountain, is his castle. It goes all the way back to scratch, when the Bluegrass was a county of colonial Virginia and logs were still green in those cabins up at Boonesborough. Then, it was every man for himself; and even after Old Virginia signed aboard the republic and spun off Kentucky as the fifteenth state, settlers were staking their claims to the flimsiest of titles—sometimes no more than the principle of first-come priority and the whack of a tomahawk on a boundary tree. Inevitably, this led to a-feudin', a-fussin', and a-fightin'. By Harry Caudill's account: "It has been rightly said there is not a survey corner in Kentucky that has not been shot over or lawed over." And inevitably, too, title confusion led to abuses in the coalfields. First came the wildcat surveyors of the 1880s, sniffing things out for the barons-to-be, chiseling the cornpatchers out of their coal-rich hillsides. Then, around the turn of the century, the coal speculators discovered a new chisel, a clever chisel, an outrageous chisel. It was known then and is known today as the broad-form deed.

As conceived and executed in the Commonwealth of Kentucky, the broad-form deed came into widespread use as a device to facilitate the coal companies' access to subsurface wealth without their having to pay a fair price for it. It worked like this. The company agent comes to the cornpatch farmer and offers, say, fifty cents an acre for the right to take his coal, when and if. Well, why not, thinks the unschooled mountaineer. After all, if the company should decide to mine someday, there would only be this one little hole in the ground. One little minehead hole leading to an underground tunnel. No more. And the mountaineer would still own the surface. The land would be *his*. Right?

It may have been remotely right, but only for a while. Then the strip-miners came into the country. Then the progeny of the broad-formed farmers woke up one morning and found bulldozers pushing *their* land around, dismantling their castles. As the land had been handed down from parent to child, so had the broad-form deed been passed from underground mine boss to strip-mine buckeroo. "I sat by the desk of Governor Edward Breathitt," Harry Caudill testified to a congressional subcommittee in 1971, "when eighty-year-old Mrs. Bige Ritchie told the governor how she stood on the front porch of her home and saw the bulldozers come to her family cemetery after coal . . . She shouted to them that the graves of her children lay in front of them, but they ignored the pleas of an old, impoverished, and helpless woman. 'I thought my heart would bust in my breast,' she told the governor, 'when I saw the coffins of my children come out of the ground and go over the hill.'"

For a generation after the coming of the strippers, Kentuckians protested the cruel inequity of the broad-form deed. In effect they were told: Tough luck, the strippers have the right to get the coal any way they want, don't get in their way, your grandpappy put his mark on this deed, it may be an *X*, but it's legal. Then, in 1984, the state legislature passed a law that would have restricted mining under broad-form deeds to methods in existence when the deeds were signed. That, in most cases, would have shut out the strippers, unless the landowner gave his consent to be stripped. But then the Kentucky Supreme Court, in a split decision, ruled the 1984 law to be unconstitutional in that it would infringe on the rights of the folks—the companies—holding the deeds. Still, the court could not help but note the obvious injustice of what it held to be constitutional. "Only Kentucky," the court opined, "has reduced the property rights of the surface owner to a mere license to occupy the surface of the land until such time as the mineral owner elects to destroy the surface in order to remove the coal."

The people of Kentucky were not content with "a mere license." Rallied by a vigorous new organization called Kentuckians For The Commonwealth, which is based in Prestonburg, in the eastern coalfields, the people turned to their legislators and demanded that a constitutional amendment be placed on the ballot to curtail broad-form strip-mining against a landowner's will. The legislators did that, and voters approved the measure overwhelmingly.

II

It is only fitting and proper that the name Caudill should appear 206 times in the slim local Letcher County, Kentucky, telephone directory, where Smiths and Browns tend to get outnumbered by Combses, Cornetts, and Campbells, and Caudills outnumber them all. In Letcher County, the clan can claim priority by birtue of one James Caudill, a North Carolinian who crossed over Pine Mountain from its tamer side in 1792, built a cabin, planted some corn, and thus became the region's first permanent settler. James begat Caudills. Down the line a few generations was Henry Caudill, a lieutenant in the Confederate Army, wounded in action and posted home to the mountains, a cripple. Henry begat Cro Carr Caudill, who went to work in the mines and lost an arm to a tipple in 1917. Cro Carr begat Harry Caudill, who went to Italy in 1943 with an M-1 rifle and got posted home to the mountains with a shattered leg. Harry begat two sons and a daughter and practiced law in mountain courthouses and served in the legislature and started writing books and articles and letters so powerful, so anguished, that scribes and commentators from across America would descend on him in droves, all begging to be shown the sorry conditions of—a Caudill phrase— "these murdered old mountains." But that was some time ago. Lately, the inquisitive visitors have been few and far between, for trends do shape the media's agenda and, alas, Appalachia is no longer in fashion.

We went out from Mayking that afternoon (and on two separate visits after that) to see what we could see of Caudill's murdered mountains. Drove up into some of the hollows, narrow dirt roads following the creeks; gray, thin-looking houses and bare-axeled, rusting cars on one side of the road, a lushness of laurel and wild rhododendron on the other; here and there amidst the squalor, incongruously, a formidable house of stone or brick, possibly a Cadillac in the driveway—reminders of boom times in the early seventies. Drove through some of the old company towns, the rows of little frame houses facing each other, mostly empty and tumbledown, jungles of vines and weeds hiding the decades. Seco, Kentucky. Born 1912, Died 1960. "See," Caudill was saying, "when you build something in the coal country and then start mining, you're just cutting the foundation out from under what you have built."

He laced his commentary with lines or paraphrases from Shakespeare, Coleridge, Toynbee, Churchill, Jefferson, Tom Paine. And every single tale had an edge of sadness, a bite of irony, a twist of humor. "Look there," he said suddenly as we approached three shacks on stilts beside the road. "When I saw these little houses here being built I asked my friend Zack Bentley, 'Uncle Zack, why are you building such sorry little houses?' Zack built to rent. 'Well,' he said, 'I'm building them for sorry little people.' He said, 'You have to match the house to the man. If you put the wrong man in the wrong house, everything goes to pieces.' He said, 'You build a good house for good people who will keep it clean and everything, you build a sorry house for a little sorry man.' Zack Bentley was the police judge. He's dead now. His brother was the police chief, and another brother was the bootlegger. The bootlegger would supply the liquor, and the police chief would arrest the people who drank the liquor, and Zack would try them. That way each of the brothers got a fee. Zack, Mack, and Hack. The three brothers, and it went on like that for twenty years."

As we drove on toward McRoberts that day, and subsequently during solo sorties elsewhere in the mountains, I was struck powerfully by images that seemed to leap right off the pages of Caudill's first book, as though nothing had changed whatsoever in twenty-five years. For all the talk of reclamation, the highlands still looked slashed and battered; the strip lines, "mazes of looped and tangled scars like great yellow snakes twisting over the tortured hills." Still, "the curse of coal etched indelibly on the land and in the hearts and faces of its inhabitants," the labor force made permanently jobless by "automation and the consolidation of mining operations," the people "listless and bitter," the creeks littered with "ancient car bodies, discarded truck beds, rusty bed springs, rotten mattresses . . ."

The prospects had seemed far better than this in what should have been the morning after *Night Comes to the Cumberlands*. But morning never came, only that first blush of dawn that the book brought with it. Later, Caudill would attribute *Cumberlands'* initial success in stirring things up to a series of articles by the Pulitzer-prizing Homer Bigart in *The New York Times*. Bigart had been posted to Kentucky to see if conditions were truly as bad as Caudill had painted them. As bad, Bigart reported, and possibly worse. The articles caught the attention of President John F. Kennedy. By one account (not Caudill's) several hundred copies of the book were ordered and distributed to key people in the Kennedy Administration. The President summoned Kentucky Governor Bert Combs to the White House, and Combs (by Caudill's account) "confirmed the grimmest aspects of the Bigart articles." Kennedy called up $45 million in emergency aid. And then he "told the governor that he had scheduled a trip to Texas to help work out some problems that worried the Vice-President, and that upon his return to Washington he would call the governor to arrange a trip to Kentucky. He emphasized that he wanted to show by a personal visit that the troubles of the coalfields had been noticed and that his New Frontier intended to provide solid and lasting help."

But of course the President never got to Kentucky, though he did return from Texas. In a bronze coffin.

Then there began what Caudill would describe as a "trek of reporters, commentators, columnists, cameramen and film directors following in the lonely footsteps of the pioneering Bigart." Here came Charles Kuralt of CBS and John Dominis of *Life* and Haynes Johnson of *The Washington Post* and Richard Starnes of Scripps-Howard, who was "so astounded and shocked that he datelined one of his dispatches 'Hellier, Kentucky, where a man can sit on his front porch and look across the threshold of hell.' " Meanwhile, Lyndon Johnson and Hubert Humphrey were declaring war on poverty, and before long VISTA volunteers and other young activists would be trekking into the hollows of Central Appalachia to patch things up. But suddenly, just when it seemed that some of the patches were falling into place, the blush went out of it all and night came once again to Harry Caudill's tortured hills and murdered mountains. Now there'd be neither time nor money for Appalachia because America had to fight a different sort of war, in a different sort of country.

"Coal miners and their sons," Harry Caudill was saying at the little veterans' memorial in McRoberts, "they seem to die in large numbers. Not just in mines. In wars. You see, they're poor. America prefers to fight its wars with the sons of poor people."

We had come up from Seco through Neon beside a scruffy-looking creek, and when I asked if it had a name Caudill said it was named Boone Fork, after Daniel Boone, "who carved his name on a tree." Boone was *here*? "Daniel Boone was everywhere," he said. And McRoberts? "Samuel McRoberts, one of those New York bankers, one of the moguls for Consolidation Coal. They built this town." Caudill turned his big Mercury sedan onto a steep, narrow road that took off along a branch of a branch of Boone Fork. "This is what used to be known as 'The Niggertown,'" he said, as we drove between facing rows of tightly spaced weatherboard houses. "After *that* word was struck from the vocabulary, they called it Colored Row. It was a separate precinct, and all these houses were occupied by black miners and their families. Some of the best people who ever worked in these camps lived here. Most of them came out of the South and had a good deal of fundamental education." And where were they now? "Dead, or moved back to the South. One man, my old friend James Thomas, had thirteen children and sent each and every one of them through college. I said, 'James, how on earth did you manage to do it?' He said, 'Well sir, I did it with a big red-edge shovel.' He said, 'I shoveled all my children right through college.'"

Back down the branch, Caudill stopped the car and pointed at an old concrete slab beside the road. "My father lost his arm down here," he said. "That's part of the foundation of the old tipple. It was an accident. This thing caught my dad by the fingers and began to pull him right up to where the wheels were turning. The foreman heard his screams and threw the switch to stop the motor, but the wheels were still turning. And this big black man who was standing on a ramp up above, working on the tipple, jumped down with a crowbar in his hands. And he ruptured himself—always suffered from a hernia because of that. And he jammed that crowbar into the wheels and stopped them and saved my dad's life. And every birthday that old man had for many years, my dad would say, 'Well, I think we ought to drive up and see Will.' Will Williams, from Alabama."

And his father? "My father got nineteen hundred dollars for his arm, discounted ten percent for cash, which meant he got seventeen hundred and ten. Then, later, the company called him in and said they wanted to run him for county clerk. He said, 'I don't have any money, I can't make a race.' And they said, 'Well, we can help you out with that.' And he ran, and won. See, back in those days, if you were living in these camps and didn't support the company with your vote, you could lose your job and house and everything."

He had told the story of the old camps so powerfully in *Cumberlands*, told how camp-towns like McRoberts had started out spic-'n'-span, the houses repainted like clockwork, the bosses distributing shade trees and grass seed. But over time it was a losing battle—spic-'n'-span versus the "monstrous coaldust genie [that] emanated endlessly from the rumbling machinery," tapped its gritty fingers against the houses, and "crept into every nook and cranny of the town." Gradually, the communities "took on that sickly hue which miners called 'coal-camp gray.'" The women fought the battle "through the best years of their lives," Caudill wrote, and some never surrendered. But many did. And "there appeared the first symptoms of the vacuity, resignation, and passivity" that marked the people who remained in the camps after the companies pulled out—"traits which could only deepen as the years brought new defeats and new tragedies."

And he had told of the great exodus in the 1950s, the miners supplanted by machines, the lure of manufacturing jobs in the big industrial cities of the Midwest, the parting cry of "I'm a-goin' to Dee-troyt!" reverberating from every hollow and hilltop. The "beginning of one of the most drastic population shifts in the nation's history," Caudill had called it, citing a 25 percent decline in the Plateau's population between 1950 and 1960. Of course, it was too early then to tell just how bad it was going to get. Caudill's home county, Letcher, had arrived at midcentury with 50,000 people. By 1970 the Census folks had trouble finding 23,000.

Many of the laments of *Cumberlands* would be articulated again and again through the body of Harry Caudill's subsequent work, and hardly a volume slipped by but that the author did not find some nocturnal, somber, or lugubrious title to establish the proper mood for it. After *Dark Hills to Westward* (1969), a novel of frontier times, came *My Land Is Dying* (1971), an illustrated polemic against surface mining throughout America. In 1974 he returned to the novel form to tell of *The Senator from Slaughter*

County who, as Anne Caudill summarizes the tale, "brings the people to dependency on government aid and the land to destruction through strip-mining." *A Darkness at Dawn* (1976) reminded Bluegrass folk in the otherwise celebratory year of the nation's bicentennial that a great challenge remained unmet in the dark hills to eastward.

For the eighties Caudill would soften his touch with two slim volumes of personal folklore—*The Mountain, the Miner, and the Lord* (1980) and *Slender Is the Thread: More Tales from a Country Law Office* (1987)—but toughen it up a bit with a footnoted history of the coal barons. *Theirs Be the Power: The Moguls of Eastern Kentucky* (1983), published by the University Press of Illinois because, of all things, the University Press of Kentucky, Caudill's publisher at the time, refused to touch it. How so? Why, because Caudill had some unkind things to say in this book about one William Sturgill, alias "Mr. Coal."

"Sturgill," he wrote, "is almost certainly the most powerful Kentuckian, with influence that reaches into coal, oil, gas, insurance, banking, tobacco, construction, real estate development, fertilizer, higher education, and railroads . . . He has been subjected to severe and prolonged criticism in the media and has survived unscathed. His strip-mines produced landslides that wrecked houses." Caudill wrote this and submitted it for publication to the University Press of Kentucky at a time when William Sturgill was sitting as chairman of the board of trustees of the University of Kentucky.

And there was *Watches of the Night* (1976), billed as an update on *Cumberlands* and arguably the toughest, angriest book of them all. In it he wrote of the coal boom of the early seventies, the "murder of a land," and the "shattering of a culture." He saw the big Macks pouring into his country, the 'dozers, diesel powerplants, high lifts, and undercutters; the big new drift mines "sunk like long spear wounds into the side of the bleeding hills." And he saw that in the thirteen years since *Cumberlands*, after interminable hearings, conferences, drafts, and reports, there had been not one significant advance in the federal effort to regulate coal strip-mining and to finance the reclamation of abandoned mines. True, Congress had passed a strip-mine bill, two years in a row. But President Gerald Ford, citing the danger of economic dislocations, had vetoed it. Two years in a row.

On August 3, 1977, Congress again passed a bill and sent it along to the new President, Jimmy Carter, who signed it into law. This one was called the Surface Mining Control and Reclamation Act, soon to be known acronymically as SMCRA, or *Smack-rah!* in the pronunciation of Bureaucratese. A reprise of earlier, Ford-thwarted legislation, SMCRA promised a brave new world to the long-sufering mountaineers of Appalachia (not to mention the ranchers of the western High Plains who had just been forcibly invited to attend the second coronation of King Coal). SMCRA was going to patch things up. SMCRA was going to bring the public into the regulatory process, set minimum environmental and performance standards to protect land and water resources from strip-mine overkill, impose mandatory penalties on the worst-case violators, and at last compel the industry to heal the festering coalfield wounds of yesteryear. In some respects, including its length (40,000 words), SMCRA was a law without precedent, and many of those who had worked so hard to bring it to fruition were rightly proud to be present in the Rose Garden when the President put his moniker on the bottom line.

But there were others who felt that SMCRA did not go far enough, that certain strip-mine practices should have been prohibited rather than regulated, that some states—Kentucky, in particular—would never by fully capable of assuming primary responsibility for enforcing the law. Confirmation of a rollback pending in Kentucky came the following year, when, according to accounts in *The Louisville Courier-Journal*, the state's top environmental official, Robert D. Bell, quit "after resisting political pressure from strip-miners and being criticized publicly by [Governor Julian] Carroll for proposing stiffer fines."

And of course no one in or out of the Rose Garden could have predicted that in less than four years the roses would be

Ronald Reagan's and SMCRA, a tinker toy for Reagan's Interior Secretary, James Gaius Watt.

In his effort to fix the law so it couldn't work, Watt went right to the heart of the matter, to the enforcement agency, Interior's own Office of Surface Mining (OSM). Watt looked upon OSM and saw that it was not good for this administration that wanted government off the backs of the people, or for this mining industry that had been riding the people's backs for so many years. So the Secretary proceeded to take his agency apart under the guise of "management realignment." In a paper for the *West Virginia Law Review* in 1986, Louise C. Dunlap and James S. Lyon of the Environmental Policy Institute charged that Watt's so-called realignment "ruthlessly forced over 50 percent of OSM's experienced personnel to leave the agency through firings, undesirable field transfers, and sheer intimidation. This misguided undertaking probably did more to permanently cripple the agency's effectiveness than any other action."

Meanwhile, Watt chiseled away at the law itself, ordering changes in the regulations that would loosen up some of the environmental standards and shut down opportunities for public participation. Citizens groups, led by the Environmental Policy Institute, sued to stop him. By 1986, according to Dunlap and Lyon, "virtually every major change sought by the Watt administration" had been rejected by the courts.

After Watt's departure from government, the Interior Department and OSM passed into the hands of like-thinking men whose dissembling ways were far more subtle. Now the official tack was to claim that SMCRA was working, when in fact it was not. On the law's tenth anniversary, OSM issued a lavishly illustrated report—a *mostly* illustrated report—purporting to show that the SMCRA regulatory program was spic-'n'-span, all-systems-go from erosion control to revegetation and wildlife "enhancement." Seeing this, Congressman Mike Synar of Oklahoma hit the ceiling. "Instead of coming to grips with their problems," said Synar, chairman of the House Government Operations subcommittee on environment, "they try to mask them with cosmetics."

Synar's disenchantment with OSM was probably exceeded only by that of Morris Udall, the Arizonan who headed the House Committee on Interior and Insular Affairs and who was universally acknowledged as the grandpappy of SMCRA. Once, at a budget hearing, Udall assailed OSM's management for its promises "unfulfilled, its mission unaccomplished." While praising the coal industry's effort as a whole in trying to achieve compliance, Udall said OSM had "shuffled paper," created confusion in a "regulatory vacuum," and racked up a backlog of hundreds of millions of dollars in uncollected penalities and fees. In fact, that other House committee, Government Operations, had just reported that of an estimated $181 million in civil penalties assessed for violations of SMCRA, OSM had collected less than $9 million—a collection rate of about five percent. In his report to the full House, Government Operations Committee Chairman Jack Brooks of Texas said he and his colleagues were unable to determine the reasons for OSM's consistent failures—"whether it is because of a fundamental lack of regulatory commitment on the part of key policymakers, the lack of effective leadership, sheer incompetence, or the lack of will."

If all of the regulatory failures could be laid at the feet of OSM, that would be one thing, and bad enough. But under the rules of SMCRA there is another partner, the state. And in all but one case (Tennessee's), the state has primary responsibility for getting out into the field to make sure that the strip-miners obey the law. One day in Washington, D.C., I dropped by the Capitol Hill office of the Environmental Policy Institute to have a talk about OSM & Partners with Jim Lyon, head of the Institute's Citizens Mining Project, and Michael Clark, a sometime reporter for Harry Caudill's hometown newspaper (*The Mountain Eagle—It Screams!*), a longtime troubleshooter for Appalachian public-interest groups, and now the Institute's president.

I asked them to what extent they felt SMCRA was effective, at least out in the field.

"That's the problem," said Clark. "We still don't know if the law is effective because it has never been fully enforced in the areas where abuse has been worst."

And where might that be?

Without hesitation Mike Clark said, "Kentucky."

"You cannot expect effective enforcement if it is left to this state," Harry Caudill had told me one afternoon as we were driving through the tortured hills of Letcher County. "The government of Kentucky is corrupt in all of its parts." I recall thinking at the time that this likely was vintage rhetoric, Caudill indulging in overkill to make a point. But that was before I put those hills behind me for a while and started poking into some of the paper hills of documents and reports that had been piling up in Lexington and Frankfort and Washington, and that clearly substantiated, though not in so many harsh words, the grievous verdict Caudill had laid at Kentucky's feet.

For perspective, there were the insightful words of Al Cross, staff writer for *The Louisville Courier-Journal*. In one piece in 1987 ("Strip-mining and politics: An ill mix for Kentucky"), Cross reported that strip-mine enforcement is "colored by the view that the state should not disrupt the industry whose taxes are most important to financing state services." Coal operators pay a severance tax of about $1.30 per ton sold. According to Cross, former Governor Martha Layne Collins described her Natural Resources and Environmental Protection Cabinet as "a service agency" for the state's industries, and then "made good on the slogan when it came to coal." Collins was replaced in the state capitol at Frankfort by Wallace Wilkinson, who had no reputation for playing hardball with scofflaws. One of Wilkinson's first official acts was to erect new signs beside major highways entering the state. WELCOME TO KENTUCKY, the signs say. OPEN FOR BUSINESS.

To hear OSM in Washington tell it, Kentucky is going gangbusters with SMCRA. No problem. In a speech to the Society of Mining Engineers, OSM Director Jed Christensen (since resigned) said: "The states have done an excellent job in implementing and carrying out these [SMCRA] provisions, and—with the exception of Tennessee, where the regulatory authority has been returned to OSM—all major coal-producing states are doing an effective job of managing the enforcement provisions of the act." So it was said by the man from headquarters. Yet out in the field, and in OSM's state office in Lexington, the evaluation of Kentucky's effectiveness has been exactly the opposite. Unlike OSM/Washington, OSM/Lexington does not play Alice-in-Wonderland with the law.

In its role as overseer of the Kentucky program, OSM/Lexington issues an annual report card on how well or poorly the Office of Surface Mining Reclamation and Enforcement, a branch of the state's Natural Resources Cabinet, has been doing holding up its end of the SMCRA bargain. While some improvement of performance has been noted from year to year, the overall grades are not good. I mean, if I were Kentucky I believe it would behoove me to go stand in the corner. Consider just two of the more glaring failures:

— In both 1986 and 1987 (let alone the earlier reporting years when conditions were worse) OSM/Lexington found that illegal mining—"wildcatting" by operators who obtain no permits, pay no taxes, and destroy much land—"has not been successfully controlled in certain regions of eastern Kentucky." *The Louisville Courier-Journal* gets more explicit: "Kentucky harbors more [wildcatters], and has had less success eradicating them, than any other state . . . No one [as of August 17, 1987] has ever served time on a wildcat strip-mining conviction."

— Year after year OSM/Lexington has chided the state for its failure to cite what to OSM inspectors are clear and obvious violations of SMCRA. For example, in the 1986 report OSM/Lexington noted that while state inspectors cited an average of 0.19 violation per mine site inspected, the ratio tripled to 0.60 per inspection when an OSM inspector went along. A full half of some 160 violations observed during joint inspections were judged by the OSM inspector to have been present, but not cited by the state inspector, during a previous state inspection when "the performance standard in question was checked as reviewed." Again, to be more explicit, Jim Lyon told me: "There are some state inspectors in Kentucky who have *never* reported a violation."

Kentucky's responses to the federal reports have ranged over the years from the bland to the ludicrous. In 1985 the state's Natural Resources Cabinet sputtered that while Kentucky may not be perfect, neither is OSM. In 1986 the state was content to "strongly disagree." In 1987 it averred that the "critical issue" was OSM's failure to understand how the Kentucky program works. Robert Knarr and Larry Grasch, the state's two top surface-mining enforcement officials that year, told me that while Kentucky certainly should and would step up the frequency of its inspections, the basic federal-state disagreement was simply a matter of how one arranged and interpreted the numbers.

However the state may strive to justify its past performance under SMCRA, there may not be much time or room left over for foot-dragging. In order to end a long-standing lawsuit brought in federal district court by the National Wildlife Federation and the public-interest Kentucky Resources Council, the state has agreed, in settlement, to take a number of steps to correct what the lawsuit alleged—a systemic breakdown in the state's enforcement of SMCRA. Congress has authorized the additional funds, some $13 million over three years, that Kentucky will need to implement the agreement.

There is one problem in Caudill country—in coalfield country throughout America—that doesn't seem to want a solution, unless the solution comes wrapped in a lot more money than the government is ever likely to spend. The problem is this multitude of old mines, abandoned and unreclaimed, on the surface and underground, posing a constant threat of landslide, subsidence, erosion, fire, acid runoff—take your pick. Kentucky alone is said to embrace some 150,000 acres of abandoned minelands in critical need of repair.

The hope had been that SMCRA would lay down the patchwork. SMCRA was to take a federal tax of thirty-five cents per ton of strip-mined coal, and fifteen cents a ton on subsurface coal, and put it into a special account from which the states would draw as they proceeded to patch their worst-case minelands left abandoned and unreclaimed ante-SMCRA, prior to August 1977.

Only trouble was this: Congress underestimated the cost of the patches, and overestimated the tax revenues that were going to pay for the patches. By most accounts, the tax will have generated up to $4 billion when it expires, by law, in 1992. That's about $26 billion short of what it would probably cost to clean up all the abandoned ante-SMCRA minelands in America. Moreover, there are constraints on the money that is available. In a Congress acutely aware of deficit spending and national debt, members have been appropriating only eighty cents of every dollar collected. But of that eighty cents, alas, about forty cents seems to get spent on internal administrative expenses, in OSM and state offices, so that only the last forty cents is left to purchase reclamation in the field.

In the drafting of SMCRA, there was an understandable eagerness on the part of its authors to avoid a new generation of abandoned minelands, to get more of the mining action into the hands of larger companies that would not only be willing to pay the costs of regulatory constraint but, given the proper incentive, foot the bill for state-of-the-art post-mining reclamation as well. The incentive was and is an exemption from one of SMCRA's toughest reclamation rules—that slopes, after mining, must be returned to their approximate original contour, no more highwalls, no more scalplocks. The exemption, of course, dictated the method, for there is only one way to strip-mine in mountain country without leaving a highwall or returning the slope to its approximate original contour, and that is to turn a mountain into a mesa by removing its head.

Increasingly over the past decade, the larger coal companies in eastern Kentucky have been turning from contour stripping to mountaintop removal out of necessity as well as convenience, for much of the best coal accessible by contouring is gone. There is no shortage of good coal under the tops of the mountains. For the most part, the regulators are delighted with mountaintop-removal projects—easier to monitor, no worries about trying to recreate and stabilize those steep slopes. Up Martin County way, near the West Virginia border, thousands of acres of once-forested hill and hollow are under conversion to flatland pasture as the big Macks rumble off with their loads of coal. "They're turning Martin County into a parking lot," says a coalfield activist in Frankfort. "There won't be a hilltop left by the time they're through." And Tom Gish, publisher of *The Mountain Eagle* in Whitesburg, sees big trouble brewing down in Harlan County, other side of Pine Mountain. According to Gish, an unprecedented mountaintop removal may soon be in the works at Black Mountain, where Arch Mineral, owned by Ashland Oil and the Hunt brothers of Texas, holds most of the subsurface rights. "If it happens," says Gish, "there goes Kentucky's highest mountain."

Caudill country already boasts a couple of blockbuster mountaintop projects, both operated by subsidiaries of Cyprus Minerals, which is a chip off the old Amoco block and, in recent years, one of Kentucky's top coal producers. At the Star Fire Mine, not far from Hazard, draglines are working over a thousand-acre site with bucket scoops that can chew up sixty cubic yards of earth in a single bite. Before the arrival of the big machines, the razorback hills topped out at a general elevation of about 1,500 feet. When the machines are gone—not to mention the coal, trucked away at the rate of 1.8 million tons a year—the general elevation will be two hundred feet closer to the sea, and the stumps of the remnant hills won't even resemble blunt instruments, much less razors.

To satisfy my own curiosity about this latest twist in strip-mine technology, I called one day in Hazard on George Campbell and John Tate, who come about as high on topless mountains as you can get. Campbell is a young Hazard businessman who, at the time, was mostly handling real estate for the Kentucky Prince Mining Co., and whose father, Roy Campbell, is proprietor of a four-hundred-acre mountaintop development with a National Guard armory, a medical center, a regional hospital, a church, and a funeral home already in place—in short, a development lacking nothing but the houses and apartments that by-and-by would furnish the bodies needed to fill the other places. Tate at the time was a property supervisor for Southern Realty Resources, Inc., the real estate arm of Cyprus Mineral's

Kentucky operations. From Tate's office the three of us drove out of Hazard on a back road toward the hamlets of Dice and Rowdy, and then turned up into a place called Pigeon Roost to have a look at the topless mountains of the Lost Mountain Mine.

We followed a gravel haulroad to a height of land. On our right were the contoured gashes and highwalls of yesteryear, an area strip-mined so ruthlessly that the writer David Mc-Cullough, in *his* piece on Harry Caudill for *American Heritage* in 1968, had been moved to describe this very same Roost as a place akin to the set for *All Quiet on the Western Front*, "only worse." And on our left was one of the dismembered promontories of the Lost Mountain Mine, losing itself by the scoopful under a dragline. No film that I'd ever seen had attempted a set like this. Beyond the mined areas, Tate parked his Bronco at the edge of a gentle grass-covered swell that had been topped two years ago. "All pasture now," said Tate, as a truck rumbled by, not with coal but with cows come for grazing. "We've made the land usable. The whole future of this region's up here, on top of these hills."

Perhaps Tate was right. I mean, who was I to say that flattop mesas belong out yonder in the big-sky West, not here in eastern Kentucky? But then who was Tate to predict a brave new world atop the topless? Tate didn't mention it, but there were and are an awful lot of people in the engineering profession who worry about these huge hollow fills where the tops of the mountains are being laid to rest. The worry is that some of the fills won't hold up to the test of time, that the so-called "durable" rock being dumped into hollows may not endure in this land of heavy rains. After all, what we are dealing with here are some of the largest earthen structures in America. If one should pop, it wouldn't be just another landslide; it could be a major death-dealing disaster. The two public-interest lawyers who forced Kentucky's hand in the settlement agreement, L. Thomas Galloway of Washington, D.C., and Thomas FitzGerald of Frankfort, have studied some of the engineering reports and have a word for the hollow fills associated with mountaintop removal. The word is *timebombs*.

III

Harry Caudill does not fulminate as lavishly as he once did upon the darker side of strip-mining in his beloved hill country. The constraints, after all, are so much stronger now than they were when night first came to the Cumberlands, and the watchdogs so much more numerous and likely to back up their bark with a litigious bite. Hardhat men think twice nowadays before broad-forming the contents of a family cemetery over the edge of the mountain.

But a Caudill without a cause? It didn't seem possible, and I soon discovered, as I toured the territory with the counselor himself, that it *wasn't* possible. If Caudill seemed to be taking it easy on the strippers, it was only because he was saving his scorn for the roadside trashers and a state government that, after all these years, still countenanced the despoliation of the region's water resources.

Caudill's scorn is supreme on the subject of trash, for as awful as its presence in the mountains may have seemed twenty-five years ago, the sheer mass of it today is probably worse, if only through the process of accretion. Especially visible is the one throwaway least likely to degrade over time—the chassis of the no-longer-usable used car. And there are thousands of them. "This is the great elephant burial ground for used cars." Caudill had told me. He explained how the coalfields became a marketplace for used cars during the exodus of the 1950–60s; how folks who couldn't afford better bought used cars for their escape to Dee-troyt and then, once there, used their factory wages to buy *up* in the vehicle world. Whereupon the discarded junker, instead of being consigned to a Michigan graveyard, would be driven home to eastern Kentucky and handed down to some needful next of kin. "The old junker would belch and smoke," Caudill said, "but eventually it would wear out and go over the bank, splash, and then they'd go get them another one."

In a speech some time ago before a group of area officials and businessmen in Hazard, Caudill said: "Eastern Kentucky is a mess. I'm thoroughly ashamed of it and humiliated by it. Yesterday I got out and drove up to Neon, and then I drove over on Number 7 in Floyd County. You know what? All the way over there it was trash, trash, trash. Trash in yards, trash in the creeks, trash by the roadsides. Quantities of trash that would boggle the mind. The biggest coal train that ever went out of here couldn't carry it."

We had driven part of that route ourselves, and I had seen the trash, and now, in the Mercury, with Caudill at the wheel, we were following a littered little road along Smoot Creek, west of Whitesburg, heading toward Premium. "That's what they call it now," said Caudill. "Premium. But it started as Dalna. It was a coal camp, and Dalna was the owner's girlfriend. After the camp closed down they called it Hot Spot—don't ask me why. Then somebody got tired of Hot Spot and named it Premium. Well, awhile back, a man came along this same road here—local man, been away up north—and he spots this sign by the road that says, LITTER BARREL 1/2 MILE. He says, 'Well I'll *be*.' He says, 'They've gone and changed old Dalna's name again.' "

Caudill's home county of Letcher was a bit of a hot spot itself in the garbage wars of Kentucky, and long under state pressure to improve its hit-'n'-miss collection program. Ruben Watts is the county's chief executive—county judge-executive is the official title—and when I called on him to speak of trash he spoke to me of his "garbage ordinance." Ruben Watts absolutely insisted that it was an *ordinance*, but in my book it was not; it was a franchise plan for private carters to collect and landfill trash from homes and business that voluntarily paid for the service. I told Judge Watts that there appeared to be a good number of people in his county who were putting their trash almost anywhere but into the landfill or back of a private carter's truck. The judge dismissed that observation, saying it was not his style to cherish taxes or regulations.

"If there's ever to be a mandatory collection program in *this* county," he said, "it will have to be by a vote of the people." Later, without a popular vote, the county *did* enact an ordinance prescribing stiff penalties for littering—but still no mandatory garbage collection.

Next county north from Letcher is Knott, and the judge-executive there is Homer Sawyer, who presides at the courthouse in Hindman. Unlike luckless Letcher, Knott does have a mandatory waste-collection program, instituted in 1987 at the behest of the freshman executive Homer Sawyer himself. Sawyer keeps a busy office, or did the morning I dropped in, with more than a few supplicants and subordinates hovering nearby, awaiting some chance to address the executive ear. Sawyer spoke proudly of his program. "Before it started," he said, "private carters were hauling about twenty tons a week to the landfill. Now the tonnage is running a hundred fifty a week."

"Where was the other hundred thirty tons going?" I wanted to know.

"Into the creek," said a hanger-on from across the room. The judge smiled at the interruption and went on to describe the program in detail. Nine vehicles involved in the once-a-week pickup, covering 5,000 households and businesses. Cost to the householder: seven dollars a month. A few folks holding back on their bill payments, but overall a break-even program. "Look here," the judge was saying. "You're going to see more and more people doing the right thing in eastern Kentucky. We're on a roll. We're moving up to be on a par with the rest of the country."

But couldn't that kind of a roll backfire? I asked. Weren't there county executives elsewhere in Kentucky who had rolled themselves right out of office on the issue of mandatory trash collection?

"I know," said Homer Sawyer. "But at a certain point you have to draw a line and—"

"And stop playing politics," chimed in that hanger-on from across the room.

On another day, in another place, Harry Caudill was speaking of his other scorn, the quality of the region's water. Of all the states of the Union, he was saying, "Kentucky is running a TV ad about it being 'a land of clear rushing waters.' But they don't show the Pampers hanging in the branches and the tens of thousands of toilets running their wastes straight out to the creek. They just call it 'Kentucky—the land of clear rushing waters.' Now isn't it strange—the land of clear rushing waters has the highest incidence of hepatitis in the country, twice the national average. That's viral hepatitis. You get it by drinking polluted water."

I had seen some of the reports. For example, there was *Drinking Water and Health in Southeastern Kentucky*, prepared by Jeanne Hibberd and William Duncan for the Mountain Association for Community Economic Development at Berea. According to Hibberd and Duncan, about 320,000 people, or 60 percent of the region's population, take their drinking water from wells, cisterns, creeks, and other untreated, unmonitored sources. Of these folks, more than 200,000 use water contaminated by bacteria. And deep in the heart of Caudill country, the situation gets even worse; one sampling in Letcher County found that out of twenty-five private water sources tested, twenty-two were polluted with coliform bacteria. On-site septic systems, the researchers found, commonly failed for want of proper maintenance or suitable soil conditions, and many of the big municipal sewage treatment plants were in violation of their wastewater permits.

"One man's septic tank," I heard Harry Caudill saying, "is another man's water supply."

Yet sewage is only part of the problem. There is also the part that comes directly from coal mining, the part that manifests itself in acid drainage (from abandoned mines), stream siltation (for want of adequate erosion controls at strip-mines), and what's known in the territory as "black water." An effluent of coal-washing operations, black water commonly contains, in addition to coal fines, trace metals and carcinogenic hydrocarbons. And why must coal be *washed*? Why, because, in combustion, washed coal produces fewer air pollutants than dirty coal. Of course, when black water escapes from the slurry pond that is meant to contain it, then what isn't supposed to get into the air gets into some creek or aquifer. It is said that somewhere on the

Licking River, north of Caudill country, there is an operator who dredges coal fines directly from the river and mines nowhere else, so bountiful are the riches of black water.

Other streams may be just as bad. The City of Hazard, for example, draws its municipal water supply from Caudill's river, the North Fork of the Kentucky. "There's no getting around it," says Mayor Bill Gorman. "When you mine the coal, you destroy the water. We have to take *our* water and rebuild it."

The way I heard it in Caudill country, trashed hollows and poisoned streams weren't the only troubles that needed fixing. What truly worries some of the people more than anything else is the sorry state of the region's schools. In our back-road travels together, we could hardly pass a schoolhouse but that Caudill would point out some failure of the educational system. The schools were not only poor, he said; they were poorly used. With few exceptions, the teachers were "noneducated." They turned out students "who don't know anything." Narrow vision and parochial conservatism ran through the system like a plague.

Once again I might have thought that Caudill was stretching it some—if I hadn't already known better. Known that one of every three adults in Kentucky cannot read or write (the lowest adult literacy rate in the country), that a high percentage of teenagers are opting to keep their own literacy skills marginal by dropping out of high school before graduation (the highest drop-out rate, I'm told, of the fifty states). As the coal seams grow thicker, the report card gets worse. Eighteen of the twenty lowest-ranking school districts in Kentucky in 1987 were located in the eastern coalfields. Of 178 districts statewide for which rankings were computed by *The Lexington Herald-Leader* (based on standardized skills tests scored by the state Department of Education), Letcher County came in 168th (up from 175th the year before), while Perry County, next-door, hove to at 171st. A few municipal systems in the region, however, fared better: Hazard's hit twenty-eighth place, up from fifty-fourth the year before.

King Coal must be held partly responsible for the rotten showing by southeastern Kentucky's rural schools, in that it contributes virtually nothing to help support them, apart from a fraction of the severance tax that filters back to the counties through Frankfort. "The moguls," says Jerry Davis, a former president of Alice Lloyd College in Knott County, "would rather buy basketball scholarships in Lexington than support education in southeast Kentucky."

But the moguls will have to mend their ways. The state's highest court has ruled that the companies may no longer sit on valuable coal reserves and continue to be exempt from paying a property tax on their unmined minerals. The free ride for the moguls had been arranged in 1976 by the Kentucky General Assembly, which set the tax rate on unmined coal at an incredible one mill per $100 of assessed value—a rate so low that the state in most cases did not bother to collect it, a rate so preposterous that the courts, goaded by Kentuckians For The Commonwealth, finally got around to ruling it an unconstitutional exemption from property taxation. (One company with reserves in Knott County valued at $1.2 million paid a property tax last year that amounted to all of $11.60.) No one yet seems to have a fix on how much revenue a new and equitable tax rate might extract from King Coal; estimates of education's share start at $30 million and range upward from there. But all the money in the world cannot guarantee better schools—not in the coalfields where political patronage, rather than professional performance, determines who uses that money to teach Johnny to read.

And then what? What if Johnny *can* read? "You could give everyone up here a college education," says R. Percy Elkins, executive director of the Kentucky River Area Development District in Hazard, "but they still wouldn't have a job. A third of our people in the coalfields are out of work. I can hire women with college degrees for minimum wage. Now isn't that awful?" Harry Caudill is a great admirer of R. Percy Elkins, who took over the helm of the district in 1970 after a term and three months as the mayor of Jenkins. In the Appalachian sector of

Kentucky, a development district serves as an inter-county regional planning and social service agency, and the one Elkins heads takes in eight counties in the watershed of the North Fork Kentucky, including Letcher. With limited resources, the district supplements the effort of local governments to keep their people on the safer side of bare survival. Last year Elkins's staff and volunteers distributed 2.3 million pounds of cheese, milk, rice, and other surplus commodities to more than 16,000 households in the district. "We've got to find an alternative employment base," Elkins says. "Coal and manufacturing just won't give us enough jobs. Maybe we've got to look to tourism. Maybe we have to prove to the coal industry that it can take some of its tremendous capital and put it not into bluegrass farms or land in Florida but right back *here*, and make a profit on it."

One evening at Mayking, while the counselor was occupied on the telephone, I asked Anne Caudill what she felt her husband's most effective role has been over the years—lawyer, writer, educator, legislator (three terms in the Kentucky House of Representatives, 1954–62). "You forgot troublemaker," she said. "Harry's always been a troublemaker. That's why he's accomplished far more outside of politics. To stay in politics, you have to get elected. To get elected you have to compromise. That's not Harry."

Almost everyone who knows the man, and admires him, agrees that Harry Caudill is a troublemaker. "He is Appalachia's premier polemicist, pamphleteer, propagandist, and prophet," says Albert P. Smith, a Lexington newspaper executive and one-time co-chairman of the federal Appalachian Regional Commission. And from the state's most eminent historian, Thomas D. Clark, this salute (in a jacket blurb for a Caudill book): "One of Kentucky's fundamental weaknesses as an organized economic and political society has been its squeamishness about facing the cold facts of its condition—the state has sweetly looked the other way while being raped. When Harry Caudill holds the mirror of actuality before the faces of Kentuckians, they will be startled to see that the image loses its bow tie and chin whiskers."

To be sure, many Kentuckians are not only startled when they peer into Caudill's mirror, but angry—at Caudill. Routinely he is castigated in letters-to-the-editor columns for giving the state a black eye. Caudill writes in *The Lexington Herald-Leader*, for example, that visible trashiness is retarding the economic development of eastern Kentucky. Chin Whiskers replies that if potential investors are taking their factories somewhere else, it isn't because of trash; it's because Caudill has poisoned the atmosphere with his negative outlook. In other words: Shoot the messenger.

Caudill's tendency to accentuate the negative has even turned off some folks who, on the issues, would otherwise have to be counted among his allies. At one conference on Appalachian problems (a conference, not so incidentally, that honored Caudill for his seminal writings), Joe Szakos, coordinator for the Kentucky Fair Tax Coalition, chided Caudill for showing eastern Kentucky through "pessimistic eyes which have been perceptive to problems but blind to solutions," and for neglecting to mention the good works of other individuals and community groups working for change—as if the common cause might somehow be served if only Caudill would be content to play Cheerleader instead of Cassandra. Indeed, a whole new generation of media-conscious Appalachian activists has come onstream in the past decade. If the few with whom I've talked are representative, an earlier breed's admiration for the old Whitesburg warrior is giving way to a kind of muted resentment that Caudill, after all these years, is still getting the ink. It is not surprising that young folks should want to reinvent the wheel; what *is* surprising is that they should believe it deserves to get oiled when they haven't yet learned how to make it squeak. "Harry Caudill has always known how to get attention for his cause, not for himself," says Elvis Stahr, who was Caudill's law professor at the University of Kentucky in the 1940s (and went on to become Secretary of the Army in the Kennedy Administration, and later a president of the National Audubon Society). "There has to be a place for the hell-raiser. That's Harry's place. No one can fill it like he can."

On the other hand, there are a few people who believe that Caudill has grown a bit quieter on the issues in recent years, and C. Vernon Cooper, Jr., president of the Peoples Bank & Trust Company of Hazard, is one of them. "I didn't like Harry Caudill when he wrote that first book," Cooper told me one morning in his office. "I thought it was too harsh. I thought Caudill went way too far in that book. But in time, he mellowed. Age does that. We all mellow. He's a good friend of mine now." Later that day, in Whitesburg, I called on Tom and Patricia Gish, the owner-editors of *The Mountain Eagle* and longtime friends and supporters of Caudill's. I asked them if Caudill had mellowed. "No," said Tom Gish emphatically. "I don't think he has, and neither have I." Then Pat Gish put in, "I can see how some people might think that Harry's gone a little soft. You get to a point where you've said the same thing for so long, you just get tired of saying it again." But Tom Gish said, "No. What's happened is that the community has simply come around at last to see that Harry was pretty much right all along."

On one matter of historical opinion, however, it is unlikely that the community will ever come around, and that is Harry Caudill's theories on the origin of the species, the Kentucky mountaineer. Hurtful enough that the sage of Whitesburg should broad-brush his Cumberland contemporaries as a down-and-out defeated people, but to declare repeatedly that most of them are descended from Elizabethan street orphans, debtors, criminals, and indentured servants would seem unforgivable. Drawing on such sources as the 19th Century historian John Fiske, Caudill posited, first in *Cumberlands* and then more force-fully in his later books, that the mountaineers hailed from a pre-dominantly urban English stock—the "mean English," Fiske had called them—that had neither the stomach for the rigors of the bloody frontier (that was for the feisty Scotch-Irish) nor the ability to compete with African slaves for work on the planta-tions of Old Virginia and the Carolinas. Thus did the mean English fall into a crack that one day would be known as Appala-chia, or so it was said. Of course others put the heritage elsewhere; Arnold J. Toynbee, being English, laid the blame on the Celts. No matter. Caudill would quote him anyway, in books, in articles, in the front seat of a white Mercury in the coal-blackened hills of Letcher County:

"You know what Toynbee said about us? He said the Appalachian mountain people are no better than barbarians. He said, I can confidently predict that before the end of this century, the hillbilly music—wild and discordant and so on—will be blaring from the great radio stations of central Europe, beginning the process of displacing Brahms, Mendelssohn, and so on with the raucous music of the Appalachian backcountry."

Toynbee said *that*?

"Toynbee said that. In the 1940s. He said the Appalachian culture is the strongest and most tenacious culture in America. And it is likely, he went on, that it will barbarize the rest of America and that America will barbarize Europe."

Kentuckians do not take kindly to the barbarian label. In Hazard, I asked Mayor Bill Gorman what he thought about Caudill and the mean English. Gorman said, "If Harry's an historian, I'm an astronaut. My people were Scotch-Irish, came over more than two hundred years ago. Hunters, they were. Came over the mountains from Virginia. My daughter went to the University of Kentucky and studied history. Harry was her professor. When she came home for Christmas, I had to give her a spanking."

Later, at Mayking, I conveyed Mayor Gorman's views to the ex-professor himself. Caudill smiled, got out of his chair, stretched his long, war-wounded leg, and disappeared into his study. When he came out, he was carrying an armful of books— *Bonded Passengers to America, White Servitude in Colonial America, Colonists in Bondage*. As we talked, he thumbed the pages of the books, making fast-penciled notes on a legal pad propped on the arm of his chair. He told me he had changed his mind somewhat on the origin of the species, that after a trip to Wales and an examination of the telephone directory of Swansea, in which the names echo those listed in the directory of Letcher County, he was willing to admit that perhaps the mountain originals were

Celts after all, though he stopped short of calling them *mean* Celts.

Presently Caudill put down his books and said, "Now I'm not saying these are Bill Gorman's ancestors, but I *am* saying that we've got eight Gorman immigrants listed as coming over in the 1700s, and all but one were indentured servants or criminals. Look here. Page 109, *Bonded Passengers*. It says 'S'—that means sentenced—'1747.' "

Who was?

"Gorman," said Caudill. "One *William* Gorman. Doesn't say what for."

There are all kinds of stories about how Bad Branch got its name, but the likeliest, from horse-and-wagon days, is that it was just a plain bad way to get over Pine Mountain from the Poor Fork of the Cumberland, of which the branch is a tributary. Near the top are some steep cliffs, and a sixty-foot waterfall before you're halfway there, and a boulder-strewn creekbed, and a lot of wet talus and big fallen trees. A bad way for serious travelers, all right, but a salubrious spot for a footloose mountain boy with a fierce imagination and a fondness for losing himself in the deep woods.

He would remember those woods—hemlocks as wide as a mineshaft, poplars as tall as the sky, thickets of laurel, bluets and trillium, ravens and trout. There were moonshiners in the mountains, then. And caves, caves with blind fish so translucent you could see their intestines. It was another world, then, up here in the woods. It hadn't been touched yet.

"They logged it off during the war," Caudill was saying in the car as we drove along the upper Poor Fork. Anne Caudill was in the back seat. We were heading toward Jefferson National Forest and the Virginia line, and somewhere along the way we would pull off and take a peek at Bad Branch. "I wasn't here when it happened," he said. "I was overseas. They logged every bit of it, and then there were fires. This was all burned out, as black as coal."

You'd never know it, I said. It comes back so fast.

"O, this is vital country," Caudill said. "Give it a chance and a little help from the Lord and you'll soon have forest back. Now see, down here, it's getting to be respectable young timber." Around another bend or two in the road, we turned off the pavement and rolled to a stop at the edge of an overgrown field. Beyond the field was a wire gate and an old logging road heading off into the woods. Caudill said, "Welcome to Bad Branch."

Much of this land that he had roamed as a boy, that had been logged and scorched and left to fend, is protected now. Some 2,700 acres of the watershed are owned or leased by The Nature Conservancy and the Kentucky State Nature Preserves Commission, which have a proprietary interest in assuring the continued existence here of several rare or threatened species, including the arrow darter, the cloudland deermouse, and the snakemouth orchid. We followed the old logging road through the woods for a hundred yards or so, and then we heard the vernal murmur of the creek, its voice rising to a tumbling roar as we came upon it. The loggers' road became a trail at this point and crossed to the other side, but the water was higher than Caudill had expected—too deep to ford. So the three of us stood there and watched the icy springs of Pine Mountain float by, and the born-again hemlocks on the other side, and the budding laurel. And then I heard the counselor's voice, the oracular voice seeking to be heard above the clamor of the creek. It was a recitation, for certain, but I could hear only fragments. Caudill's face was quartered upstream, as though he were addressing the mountain.

On the way back to the car, I asked for an encore. He said, "And here were forests ancient as the hills, / Enfolding sunny spots of greenery."

What's that?

"Kubla Khan," said Anne Caudill. "Coleridge's vision in a dream."

"And 'mid these dancing rocks at once and ever / It flung up momently the sacred river."

I said, "How do you remember all this stuff?"

He said, "When I was in school we had to memorize reams of

verse. They kept a big yardstick, and if you didn't learn, they'd whack you. Whack, whack, whack. That would make you *learn*."

Anne Caudill was grasping at the corner of another line. "A holy place," she said. "How does that go?"

"It was a miracle of rare device, / A sunny pleasure dome with caves of ice."

A splendid moment, Caudill reciting his Coleridge at Bad Branch, his face lit up with the romance of it all. I would frame the scene in my memory and take it home with me from the mountains as a hedge against his other dreams, his nightmares, his apocalyptic visions. There were no sacred rivers running through the crystal ball that Caudill held, only the topless mountains where the rains carved new channels through the jumbled spoil and unholy streams flowed out from the ruined land to plague the lives of millions. And there were no miracles of rare device.

"There is a major eastern Kentucky coal operator whose ancestors have lived in the hills for many generations," he had written in the last paragraph of the last page of *Theirs Be the Power*. "Like the men who work in his mines, like those who illuminate their homes with the power from the coal his miners dig, like all mankind, he is locked into an industrial system he deems unstoppable. 'I wish it could be avoided,' he said wistfully, 'but it cannot. Only God could stop it with a miracle, and I do not believe in miracles.' "

I was mulling that when we went through the gate and got in the car and at last drove away. We rode in silence for a while until Caudill said, "You know, when Anne came over here the first time, my young wife was so innocent. She'd had a sheltered life in Cynthiana. That's in the Bluegrass. She'd never seen men tearing up the country before. She came up here to this scorched and blackened earth and—"

"Flowers!" Anne Caudill cut in from the back seat. "Look here, on the right. That must be cinquefoil."

"Looks like it," I said.

"Looks like trash to me," said the driver.

"That's always his outlook," Anne Caudill laughed. "He *always* sees the trash."

BRUSHPOPPIN'

THE

SLICKROCK

On a clear day—and some days come mighty clear in southern Utah—you can see straight out to the edge of forever. Forget it if chance should take you down a slot canyon with walls of red sandstone pinching the view; or out on some mile-high mesa, the pinyons and junipers slapping your shanks. You have to get higher than that, up eight or nine thousand feet, up on the brow of the Aquarius Plateau maybe, up Powell Point with the tip of your nose sighted in on Kaiparowits country, up in the aspens on Boulder Mountain, looking east across the Circle Cliffs and the snaggle-tooth rim of the Waterpocket Fold, and liking the snow on the caps of the Henry Mountains but wishing they were not in the way because without them the edge of forever would roll on to the Dirty Devil and the great Colorado, to the glacial cirques of the far La Sals, to the gossamer flats of the Great Sage Plain. Out there or over here somewhere, in one direction or another, the maps speak of such lively places as Death Ridge and Carcass Canyon, Fiftymile Mountain and the Sweet Alice Hills, Fiddler Butte and Tarantula Mesa, Studhorse Peaks and Donkey Meadows and Rat Seep and Hell's Backbone and Choprock Bench and Beef Basin, Robbers Roost and Horsethief Point, Old Woman Wash and Cad's Crotch, The Cockscomb, The Fins, The Maze, The Wickiup, The Needles, The Gulch, The Blues. The sassy names dance on across the land. Forever is hardly big enough to hold them.

This is a fine sort of country, for wilderness. There are some folks (partisans, to be sure, mostly of the outlander stripe) who will tell you that these buttes and canyons constitute as grand an assemblage of roadless areas as any in America, and, so saying, offer no apologies to Alaska. But why pick a fight over apples and oranges? Southern Utah stands to be counted in its own right. It qualifies. Its backcountry (there's hardly any *front*) has all the necessary credentials for statutory Wilderness—millions of acres of forest, parkland, and public domain ready to put in the uppercase *W* as soon as Congress says the word; a territory once described by writer Edward Abbey as "the least inhabited, least inhibited, least civilized, least governed, least priest-ridden, most arid, most hostile, most lonesome, most grim bleak barren desolate and savage quarter of the state of Utah—the best part by far. So far."

Over the years, the canyon country has survived recuring efforts to tame its wildness. Well, most of it has survived. So far. Glen Canyon did not survive. Glen Canyon was the place no one knew, and because of that, no one now will *ever* know it, for it lies in the deep, deep waters of Lake Powell. Meanwhile plans are afloat to flood the rest of the territory with paved roads, coalfields, slurry pipelines, range improvements, and assorted projects calculated to ream uranium, oil shale, tar sands, carbon dioxide—you name it—right out of the wildest niches of the public domain. And that's only for openers. The worst news is yet to come.

The worst news has to do with some of the people who are trying to call the shots on what happens out there between Boulder Mountain and the edge of forever. Some of these people who would shape the configuration of uppercase Wilderness in southern Utah don't much like the idea of uppercase Wilderness anywhere. Some of them have nothing but contempt for uppercase Wilderness. Some of them run the towns and counties of southern Utah. Some of them belong to Utah's congressional delegation. Some of them work for the Bureau of Land Management of the U.S. Department of the Interior, the agency in charge of most of this land—and of defining what does and does not qualify for the big *W*. Add to that eight years of an anti-wilderness Reagan administration—particularly in the persons of Interior Secretary Donald Hodel and Bureau Director Robert Burford—dedicated to the proposition that resource management is one big game of Sagebrush Monopoly and you begin to get the message.

So here I am to fill in some of the details. About the country itself and how it came to be the way it is, and where the lines of wildness and solitude have been most curiously jiggled on the Bureau's maps, and how the Brushpopper came by his name, and why the Bureaucrats are huffing and puffing to blow down Clive Kincaid's house, and what makes Calvin Black of Blanding run, and about Arch Canyon and why one has to do a place like that the right way or not at all, and maybe, too, about the edge of forever, if we should be so lucky to get that far. Let's go.

I

There are as many different ways to parse this canyon country as to skin a cat, and I suppose that any one is about as good as the next. For atlas definition, I like to start out on the west side and run my line up U.S. Highway 89, from Kanab more or less to Panguitch, and then string it northeasterly, cross-country, through the high plateaus, past Cathedral Valley and the San Rafael Swell to the Book Cliffs. It is said that the Book Cliffs constitute the longest continuous escarpment in the world, some 250 miles from Price, Utah, almost to Grand Junction, Colorado. But that's too far for our purposes, so I'll leave the cliffs near the Colorado border and drop south along the edge of the La Sal and Abajo mountains until I hit the San Juan River, and then hightail it for sundown across the top of Navajoland back to Kanab. That's the canyon country. Geographers, eschewing the atlas and drawing their boundaries more precisely along physiographic lines, refer to the general region as the Canyon Lands Section of the Colorado Plateau; the Plateau being that larger province that falls between the Rocky Mountains and the Great Basin and includes, among its other subdivisions, the Uinta Basin to the north and the Grand Canyon country to the southwest. Grand Canyon country, then, should not be confused with *our* canyon country.

So there it is, about 15,000 square miles of slickrock and sand, enough space to bed down Massachusetts, Connecticut, and Rhode Island, with room to spare. Around the edges of this territory are the towns of Torrey, Green River, Moab, Monticello, Blanding, and Bluff—despite their big Mormon families, not even 20,000 people all told. Within the territory are the villages of Escalante, Boulder Town, and Hanksville; the hamlets of Bryce Valley, the marinas of Lake Powell, a few sparsely staffed units of the national parks system, and maybe a dozen ranches—not even 2,000 people. You are talking elbow room, now, like about one pair of elbows to every 4,800 acres.

Aridity is what makes this country tick; aridity, time, and the erosive rivers. Think of it as a great high desert lying in the rain shadow of much higher country roundabout. What falls from the sky on that shadow is not much, fewer than ten inches of rain or snow a year, and nearly all of that is soon sucked up by evapotranspiration. But in the mountains where the rivers begin—in the Wind River Range at the head of the Green, in the Uncompahgre, font of the Dolores, in the San Juans, in the highest Rockies that turn the Colorado loose to gather all the other streams—there the snowfall is prodigious. And the results fascinating, and best described by the man who put this country on the map, none other than the one-armed Major John Wesley Powell. The summer sun, wrote Powell in an account of his river-borne exploration of the canyon country in 1869, unleashes the snowpack "in millions of cascades. A million cascade brooks unite to form a thousand torrent creeks; a thousand torrent creeks unite to form half a hundred rivers beset with cataracts; half a hundred roaring rivers unite to form the Colorado . . . Now, if at the river's flood storms were falling on the plains, its channel would be cut but little faster than the adjacent country would be washed, and the general level would thus be preserved; but under the conditions here mentioned, the river continually deepens its bed; so all the streams cut deeper and still deeper, until their banks are towering cliffs of solid rock. These deep, narrow gorges are called"—now hold on, for few Anglo-Americans then had even heard the word—"canyons."

There are more canyons than a person can count, or name, and they come in all shapes, sizes, and colors. Canyons like cracks, so narrow at rimrock that a man, on the bottom looking up, has trouble finding the sky. Sinuous canyons that writhe and meander. Straightaway canyons, slick as a piston. Awesome canyons a thousand feet deep. Red, white, and blue canyons—blue, or lavender, from a desert varnishing of manganese oxides. Box canyons and side canyons and sides-off-the-side-of-a-side canyons, all with their tails to the high ground, their heads atilt toward the Colorado.

As the country falls away into its canyons, so does it climb here and there to substantial heights above what Powell called "the general level." Or, as another early rover saw it, "Why, there's as much country standing up as there is laying down." Standing tallest are the isolated clusters of interior mountains, the aforementioned La Sals, Abajos, and Henrys, each of which lofts a peak or two above 11,000 feet. Geologists call these mountains laccoliths (from the Greek, meaning stone cisterns). In effect, they are volcanoes that never quite blew their lids; instead, the rising lava formed blisters under the skin of the overlying sedimentary rock.

Next in order of presence above Powell's general level are the extraordinary cliffs of the canyon country: the Book Cliffs, already cited, and in places they do indeed resemble a rough-cut row of volumes on a library shelf; the Grand Staircase, which begins at the southern rim of the territory with the Vermilion Cliffs and then steps *in seriatum* over the White and Gray cliffs to the Pink Cliffs at the edge of the Paunsaugunt Plateau; the Straight Cliffs, which delineate the eastern escarpment of the Kaiparowits Plateau; the Circle Cliffs between the Henrys and the Escalante country; and the Orange Cliffs west of the confluence of the Green and Colorado rivers. And hardly to be outshone by the colorful cliffs are the upwarps—fangs of steeply tilted and eroded rock, monoclines in the parlance of geology, such as Comb Ridge and the San Rafael Reef, and, most spectacular to my eye, the thousand-foot-high jaw of the Waterpocket Fold. Not to mention some of the more common protuberant features, namely the monuments and buttes, the arches and the natural bridges, the little stone fins and shiprock spires that, in aggregate and in combination with the major landforms, give this canyon country an unsubtle texture duplicated nowhere in the world.

With plants and animals the territory comes about as well endowed as one might expect in a land of little rain, though in places the endowment can greatly exceed the expectation. There are barrens to be sure, some moonscapes, stark and brittle badlands where little but lichens will grow. But for the most part, the mile-high general level of the country falls within the great Southwestern botanical zone known as the pinyon-juniper belt. Pinyon pine and Utah juniper, to be more precise. Scratchy yet lovely little trees befitting the sand and the slickrock, resinous and fragrant, widely spaced, usually in mixed stands, and variously mixed up, depending on site and soil, with sagebrush, snakeweed, squawbush, prickly pear, cliff-rose, yucca, and buffaloberry, among the other attendant species. Down in the canyons, along the perennial streams, one encounters the Fremont cottonwood, the tamarisk (a runaway exotic), and sometimes a garden of wildflowers, hanging upside down from a seep in a sandstone ledge. Going the other way, ponderosa pine and gambel oak poke into the upper range of the pinyon, Douglas-fir pops up beyond the ponderosa, and spruce stand sentinel on the lids of those unblown volcanoes.

As for creatures, the territory provides habitat for modest populations of this and that. Mule deer are the predominant large animal and of sufficient number in some precincts to twitch a mountain lion's tail. Yes, there are still some of the big cats left—as many as 2,000 in the state of Utah, in fact—and some elk in the Book Cliffs, and some transplanted bison in the

Henrys, plenty of desert bighorn sheep in the wildest niches, and coyotes and foxes and owls and eagles and hawks and peregrine falcons and lizards and snakes, among other good things that fill up their trays on the slickrock food chain.

But neither wildlife nor wildwood is the main draw here in canyon country. What sets this territory apart—what lures camera-toting pilgrims from the four corners of the earth, what justifies the presence of such five-star national parks as Arches and Canyonlands and Capitol Reef and Bryce Canyon—are the rocks, the cold, inert, unblinking, eroding rocks in all their sculptured and stratigraphic glory. Learning how to read these rocks is the consummate challenge facing every traveler in canyon country, for one can hardly ignore them, or fail to wonder what tales their turning pages have to tell of a time when the whole world sat at the very edge of forever.

And there is this, too, about the rocks: They tend to make a person think big. In the 1930s, for example, more than a few people thought it would be a grand idea if almost half of all of this territory, from the Straight Cliffs east to the outliers of Moab, were placed under the protection of the National Park Service. The idea was to have a park befitting the sand and the slickrock, a park (actually, a national monument) bigger than any other in the world; and it would be named after the little town, the large canyon, and the eighteenth-century exploratory priest, Escalante. But like most big ideas, this one slipped through a crack, the Depression, and when it came out the other end, it shattered against some tougher ideas such as ranching and mining and damming the glens of the runaway rivers.

Now there is another idea. It is to pick up as many of the old pieces as are still lying around untarnished and put them together again, not as parks but as uppercase-*W* Wilderness. Of course, if there can be another idea, inevitably there must be another crack. This one is called the Utah segment of the wilderness review process of the Bureau of Land Management.

On the last day of January 1986, there emerged from the Utah State Office of the Bureau of Land Management in Salt Lake

City, a massive document purporting to represent the Bureau's best thinking—its biggest idea—as to how the lines of proposed wilderness might be drawn upon the maps of its 22-million-acre federal estate. Packaged in six separate volumes, weighing eighteen pounds, and running into hundreds of thousands of words, the *Utah BLM Statewide Wilderness Draft Environmental Impact Statement* remains a kind of "War and Peace" of the canyon country, although no one yet has come to the part about peace. As long as the poles of perception remain so far apart on this issue, no one will.

In sum, the Bureau's best thinking analyzed some 3.2 million acres in eighty-two Wilderness Study Areas, mostly in the southern part of the state. Of these, the Bureau proposed to recommend to the Secretary of the Interior 1.9 million acres in fifty-eight study areas as lands suitable for wilderness designation and the remaining 1.3 million acres as lands "nonsuitable" for wilderness but, by inference, perfectly suitable for just about everything else. The document analyzed certain environmental consequences of the proposal, as well as alternative actions ranging from "No Action/No Wilderness," which would have pleased most Utah politicians, to "All Wilderness/Designate 3,231,327 Acres," which would have sent the politicians right up their walls. Of course a good many conservationists would be climbing walls in either event. To their way of thinking, or at least to the way of thinking of the two-score organizations comprising the Utah Wilderness Coalition, suitable designation for Bureau roadless areas should not begin with 1.9 million acres, or even with 3.2 million. The Coalition had already drawn its own bottom line—and that one stood at 5.1 million acres.

To understand how the Bureau and the Coalition could arrive at such disparate numbers, one must turn back the clock to 1976, a full decade before the Bureau released its draft recommendations. That was the year of FLPMA (*flipma*), shorthand for the Federal Land Policy and Management Act of 1976 (hereafter the Act of '76), which set in motion a number of official actions, including a "wilderness study" process that was supposed to help Congress decide what areas to designate as upper-case Wilderness. These study areas were referred to as WSAs.

Identifying and managing statutory wilderness was not a part of the Bureau's mandate before 1976. The big *W* was for for-esters and park rangers to think about. Then the Act of '76 came along and put the Bureau on the wilderness team. The Act di-rected the Secretary of the Interior to take a careful look at the Bureau's domain, to identify the roadless areas of 5,000 acres or more that might qualify as additions to the National Wilderness Preservation System, to have those WSAs studied intensively, and, after further analysis, to make recommendations for wil-derness designation. Under the law, the Secretary of the Interior has until October 21, 1991, to convey those recommendations to the President, and the President then has two years to get them, or some reasonable executive facsimile, to the Congress for enactment.

The initial phase of the Bureau's inventory got under way in 1978. Using such objective criteria as relative size and degree of naturalness, the Bureau weeded out the areas it deemed unwor-thy of further review. Then, a year later, it moved on to what would be billed as the "intensive" inventory. Here some subjec-tive standards were applied to the process—standards, for ex-ample, that gave the Bureau great latitude in interpreting what might constitute an "outstanding opportunity" for solitude or for "a primitive and unconfined type of recreation." A roadless area had to have at least one of these characteristics or, under the Act of '76 and the Wilderness Act of 1964, it could not qualify for the big *W*. And this was just dandy for the Bureau because now a district manager could jettison a roadless area simply by deciding, however arbitrarily, that its opportunities for solitude and primitive recreation were not outstanding. Of course, the *purpose* of a decision to jettison an area was anything but arbi-trary. As a number of witnesses would later bring out at Con-gressional oversight hearings and in depositions to the Interior Department's Board of Land Appeals, the Bureau had a very clear and direct purpose for excising a number of roadless areas otherwise held in the highest esteem. Its purpose was to preserve for miners and county commissioners, and for generations of miners and county commissioners yet unborn, the right to exploit the jettisoned areas' resources, for, in truth, once the threat of the big *W* was out of the way, opportunities for a primitive and unconfined type of exploitation would be absolutely outstanding.

Macabre tales from the Utah inventory are legion, but to illustrate the sins of omission, perhaps two may suffice. The first comes from the golden pen of the Utah writer Ray Wheeler, in a splendid roundup for *High Country News*. In this account, Wheeler tells of a woman named Debbie Sease (now a lobbyist for the Sierra Club in Washington, D.C.) who accompanied Gary Wickes (then the Bureau's state director) on a tour of roadless areas under review. Sease is quoted as saying: "We stood on the edge of—far as the eye can see—incredibly beautiful, utterly wild land. Miles and miles and miles of beautiful Utah scenery. And I would say, 'Gary, why are you eliminating this?' And he'd say, 'Because there are no outstanding opportunities for primitive recreation.' And I'd say, 'And there's no opportunities for solitude either?' And Gary would say, 'You're right. You can have solitude here, but it's not outstanding solitude.' "

Janet Ross of Monticello offers the second testimonial. Ross is a pedigreed outdoor educator, a leader of wilderness river trips, and, nowadays, chair of the board of directors of the Southern Utah Wilderness Alliance, in which capacity she is largely preoccupied with undoing the official sins of yesteryear. For half of one of those years—1979 to be exact—Ross herself worked on the Utah inventory as a seasonal wilderness specialist attached to the Bureau's San Juan Resource Area Office. Her personal account of the Bureau's effort to undercut the process is contained in affidavits on file with Interior's Board of Land Appeals.

"It is my experience and professional judgment," Ross declared in one deposition, "that we did not perform and were not allowed to perform a competent wilderness inventory. The result was that substantial wilderness-quality acreage was arbitrarily excluded from further study and proper consideration."

Inadequate staffing—three employees, including herself, to inventory half a million acres—was only part of the problem. "From the highest state levels of BLM down through the area office there was little support or interest in the concept of wilderness . . . Field employees who expressed even mild leanings toward wilderness or particular units were accused of being 'too biased'. . . . The message was clear on two levels: (1) unlike other BLM missions (range, etc.) we were to suppress our commitment to this mission; and (2) our supervisors already had."

In one particular case, Ross and her two colleagues were ordered to evaluate an 80,000-acre unit on Mancos Mesa "entirely by helicopter, as the area was 'too big' to do on foot"—and all of this in a single day. The inventory team recommended that the mesa be classified a WSA. "Due to its vast size and inaccessibility," the team reported, "this area offers great solitude." Nevertheless, the Bureau excluded Mancos Mesa from further review (a decision later reversed by the Interior Board of Land Appeals). The solitude, it decided, while perhaps great, was not outstanding.

The astonishing thing is that so much of the damage was inflicted while the environmentalist Jimmy Carter still sat in the White House. Here were all these tree-huggers in high places at Carter's Interior Department on C Street, yet out there in Utah the whole process they had put in place was being busily subverted by the locals. Then, 1981, in came Ronald Reagan and suddenly the tree-huggers were being replaced by sagebrush rebels and privatizers, including a ranching man named Robert Burford, who moved into the top spot at the Bureau, thereby sitting at the right hand of Interior Secretary James Gaius Watt.

In July 1985, after a round of appeals had managed to restore to WSA status at least some of the left-out roadless areas, the Southern Utah Wilderness Alliance, The Wilderness Society, the Sierra Club, and the National Parks and Conservation Association (the nucleus of the Utah Wilderness Coalition) brought forth at a press conference in Salt Lake City their own statewide proposal, conceived in liberated audacity and dedicated to the proposition that a total of 5.1 million acres deserved wilderness designation—including those two million that had disappeared through the cracks of the Utah study process. (Note: The statewide figures used here, both the Coalition's proposal for 5.1 million acres and the Bureau's draft call for 1.9 million acres, include several hundred thousand acres of roadless areas in the Great Zion and West Desert regions, both of which lie outside the boundaries of canyon country as I have defined it.)

Unlike the Bureau's fragmented and insular approach to wilderness in southern Utah, the Coalition proposal sought to preserve the canyon country as a single physiographic entity, a macro-ecosystem, a great web of protected land such that when you tried to pick out any one unit by itself you found it hitched to everything else in the canyon country, including its national forests (some 700,000 acres) and its national parks, monuments, and recreation area (1.9 million acres, and more than two-thirds of *that* already recommended as additions to the National Wilderness Preservation System). But then Burford's Bureau rolled out its own vision of the territory, its eighteen-pounder, its *Statewide Wilderness* draft, its War Without Peace. Differences of opinion only begin with the statistics.

Consider the Book Cliffs, that world-class escarpment running across the top of the territory. The Coalition proposes more than half a million acres of wilderness here. The draft recommends fewer than 300,000 acres. Three entire WSAs—Coal, Flume, and Spruce canyons—are dropped through a crack. They shatter on the draft's finding that this is an area "known for hydrocarbon potential." Coal, oil, gas. No Action/No Wilderness. In the Desolation Canyon area, where the Green River carves its deep and turbulent passage through the cliffs, where the one-armed Powell lost a couple of oars, where the Coalition calls for designated wilderness, Burford's Bureau gives a "high favorability rating" to the prospects for coal and hydropower—and good-bye to sixteen miles of wild river.

Consider the San Rafael Swell, that great eroded uplift with its sickle-blade reef, its Red Desert and Muddy Creek and rainbow badlands. Long considered an area worthy of national park status, the Swell embraces some 650,000 acres of Coalition wilderness. Yet for many of those acres the draft places a higher value on coal, tar sands, and accessibility for dirt bikes and other off-road vehicles.

Moving counterclockwise across canyon country, we arrive into the subregion of the Kaiparowits Plateau and the canyons of the remote and wild Paria River. Eight hundred thousand acres of wilderness, the way the Coalition sees it; a bit over 200,000 in the opinion of the draft. Why? Because of coal, again. And maybe a little uranium. And possibly a bit of range improvement, here and there.

Things are looking better in the subregion of the Escalante, though not by much. Here the two sides are fairly close along the main stem of Escalante Canyon, but poles apart in some of the side canyons and up on the benchlands. Apparently because a portion of one key WSA overlaps an area "considered to have a high certainty for the occurrence of large deposits of uranium," the draft recommends No Action/No Wilderness for some 26,000 acres around Scorpion Flat and Brimstone Gulch, acres it otherwise enthusiastically applauds as having high wilderness and aesthetic values.

Swinging east, we'll skip over the Henry Mountains–Dirty Devil complex (saving it for a closer look, later on) and pause instead among the wonders of the Cedar Mesa country, a territory noted especially for its treasure-trove of Anasazi ruins. Some of the major conflicts here go back to the Bureau's inventory, when it declined even to consider as WSAs such gems as most of Arch Canyon and all of Comb Ridge and Harmony Flat. Also at issue are the Dark Canyon and Mancos Mesa areas, where, the Coalition alleges, the Bureau has pinched the potential with "exaggerated claims of impact" in some places, and "understated wilderness values" in others.

And finally, last stop on our way back to the high-noon Book Cliffs, we arrive in the Canyonlands, precinct of exquisite roadless areas abutting the national park of that name (and Arches, too) or tucked into that slickrock maze along the Green and Colorado rivers. Put the *W* to 481,990 acres, says the Coalition;

hold it at 135,365, said Buford's Bureau. If the Bureau prevails, good-bye to wilderness for Hatch Wash and Harts Point and most of Indian Creek and all of the Mill Creek and Negro Bill Canyon WSAs next door to Moab, where Grand County buckeroos sought to preempt any designation by bulldozing jeep trails. But possibly the saddest loss of all would be the evisceration of Labyrinth Canyon, just upstream from Canyonlands Park on the Colorado River. Here the Bureau has seen fit to recommend for designation only a fraction of the total roadless area, bisecting the canyon and excluding its entire eastern flank. "River travelers," the Coalition noted in an early critique, "cannot understand how the west bank is wilderness while the BLM claims the equally natural east bank 'clearly and obviously lacks wilderness characteristics.'" The mystery was easily solved. Right there in the War Without Peace draft was the simple statement that, while no plans existed to construct hydroelectric projects along this stretch of the river, hydropower would have to be rated highly.

II

The idea was to do the country in a week. It was a bad idea. A gadabout person could not do this country in a year, maybe not even in a lifetime if he should measure the doing canyon-by-canyon right down the line. There is too much of it. So you take what you can, where you can, when you can, and hope that enough of it rubs off on you to last until the next time. If you should be so lucky.

My own luck has been pretty good, though it took me long enough to get into the territory to discover what I had been missing. At first I could only sniff at the tamest edge of it. This was in the Fifties, when I was gumshoeing for a little daily newspaper beyond the Four Corners in Navajo country. You needed plenty of time, then, to explore *either* country, and one free day out of seven didn't exactly set you up for a proper expedition. But I knew this other country was out there, beyond the spires of Monument Valley and Navajo Mountain, the tribe's holy place, and I promised to post myself across its border someday.

And finally got the chance to do that fifteen years later—several sorties, in fact, into the slickrock funhouse around Canyonlands National Park, remanding myself into the custody of that seasoned canyoneer and campfire raconteur Kent Frost of Monticello. And then there was one more journey to the canyons, about the same time that Congress was putting the Bureau into the wilderness business with the Act of '76. That time I had stood at the edge of the Waterpocket Fold and watched the sun rising out of the Henry Mountains, the shadows reaching out under Tarantula Mesa, the great rift trench of the Fold itself curving down to the red rocks at Bullfrog Bay. It was the kind of morning, at the kind of place, that tightens the skin over one's temples. My temples, anyway.

And now I was going back to do the rest of it, in a week. Pick up a jeep in Grand Junction and skedaddle down the Western Slope; grab some gear and grub and go out to the little airstrip north of Moab and wait for a little plane to bring my big friend The Brushpopper out of the sky. The jeep was my idea and it was a good idea, since we had only a week, but I think it embarrassed The Brushpopper. I'll try to explain why.

First of all, for reasons not germane to this tale, the true identity of my traveling friend must be withheld. Anonymity has to run in one of two directions: either to a pseudonym, or to a nickname. Since I abhor pseudonyms, I had no alternative but to go the other way. And what a hard way it was until, at the end of our first long day, some five jeepless miles up a canyon in the Book Cliffs, my companion took leave of our campsite and disappeared into the pinyons, scrambling, solo, for rimrock. And what the hell had he been doing, I wanted to know when at last, and just in time for supper, he returned from his hike.

"Been brushpoppin'," he said.

"Which is . . ."

"Which is cowboy talk," he said. "Cowboy goes up the side of a canyon after some lost cow, that's brushpoppin'. There was a saying that you could always tell when a cowboy'd been brushpoppin' if he came back with enough wood jammed into his saddle tree to cook dinner with."

So The Brushpopper he'd be, though for some reason he never quite took to the name as eagerly as he pursued the activity. Every chance he got, he'd scramble away from the jeep, into a canyon or out on some ledge. It was as if he were trying to make up for lost time, which in fact he was. Having spent the worse part of his years as a fellow of rather limited ambulatory experience, as an armchair, or barstool, elitist, if you will, The Brushpopper had recently undergone a change of life and become—transmogrified—a compleat walker, seeker of solitude, a bagger of boondocks. Any or all of which does not incline one to be favorably disposed toward traveling about in a motor vehicle, especially in wild country. Moreover, The Brushpopper was painfully aware, as I am, that cityslick boosters of uppercase Wilderness who fly into little airports and then go popping around in jeeps always seem to catch the thickest flak from local-gentry wilderness bashers—their theory being, bygawd, if you want wilderness so much then you should bloody *walk to it*. (The antithesis of this, and I've heard it from more than a few conservationists, is equally illogical: Okay, if you hate wilderness so much, and love pavement, then you should bloody well *move to the city*.) Well, you can't please everyone, can you? And besides, we only had this one week.

From the Book Cliffs, we scoot over to the San Rafael Swell and cross its reef through the wash south of Temple Mountain—scarred and battered Temple Mountain with the holes in its sides where they mined uranium for the Manhattan Project, took it right out of the mountain's red-green Chinle shales and packed it off to . . . where? Alamogordo? Hiroshima? Nagasaki? The little black holes in the rock do not suit this country. But it is not too hard out here to get away from them, to turn the corner, cross the head of Wild Horse Canyon and swing down along the edge of the 25,000-acre Crack Canyon WSA and then pull over and leave the jeep and head for the Crack that slices right through the San Rafael Reef, three hundred feet deep in one place, and just wide enough for a horse and a rider with concave knees. Head for—and then stop. There are rainclouds overhead, black as the empty mineheads, and though I have never experienced a flash flood in canyon country, I have heard enough to believe that even long shots should be avoided, especially in a canyon called Crack. The Brushpopper is no dummy about floods either, but I have reason to suspect he harbors a certain predilection for risk. To save face I look at my watch and say we had better be going in any event, if we want to get down to the Dirty Devil by dark.

John Atlantic Burr was born on the briney, bound for the promised land. And that's how he got his middle name. Across the Alleghenies and the wide Missouri, through tall grass and short, his parents bore the twinkling lad all the way to Koosharem in Fishlake country, northwest of the canyons, backside of the high plateaus. Formal histories of the territory hardly give the time of day to John Atlantic Burr; after all, he never grew up to be President or Bishop or a general in the Army, just a stockman, a cowpoke, a six-shooter type who blazed a trail for his cows through the Circle Cliffs. But Old John sure caught the fancy of cartographers, for his name is sprinkled all over the place. Burrville. Burr Trail. Burr Pass. Burr Desert. Burr Point. For all I know, there could be other Burrs that are *off* the map, like the John Atlantic Burr ferryboat that plies the blue waters of Lake Powell out of Bullfrog, where the herds used to drink when the water was brown and the place was Glen Canyon, as, by all that is right and decent in nature, it ought to be yet.

We have come down through Hanksville and off the pavement east of Bull Mountain, in the Henrys, and across the red dust and purple sage of the Burr Desert toward the point—the Burr Point, of course—that overlooks the grand jigsaw of the Dirty Devil. Why Old John drove his stock thisaway is beyond me, if indeed he ever did. Except for the low sage to hold the sand in place, this has to be one of the sorrier cowpastures ever, though I expect it was a bit lusher a hundred years ago, before the free-ranging herds began taking their toll. That was about Burr's time, too, the Eighties. They say his summer range was up on Boulder Mountain and he scratched his trail through cliffs and canyons in order to winter his steers out here or down on the big river at Bullfrog. It was Butch Cassidy's time, too, and the Wild Bunch up at Robber's Roost, on the far side of the Devil, were mavericking strays and making life miserable for honest drovers before turning to holdups and bank heists; so that maybe Burr just put his name down here in the dust, patted his holster, clicked his spurs, and trotted off to some safer home-on-the-range. Or maybe he didn't.

The Dirty Devil. The legends hold that Major Powell's men named it. Coming down the Colorado, low on provisions, they could see the mouth of this tributary river approaching on their right, and called out to the scouts in the lead boat, "Is it a trout stream?" The answer came back: "Naw! It's a *dirty* devil." That was because of Muddy Creek, which, when it's running, throws a load of badland silt into the mountain-fed Fremont River at Hanksville, and therein becomes the Devil itself. And what an incredible incision so little water and so much silt have made in the rocks—a mini Grand Canyon, one counselor had called it, you just wait and see. Well, we waited and now, here at Burr Point, we see; see the ancient siltstone rimrock suddenly opening into a great abyss, and the Navajo sandstone below, and then a thin bench of red Kayenta, and the long cliffs of Wingate falling down, down, down to the Chinle crumbling away underneath, and maybe a streak of Moenkopi bottoming out, and at last the khaki scalpel of the river, twisting and turning, probing for bedrock fifteen hundred feet below our perch.

We have come not only to praise the Devil but to bury it. In a figurative sense, of course. To do the real number, one would have to invoke either an act of God or an irreversible decision by the Bureau of Land Management to gerrymander side canyons, satellite benches, and a stretch of the river itself right out of protective wilderness custody and into the hands of . . . whom? A wild bunch of tar-sands rustlers? Possibly. Who knows? Only Burford's Bureau knows why, as I stand here at the Burr, I can look upstream past Ibex Point and see nothing but Bureau-endorsed wilderness, while across the chasm on Sam's Mesa and for a long way downstream there is nothing but this huge hole in the Bureau's process—no, not a hole, a gravesite big enough to swallow Sam's and Happy Canyon and The Big Ridge and Fiddler Butte and The Block; can't see it all from here, too far away, but I know they're out there, and just as wild as anything to which the Bureau has given a nod.

On paper, of course, it looks a whole lot better. On the paper of War Without Peace, it looks at first as if the Bureau has tossed in its lot with the tree-huggers after all, for here is a 61,000-acre Dirty Devil WSA with an "All Wilderness" recommendation, and a 25,000-acre French Spring–Happy Canyon WSA in which the Bureau appears to favor 11,110 acres for designation, and finally a 73,100-acre Fiddler Butte WSA in which the Bureau recommends 32,700 acres as wilderness. That's what you get in a cursory glance at the impact statement. But look again. Look again and you see that Fiddler Butte isn't even included in the Fiddler Butte proposal; it has been excised "to reduce tar sand conflicts." Look again and you see that the proposed 11,110-acre French Spring–Happy Canyon Wilderness is a mistake, a slip of some intern's pen (the Bureau says), an entry for the errata sheets (0, so *many* errata). What the Bureau really means to propose for French Spring–Happy Canyon is *zero* wilderness.

But why? Why is so much of this whole Dirty Devil corridor unsuitable for wilderness designation? Why, because of those tar sands. Because Interior Secretary Donald Hodel, one of Watt's successors, has declared mineral development to be the top priority for Bureau lands, and because there is this paper concept called the Tars Sands Triangle, which overlaps much of the corridor. No matter that the conversion of tar sands into oil in the United States is widely considered an alchemist's pipedream that is likely to make neither dollars nor sense. If there is the remotest possibility that a mineral or energy resource might be developed some day, Hodel's Interior Department is not about to lock it up and throw away the key. It is going to keep the options open, such that, in this particular case, should tar sands development ever become economically feasible, the Devil will have an altogether different meaning attached to its dirtiness, what with all the injection wells, storage tanks, stream generators, coking plants, and hard-top roads already envisioned by at least one major energy consortium. Now, *there* would be one dirty Devil, for certain.

Tonight, at Burr Point, it is a blustery Devil under a west wind off the snow-capped Henrys, and all those miles of hot, red dust between here and the mountains cannot soften the chill. We have made our camp out of the wind on a ledge below the rim, savaged our rations of tortillas and kabobs, denounced the gerrymanders of Burford's Bureau, and saluted the stars. Now The Brushpopper is making noises about descending fifteen hundred feet to the river, just to get warm.

You don't have a flashlight, I tell him.

He'll use the stars, he says. I know he's bluffing. He's all zipped up in his mummy bag, preparing to snore. Not quite. Now he wants to know if I know what.

What, Old Brushpopper?

The sky, he says. The sky has no lid on it.

In olden days, between the demise of the Anasazi cliff dweller and the arrival of the lonesome cowboy, the biggest idea for the canyon country was to find a way to get across it, or around it. Most folks then didn't care much about solitude, nor much about tar sands either, though a handful did care about beaver and gold. The first ones through were a couple of friars, Dominguez and Escalante, sanctioned to explore for a route linking Santa Fe to the precincts of Monterey in California. This was in 1776, about the time George Washington was being routed himself, a world away at a place called Long Island. The friars never reached California, but in their long loop homeward crossed the Colorado at a point now flooded by Lake Powell, and thereby touched the hems of their robes to the edge of the territory. A lifetime later, John C. Frémont of the Army Corps of Topographical Engineers brushed the opposite edge, on the north side. He was looking for a route, too, a mythic river road that wold float Manifest Destiny straight to the tides of the Pacific. And a few years after that another topographer, one John N. Macomb, came to discover the most direct route between the new Mormon settlements in Utah and the old Spanish communities of the Rio Grande. Macomb did not care much for southern Utah. He declared he could not conceive "of a more worthless and impracticable region than the one we now find ourselves in." There is no accounting for taste.

The Mormons, of course, put an end to this terrible habit of using the territory as a stepping stone to somewhere else. The Mormons liked the country, and still do. They started poking down this way from the Great Salt Lake as early as 1855. This caused a stir among the locals, first among the Utes and then among the Navajos. But the Mormons were pretty firm about what they wanted to do (and still are), and by-and-by they were dug in along the lee of the high plateaus, and down the wild Paria in places, and out from Boulder Mountain across the northern foothills of the Henrys. To settle the far southeastern corner of the kingdom, the Saints dispatched a train of eighty-three wagons and a thousand head of stock cross-country from Escalante to what is now Bluff, in the Cedar Mesa country. The path today is known as the "Hole-in-the-Rock Trail," because that's what the pilgrims had to do—dynamite a hole in the side of Glen Canyon, a chute just wide enough for wagons, so that they could get down to and across the Colorado, bound for this new promised land. And they got there, too, though it took a whole winter.

Now if The Brushpopper and I had *that* kind of time, we could begin to do the country right. As it is, we have already shot two whole days getting from the Dirty Devil to the Escalante, with no wagons or livestock to slow us down, and no need to blast holes in the rock with dynamite, though some of the people in Garfield County here think a little more blasting might be a good idea, especially along the road we've been traveling. Namely the Burr Trail. People in Garfield don't think much of the Burr as an improvement. I wonder what Old John Atlantic would have to say about that.

To get here from the Dirty Devil, we were obliged to backtrack from dust to pavement and head south, down between the big Henrys and the Little Rockies to Bullfrog, where we marveled at the wonders of the Lake Powell Yacht Club (high and dry and miles from the water at the edge of the Cane Springs Desert) and sundry other amusements of Del Webb Country (Del Webb people being the entrepreneurs of Bullfrog Marina). Then, putting all of that behind us, and none too soon, we proceeded up a graded gravel road, first leg of the Burr Trail, into the Waterpocket Fold. No matter the pressure to be somewhere else, one must spend time with the Fold. It is not to be missed, especially if one can arrange to be at the Strike Valley Overlook for sunup or sundown, as I had that time once before, that time of the tightening of the temples. This time, alas, we missed the sundown show, but we did manage to catch the Fold unfolding under early morning light, and, as before, the view was magnificent: The backlit Henry Mountains—Ellen, Pennell, Hillers, Holmes, Ellsworth—wrapped in blue gauze; those flat-top mesas—Tarantula and Swap—leaning our way; the valley of the Fold with its spine of white rocks—the Oyster Shell Reef—and then the toothy, convoluted, upside-down sandstones defining the monocline's western edge.

Only this time was different. Since my last visit, the Bureau had cast its appraising eye upon the other side of the Fold and decided that the country over there was, insofar as wilderness might be concerned, less than outstanding.

For starters, during the inventory process, the Bureau had sliced from a 140,000-acre roadless area one slim ghost of a study area, the Mt. Pennell WSA, weighing in at some 27,000 acres. Conservationists appealed. The Board of Land Appeals instructed the Bureau to bring the WSA up to snuff at some 74,000 acres. Having done that, the Bureau in its draft environmental-impact statement simply threw the whole baby out again, prescribing *zero* wilderness for the Mt. Pennell unit (though another slip of some intern's pen—shades of Happy Canyon—garbled the Bureau's intent; o, *errata*!). And why no wilderness? Why? Because the Bureau concludes that "Pennell would not contribute sufficiently to the diversity of the wilderness system to outweigh other resource considerations." Which means, there are those miners and cowboys again. And where there are cowboys, there are cows.

From the Strike Valley Overlook, it is easy enough to miss what the Bureau has done to the other side of the Fold, on behalf of the cowman and his cow. The top of Tarantula Mesa, for example, is just a bit higher than Overlook eye-level, so that you need better loft—an airplane will do—to comprehend the meaning of range improvement, as executed by the Bureau of Land Management in southern Utah under the approving eye of old cowman Robert Burford. What it means in the Henry Mountains is the destruction of the pinyon-juniper forest. And all that is needed to convert the forest into pasture is two government bulldozers with an anchor chain strung between them, a bucket of grass seed, and fistful of *your* tax dollars. In pointy-toe-boot circles, the procedure is known as chaining.

Chaining has already scarred much of the Henrys and their satellite benchlands, and more destruction is on the way. If the numbers can somehow be justified—it beats me how they possibly can—several thousand acres of pinyon-juniper will soon be chained and otherwise "reclaimed" at a cost of $321,000. And the purpose? Why, to increase the mountains' carrying capacity, to provide for some 2,000 additional animal-unit-months (the amount of forage needed to sustain one cow plus one calf or 6.2 sheep for a month). This breaks out at about $160 per cow/month, a figure that seems outrageously high. According to Rodney Greeno, issues coordinator for the Southern Utah Wilderness Alliance, the National Park Service is currently buying ranchers out of grandfathered grazing rights right here in Capitol Reef National Park at the rate of $52 per cow/month—less than a third of what the big-spending Bureau proposes to drop for its animal units.

Moreover, there is an astonishing subsidy built into this program. Of the $160 per-unit cost, the Bureau's share (the taxpayer's share) is 60 percent, or $96. The cowman—the permittee, if you will—pays a bit under 9 percent, or only about $14 per unit, and the state of Utah picks up the balance. How about *that*? Remember it the next time you count your change at McDonald's. Thanks to Burford's Bureau, you will already have paid for the Big Mac hamburger—with your subsidy.

Enough of that. The chains and cows are behind us. We have come across the territory to camp at last on a sandbar beside the gin-clear waters of the Escalante. Cottonwoods to the right of us, pinyons to the left. Across the river, a canyon wall as slick as quicksilver. We are at the edge of solitude; not outstanding solitude, mind you, because the trailhead is but a hop and a skip away, and such is the Escalante's five-star reputation, more backpackers are hopping and skipping past our campsite in an hour than we have seen in four days of canyon crawling elsewhere.

Still, it is a salubrious spot—and all the more appreciated since The Brushpopper and I must go our separate ways tomorrow, his time in the canyons cut short by events in the world he left behind. But first, in the morning, we will pack out of here and go to the airstrip outside the town of Escalante and fly over some of the country we missed on the ground. And then I will spend some time with Clive Kincaid, who is the most unwelcome man in the territory. Until Kincaid rose to prominence, the meddlesome and tree-hugging actor Robert Redford held the title of Most Unwelcome (mostly because of Redford's eloquent opposition to a coal-fired powerplant on the Kaiparowits Plateau). In fact, it is said that the good people of Escalante Town would have unwelcomed Robert Redford by lynching and burning him in effigy, if only the folks in Kanab hadn't got the idea first. It was some time after this ripple of ill will that a bolt of lightning struck the Escalante area office of the Bureau of Land Management, and burned *it* to the ground. The Lord works in mysterious ways.

III

"So I approached the Sierra Club and The Wilderness Society," Clive Kincaid was telling me that next afternoon on Boulder Mountain. "I'd been working with them a lot as a BLM bureaucrat, trying to involve them in the Arizona wilderness program, and I told them that I was going to be quitting. After a year of the Watt administration I just had to. And they asked me if I would go into the Four Corners Region and determine whether there was any pattern of abuse of policy. So I did that. I left in

October of '81 and first went to New Mexico and spent several months, and then to Colorado, and then I just drove across the border—I'd never been to Utah before—and kind of went past Monticello and saw those first red rocks and I was blown away. And that's what started this odyssey to uncover what clearly has been a very well-coordinated and direct campaign to corrupt and limit the wilderness review process here in the State of Utah."

We sat on the side of Boulder Mountain, at an overlook off the high road to Torrey, and the whole vast arc of country that once might have been—that still could be—the greatest park in the world unrolled before us in a diorama of a hundred different colors and configurations. From the Moroni Slopes at nine o'clock north, the arc curved behind the high-noon Henrys all the way to the cone of Navajo Mountain, hunkering in a shimmer of haze, three o'clock south. And splitting it all in half, or at least the foreground of our view of it, was the thin red line of the Burr Trail, picking its way out of the Fold through the Circle Cliffs.

We had taken the bird'seye view in the morning, in a six-seater aircraft out of Escalante, courtesy of that nonprofit airlifter of ecofreaks, Project Lighthawk, out of Aspen, Colorado. Pilot Bruce Gordon was at the controls, Clive Kincaid beside him with the running commentary, The Brushpopper and I in the middle pew, and Wilderness Society field representative Mike Medberry of Salt Lake City and Gordon's colleague, photographer Andre Ulrych, holding up the tail. We had sought and attained altitude over the Kaiparowits, gazed upon the Paria, the Grand Staircase, the Cockscomb and the Wahweap; east with the wind over the Escalante canyons, Stevens Arch, the Fold, and Tarantula Mesa, where at last we saw what chaining really looks like. It looked like hell. "This is the land of the big mistakes," Kincaid had said from the co-pilot's seat as we flew from the mesa over the saddle between Mts. Ellen and Pennell. "Someone does something illegal in a WSA and it's called a 'mistake.' Then the BLM reclaims the mistake. Look here. Here's their reclaimed chaining and over there is their reclaimed drill pad. And their reclaimed road. Figure it out for yourself."

Now, sitting with him on the side of the mountain, I had my mind full just trying to figure Kincaid. Who *was* this latter-day Muir-of-the-Desert, this apostate bureaucrat, this whistleblower? And why were folks on the other side saying such terrible things about him? He didn't look like some wilderness squatter to me—but then he didn't look like an alumnus of the Bureau of Land Management either. He talked, I listened.

He had come out of the University of California at Los Angeles, straight from the campus to a district office of the Bureau in Arizona. He worked as a planning coordinator; his wife signed aboard as the district archeologist. It was the year the Bureau joined the wilderness team. By and by the Phoenix district was looking for someone to handle its inventory, and Kincaid got the job. "Had a wonderful time. A helicopter and airplane at my disposal, and eventually I had something like thirteen people working for me." Then Burford sat at the right hand of Watt. Kincaid bailed out and began his sleuthing for the tree-huggers.

"It didn't take me long to figure out that something very strange had happened in Utah," he said. "Systematically, the Bureau districts had gone about trying to eliminate from wilderness study well-known resource complexes through any machinations they could come up with, whether it was simply saying, 'Well, this is a nice opportunity for primitive recreation, but it's not an outstanding opportunity,' or simply dropping entire areas outright, or excising portions of areas that people for some reason or another didn't question. Anyway, I ended up spending a year of my time and money piecing it together, and it turned out that all those eliminated areas were full of mining claims or coal seams or oil leases or whatever. See, they were smart. They cleared the decks early. They knew to get the problem children out of the way. They tried to do that, and they did."

But why? This hadn't happened in Arizona or New Mexico. Why Utah?

"Utah is Utah," said Kincaid. "Utah was invaded by the United States Army in 1858 to put down the Mormon insurrection. And the inculcated hatred of the federal government because of that is something that will not leave the consciousness of some of these people for another five hundred years, if they're here that long. Look. When I worked for the Bureau in Arizona, nobody wanted to come to Utah. I never understood why. And then I came to Utah myself and met enough BLM people to find out what was going on here. What was going on was that local boys that go to Utah State or some of the agricultural colleges and then go to work for the BLM—they don't want to go to California or Montana or Wyoming. They want to stay right here in Utah. So you had this extension of the local culture into the agency. You had an absence of any kind of pluralism on one hand, and on the other this overwhelming, lopsided cultural layer dovetailing with the political structure of the state. Look at the district managers. Throughout the Bureau, the average turnover of district managers is something like two to four years. In this state, it's thirteen years. A boy comes here that grew up in the neighboring county, went to school in the area, becomes a BLM man, never leaves the district, works his way up, one job to the next, gets into management and stays for his whole bureaucratic career. So. The U.S. Army invaded Utah and the federal government took over all of the land that was the Kingdom of Deseret. But you know what? Ultimately, in their own way, the people here got it all back again. It's really fascinating."

It was *very* fascinating, but we had to get on to other things. So he talked for a while about the Southern Utah Wilderness Alliance, which he helped to launch with a little newsletter published out of Boulder Town, in 1984. The start-up circulation was all of five. Now the Alliance counts a membership of 1,500. And then he spoke of that thin red line below us, the Burr Trail.

The Brushpopper and I had done the Trail, as I mentioned earlier. It is a splendid road, a bit too precipitous for my acrophobic tastes where it climbs the switchbacks up the side of Waterpocket Fold. A bit too slow and bumpy if you happen to live in the lee of the high plateaus and own a powerboat and want to haul it on weekends directly to Bullfrog Marina, instead of taking the long way around, by hardtop through Hanksville and Ticaboo. But it is a scenic road for certain—possibly the most scenic, Brushpopper and I had agreed (and we rarely do), in all of America. And because many folks hold the Trail in the same high esteem, and note that it also happens to cruise past a couple of WSAs, while others would have it the opposite way, unkinked and unwrinkled, with hardtop pavement as smooth as a canvas mat—because of all this the Trail has been on and off the litigious ropes like a punchdrunk contender. Last I heard, the hardtoppers were ahead on points, the courts giving Garfield County a right-of-way on the Trail; but it's still unpaved and the Trail-lovers plan further moves.

And finally Clive Kincaid was speaking of his home, which is down there in the arc somewhere beyond Boulder Town, just off the Burr Trail, and which he built himself, and by the sweat of his brow, of native stone. I had heard about Kincaid's house. It was almost as famous—or infamous, depending on your point of view—as he was. I had asked him why he had left the Wilderness Alliance as executive director, and he said, "The biggest single factor is what happened to me with my house."

The word around the territory—word emanating even from folks who are not altogether admiring of Clive Kincaid—was that the Bureau was out to "get" him, run him out, pay him back for all the trouble he'd caused. So I asked if the Bureau had actually "jiggled" a property line to make it appear he was squatting on public land.

"Yes and no," he said. "They came in and did a survey and it appears that they are correct on one point—that half my house, about six hundred square feet, is on federal land. But what they did to crucify me in the press was to jiggle a *wilderness* line, to make it appear I had built my house in a wilderness study area."

So where did it stand, now, with the Bureau?

"They've given me an order to destroy the house. I'm appealing. Destroy it? I put a hundred and fifty tons of stone in it."

The Bureau's people in Salt Lake City deny that any lines have been jiggled in the Kincaid affair, but confirm that the house will indeed have to be moved or destroyed if the Board of

Land Appeals finds in the Bureau's favor. "This has been at least as difficult for us as for Mr. Kincaid," said Bureau spokesman Jerry Meredith, "especially with all these people wrongly accusing us of harassing the man."

With 7,884 square miles, and that doesn't count any of its vertical surfaces, of which there are many, San Juan County is the largest county in the territory, the largest in all of Utah. It is also the poorest county in Utah, at least insofar as one measures personal income and relative numbers of people who fall through that crack called poverty. Much of the poverty is concentrated among the Navajo people, who make up about half the county's population of 12,000 and reside for the most part on reservation lands south of the San Juan River. North of that river, the only major employers are the school systems, a uranium mill outside Blanding, and Hall's Crossing Marina, on Lake Powell. Oil and gas are big in the county—it is the state's leading producer, in fact—but the industry does not produce many jobs. Same goes for cattle—big and consistent, but precious few jobs. Some people say, though not too loudly or openly in local circles, that the last best hope for San Juan County's economic survival is to capitalize somehow on its real wealth—the buttes and canyons and Anasazi ruins that are scattered prodigiously and beautifully across the Cedar Mesa country at the county's core.

To test such an idea against the reality, I had left Clive Kincaid on the side of Boulder Mountain and come the very long way around, through Hanksville the hardtop way, to Blanding, which, with 3,600 souls to its name, is San Juan's largest municipality. In Blanding I called on Harold Lyman, who runs the San Juan Jobs Service Center and is a direct descendant of the Latter-Day Saint who founded the city at the turn of the century. Lyman said, "Every day I sit here talking to people who don't know where their next meal's coming from. And then there's the backpacker. Why, you know he probably flew a jet into Salt Lake City and rented a car and drove down here on a paved highway, and now he wants to hike the Grand Gulch and not be bothered by off-road vehicles." So Lyman had figured me out. Then he said, "The environmentalists are always trying to tell us to develop our tourist economy. And when we try to do that, they object to that, too. Besides, we cannot survive on tourism alone."

A hop down the block at the Elk Ridge Restaurant, I spent some time with Calvin Black, who owns the restaurant and a fine motel nearby, and Hall's Crossing Marina up at the lake, and interests in other things; and is a longtime county commissioner, running this fall for a shot at the state legislature (he's been there before), and a member of Interior Secretary Donald Hodel's National Public Lands Advisory Council, and thinks that the 1.9 million acres recommended for uppercase Wilderness in *War Without Peace* is just about 1.9 million acres too many. Cal Black is a real veteran of the canyon battles, an articulate and rational spokesman for a constituency that sometimes prefers to foam at the mouth. Once upon a time, Cal Black told Edward Abbey that with so much of the territory locked up in parks, and no jobs available, San Juan County had but two significant exports—empty pop bottles and its own children. That was almost twenty years ago and Black, not without some justification, still believes it.

"Tourism is wonderful," the proprietor of Hall's Crossing Marina was saying, "but—" and now the county commissioner in him took over—"it is not a good single-base economy. Just look at Garfield County, other side of the lake. Garfield has or is next to the most developed accessible parks in the state of Utah. Bryce Canyon is in Garfield and Glen Canyon Recreation Area is substantially in Garfield, and I'm not even counting Capitol Reef. Zion and Cedar Breaks are just to the west of them. So Garfield County has the best-known, most-visited parks in the state. Now, there is the epitome of building tourism, and all the benefits that the environmentalists always talk about. Yet Garfield County has not been allowed to have coal development. Limits on oil and gas. Timber sales appealed. All they've got is agriculture, a little sawmilling, and tourism. They now have 50 percent of the population they had fifty years ago, which means they've lost half of their seed and all of their increase. They have the highest average unemployment in the state. If you take out the Indian component in San Juan County, Garfield has the lowest per capita income in the state. Now, if that's what tourism does for you and you can't have anything else, I'd rather have 'anything' else. If I had to make a choice. But what I am saying is that you can have both."

I told Cal Black that most environmentalists probably wouldn't agree with him about the prospects for "having both," but that a few were finally sending out some positive signals on the tourism issue, instead of bleating instinctively every time some local booster suggested a plan to bring more tourists into the territory. Clive Kincaid, for example (though I didn't mention this to Black), old Mister Most Unwelcome himself, had spoken to me of the need to accommodate tourism in a significant way—significant enough to serve as an economic alternative to hit-'n'-run resource development. And if that meant paving some road, so be it. And Ken Sleight, the river-runner and pack-trip outfitter and perennial foe of wilderness bashers— even *this* one was talking accommodation. "We've got to help develop the small towns," Sleight told me. "I mean, do they *really* want a small jetport at Hall's Crossing, or at Blanding? Tourism should be directed at the towns, not Lake Powell. By concentrating on Lake Powell, all you do is turn the towns into piss stops—just like a freeway passed them by."

But I didn't tell Cal Black about that either because Black has no use for Ken Sleight, partly because he views Sleight as a lot of trouble in his own right, partly because Sleight is a good buddy of Ed Abbey, who wrote that seditious book about a monkeywrench gang, and partly because, in Black's view, if it wasn't for people like Sleight and Abbey, San Juan County would have something to export beside empty pop bottles and its own children.

I had planned from the start to save Arch Canyon for the last stop. Everyone—Medberry, Kincaid, counselors to The Brushpopper—had given the place five stars, the highest rating. It just had to be experienced, this canyon that came down through orange sandstones in the Cedar Mesa country between Blanding and Natural Bridges National Monument. Ray Wheeler, a lively wordslinger if there ever was, had whetted my appetite with one of his "magic carpet rides" in that newsletter put out by the Wilderness Alliance: "We're skimming south over the level, forested surface of Elk Ridge . . . Suddenly the land drops away into a breathtaking thousand-foot-deep gorge. Virgin ponderosa line the canyon floor and cling to its walls. Below us are plunging cliffs, narrow ledges, buttes, pinnacles, buttresses, and alcoves. A massive sandstone arch wings by, holding a slice of sky in its armpit . . . Where the snowmelt funnels down off the rim, we can see a dozen stupendous waterfalls . . ."

Now how could anyone pass up a treat like that? The canyon's praises had been sung in high places ever since National Park Service Director Stephen Mather posted a scout this way in 1926 to check out some prospects for national monumenthood. "This canyon is one of the most beautiful I have ever visited," the scout flashed back to Mather. "It would be a shame to have it get into the hands of exploiters." But, alas, as happens so often, the good suggestion fell through a bad crack. Impossible, said the crack. It cannot be done because part of the canyon is under the jurisdiction of the U.S. Forest Service (about 13,000 acres of Arch's roadless area are in Manti-La Sal National Forest, about 8,000 under Bureau control). Thus, a line drawn between two federal departments, Agriculture and Interior, became the Catch-22 for Arch Canyon. Agriculture's Forest Service wouldn't consider its share of the canyon for wilderness designation in 1984 partly because Interior's Bureau of Land Management had jurisdiction over the other part of the canyon and had already decided that its 8,000 acres were unworthy of wilderness study. And the Bureau had come to that astounding decision how? Well, how about partly because Agriculture's Forest Service had jurisdiction over the other part of the canyon?

So I was all set to hit Arch Canyon, last stop and maybe last chance, too, before the exploiters got to it. Mike Medberry had fixed me up with the appropriate maps, had penciled in where one leaves the jeep in a grove of giant cottonwoods and slips in through the slot at the canyon's mouth, and then, farther up, starts scanning the south-facing walls for those thousand-year-old Anasazi cliff dwellings. Just a few hours in from the trail-head, Medberry had said, and I'd start to get the feel of the place. An overnighter would be better, but if you're in a hurry . . . Get the feel of it and then split for Ken and Jane Sleight's Pack Creek Ranch up near Moab, a western sort of country inn (and five stars, in my book) that would put me in striking range of tomorrow's flight from Grand Junction. Get the feel . . .

But wait a minute. After almost a week of hit-'n'-run feels for the Book Cliffs and the San Rafael and the Dirty Devil and the Escalante, did I deserve yet another at a place that some folks were calling the jewel in the crown? I mean, what would Ken Sleight or Ed Abbey think of some visiting fireman who did Arch Canyon in the elapsed time of a motion picture (and not "War and Peace")? I was driving west from Blanding toward Comb Ridge to try to do just that and suddenly I pulled over and stopped because someone was knocking at the windows of my mind. It was that seditious fellow Abbey, speaking from his introduction to *Desert Solitaire*. Abbey was saying, *Do not jump into your automobile next June and rush out to the canyon country hoping to see . . . you can't see anything from a car; you've got to get out of the goddamned contraption and walk, better yet crawl, on hands and knees, over the sandstone and through the thornbush and cactus. When traces of blood begin to mark your trail you'll see something, maybe. Probably not.*

All right. I would save Arch Canyon. I would turn around right here and go the other way, to the edge of the territory, to the outliers of Moab, to Pack Creek Ranch and the pavement to Grand Junction, and someday I'd come back. I mean, why not? Sure, there were places—and maybe Arch Canyon was one of them—that might go down the tube for want of protection. But would the Bureau dare risk the lightning? "Time is on our side," Brant Calkin had told me in Escalante. Calkin was bucking for the title of Mister Most Unwelcome, now that he had replaced Clive Kincaid as director of the Southern Utah Wilderness Alliance. A former national president of the Sierra Club, Calkin had served in the canyon trenches as long as Calvin Black, on the other side. "Listen," Calkin said. "If I've already outlived some of the bastards, and I have, time *has* to be on our side."

And there was Darrell Knuffke, The Wilderness Society's regional strawboss in Denver. Knuffke had said: "Support for wilderness is growing daily in Utah. Those politicians who stomp their feet and shout, 'No Wilderness!' cannot prevail."

So, all right. If these professional optimists were right, then I could just tuck Mike Medberry's annotated map into my armpit and—someday—come back and do Arch Canyon the right way, though probably not on my knees. I would take a week, slow, walking from pinyon to ponderosa, and maybe every night I would discover what The Brushpopper had seen on that ledge above the Dirty Devil, a sky with no lid on it; and maybe, too, if I was *really* lucky and got into the canyon far enough, I would find where the edge of forever comes down, and finally touch it.

ALASKA 1977:

WHERE HAVE ALL THE

TUTTU GONE?

In Alaska, English-speaking people have no special name for the place. Possibly because it is so vast, most take their cue from the compass and call it the Northwest, which explains nothing, except where it's at. Around the place are three natural, and one unnatural, boundaries: the Arctic Ocean on the north, the Chukchi Sea on the west, the Koyukuk River more or less on the south, and on the east, the corridor of the trans-Alaska oil pipeline. And all of it hangs unevenly from a serrated skewer, the Brooks Range. Overall, the area encompasses some 140,000 square miles, just a few sections shy of the girth of Montana, fourth in size of the United States. It is not an especially hospitable place, Northwest Alaska. Not if you prefer velvet convenience and push-button ease. Consequently, as well as for reasons of economic opportunity, this is the least populated place of its size in the nation. The entire city of Anaconda, Montana, for example, could not even double its population if, suddenly, it were to roll out the welcome mat for all of Northwest Alaska's 9,000 residents, who are mostly Eskimos and Indians and sourdough loners in a score of villages scattered from Kotzebue to Anaktuvuk Pass and north down the long Arctic Slope into Barrow.

It is raw, lonely country, all right—surely among the best kinds of country remaining for people who, by choice or tradition, would live by the fat of the land. Or, for that matter, by the lean. Fat or lean in most places is generally subject to the vicissitudes of nature. In the 49th State, however, there has lately been another factor: the vicissitudes of human judgment, notably within the highest echelons of the Alaska Department of Fish and Game.

Socially and geophysically, perhaps it is absurd to set the Northwest apart from the rest of Arctic Alaska. From the perspective of village and regional jurisdictions established under the Alaska Native Claims Settlement Act of 1971, the authentic divider parallels the Brooks Range crest, and everything north of that, from Chukchi to Yukon Territory, is Arctic Slope. Similarly, the Alaska Game Board acknowledges a certain cohesiveness north of the mountains, and therefore designates the entire Arctic Slope as a separate game-management unit, Number 26. The fact of the matter is that the Northwest as defined has no validity as a region except in one way; and that is the way it defines and coincides with the range of the Western Arctic caribou herd.

There was a time, once, when the Western Arctic herd was by far the greatest caribou herd in North America. Upward of 300,000 strong, the animals grazed freely across the permafrost prairies, along the spruce-fringed valleys of the Kobuk and Noatak rivers, across the mountains to the calving grounds on the Slope, and down the Colville Valley to the tundra shore of the Beaufort Sea. As with the Porcupine herd to the east, it may have seemed to some generations of Arctic rovers that this herd too, in the words of Canadian biologist George Calef, was "beyond counting." But the rovers were wrong. For when the scientists got around to it—when the game managers in Juneau finally *allowed* them to get around to it, being otherwise preoccupied with the fate of ungulate populations more convenient to such seats of sport-hunting power as Fairbanks and Anchorage—they discovered that the once-great Western Arctic herd was on the skids. In just five years it had tumbled from a quarter-million animals to a hundred thousand; and in the sixth precarious year, 1976, it had tumbled again—to some 50,000. Suddenly, the fat of the land had gone miserable and lean.

In October 1976, Alaska Governor Jay S. Hammond dispatched to the U.S. Department of Agriculture in Washington, D.C., an urgent request that the Northwest be declared a disaster area. Hammond was gravely concerned about a possible shortage of protein among the Native peoples. He asked that emergency food stamps be made available to them. In Washington, the bureaucrats who process such requests ran stony eyes over Hammond's application and pronounced it preposterous. Acting Agriculture Secretary John Knebel dutifully drafted a response, saying the request could not be granted because statutes governing such designations limit their application to "natural" disasters. It was suggested by indirection that if Hammond wanted extra food stamps in Northwest Alaska, what Northwest Alaska needed was a first-class flood, or possibly an earthquake high on the Richter scale. But Hammond did not have such a classic catastrophe to complain about. Hammond had only the inexplicable decline of the Western Arctic herd, and the specter of nutritional hardship certain to befall Native Americans faced with severe new limits on the harvest of caribou by subsistence hunting.

One can only imagine the difficulty Washington bureaucrats must have had trying to comprehend this situation. After all, the caribou was a *game* animal, not a crop. Subsistence? Rubbish! In the twentieth century, one did not eat wild meat procured in the boondocks; one ate USDA-approved feedlot beef procured from the supermarket. Yet here was Hammond going on about caribou as if a quarter of his state had just been ravished by a plague of locusts. In Alaska, one state official charitably credited the federal grantsmen with a shrewder understanding of the problem. "I expect," said Game Board Chairman Samuel Harbo of Fairbanks, "that the feeling in Washington must have been that this is one disaster Alaska has clearly brought on itself."

In fact, if not in law, the disaster of the Western Arctic herd has already touched a number of disparate victims. Consider the wolf. Because the caribou has crashed, so, inevitably, must the wolf, though not necessarily from hunger. In keeping with its unofficial policy of holding the wolf accountable for a disproportionate share of what too often is the result of human excess or oversight, the Game Division of the Alaska Department of Fish and Game once again has dispatched shotgunners into the skies with orders to destroy up to 80 percent of the wolves on the south slope of the Brooks Range, the idea being to relieve pressure on the dwindling herd. Last year, faced with moose declines in the precincts of Fairbanks and Anchorage, the division authorized a similar wolf hunt. Critics of this program were advised not to worry. Alaska, it was said, was not about to extirpate its wolves; it was taking only two percent of them on two percent of its land. Yet now, with the old hunt continuing and new ones under way not only in the Northwest but in southeast Alaska as well, the rational critic is entitled to wonder where and when this systematic killing of wolves is going to end.

Consider, as victim of its own contrivance, the entire game-management establishment of Alaska—the legislators, the administrators, the lobbyists for liberal limits and seasons, the good ol' boys who, in recent years, have swaggered from one wildlife crisis to the next on the frail assumption that the demand for game in this great land could never exceed the supply. And if something did happen to go wrong—well, one could always blame a good part of it on the wolf. Or, in the present instance, on the Natives. And one could also blame it on no money. The way some veterans tell it, "research" of late has become a dirty word at budget hearings. "Management" is the cry. Mention research and the guardians of the Game Division's coins draw the purse strings taut. And what does the Game Division say when this or that ungulate herd is suddenly pinpointed at the brink of collapse? It says, "Ah, but we had no money to monitor the herd." Yet after the crash, the same kind of money, or more, is suddenly made available to monitor the wolf with the business end of a 12-gauge shotgun.

And last but by no means least, consider the people: the In-upiat Eskimos and the Athapascan Indians of the upper Ko-yukuk. Consider the tradition and the need. For centuries, for millennia, these people have depended on caribou to supply them with protein as their stocks of dried salmon and whitefish ebbed in the winter. Indeed, the historic presence of the caribou and the pattern of the herd's migration routes are partly respons-ible for the locations of many inland villages. But now, because of the fall of the Western Arctic herd, the laws have been changed. Where early last year there was no limit on how many caribou the people might take, now an Eskimo hunter, if he is lucky enough to hold one of the precious permits, may take only one bull. As the days grow longer now, as the vernal sun swings higher in the Arctic sky, as the stocks of salmon sink lower in the log houses of Shungnak and Allakaket, there will be hard times. No one will starve. There will be few, if any, distended bellies in the barren-ground villages. Notwithstanding the adverse ruling by Secretary Knebel, aid did come in the winter from the great white fathers in Juneau and Washington. Food stamps. Beef at bulk rates. And welfare. But the people do not want beef and welfare. The people want caribou. And for lack of it there is and will be pain. Not in the gut; in the heart, in the timeless marrow of their cultural pride.

I

It is said that caribou have been human provender almost since upright biped types first discovered that sticks and stones can break a fleeing prey's bones. The antlered creatures etched in limestone caves by Cro-Magnon artists no doubt were modeled after ancestors of the present breed, of which there are nine sub-species including the one in Alaska that is known to taxonomists as *Rangifer tarandus granti*, the barren-ground caribou. Exactly when *Rangifer* arrived in North America is unclear. How it got here is how almost everything else of Eurasian origin got here—across the tundra bridge on the Bering Sea. And close on the caribou's hooves came bronze-skinned Paleosiberian hunters, most of whom pushed south and east, exploiting other ungulate herds across the continent. But some of the hardiest hunters remained, establishing a culture that in time would be known as Inupiat. In the summers, the people pressed inland in quest of hides and red meat that did not taste and smell of the sea. And since neither taxonomy nor classical Latin had yet been invented, the summer people who looked on the caribou with favor did not have to split hairs or twist tongues. They simply called the animal *tuttu*; and down through the summers and winters of prehistory to modern times, along with the seal and salmon, tuttu has been the Inupiat staff of life.

Archeological excavations at Onion Portage on the Kobuk River reveal that the ancestral Inupiat of five to ten thousand years ago were heavily in debt to tuttu. Among other things, caribou provided these early hunters with their most effective weapons: antler spearheads. The people of Onion Portage flourished for generations beyond counting, then strangely disappeared from the Kobuk Valley for some 2,000 years. Why they left the region is not clear—a climatic trauma, perhaps, or possibly some erosion of their food base. In any event the excavations reveal a number of lean times, some lasting for several centuries, when it was unprofitable for the ancient ones to reside in the Kobuk Valley. More than likely, as the tuttu went, so went the people.

Apparently, both caribou and Inupiat were doing quite well by each other when, in the middle of the nineteenth century, the first white sails of Yankee whalers hove to off the Northwest's shores. The whalers brought many ingenious devices with them, including the rifle, which could speak of death from a greater distance than the antler-horn spear. In fair exchange for furs, the whalers supplied the barren-ground people with rifles and asked them to go to the mountains for meat that did not taste or smell of the sea. And whether it was this, the filling of whaleship larders with caribou meat, or some natural factor that afflicted the herds, no one today can be sure; but by the 1880s, tuttu was hitting the skids. And once more the Inupiat Alaskan knew what it was to be *nigisuliq*—hungry. In the central Brooks Range, near Anaktuvuk, the mountain people who call themselves Nunamiut deserted their sod houses and followed the rivers north to the Beaufort Sea. They would not return to the mountains until the 1930s, after tuttu had tumbled and recovered its numbers once again.

The years following World War II brought great and lasting change to the life-style of the barren-ground people. Now, it was no longer so practical to pack up one's belongings on a sled, to travel nomadically in order to capitalize on some seasonal shift in the availability of game. The village roots were running deep. There were airstrips and bush planes bringing mail. There were radios and stoves that burned oil. And white eyes looking for oil under the permafrost. And rumors of a highway from Fairbanks north to Prudhoe Bay. And finally, in the 1960s, the great white silence of the Arctic was shattered by the *braaaaaap* of the snowmobile. For the Eskimo hunter, this was the most ingenious device since the whalers had arrived with rifles. The machine would change everything. At speeds of 60 miles per hour or more, at effective one-day ranges of 150 miles outward from any village, snowmobiles would soon reshape all the ancient rules of subsistence. No one knew it at the time, but the machines would also help to shape the fate of the Western Arctic caribou herd.

At the time, the herd had never seemed healthier. Game biologists estimated its numbers in excess of 300,000. There had been a succession of mild winters. In the Brooks Range, predator populations were low after a decade of poisoning, trapping, and aerial shotgunning by agents of the U.S. Fish and Wildlife Service. "For the herd in the 1960s," one biologist recalls, "everything was coming up roses." But the roses were growing in the thin air of speculation. One optimistic report on the Western Arctic herd by Game Division staffers conceded in 1966 that much of the data was second-hand, that because "project personnel were involved in the Kenai caribou transplant and the Nelchina calving studies, little information was obtained on Arctic calving success." As for the potential impact of the snowmobile, the report speculated that more machines would mean fewer dogs in the villages, and, consequently, fewer caribou taken for dog food. "In any case," the report concluded, "under present conditions of the high caribou population in the Arctic, it is improbable that either technological change such as has occurred with the introduction of the snowmachine or even a sizable increase in need for caribou meat because of local human population growth will seriously threaten caribou survival in the near future."

In the summer and fall of 1970, Game Division biologists applied to the Western Arctic herd a relatively new method of assessing ungulate populations. Aerial photos were taken of the post-calving aggregation, and a cow–calf ratio was obtained from observations on the ground. Then, in October, an age–sex ratio was obtained in a composition count of a representative sample of animals. From these two counts, biologists extrapolated a total population for the herd of 242,000, down some 19 percent from previous estimates. Later, in a progress report that year, biologist Robert E. Pegau noted that "an accurate estimate of the total harvest cannot be obtained." Yet the same report found that "the current harvest is only minimally affecting the population. It is recommended that the liberal season and bag limits remain unchanged." Pegau echoed that recommendation in 1971. A year later, he wrote: "The overall harvest in 1972 was higher than normal as the caribou were accesible to hunters in several of the larger villages. The present harvest level has little effect on the large Arctic caribou herd. It is recommended that the liberal seasons and bag limits remain unchanged."

Others who had been afield at the time did not easily toe the Game Division's optimistic line. Among the dissenters was David M. Hickok, then science advisor to the Federal Field Committee for Development Planning in Alaska. Hickok had traveled extensively among the Inupiat villages in the 1960s, gathering data on subsistence life-styles and the human carrying capacity of the Arctic environment. In the villages, Hickok talked with white-haired elders who remembered how, before the caribou crash of 1927, the numbers of the herd had seemed beyond counting, as they did now. Afield, he watched the great migrations and was struck by the erratic behavior—the panicked appearance—of individual animals. He noted, too, that small subherds were establishing themselves in alien localities in the same patterns that had preceded the collapse of the herd 40 years earlier. And in the library, Hickok found dog-eared journals revealing that similar aberrations had been observed in the herd before its decline in the late 1880s.

In October 1969, in an address to the Alaska Geological Society. Hickok said of the Porcupine and Western Arctic caribou herds: "I predict to you flatly that these populations will crash dramatically in the next few years. In fact, there is some evidence available which suggests this decrease has already started. This has happened regularly through recorded time every 30 to 40 years—and we have no wildlife-management techniques to cope with the situation."

In Juneau, the wildlife managers shook their heads in disbelief and went on dreaming. Of roses.

Sweet dreams and rosy visions of wildlife plenitude seem to have dominated the subconscious of the Alaska Department of Fish and Game in recent years. It was as if, in their eagerness to satisfy the expectations of licensed constituents, the game managers thought they could somehow *will* sustained yield simply by believing dogmatically in the capacity of ungulate populations to benefit from human harvest. Thus did the department evolve what some of its critics now call a policy of "crisis management."

The first major crisis of the decade unfolded in the great mountain-rimmed basin northeast of Anchorage, on the range of the Nelchina caribou herd. In 1962, biologists had estimated the herd to number some 70,000. The Department of Fish and Game figured this was a rosy number, possibly even a few too many for the range to carry. So in order to keep the range uncrowded and its constituents happy, the department availed itself of public-service time on the radio and, as the migrating herd approached a highway crossing, announced the best location to set up an ambush. According to Jim Pitts, a former bush pilot and frequent commentator in the Anchorage press, "massive numbers of hunters" turned out on snowmobiles. "Result:

endless lines of caribou carcasses and entrails along Unit 13 highways." In 1973, state biologists took a census. Crisis! The Nelchina herd somehow had crashed to 8,000 animals. And as emergency orders were rustled up to save those survivors, lo and behold—another disaster. East of Fairbanks in the Tanana Hills and on the Klondike Plateau, the Fortymile caribou herd, which had numbered 50,000 in 1953 and was consistently subjected to hunting and predation pressures, suddenly crashed to a low of 6,000. How could it be? Where, they asked in Juneau, where have all the caribou gone?

Not to mention the moose. Where were the moose? In Game Unit 20A, they were down from 12,000 to 3,000 in only six years. They were down in Game Unit 13. And down in Game Unit 5. The blush of the rose was now on the cheeks of the game managers. And as the crises were piling one upon another south of the Yukon, what news from the north? How fared the great caribou herd of the Arctic, the one of which it had been said that neither technological change nor an increased demand for meat could threaten its survival, the one for which liberal limits and seasons had so heartily been prescribed? From Fairbanks in the fall of 1975 came an answer: The Western Arctic caribou herd was headed for trouble.

In his report on the status of the herd, biologist Jim Davis noted that the findings were somewhat tentative. Attempts at a photo census that summer, he said, had been unsuccessful because the caribou had failed to form their normal post-calving aggregations. Fewer than 45,000 adult animals had been observed from aircraft in a day's overflights of the calving grounds and adjacent portions of the summer range. There was, moreover, a possibility that "use of the 1970 composition figures for extrapolation may have resulted in a substantial overestimate of total numbers." Several formulas were applied to the data. Estimates were recalculated. "Our best approximation," reported Davis, was 100,000 animals (down from 242,000 in 1970). Assuming such a herd size, he added, "it can be calculated that total mortality from all causes must not exceed 6,800 animals if the herd is to remain stable in numbers." Yet already, in just September and October of that year, the Native villages had taken almost 6,400 animals from the herd; and projections of wolf populations indicated that four-legged predators might take 15,000 caribou over the course of the year. "Clearly," warned Davis, "either wolf [-caused] mortality or hunting mortality alone will greatly exceed the annual increment to the population this year; all mortality combined will greatly reduce the population . . . Some precautionary measures would seem to be timely and most appropriate."

After the recent succession of ungulate disasters—the Nelchina and Fortymile debacles, the moose collapse in Game Unit 20A—proprietors of Alaska's wildlife resources were hardly of a mind or mood to own up to yet another burdensome loss. Still, there was no ducking Jim Davis's grim call for precautionary measures. And so, in issuing new regulations for the 1976–77 year, the Game Division and its board imposed on the Western Arctic caribou harvest the first restrictions in nearly 20 years. There would be a new limit of 15 caribou per hunter. The season would be closed from June 1 to July 15 and for 17 days at Christmastime. The herd must be saved. But would it be saved? Could it be saved with a bag limit that more or less approximated the average annual take of the Native hunter under the old no-limit system? Could it be saved with closures in June and December? In fact, few Northwest people hunt caribou in midsummer anyway, because they are too busy trying to catch fish; nor at Christmastime either, for the simple reason that, except for an hour or two at noon, there isn't enough daylight to sight a rifle. So much for "timely and appropriate" action.

Even before the new regulations could be promulgated, the Department of Fish and Game proceeded along another course of action, the memory of which, even to this day, leaves some Alaskans bitter, angry, and confused. To comprehend the source of this confusion, one must first understand the departmental mood prevailing in the spring of 1976. The mood, in short, was touchy. Game Division Director Robert A. Rausch, whose headquarters are in Juneau, was inclined to feel that he and his people had been taking some bad raps. There had been much flak from the Lower 48 over Rausch's wolf-control programs, and much flak from within the state over the tumbledown status of the game herds. In the Northwest, it was thought, the Natives were growing restless. According to one aide, there were reports from Kotzebue and Barrow that certain Native leaders might resist any regulated reduction in the caribou harvest. Kotzebue and Barrow, said the aide, are regarded by some top game officials as "the Berkeleys of the North." If there was going to be trouble over caribou, those were the places where the trouble would start. So the strategists in Juneau settled on a plan. The idea was to give the Natives a warning they would never forget. The idea was to send the Game Division's Arctic representatives to the villages, to have them state in no uncertain terms that the Western Arctic caribou herd was in grave peril, and to suggest, in terms purposefully uncertain, the division's intent, if necessary, to close the caribou season altogether. Zero bag limit, and let the chips fall where they may.

It is almost impossible now to reconstruct with a degree of accuracy exactly what happened next. There have been so many accusations, denials, contradictions, and passed bucks that the sequence of events and the burden of responsibility begin to blur. One is reminded of *Rashomon*. No matter. Suffice it to note that the division's men did indeed go to the villages to speak about caribou and "options"—one option being a closed season. In the villages, in the thin wood houses of the Inupiat, the people listened. The hunters listened and wondered how this could possibly be. Then the men who spoke of options went away. And what did the hunters do? The hunters grabbed their rifles, fueled up their snowmobiles, and—determined to get what they could while the getting was good—promptly set off cross-country toward the nearest straggling bands of the Western Arctic caribou herd.

II

In certain romantic circles nowadays, it is popular to assume that waste is an invention of the twentieth century. To be sure, we are infinitely more skilled at wasting than we used to be. Waste is the potting soil of modern society. A city's worth is measured by the depth and breadth of its sanitized landfill middens. Energy is transferred in the most profligate ways. To preside with knife and fork over one calorie of feedlot beef, we burn ten calories of energy transporting it to table. Cost–benefit ratios made better sense in olden days. Before snowmobiles, for example, ten calories of wild meat could be brought to table in exchange for just one calorie of human footpower, or so say the theoreticians who calculate such things. But still, there *was* waste.

Among the most prodigious wasters were the pennyskin Asian hunters who poured across the Bering bridge and, leaving Alaska to the Eskimo, proceeded south and east to the happy hunting grounds of the Great Plains. And there, where the rolling plains drop precipitously into river-carved canyons, the hunters procured calories by driving entire herds of Pleistocene shaggies over the cliffs. In the Arctic, northern hunters developed similar methods of harvesting game. Bands of caribou were herded into lakes, then speared by men in kayaks. Great corrals were constructed. Two lines of earthen mounds converged on each corral, like a funnel. Once the driven caribou had entered the funnel, women and children concealed behind the mounds would stand and shriek, driving the game deeper into the trap. Then the funnel would be plugged with dummies made of willow bundles; and within the corral, amid the panicked and thundering herd, camouflaged Eskimo hunters would rise, as if from the earth itself, and proceed with the slaughter.

As on the plains, such methods frequently resulted in a surfeit of calories and hides, more than the people could possibly carry away for their collective use. But there was nothing deliberately wanton in these slaughters. Given their knowledge of the uncertain cyclical beneficence of nature, the early hunters were simply doing what subsistence peoples had been doing—and continue to do—since it first occurred to the human mind to plan ahead. When game beyond counting is here today but gone tomorrow, you do not dally. You trade in one old calorie for ten new ones. You get while the getting is good.

And so, inevitably, it was said in Juneau in the spring of 1976 that the people of Kotzebue and Noorvik and Kiana and Kobuk and Shungnak and Ambler and Anaktuvuk and Barrow were "wasting" the resources of the Western Arctic caribou herd. In a report requested by the State Senate Resources Committee, biologist Jim Davis assembled a virtual chamber of statistical horrors. In late March, he said, 152 caribou "kill sites" had been inspected in the lowlands between Noorvik and the Kiana Hills. Half the carcasses were either unused or, because of scavenging by ravens and foxes, unusable. Davis reported that on May 6, during flights over adjacent lands near the Kiana Hills, observers counted an additional 400 carcasses—this being after an early thaw when retrieval of meat by snowmobile was "extremely unlikely." From Onion Portage on the Kobuk came a somewhat belated account of 500 caribou slaughtered by boat hunters, of carcasses floating downriver. Another report came to Davis from Arctic Village, within the range of the Porcupine herd. At Arctic Village, it was said, Fort Yukon Air Service had refused to land its planes until 17 odoriferous caribou carcasses were bulldozed off the runway.

And from almost everywhere in the Northwest came reports that village elders, whose days afield had ended before the advent of the snowmobile, were deeply distressed by the mechanized ways of village youths. There were complaints that some young people were pursuing caribou on their machines, "flock-shooting" point-blank with small-caliber weapons, going away with only the choice parts of the fattest animals, leaving the gut-shot and the cripples behind untouched by the skinning knife. One youth from Kotzebue, it was said (though not by Davis), took 53 caribou by snowmobile, but retrieved only three.

And all the observations and hearsay seemed to implicate the Native hunters, as if somehow they alone had cornered the market in waste. It hardly seemed possible. In December, I spoke with a white man in Kotzebue. I asked him what he knew about slaughter and waste. He is in a profession, this white man, providing a valuable service to persons of marginal means. He is not himself a subsistence person; the government pays him a salary that no doubt is in excess of $25,000 a year. In answer to my question, he said that he could speak only for himself. Yes, he knew about slaughter. Once, he said, he and several companions with snowmobiles had taken 31 caribou. "In a single morning," he added. "We got them in a surround. I felt like a bloody buffalo hunter."

I asked him why he had done this. He shrugged and looked away across the room. "It was a no-limit situation then," he said. "The Game Division was virtually saying, 'Go ahead. It's legal.' So that's what we did."

Now it was Davis again, reporting from Fairbanks on the July 1, 1976, status of the Western Arctic caribou herd. Jim Davis, bearer of sad tidings, announcing that the herd which had numbered 100,000 animals only one year earlier now appeared to have dwindled to 52,000. "Simple arithmetic and computer simulation models tell us," said Davis, "that the herd will decline if more than 1,500 cows are taken by humans and predators in the following year." Officials in Juneau were stunned. The director of game turned to the commissioner of fish and game. The commissioner turned to the Game Board chairman. The chairman turned to the governor. And the governor turned to Washington, D.C., asking that Northwest Alaska be declared a disaster area. Meanwhile, by emergency order, the recently adopted 15-caribou-per-hunter season was officially closed, pending public hearings by the Game Board in Fairbanks in September.

Out of the Fairbanks hearings came a new set of emergency regulations. In the game units embracing the range of the Western Arctic herd, from September 25 to March 31, bull caribou could be taken by permit only. One permit, one caribou. Only 3,000 permits would be issued by the Game Board. For each village there would be a quota based on recommendations by Native corporations and village councils. The quotas would reflect such considerations as population, availability of alternate food sources, and local employment opportunities. The councils, in turn, would distribute permits to individuals on the basis of need. The regulations further stipulated that henceforth there would be no use of caribou meat for dog food or trapline bait.

There would be no more caching of carcasses; meat would be removed "immediately" from the field. There would be no aerial reconnaissance followed by hunting in the same day. As for dealing with other predators, the Game Division would attempt to reduce the wolf population in the herd's winter range by as much as 80 percent. With full success, this could amount to a kill of 800 wolves. The hitmen would be private pilot-gunner teams working under state-issued permits.

And then, the reactions.

In Juneau, remembering the earlier furor over wolf hunts near Fairbanks, aides to Governor Hammond anticipated a new flood of angry letters from the Lower 48. This time they would be prepared. A form reply was drafted for the governor's signature. Thousands of copies were mimeographed and stacked at the ready in a capitol stockroom. But by year's end, the anticipated deluge of protest had amounted to only a trickle. The environmentalists seemed to be holding back. "This time around," said one state bureaucrat, "they're caught in a bind. It's a complex issue. How can you love the wolf and the Eskimo at the same time?" Indeed, Hammond's mimeographed explanation had touched on this conflict. The wolf, he asserted, had been taking up to 15,000 caribou from the herd every year. The Natives had been taking 25,000 but were now restricted to a harvest of 3,000 bulls. "This harvest," wrote Hammond, "constitutes an extremely important source of food and livelihood for these people . . . In those villages where beef *may* be available, the costs range from $2.07 to $6.15 per pound depending on cut, and that assumes the availability of employment opportunities which generally do not exist. The village of Anaktuvuk is entirely dependent on caribou, having taken approximately 1, 000 per year in the past. They presently have been allocated 340 permits by the Board of Game. Curtailment of caribou harvest of this magnitude will severely impact the residents of the Western Arctic, but are deemed necessary if we are to save the herd."

From the Native community, reactions were mixed. Some village leaders expressed skepticism at the Game Division's most recent caribou census. During the summer, some said, they had seen animals beyond counting on the Arctic Slope. Others wondered bitterly why, if the herd truly had been tumbling down over the past six years, the Game Division had not warned them earlier of the decline and imposed some moderate restrictions on their harvest. And the answer most often supplied by their colleagues was that there had been no early Western Arctic caribou warnings because the state biologists were too busy counting moose down south for the sportsmen of Fairbanks and Anchorage. Still, however bitter, most Natives seemed willing to comply with the new regulations. As the long darkness of winter approached, the villagers turned toward their leanest season with a stoic bravura that no doubt has characterized all barren-ground peoples since ancient times. It was going to be bad, all right; but not as bad as Philip Smith, the director of the Rural Alaska Community Action Program (RurAL CAP), had said it would be. Smith's reaction to the regulations had been rather extreme. The way Smith saw it, by winter's end the game managers would stand convicted of "genocide."

In the quota shuffle, moreover, a number of villages had been excluded, notably the Athapascan Indian communities of Alatna, Allakaket, Huslia, and Hughes on the Koyukuk River. The leaders of these villages had not been present at Fairbanks in September when the permits were allocated. The Game Board had therefore assumed that the Koyukuk people did not need caribou permits, that because of their subarctic location they could subsist just as well on beaver and moose. But this was not so, the Game Board was told when it met in December at Soldotna on the Kenai Peninsula. Speaking on behalf of the Koyukuk communities, Mitch Demientieff, executive vice-president of Tanana Chiefs Conference, explained that the villagers were sorry they had not attended the hearings in September. Freeze-up, he said, had not come in September to the Koyukuk, as it had in the north, and therefore the people were otherwise occupied with subsistence, seining and drying Koyukuk salmon. Demientieff further explained that his people could not subsist on salmon and beaver and moose alone, nor on store-bought meat, for that matter. Demientieff spoke of Kotzebue, which had been allocated 696 caribou permits and yet had available to it five and one-half times as many salmon as were available to the Koyukuk villagers, who had been allocated zero permits. In fair consideration of their need, said Demientieff, the people of Alatna, Allakaket, Huslia, and Hughes should promptly receive 450 caribou permits. Promptly, he added, because already the southern flankers of the migrating herd had arrived at the banks of the Koyukuk. "Right now there is meat in the woods," said Mitch Demientieff. "But no one can hunt it."

The Game Board was sorry. The board said it could issue no more permits. More permits, and the herd would be finished. The September allocations had been based, in part, on the tradition of "Native sharing." Barrow, for example, had shared some of its permits with Anaktuvuk. Could not Allakaket and Alatna go to Kotzebue and beg for similar generosity? Kotzebue so far had issued only 89 of its 696 permits. Did not Kotzebue therefore have permits to spare? No, Kotzebue did *not* have permits to spare. Willie Goodwin, a Native official from Kotzebue, had explained it a few days earlier at a conference in Fairbanks. The caribou bulls were still in rut. In rut, he said, "the bulls are skinny and the meat stinks. The real hunt will start in March." Game Director Rausch, in Soldotna, agreed. "The people of Kotzebue look at these permits as money in the bank," said Rausch. And besides, no one knew better than Mitch Demientieff that sending Allakaket to Kotzebue was not quite the same as sending Anaktuvuk to Barrow. Anaktuvuk and Barrow have strong cultural and kinship ties. Both are Eskimo communities, as is Kotzebue. But Mitch Demientieff and the people of Allakaket are Indian. There is a difference. Even in the north country. *Especially* in the north country, when the fat of the land has gone miserable and lean.

By and large, the members of the Tanana Valley Sportsmen's Association are neither Indian nor Eskimo. Mostly, they are the good ol' boys of North Star Borough and Fairbanks, and they are fundamentalists when it comes to defining and defending a good ol' boy's constitutional rights. Namely, the rights of one Mark A. Wartes, a white man who is said to reside somewhere on the Colville River delta. Come now in December to the Alaska Superior Court, Fourth Judicial District, the plaintiffs, Tanana Valley Sportsmen's Association, and Mark A. Wartes, alleging that between September 22 and October 11 Wartes was denied by the state fish and game representative at Nuiqsut a permit to hunt caribou, for the reason that Wartes is neither a Native nor a member of a Native corporation. And further alleging—inasmuch as the Alaska constitution holds that wildlife shall be reserved to the people for their "common use"—not only that such action by the state is in violation of said constitution but that the Alaska Department of Fish and Game has no legal authority whatsoever to issue permits for the taking of caribou solely on the basis of need. In short, a lawsuit demanding that the court restrain the state from enforcing its Western Arctic caribou regulations. A decision is pending.

So it could be said of the September regulations that no one—neither Tanana sportsmen nor chiefs, Eskimos nor Indians nor remote urban admirers of Arctic wolves—had reason to cheer. Especially cheerless were the wildlife managers. In a personal report to headquarters in October, Carl Grauvogel, the Game Division's fieldman in Nome, summed it all up. The past year, he wrote, "has been a time of turmoil, misunderstanding, distrust, and outright hatred"—much of it, Grauvogel added sagely, having been directed at the Alaska Department of Fish and Game.

One of the most popular games in Alaska these days is armchairing the decline of the Western Arctic caribou herd. It is popular because, inasmuch as full causes and effects are still unknown and likely to remain so, how can one lose? The only losers are the caribou, the subsistence people, the game managers, and the ecological stability of 140,000 square miles of wild America.

Nevertheless, a theory is adrift that predation by man and wolf alone could not have tumbled the herd so swiftly and dramatically. Perhaps, some observers speculate, the abortion-inducing disease brucellosis may have been a significant contributing factor. Possibly—and yet what little empirical data exists indicates a moderate incidence of this undulant fever within the herd. Then maybe, others say, maybe somewhere along the line an entire cohort of calves was wiped out by a natural calamity— a mass drowning, perhaps, in the swift high waters of some river athwart the migration route. Or possibly it was the range, though there has been little evidence of overgrazing. Could it be, as David R. Klein of the University of Alaska sometimes wonders, that the fragile tundra lichen, a prime caribou staple, has become contaminated? But by what? Radioactivity from nuclear tests in Asia? Atmospheric fallout from smokestacks in the Urals and the Ruhr? Take your pick. It doesn't matter. You can't lose. No one knows.

There is, on the other hand, a good deal of hindsight knowledge about the decline of wisdom within Alaska's game-management establishment. It is said, for example, that the Game Division's gravest miscalculation was assuming in the late 1960s and early 1970s that the snowmobile would have no detrimental impact on the herd; indeed, that the impact might be beneficial inasmuch as more machines would mean fewer sled dogs eating caribou meat in the villages. "The snowmachine backfired on us," says Game Board member Jim Rearden, a Homer outdoor writer. "It simply made the hunter far more capable of killing large numbers of animals." Robert Hinman, the deputy game director, apparently agrees. At a symposium in Fairbanks, Hinman described the snowmobile miscalculation as "our basic error" in managing the Western Arctic herd. In fact, there were a number of basic errors. Another was the Game Board's lethargic response to Jim Davis's 1975 census, the one which showed a herd of 242,000 animals reduced to 100,000 in only five years. "When the count was 100,000," says game biologist Don McKnight of Juneau, "we were already into a disastrous situation." Another biologist says privately that if the board had taken emergency measures at that time, instead of waiting a full year, "we could have gained seven to eight years in the process of trying to rebuild the herd. Now it may be too late."

And why didn't the board act sooner? "It felt it didn't have enough solid information," says Fish and Game Commissioner

James Brooks. "It didn't know how far it ought to go. The response turned out to be feeble."

No doubt a third basic error was Juneau's decision to allow four critical years (1971–74) to slip by without taking a full-scale aerial census of the herd. "We didn't have the money to do that every year," says Bob Hinman. Given the high price of aerial operations north of the Yukon, he adds, an aerial census and follow-up composition count now cost about $70,000. Okay, so the Game Division didn't have the money to do that every year. Yet somehow it did obtain and spend $70,000 last year to remove wolves from the moose-deficient precincts of Game Units 13 and 20A downstate.

I suppose, insofar as money is concerned, that it is simply a matter of covering one's priorities. A year ago, for example, Game Board member Darrell Farmen of Anchorage wrote a letter to Jay Hammond. Farmen said he wished to support "Jim Rearden's idea of retaining a top notch public relations firm in the Washington, D.C., area to present Alaska's program for managing fish and wildlife resources to the nation." Farmen explained that this would be accomplished through the national media. Then he added:

"The wolf controversy limelights the desperate need for Alaska to go on the offensive in a program of this nature. We are unable to properly manage our fish and wildlife resources due to the emotional and hysterical drivel being presented to federal agencies, the U.S. Congress, and the general public by well-financed groups opposed to any utilization of wildlife resources." In closing, Farmen asked the governor to authorize "a minimum of $300,000 to start this project." Three hundred thousand dollars requested for national public relations, but not an additional penny for research to help cancel the disappearing act being played on the tundra plains of the Western Arctic.

And let us not overlook the wolf. What do the downstate aerial wolf hunts of last year tell us about a new removal of "excess" wolves in the Northwest, and about its probable effect on the Western Arctic herd? Will fewer wolves mean more caribou? (I hear an echo: *Will fewer sled dogs in the villages mean more caribou?*) The data is scant. In the area encompassing Game Unit 20A, where hunters and trappers on the ground last year took some 70 wolves in addition to the 66 killed from the air, preliminary reports indicate improvement in the survival rate of moose calves. Game Director Rausch proudly predicts an improvement over the previous year of 300 percent. A number of wolves also were killed last year in Game Unit 13. In December, Rausch declined to comment on moose calf survival in Unit 13. He said he had not yet seen any data. Yet the very same day Game Board Chairman Sam Harbo allowed as how it was his understanding that early data from Unit 13 showed little improvement in the calf survival rate—a possible reflection that Unit 13 wolves had been taking a bad rap, or rather a load of buckshot, for predation partly attributable to grizzly bears. So it goes in the complex business of manipulating wildlife. And besides, comparing game units can be almost as risky as extrapolating moose calves into caribou.

Where the wolf is concerned, it seems risky to be extrapolatory about anything. But, alas, for want of time and money to extend the necessary *in situ* research to so vast a territory as the Western Arctic herd's range, the Game Division has gone the short route again, eliciting from its most qualified but currently desk-bound wolf biologist a population projection based, in the researcher's own words, on "an educated guess." The biologist is Robert O. Stephenson of Fairbanks. If one must settle for an educated guess about Arctic wolf numbers and feeding habits, I would rather it be from Stephenson than anyone else in Alaska. Stephenson has been studying the wolf in Alaska since 1970, and not always from behind a desk. And he has a large, positive concern for the wolf's future.

From his own earlier density studies near Anaktuvuk, from Canadian studies and talks with other biologists working in the North, Stephenson developed a fairly elaborate set of assumptions. He projected a population of 320 wolves in Game Unit 26A, on the North Slope, and 986 wolves in Units 23 and 24 south of the Brooks Range crest, for a total of 1,306. The three units embrace all but 18,000 square miles of the Western Arctic herd's traditional range. Among other things, Stephenson figured that caribou constitute 50 percent of the winter diet of all wolves within the range; and 50 percent of the summer diet of all wolves on the Arctic Slope and of one in ten of the wolves to the south. He assumed that each wolf was obtaining meat of a volume somewhere between the minimum maintenance requirement of 3.5 pounds per day and a maximum of 6 pounds per day. Thus, according to Stephenson's mathematical calculations, the 1,306 wolves of the Northwest annually were taking a minimum of 6,794 caribou, a maximum of 11,551 caribou, or a number of caribou in between. He further noted that field data on the mortality of the 1975 calf cohort showed a loss of almost 72 percent, with wolves presumably accounting for about one in five of the lost calves. Yet even if overwinter calf losses could be reduced this year to 35 percent, said Stephenson, only about 8,250 yearlings would be present in the herd in October 1977. This number, he said, would barely exceed the minimum anticipated losses of adult caribou to wolves and humans—and additional sources of mortality, which are almost certain given nature's ways, could wipe out any fraction of increase in the size of the herd.

So now, as the hours of daylight stretch deep into the Arctic afternoons, the Pipers and the Cessnas are flying again out of Bettles and Kobuk and Kotzebue, one man at the controls, the other behind him with a 12-gauge shotgun poised at the cockpit window. They are aiming to take up to 80 percent of the 986 wolves Stephenson figures are scattered across the 74,000 square miles of Game Units 23 and 24. Educated guesses say they will not succeed.

"For every wolf I see, I must fly over three or four I can't see," Warren Thompson was saying. Warren Thompson is a bush pilot. He is said to be one of the few white men with a cabin on the Noatak River. He knows the country. And he knows the wolf as only a hunter can. In December, I flew with Thompson out of Kotzebue. He had been hunting wolves, under state permit, for a week. The snow was not good for tracking and the daylight was thin and short. Thompson was waiting for March.

I asked him if he thought removal of 80 percent of the wolf population was a reasonable goal. "Impossible," said Thompson. "Even if we *could* take that many, I'd hate to see it. It's too much. And besides, I don't think wolves played a significant part in the crash of the herd. Three to four years ago, the caribou and the wolf were stabilized."

If not the wolf, I asked, then what?

We were flying low, approaching an airstrip, and suddenly Thompson jabbed his finger toward the ground. "There's what," he said. Below us, multiple tracks of snowmobiles pointed east, up the Kobuk Valley, toward the wintering herd.

III

NANA is the acronym for Northwest Alaska Native Association, one of twelve regional authorities created under the Alaska Native Claims Settlement Act of 1971. The region embraces 36,000 square miles in the southwest quadrant of the range of the Western Arctic caribou herd. Within the region are some 4,000 people living in twelve villages scattered from Deering on the Seward Peninsula north to Point Hope and east to Kobuk. NANA's Regional Corporation is headquartered in Kotzebue, along with half the people. Kotzebue is only 200 miles from Siberia. Ten times 200 miles is the distance to Seattle, from whence, by sea, comes the principal commerce. The port of Kotzebue is therefore a very busy place, but only for three months in the summer. The rest of the year the port of Kotzebue is locked in ice. There is daily jet service into Kotzebue, and small planes service the villages biweekly. There are no roads to or within the region. Travel is mostly by snowmobile and motorboat. A gallon of gasoline in some of the villages costs $1.50. A can of corned beef priced in Anchorage at $1.09 sells in Kotzebue for $3.25. In Selawik, bacon is $3.25 a pound. When people eat bacon in Selawik, or corned beef in Kotzebue, they are mostly eating the freight.

For all its disadvantages in the cash economy, the NANA reion could be a rich one indeed—especially if one were to scratch its frosty surface. There is oil shale north of Noatak, asbestos near Kiana, coal and nickel at Ambler and Kobuk, copper and lead south of Shungnak; and almost anywhere from the Waring Mountains to the floor of the Chukchi Sea is the glimmering promise of petroleum. These riches are well known to people from beyond the NANA region—people in corporate and government offices, people in Juneau and Seattle and Washington, D.C. And so, not surprisingly, there has lately been much talk of a highway. A highway from Fairbanks to Kobuk, from Kobuk to Kiana and Kivalina on the sea. But the people of NANA are not entirely sure the highway would be a good thing. Yes, the highway would facilitate the unlocking of mineral treasures; but it would also bring hunters and fishermen from the Interior. It would bring the sportsmen from Fairbanks who believe that all the wildlife shall be reserved to all the people for their common use. And it would bring an almost certain end to the old ways of life—ways not of copper and asbestos and freight-fattened bacon, but of berries and salmon and fat caribou.

Between the old ways and the new, NANA treads a razor-thin line. Board Chairman Robert Newlin, an Inupiat from Noorvik, speaks to his people of working to ensure a continuance of the Eskimo way of life. "Our success in the future," he likes to say, "depends on the strength of our past." The 1975 NANA annual report features on its cover a photograph of barren-ground caribou. Overleaf is the corporation logo: an aggressive-looking Eskimo hunter cum harpoon. "NANA is all of us together as one hunter," the copy reads. "As one hunter is small and insignificant compared to our environment, so is NANA when compared to the corporate and governmental environment in which it must hunt successfully to survive."

So far, NANA the hunter has survived. Among its various past and present profit-making subsidiaries are NANA Oilfield Services Inc., operator of a 242-person Alaska pipeline camp at Deadhorse and licensed distributor for Standard Oil Company of California at Prudhoe Bay; Arctic Utilities Inc., sole provider of electric power at Prudhoe Bay; NANA Commercial Catering, provider of commissary services at Alyeska's Sheep Creek camp near Valdez; NANA Security Systems Inc., watchdog of law and order at fifteen pipeline camps and pump stations north of the Yukon; NANA Environmental Systems Inc., designer, builder, and operator of sewer and water systems at Prudhoe Bay; NANA Construction Company, builder of Anchorage International Airport's new FAA control tower, among other projects; Jade Mountain Products, with placer claims on an estimated 200, 000 tons of jade in the upper Kobuk Valley; and, last but not least, the $3 million, 53-room Nul-Luk-Vik Hotel in Kotzebue where, beside a window in the waterfront restaurant, one can alternately watch snowmobiles racing under a full December moon and marvel at a menu that offers both escargot and reindeer stew. For the fiscal year ending June 30, 1973, NANA's bottom line showed a deficit of $2,000. Just two years later it was in the black with a profit of $1.6 million.

The pace may be slowing down. Much of NANA's profit activity has been associated with the oil pipeline, which is nearing completion. At the peak of construction, NANA had 175 men on that job; by December 1976, the work force had dwindled to a dozen. Moreover, in many of the NANA ventures there has been little employment opportunity for the NANA Native. Most of the operations are outside the region, and most of the jobs require skills that the Native does not yet have. As of March 1976, for example, only 32 of NANA Security Systems' 116 employees were Alaskan Natives, and not all of these were residents of the region. There have been problems as well closer to home. The salmon run last summer was not productive. There were fewer jobs with the commercial fishery at Kotzebue. Some men went away in the summer to fight fires in the south. And then came the rulings in September, and the caribou permits. But the NANA profits, large or small, would not solve *that* problem; nor would they solve the problem of subsistence in a region where, for nearly half the population, the median family income is well under $5,000 a year.

Subsistence these days is much on the mind of NANA President John W. Schaeffer, who oversees his region's far-flung affairs from an office on the second floor of the Nul-Luk-Vik Hotel. Born in Kotzebue, Schaeffer is a tall, soft-spoken self-described "high school dropout" who graduated from Officer Candidates School at Fort Benning, Georgia, and now holds the rank of lieutenant colonel in the Alaska National Guard. (The Guard still looms large in the imaginations of Eskimo males of an age to remember when there were "armories" in every village, and rumors of Japanese regiments on every Aleutian island.) Like his colleague Robert Newlin, Schaeffer walks that thin line between the old and the new. He is in no great hurry to embrace mineral development and highways. He would rather discuss NANA's growing reindeer herds: 3,000 head, with a goal of 2,000 more "to make it pay," the meat butchered on the range and sold by the herders for 85 cents a pound, and plenty of trouble from the wolves.

"Living off the land is part of our culture," John Schaeffer was saying one afternoon in Kotzebue. "As long as possible, we have to give our people the option of choosing which way they want to go. The people have to make their decision. Then we in NANA can make ours."

A question from the visitor: If they choose to go away from the subsistence life-style, what then?

"They cannot go from it entirely," said Schaeffer. "The importance of it will always be there. Subsistence is more than just eating."

Subsistence, *n.* 4. means of supporting life; a living or livelihood. *The Random House Dictionary of the English Language.*

— In this section "subsistence hunting" means the taking of game animals by a state resident for food or clothing for personal or immediate family use. *Section 16.05.257 of the Game Laws of the State of Alaska.*

— By the state's definition all resident sportsmen are subsistence hunters. But there is no such thing as true subsistence in Alaska anyway. Our welfare agencies have changed all that. They take care of you. *Tom Scarborough of the Tanana Valley Sportsmen's Association.*

– Subsistence is such an emotional issue up here. The competition for game has created tremendous hostility. *Celia M. Hunter of the Alaska Conservation Society, and president of The Wilderness Society.*

– The Natives are riding on subsistence, and that's the wrong sled. I don't qualify for their privileges, but I sure as hell qualify for paying the taxes. *An Alaska Department of Fish and Game employee.*

– Within legal constraints, fish and game will be allocated to subsistence users on the basis of need . . . The Board and Commissioner also understand that subsistence requirements will not affect all resources in all areas equally, and recreational and commercial uses will continue where and to the extent that they do not interfere with or jeopardize subsistence resource use. *1973 Policy Statement by the Commissioner and Alaska Board of Fish and Game.*

– Subsistence use has always been a natural part of true wilderness, contrary to today's popular notion of wilderness as ". . . a place where animals live, but people only visit." *Alaska Conservation Society Position Paper on Life-styles, Subsistence, and Hunting.*

– There are two fundamental ways of valuing an activity such as subsistence hunting, fishing, and gathering. The first is to put a value on the other activities which cannot be undertaken because the person is busy subsisting. For example, if a person is a subsistence hunter year-round, but could have a job paying $10,000, the value of subsistence hunting could be construed as $10,000. This approach collapses in NANA Region for the simple reason that jobs here are not available. For large numbers of people, the only alternatives to subsistence are to leave their homes for an alien environment outside the region, or else to die. It is quite difficult to put a value on either of these "alternatives." *A 1974 Report by the Mauneluk Association et al.*

– I don't believe in subsistence as a special right. Why, you can't even define it. *Robert Rausch, game director.*

Rausch had had a bad day. The Game Board was meeting at Soldotna. They were rehashing the caribou figures and listening to Mitch Demientieff petition for Koyukuk permits. Now the afternoon session was over and the evening meeting was about to begin. Rausch sat at a table in the lounge of the International Hotel's Riverside House restaurant. Waitresses moved back and forth through the dining room, bringing on twelve-dollar steaks and bearing away the picked-over plates of the belly-filled. Rausch had no time for steak. Instead, he ordered a bacon, lettuce, and tomato sandwich and a very dry martini. He looked at his watch. He entertained in desultory fashion a few questions from across the table. He sipped his martini. It had been a bad day. Trustees for Alaska had just unloaded on the Game Board a scathing critique of the state's caribou management. Trustees is a relatively new environmental voice in Alaska, and few, if any, of the Game Board members had ever heard of it. Indeed, some members might not have bothered even to read the critique but for the happenstance that their eyes, running down the list of Trustees on the covering page, came upon such names as Ian MacTaggart Cowan and Douglas H. Pimlott, neither of whom are Alaskan (both are Canadians) but who nevertheless are regarded most highly in international wildlife-management circles.

Cowan and Pimlott, of course, were not the authors of the critique; the author was Wilson A. Rice, Trustees' executive director. Rice charged, among other things, that "had adequate research been done several years ago, in all likelihood the draconian management programs which have now been imposed could have been avoided." Alaska, he added, "may understandably be several years behind in women's fashions and the latest nightclub crazes, but there is no excuse for fish and game policies which represent a body of knowledge long out of date." And so on. Rausch had heard it all before, in other language. Now, perhaps, he was less concerned about Wilson A. Rice than about Ruby I. Compton of the Natural Resources Defense Council in Washington, D.C. Compton, on behalf of Defenders of Wildlife and the Alaska chapter of the Sierra Club, had sent a letter to

U.S. Interior Secretary Thomas S. Kleppe, outlining a number of legalistic reasons why Interior's Bureau of Land Management was duty-bound to prepare an environmental-impact statement on Robert Rausch's caribou–wolf management plan for Northwest Alaska.

Then the talk at the table in Soldotna turned to the problem of the Koyukuk villages and why it was that the Kotzebue hunters did not want to use up their permits on caribou bulls that were stinking of rut. Rausch looked at his watch, sipped his martini, savaged a corner from his BLT, and said, "You're not hungry if it has to taste good."

Skeeter Mulloy is an Eskimo woman employed by RurAL CAP to administer village nutrition programs for Mauneluk Association, NANA's nonprofit social service affiliate. Nutrition programs are new in the NANA region. They are very much on the modern side of the razor-thin line, along with food stamps and welfare application forms. Mulloy is a bright cheerful person who is in the habit of signing off her letters and memos to the villages in a bright cheerful way. *Aarigaa taikuu*! she writes, in Inupiat. In English this means: "It is good. Thank you."

Last winter, shortly before Christmas, Skeeter Mulloy had reason to be cheerful. Something *was* good. RurAL CAP had just allocated to the NANA region a grant of $36,000 to help alleviate the protein shortage; and it was her responsibility, together with other Native officials in Kotzebue, to redistribute the funds, on the basis of population, to a nutrition committee in each village. In a memo to village administrators, Skeeter Mulloy explained that the funds could be spent either through a food-voucher system, utilizing village grocery shops, or by direct purchase of beef in bulk quantities. NANA had a friend in Anchorage, a certain wholesaler willing to provide beef at about 80 cents a pound, plus 22 cents the pound for air freight. (Always, the freight.) This would mean about nine pounds of beef for every man, woman, and child in the region; actually, more than that, since not everyone in every village would qualify. If the program went smoothly, something other than dried salmon would be on the tables for Christmas. It would not be the preferred tuttu, of course. It would be tame and weak-tissued and flat on Inupiat tongues. But at least for a while, for a month perhaps, there would be meat that did not smell of the sea. *Taikuu*.

Thomas Punglaik is an Inupiat hunter. Or, rather, he *was* a hunter before the emergency regulations in September. And he will be one again in March, by permit, with the savory fat once more on the backs of the caribou bulls after rut. On December 9, I spoke with Punglaik in his home village of Noorvik, east of Kotzebue in the delta of the Kobuk River. Because of its proximity to Kotzebue, Noorvik is farther on the modern side of the razored line than any other village in the Kobuk drainage. And with a population of 500, it is also the largest. In the "new" village, as opposed to the "old," which dates to 1914 and sits higher on the Kobuk River bluff, one encounters a modern high school where Punglaik occasionally obtains part-time employment in maintenance; a new eight-room NANA hotel, where Punglaik and I conversed; and 20 new housing units hooked into a sewage treatment plant, which is also new, as is the post office. For the most part, the rest of Noorvik is old, if not in years and condition, then at least in spirit: sled dogs chained in the 45-below-zero cold, meat sheds raised on stilts, with a few furs hanging outside and the padlocked doors not revealing what sort of meager provisions might lie within. "Between now and March," Thomas Punglaik said, "it's going to be plenty rough for people out of work." And, except for the odd jobs, he is one of them.

Punglaik is head-of-household for a family of seven, including his father. He lives in one of the newer houses. To heat the house with oil costs $100 a month. Electricity costs $50 a month. There is a $30 charge monthly for water and sewer service. Cable television is $15. These are the fixed costs only, and they amount to $2,340 a year. Punglaik can earn $2,340 doing odd jobs—maintenance in Noorvik, construction in Kotzebue. But what does he use for groceries?

"Before September," said Punglaik, "my family used 15, maybe 20 caribou a year. And we have no dogs. Moose, we use a little. But it is difficult. You have to travel very far. You burn a lot of gas. And rabbits. There are plenty of rabbits this year, and we snare them. But there are plenty of foxes, too, so there go our rabbits."

Thomas Punglaik holds three of Noorvik's 260 allotted caribou permits. In March, he plans to go by snowmobile to the far side of Selawik, to the flats where, in other times, one could take many caribou. This year, if he plays by the rules, Thomas Punglaik will take only three. "Last year," he said, "we heard rumors that the season would be closed. So the people went out and shot plenty. I told the game warden once, 'If my kids are hungry, I will take what I need to feed them.' I will go by the law, but not if my kids are hungry."

I said good-bye to Thomas Punglaik and walked out of the village through stunted spruce to the airstrip. It was getting dark. Warren Thompson, the wolf hunter, came down from the sky in a Cessna. I got in beside him, and we flew away. As the plane banked over the Kobuk River, heading west, we could see the little lights of Noorvik on the bluff above the river, the great deltaic plains rolling off to the north where Jim Davis had counted the unretrieved carcasses, and beyond that, the ice-blue hump of the Kiana Hills. It was raw, lonely country, all right. And it would be a long time of hell freezing over before the people of this country could ever again say of the Western Arctic caribou herd, *Aarigaa taikuu, Tuttu*! It is good. Thank you.

ALASKA 1987:

LEGENDS FROM AN

ESKIMO GARDEN

In June 1987, I was one of four writers who joined Audubon *editor Les Line at a camp on the Jago River, on the coastal plain about half-way between the Beaufort Sea and the Brooks Range of Alaska, at the epicenter of the Arctic National Wildlife Refuge. Our collective assignment was to examine the values at risk in the Reagan administration's plan to open parts of this vast wilderness to oil exploration and development. My own particular mission was to assimilate a sense of the place, that I might better understand why, even on this remote fringe of the continent, it is still true that the only thing people ever learn from history—I paraphrase the economist Paul Taylor—is that they learn nothing from history.*

For the longest of times, it was a place no one knew, an empty quartet, a land without legends. Legends exist only in language and language needs people to speak it, and all of the people, though there weren't very many, were going the wrong way. They were coming out of the old world into the new, and when they saw all this ice, and no sun in the wintertime, they kept on going. Thousands of years would pass before any people would pause long enough to learn how to live with this ice. It is a puzzlement as to how exactly they called themselves; probably, like every other race perceiving its homeland as the center of the universe, they called themselves The People and let it go at that. In time, their successors would be known as Inupiat, and a tongue-clacking language would begin to put names on the land—practical names reflecting how a certain place looked to The People, or what it might yield for the empty plate, or how it came to be stamped with the imprint of legend.

This is how it was until the Europeans came into the country. The Europeans did not want to learn to live with the ice. They only wanted to map it in order that they might pass through to some farther place, or, barring that, take what little the land had to offer. The Europeans did not like to see all this blank space on their maps of The North, and since they could not pronounce the tongue-clacking words, much less understand them, they began to fill up the blanks with their own language, which in most cases turned out to be English. These words did not describe places. These words celebrated the genealogy of captains and admirals of the ocean seas, knighted patrons of empire, and lively ladies, mostly English. Thus the nomenclature imprinted on much of the New World Arctic ignores the perceptions of The People, and bows instead to the memory of Baffin and Banks and Bathurst and Barrow and Beaufort and Belcher and Bering and Booth and Buchanan.

There is at least one region in the Arctic, however, where both languages—English and Inupiaq—appear on the maps. It is the country that is known as the North Slope in general and the Arctic National Wildlife Refuge in particular, or rather that part of the refuge falling between the Brooks Range and the Beaufort Sea. Here, there is much English sprinkled across the high ground and along the sea, while Inupiaq seems to have run up the score on the braided rivers of the tundra plains, in between. A few places carry names in both languages; occasionally in a third, which, having no linguistic authenticity whatsoever, suggests a kind of phonetic hybrid—part Anglified Russian, part Drugstore Eskimo.

Every name on the map has a story to tell, a legend to reveal. Here, from the Slope, are a few of them. Perhaps one or two hold answers to questions we had damned well soon be learning to ask. I mean about oil, and wilderness. In whatever language.

I. PATTAKTUQ

When The People speak of Pattaktuq, they refer to the place "where the waves splash, hitting again and again." It is a splendid image, especially from a seacoast locked so much in the ice, yet American cartographers prefer to call it Gordon, after the Scot who came here to trade in 1917. Strange, that the mapmakers should prefer commerce to the concert of the sea.

Pattaktuq sits on the east side of Demarcation Bay, hard by the boundary separating the state of Alaska from the province of Yukon. There are sod and timber house ruins here, and graves, probably from before Gordon's time. The People lived here, once, and some still come back from far away to hunt and fish.

In Gordon's time, or shortly after, there was an Eskimo trapper called Putugook who lived nearby, and a white fellow down the bay known as Old Man Store. It is said that Putugook was a great trapper of wolves, that he knew how to fool them with a howl from his throat. It is not said precisely how he came by his name, for Putugook means Big Toe, though it sounds more Drugstore than Inupiaq to me. As for Old Man Store, and that's all the name he had, hardly anything is known, except that he may have been a whaler from Herschel Island. At Demarcation Bay, the old man trafficked in furs and caribou meat and kept his business cottage-industrial and died with his boots on about 1928.

[These are details. Not mine, The People's. The People passed them on to the researchers Michael J. Jacobson and Cynthia Wentworth, who, at the behest of the U.S. Fish and Wildlife Service, prepared an excellent report on subsistence values in this region in 1982; and to the ethnohistorian David Libbey, whose cultural resource survey appeared a year later under the auspices of the North Slope Borough Planning Department and the National Park Service. My part of it is simply to arrange some of the details and pass them down the info-line. You have to keep a legend moving. Memories are so short nowadays.]

Tom Gordon of Pattaktuq. His first wife, Apayauk, had died in childbirth. His second wife was Mary Agiak, the woman who could talk with the birds. Some of their children would remember the Indians who came to trade from beyond the mountains, firing three shots in the air, at a distance, to assure Old Tom they were up to no mischief. And the Scot shot back, three times in the air, welcome. In 1923 Gordon opened a second trading post at Barter Island and left his oldest son, Mickey, to dicker with mountain Indians at Demarcation Bay. Mickey had named his own oldest son Tommy, after the Scot, but threw in Uinniq, as a middle name, so that no one would forget there was still much Eskimo blood in the boy's veins. *Uinniq* is an Inupiaq word used to describe unsafe ice, which was how things were at the time and place where the boy was born. Tommy O, some people called him. The rest of this Pattaktuq story is his.

Growing up at Demarcation Bay, and even later when he lived elsewhere along the Beaufort coast and used this place only as an occasional camp, Tommy O was quite a hunter. He could catch almost anything—brant and old-squaw, when there were shells for the shotgun, and Dall sheep in the mountains up the Kongakut River, when there were cartridges for the rifle. And sometimes in April, if the ice was not *uinniq*, he would strike due north from the bay, maybe thirty miles, to hunt polar bear. Some of the hides he sold to the Norwegian trader John Olsen at Uqsruqtalik, one dollar the running foot.

Like so many of the paniks—the white men—in Alaska in those days (and maybe in our own time, too), John Olsen wanted to strike it rich. Trouble was, trafficking in bear hides was no way to go about it. So every spring the Norwegian would mush up the Okpilak River to prospect for gold. Sometimes he would ask Tommy O to come with him, to help haul his supplies. According to Jacobson and Wentworth, "Olsen would never let Uinniq know the exact locations where he was prospecting in case he [Olsen] made a big discovery." Apparently, neither Olsen nor anyone else—panik or Eskimo—ever did strike it rich on the Okpilak. Not in gold, anyway.

One day in the growing-up years Tommy O and his father came upon an old tusk sticking out of the gravel near a survey marker on the international boundary. It wasn't a walrus tusk, walrus being rare on the shores of the Beaufort Sea. This rotting tusk represented something extinct. It was the ivory ghost of a mastodon, probably from a time when the first old world people passed by in their search for the wintertime sun. Tommy and his father took a piece of the tusk, only twenty to thirty pounds it was, back to Pattaktuq and kept it among their other artifacts of collectible antiquity, such as arrowheads and spears.

One day in the grownup years, soon after ownership of the trading-post house at Pattaktuq had passed on to him (though he used it only as camp then, being a resident of Herschel Island), Tommy O stopped by the old place and was not too surprised to discover—open doors are the policy north-of-tree-line—that someone had been sleeping in his bed. What did surprise him, however, and sadden him deeply, was that this someone (who turned out to be a panik surveyor) had stolen away with his artifacts, including the mastodon relic. This was sometime in the 1940s.

In the 1950s DEW came to Demarcation Bay. DEW, in drug-store-cowboy English, means Distant Early Warning Line. To make itself comfortable and well padded at the bay, DEW, helped itself to gravel from the erodible seashore near Tommy's place. One day Tommy returned to Pattaktuq only to discover—and without any early warning by official mail—that DEW had helped itself to so much gravel, the house his grandfather built had washed away into the Beaufort Sea.

What Tommy Uinniq Gordon did at that point is not recorded. I can only guess. I guess Tommy sat down on the gravel shore where his place used to be and, if the time was right for it, listened to the waves splash, hitting again and again.

2 . NORTHWEST PASSAGE

To the best of my knowledge, the Northwest Passage does not appear on any map, and Eskimos have no word or phrase to describe it, since it was only a white man's concept and a foolish one at that. Still, one cannot treat of this part of the world without touching on the Passage. The quest for a Northwest Passage was the very first carrot on the Arctic Slope's stick.

Ever since Pytheas of Massilia set sail through the Gates of Hercules for Thule, Europeans have looked to the North and West in awe and wonder. "In the attic of the world," noted the writer Jeannette Mirsky, "were the paraphernalia for those who dressed up everything in the glittering garments of their imagination." For example, it was imagined that one might find a shortcut to Cathay by sailing around the attic of North America. Sebastian Cabot was the first to try, and the first of many to fail. He returned with tales of a sun that shone on his ship for a month without setting. In 1576 the Virgin Queen dispatched Martin Frobisher across the North Atlantic in search of a passage to India. Frobisher brushed the tamest edge of it and returned with some fragments of rock believed to contain gold. On his second voyage the great navigator was licensed "for the searching of ore," thereby establishing a time-honored precedent: Exploit now, explore later.

For two hundred years English and Dutch navigators chipped at the eastern gates of the Northwest Passage, while Russians chipped away from the west. Soon the English became more obsessed with catching polar whales and rendering their blubber to fuel the street lamps of London, while the capitalist Russians dipped themselves in otter skins. Between their various plunders, the old salts nonetheless found time to paste a name or two over some blanks on the map. By the dawn of the 19th Century, the northwest coast of Alaska had already been charted—kudos to Captain James Cook—past Kotzebue Sound and Point Hope to Icy Cape; and a Scotsman named Mackenzie, trekking overland, had followed a fabulous river to the shores of the Polar Sea. This left a gap, at the western end of the Passage, of some seven hundred miles. Arctic Slope, Beaufort Sea, Terra Incognita.

From the high chambers of the Admiralty, Sir John Barrow scolded the government. The gates of the Northwest Passage lay open, he thundered. England must not risk the world's laughter by dallying a the threshold.

3. NAALAGIAGVIK

Naalagiagvik is the place "where you go to listen for whales." It is located about five miles west of Barter Island, on the smaller island called Arey in honor of the whaler and prospector who spent some time there. Arey's name is on all the official maps. Naalagiagvik isn't.

Many years ago, going way back, some of The People made their home at Naalagiagvik in order that they might not only listen for whales but subsist on them, too. The exact dates of habitation are not clear, though some of the irregular sod mounds examined by scholars appear to resemble ancient sites uncovered at Barter Island in 1914 by the Canadian anthropologist Diamond Jenness. At Barter, Jenness had deduced from an absence of iron and other panik-trade objects that some dwelling sites might be two hundred years old, while others might be twice that. "We suspected," Jenness wrote, "that the inhabitants had hunted whales during the summer months, because . . . inside many doorways we found a whale vertebra which the inmates had used as chopping block and, behind some of the houses, open fireplaces where they could have rendered down the whale blubber."

It is almost beyond imagining, to think of Stone Age Eskimos in skin boats pursuing and catching the great leviathan of the Beaufort Sea—Agviq, the bowhead whale. In historic times, before commercial whaling had taken its toll, bowheads were measured at lengths exceeding sixty feet, at weights surpassing eighty tons, at yields producing six thousand gallons of rendered oil. To listen for the whoofing song of such a creature, to raise the hunter's call to arms, to watch pursuing paddles flash like mirrors in the sun—all of that was to be among The People at Naalagiagvik, then, before iron.

Iron brought much gain to The People, but it also brought a certain loss, for among its bearers were panik whalers who would not only rob the Eskimo of his Agviq, but put upon the Arctic shore a stain from which it would not soon recover. As in the search for a Northwest Passage, the commercial slaughter of bowheads began in the eastern Arctic under Dutch and English flags. Whale oil, or "train" as it was called, was the principal illuminating fuel in Europe in those days; and bone, the bowhead's flexible baleen, was much in demand for the manufacture of umbrella ribs and fishing rods and tongue scrapers and stays for the corseting of busting-out-all-over British bodices.

It is recorded that sometime near midpoint in the 19th Century, a Yankee whaler from Sag Harbor, New York, sailed through the Bering Strait and, much to his surprise, discovered that herds of bowheads pastured here as well as in the depleted slaughterhouse between Greenland and Hudson Bay.

Slaughterhouse II. The Bering-Chukchi-Beaufort seas. Three thousand bowheads harpooned with iron in a single season, almost all under flags of the red-white-and-blue. With ships displacing four hundred tons and hulls of double planking to withstand the ice, many of the whalers wintered over. Toward the end of the century Herschel Island, east of Demarcation Bay, became, in the word of the English writer Sam Hall, "the Klondike of whaling." The Americans dispensed firearms and whiskey, and taught the Eskimo to distill a demon from molasses. And inevitably, the Yanks left behind among the Eskimos a fatal legacy of influenza and tuberculosis and—how did they call it?—social disease. By 1910 Eskimos of the Herschel Island–Mackenzie Delta region had dwindled down to a precious few. As for bowhead whales, who could say? By 1910 they were too scarce to count.

Nowadays, Eskimos from Barter Island come to Naalagiagvik to catch waterfowl in the spring and char and cisco in summertime. They do not spend much time listening for whales, though a few bowheads are still taken, year to year, luck and the quotas permitting. Possibly, among old-timers, Naalagiagvik is thought of more often as the place where Agiak Gordon, second wife of the Scotsman, spoke with the birds. Antiquity, it seems, was much on the woman's mind. Walking among the prehistoric ruins of Naalagiagvik. Agiak would speak to the birds in Inupiaq, saying that she wanted to know where the artifacts were buried. A bird would answer by flying directly to the spot and flapping its wings. Then Agiak would dig in the tundra sod, and it worked every time. Her collection grew and grew: whalebone tools and utensils and gewgaws of every description. But no umbrella ribs. No tongue scrapers. And no corset stays.

4. FRANKLIN

At Spilsby in Merrie England, his boyhood playmates contemplated the future and threatened to better him in fame and glory. Not to be outdone, Franklin told them he would get a ladder and climb higher than anyone in the world had ever been, all the way to heaven. Alas, on his way to the top, Franklin discovered that his own particular heaven would be very cold indeed, at least as cold as hell can be hot.

Sir John Franklin of Spilsby (1786–1847). Cabin boy to Australia (1801). Subaltern to Lord Nelson on the *Bellerophon* at Trafalgar (1805). Sailor in futile search of the North Pole (1818). Survivor of an abominable expedition to the Polar Sea (1822). Northwest Passenger to the gap between the Arctic apogees of Alexander Mackenzie and Captain Cook (1826). Governor of Tasmania (1836). Pilgrim to heaven (1847).

Franklin. The name is as common as any upon the latitudes of The North. It signifies capes, districts, mountains. The Franklin Mountains. With the Romanzofs next door, they are the attic of the Brooks Range, the roofgarden of the Slope, the apogee of the refuge. Only one peak in the Romanzofs is closer to heaven than the highest of the Franklins, but only by forty feet. Not that it matters. Sir John's mission was not to measure mountains but to close the gap. Official instructions came from Downing Street, the desk of Bathurst of the Admiralty:

31st Jan., 1825

You are to proceed with your party by the Packet from Liverpool to New York, and from thence make the best of your way to Lake Huron, where the stores necessary for your journey have already been sent. Embarking in Canoes, you are from thence to follow the water communication to the western side of the Great Bear Lake, where you are to establish your winter-quarters.

Early in the Spring of 1826, you are to proceed down the Mackenzie River with all the necessary stores and provisions, in order to be prepared to take advantage of the first opening of the ice on the Polar Sea, so as to enable you to prosecute your voyage along the coast to Icy Cape, round which you are to proceed to Kotzebue's Inlet, where you may expect to find His Majesty's ship, *Blossom*.

July 1826. The expedition has arrived at the Polar Sea. Two longboats, the *Lion* and the *Reliance*. Coxswains and bowmen, middlemen, marines, one carpenter, a friendly Esquimaux called Augustus, a naval lieutenant named Back, and John Franklin, Captain R. N. There is much adversity. The water is shallow. The fog is dense. The ice is fickle. And some of the indigenous Esquimaux are not as friendly as Augustus. Farther west, conditions begin to improve. It is noted that the Natives are in possession of iron, though not of British manufacture, not of the kind available at the counters of the Hudson's Bay Company. It is supposed that these articles are obtained from Esquimaux far to the west who in turn trade with *Kabloonacht*, Siberian paniks, Russian fur merchants.

Onward, past Demarcation Point and Icy Reef to Barter Island. In his narrative of the journey, Franklin will remember it as

a collection of tents planted on a low island, with many oomiacks, kaiyacks, and dogs around them. The Esquimaux being fast asleep, Augustus was desired to hail them, and after two or three loud calls, a female appeared in a state of nudity . . . The whole space between the tents and the water was, in a few minutes, covered with armed, though naked, people . . . We then learned that these were the people who had conveyed the furs,

Alaska 1987: Legends from an Eskimo Garden 209

&c., from Herschel Island, and that the exchange with the western Esquimaux had been made at the place where they were encamped, only a few days before. They intended to commence their return this day to Herschel Island, where the iron and beads would be distributed among their relations.

And he will remember how, on Wednesday, August 16, 1826, he is forced to consider the wisdom of continuing on. The expedition is now but halfway from the Mackenzie River to Icy Cape. It has taken an entire month to explore but ten degrees of longitude. The summer is nearly at an end. Daytime temperatures have not topped 37 degrees in some time. Ice forms in the water buckets at night. The coast ahead is Terra Incognita. The risk is great. He remembers the previous expedition to the Polar Sea (1819–22), down the Coppermine, the flight from famine, the diet of lichens, the long cold, murder and cannibalism and execution. It must never happen like that again. The orders from Bathurst are explicit:

> If you should make but slow progress . . . so that it remains doubtful whether you will be able to reach the neighbourhood of Kotzebue's Inlet the same season, you are not to consider yourself authorized to risk yourself and party to the chance of being obliged to winter on the coast, but commence your return about the 15th or 20th of August to the established winter-quarters on Bear Lake.

In the evening Franklin announces his decision to the men. The wind changes to the northeast after midnight. There are violent squalls. Fog in the morning, afternoon clearing. From the shore of Return Reef, Franklin spies the most westerly point in view, names it Beechey after the captain of HMS *Blossom*, and declares his discoveries terminated. On the 18th, the *Lion* and *Reliance* turn tail for the Mackenzie across a shallow inlet. He calls it Prudhoe Bay.

5. UQSRUQTALIK

Uqsruqtalik is a point of land located about ten miles east of the mouth of the Jago River. The Jago has its own story, and that comes next. This part is for Uqsruqtalik, "the place where there is oil on top of the ground."

Franklin may have seen it. He camped here heading home from Prudhoe Bay, though he called it by a different name: Point Griffin.

Oil seeps are not uncommon along this coast. Here, and at Angun Lagoon, the petrol is said to seep to the surface of the earth, where it turns into brittle pitch in the winter; into sticky tar, summertime. Years ago Eskimos came to such places to harvest the pitch for their stoves. Tommy Uinniq Gordon told the researchers Jacobson and Wentworth that he chipped pitch for his stove at Pattaktuq. But it was very dirty, he said. It could turn the outside of one's house black. You could smell the smoke ten miles away. Of course, those days, the preferred fuel was wood. But wood was scarce. Apart from a few scraggly toothpick willows, there were no trees to speak of north of the Brooks divide. Yet there was driftwood along the shore, which made the old-time Eskimos suspect that wood, like money, didn't grow on trees after all; it grew at the bottom of the ocean. Or it came to the Arctic on the floodtide of the great Mackenzie—a logical and correct solution to the puzzlement of driftwood, though not as intriguing as the mythic forests of the sea.

A few words, now, as to why John Franklin called this place Point Griffin instead of Uqsruqtalik. It seems that John Franklin could not go to the Polar Sea without naming some feature after an English lady. Having done that, John Franklin would then sail home and marry her. First, it was Lady Eleanor Anne Porden, the poetress. When Franklin mushed down the Coppermine to Coronation Gulf in 1821, he spied upon the horizon an archipelago of islands and promptly named them for Miss Porden—possibly to reward the lady for having honored him with a sonnet that celebrated an earlier Arctic voyage. In the verse Miss Porden supposes to be an Eskimo girl pining away for her gallant Englishman:

Return! and the ice shall be swept from thy path:
I will breathe out my spells o'er the land and the sea.

Alaska 1987: Legends from an Eskimo Garden 211

Return! and the tempest shall pause in his wrath,
Nor the winds nor the waves dare be rebels to thee.
. . . By the lake, by the mountain, the forest and river,
In the wilds of the North, I am thine, and for ever!

Franklin married Miss Porden in 1823, and, according to one biographer, it was a happy union in every respect save one. The lady was not well. In fact, the lady was to breathe her last even as the Captain stood six days out from Liverpool, bound for the Arctic at Bathurst's behest to close the gap in the Northwest Passage. News that he was a widower did not reach Franklin until he was deep into fur country. In her memory he would raise upon the shores of the Polar Sea the Union Jack that she had sewn for him. It was the custom, those days, for the ladies to sew flags for their departing officers, the better to bring them Godspeed. In the event that God's speed went adversely for the officer, the flag could be put to good use—draped over his coffin, for the burial at sea.

In any event, John Franklin recovered from his loss and went on to name Uqsruqtalik Point Griffin, after the beautiful and vivacious Jane Griffin of Bedford Place, whom he would take as his wife upon his return from The North. It was a perfect union in almost every respect save one. The Captain's days were numbered. Shortly before the knighted explorer sailed away on his final voyage to the Arctic heaven, it is said that Lady Jane put the finishing touches to his Union Jack. Franklin at the time was stretched out on a divan, taking his ease. For whatever thoughtless reason, Lady Jane suddenly threw the flag across the sofa. It fell on her husband's supine form like a shroud.

"O Jane!" the Captain cried. "What have you done?"

6. THE JAGO

The rivers of the North Slope tumble down from the mountains and out across the plains to the sea. There are many. Some, such as the Clarence, the Canning, and the Colville, are named after Union Jack paniks. Most carry Eskimo names: Egaksrak, Niguanak, Aichilik, Katakturuk. And a few riverine monickers come over the drugstore counter: Jago, for one; Hulahula, for another. Let's save the Hulahula and start with the Jago, okay?

There appear to be some differences of opinion here. One version has it that Jago was a Norwegian trader who went broke trying to operate an aquavit distillery somewhere nearby. It sounds preposterous, and probably is. In any event, spirits of one kind or another seem closely connected with the name, and the place. One commonly held belief is that Jago derives from Jags, a nickname. Panik whalers put this name on a Native who drank much whiskey to screw up his courage. The Native needed to screw up his courage in order to be the first to brave the evil spirits that are said to dwell along this river. And there the tale seems to hit a dead end, though I sure would like to know more about the devils of the Jago Plains. This is one of the places where certain folks would like to turn wilderness into an oilfield. It sounds like a stupid idea to me. I mean, what if there *are* devils?

Just east of the Jago River Delta, on a spit of land called Martin Point in English and Tapquaraq in Inupiaq, are the ruins of a cabin trading post once occupied by the prospector Gus Masik. An Estonian, Masik had apprenticed in the Arctic with Vilhjalmur Stefansson. He was a man of great physical stature and endurance, was considered one of the best dog mushers in the territory, knew how to make passable whiskey in a five-gallon still, and, like the trader Olsen at Uqsruqtalik, believed he would strike it rich someday with North Slope gold. Masik and Olsen, and Tom Gordon at Barter Island, and Henry Chamberlain at Brownlow Point, and Jack Smith at Beechey Point were the main players in the last big boom to hit this country, at least the last before oil. But gold it wasn't. It was fur.

The Slope had missed out on the real Alaskan fur heyday in the 19th Century, partly because of remoteness but also because, in relative terms, the Slope offered few furs. Except for one species: the Arctic fox. Tigiganniaq, they call it in Inupiaq. Tigiganniaq's skin of soft white fur did not come into fashion, Outside, until about 1910, and then the Edwardian equivalents of Fred the Furrier couldn't get enough of it. And that was good news for The People, because 1910 was about the time commercial whaling hit the skids in the Beaufort Sea, whereupon the many Eskimos once employed in that industry found themselves without means to purchase flour and cartridges and other sundries to which they had become accustomed under the umbrella of the baleen economy. Thus did The People obtain a new currency, the fox. And thus began the reign of the inshore trader.

It was a short and not altogether happy reign, the Arctic fox being an up-and-down-numbers sort of critter, too much dependent on up-and-down lemmings and ground squirrels. And fashions Outside being what they are, white fox fur soon lost currency as cityslick ladies switched their allegiance to ranch-raised mink. This happened about 1937 or so. By this time, most of the inshore traders were getting old and lame. Or dead. Gus Masik would survive enforced retirement for quite some time—in Seattle. But not Tom Gordon, killed by a stroke in '38. And not John Olsen, dead of pneumonia in '42.

Came a lean time with the traders gone. Then one morning The People woke up and found themselves covered with DEW.

7 · POINT COLLINSON

The Point pokes out into Camden Bay near the mouth of the Katakturuk River. Eskimos call the place Nuvugaq; some of their ancestors lived here in times long ago. There were traders and explorers, too—Jack Smith, before he left for Beechey Point, and Vilhjalmur Stefansson, and Roald Amundsen, who was the first end-to-ender through the Northwest Passage in 1906. And there was Collinson, Captain Richard Collinson of HMS *Enterprise*, come to the Beaufort Sea to answer a question the whole world then (1850–55) was learning to ask: Whatever happened, in the Passage, to Franklin, now that the Old Salt was so long overdue? Collinson found no trace of Franklin at the Point, and left no traces there of his own. About all you can see now, or might have when the ethnohistorian David Libbey passed through, are the abandoned hulks of a DEW station, code named POW-D and built circa 1950–55. What strange and curious things come to pass, just in the course of a single century.

O Jane! What have you done?

There were two ships. The *Erebus* and (alas!) the *Terror*. There were one hundred and twenty-nine men, including the skipper, Sir John. Against the ice there were sheets of iron upon the ships' bows. Against the cold, a hot-water system for heating the cabins. Against the clock, three years' provisions. Thirty tons of beef and pork. A thousand pounds of mustard, and seven thousand of tobacco. Two organs. A hundred copies of the Holy Bible (required reading for entrance to heaven). And there was one mission. To skewer the Northwest Passage, end-to-end. To sail west from Baffin Bay to the Bering Sea.

Return! and the ice shall be swept from thy path.

Late in July 1845, the master of a whaling vessel encountered the good ships *Erebus* and *Terror* moored to an iceberg at the northern end of Baffin Bay, awaiting the breakup of pack ice and safe passage west into Lancaster Sound. The whaler entered the location in his log and sailed away. It was the last fix, the final contact.

No one seriously expected Franklin to appear off Alaska in a year's time, not even in two. But when the summer and fall of 1847 passed without a whisper of his whereabouts, the Admiralty grew anxious and began to lay plans for his relief. All of the plans were optimistic, and all but one were aimed at the wrong end of the puzzle. By summer 1848 three separate commands had set sail for the Bering Sea, and a fourth was trekking overland through Canada to scour the northern coast in longboats. The fifth effort, commanded by Sir James Ross, sailed directly to Lancaster Sound, hoping to pick up a spoor at the last known fix. Ross carried a letter for Franklin from Lady Jane, who was the greatest optimist of them all.

My dearest love: May it be the will of God if you are not restored to us earlier that you should open this letter & that it may . . .

Ross arrived back in London in 1849. So dreadfully sorry, he said, returning the undelivered letter to Lady Franklin. Not a trace. Not a whisper. The Bering and Canadian relief parties began straggling home the following year. Not a glimmer. Not a clue.

By 1850 the Admiralty was offering a reward of twenty thousand pounds to any ship that might bring this costly search to a satisfactory end. To the Arctic labyrinth that summer went no fewer than six seperate expeditions, involving some ten ships, including Lady Jane's personal ocean-going yacht and the HMS *Enterprise*, Richard Collinson, commanding.

Soon the United States joined the hunt. Caches of supplies were deposited at strategic places. Signal rockets were fired into the Arctic air. Astrologers were consulted. Clairvoyants gazed into their crystal balls. Each succeeding year saw more expeditions, more ships, more blanks covered up with names on the map. But no *Erebus* and *Terror*. No Franklin. No clue.

But soon—though not soon enough for the lost men—the clues began to trickle out. From Eskimos, and some of their artifacts, which included naval officers' silverware bearing the original owners' family crests. From memoranda buried under stone cairns. From deductive geographic reasoning. From the trail of graves and skeletons heading ever south, and never getting there. The precise details are not germane to *our* map. It happened so far away. This much must suffice:

Beyond Lancaster Sound the Franklin expedition had wintered uneventfully, and pushed on. West the two ships pressed, seeking the fabled passage that would bear them on to the golden light of the Bering Sea. Then, in September of '46, twelve miles north of King William Land, a spiderweb of ice closed in around them, a web that would hold fast even through the summer of '47. Already three men were dead, of unrecorded causes. The fourth to die, on June 11, was Sir John Franklin. Cause unrecorded. O Jane.

Another winter in the ice. Twenty more dead, poisoned by the putrid provisions. A decision to abandon the ships, to strike out across the ice for Canada. Then the winding spoor of flotsam and jetsam—tents, axes, rifles, tunics, silver spoons. Men with the bleeding gums of scurvy did not need silver spoons.

They needed graves, and ladies to weep for them. Of the one hundred and five who began the ghastly trek in April 1848, not one survived to tell of it.

England refused to believe in no survivors, and the search went on. But in callous America, a certain segement of the public had become bored with the subject of Franklin even before news of his fate was widely known. In Concord, Massachusetts, a man named Thoreau was scribbling some final thoughts for the concluding chapter of a book that Ticknor & Fields would publish in 1854. The book was about the geography of a little pond, and about the mapping of the undiscovered countries of the human mind. Now, in his final draft, Thoreau added a thought:

> Is Franklin the only man who is lost, that his wife should be so earnest to find him?

8. THE HULAHULA

No, Inupiat women do not wear grass skirts. But Polynesian men once wore sealskin mukluks. And that, according to one version of the story, is how the river got its name. You see there were these whaling ships locked in the ice off the mouth of the river, and mukluks were not enough to keep the able-bodied Hawaiian seamen warm through the long winter months. So what did the Hawaiians do to get warm? You got it! They danced the Hulahula.

It is a good, strong, dancing river, the Hulahula, and for many of The People who live today on Barter Island, near the river's mouth, it is an important handrail into the country where The People hunt and fish. Along the Hulahula there are grayling and char to be taken through the ice in the places The People call First, Second, and Third Fish Hole, using the English words because, along a Polynesian river, why muddy the waters with Inupiaq. But here and there, of course, they do, especially at that headwaters place called Kanich, meaning "source of the river." Kanich is a favorite place of The People. It is tucked way up there in the mountains, in a horseshoe valley between the Romanzofs and Franklins, and is probably about the best place of all in the territory if one is hungering to savor Imnaiq, the succulent Dall sheep. Scores of the critter can be seen on the slopes above Kanich. And over the ridgeline is a canyon known as Two Hundred Sheep Creek.

More than anything else, though, the Hulahula is a handrail to caribou, Tuttu, the bread of life. From camps along the Hulahula the caribou hunters fan out, over toward the Sadlerochit or east to the Okpilak drainage, even to the Jago. As fox was once currency for the cash economy, so always has Tuttu been top staple in the economy of subsistence. But like anything else, subsistence has its ups and downs. Many years ago, when subsistence was down, The People were invited to experiment with reindeer herding. The experiment failed. Now the technologies of subsistence are somewhat more sophisticated, to say the least. And if the game is there, The People have a better chance to get it. *If* the game is there.

In 1979 Archie Brower, then mayor of Kaktovik on Barter Island, testified at a hearing on proposed oil-lease sales in the Beaufort Sea. Brower spoke of subsistence. "The Brooks Range all the way to the ocean is our garden," he said. "We feed on that." The proposal then was to drill for oil on the edge of the garden. What strange and curious things come to pass, and in less than a single decade. Now the proposal is to spade up the garden, and drill *there*.

9 . KAKTOVIK

One day The Man From Outside went to Kaktovik to find out how The People felt about oil, and then, flying out, to see what their garden looked like with so many sheep on the vine up at Kanich, and Tuttu with calves ripening out on the Jago Plains. (Since The Man's name cannot be translated into Inupiaq or Admiralty English, let's call him The Outsider and let it go at that, okay? Besides, he's only a journalist.)

Coming in the first time, The Outsider could see Kaktovik from many miles away, even though it is a small village, with hardly two hundred souls to its name. What gave Kaktovik away on the flat horizon at the edge of the sea was DEW. DEW had its rabbit ears trained on the sky toward Siberia, and such better-to-hear-with big ears The Outsider had never seen. Later, reading the report on Kaktovik subsistence by Jacobson and Wentworth, The Outsider discovered that before DEW came to Barter Island the biggest act had been Old Tom Gordon's trading post, built in 1923. The Eskimos had called it Iglukpaluk, meaning "big house seen from far away." Now the undisputed Iglukpaluk of Barter Island was this pair of rabbit ears, listening for bad medicine in the sky.

There was much The Outsider had to learn about Kaktovik. First he learned that the name Kaktovik is Drugstore Eskimo, a phonetic rendition of Qaaktugvik, which is a word the people from DEW could not easily roll off their tongues. Qaaktugvik means "the seining place."

Next, The Outsider learned that Koktovik sure has been around a lot, and kicked around a lot, too. Just since 1946 the village has been relocated on Barter Island three times. If The Outsider had known some historical geography when he first stepped out of an airplane onto the island's gravel runway, he would have understood that he was then standing upon the location of Kaktovik I. Kaktovik I had to go away when the United States Air Force decided to bury the site under an airstrip for its DEW Station in 1947. Better than The Outsider telling how such an outrage could happen in a democracy, let's hear it from historian J. M. Nielson's 1977 monograph on the subject of Kaktovik relocations:

> The Air Force abruptly informed the stunned residents that they would have to move immediately, presumably under authority of PLO 82 of 1943, which had withdrawn lands in connection with the prosecution of the war. No specific military withdrawal had been made. Bulldozers hauled the dozen sod and driftwood structures and several frame buildings 1,650 yards up the beach . . . Dismantling of their village caused the Kaktovik people considerable grief, hardship, and dismay . . . However, it was almost impossible for the villagers to effectively protest the move be-

cause very few spoke any English or understood what was happening, or why.

The People resettled themselves at Kaktovik II, hoping that, with dismay behind them, they at last might seize the day and live happily ever after. Yet according to J. M. Nielson:

> The village was relocated again in 1953 because of changes in the DEW Line layout and new road construction. This move was accomplished in the same manner as the previous one, with the new site located farther to the west and a little farther back from the beach.

At Kaktovik III, The People lived not so happily ever after because the site selected for them was prone to flooding and because, inevitably, the Air Force was desirous of expanding its facilities once again. And once again (1964) the villagers were moved. Not far. Just far enough so that if you are keeping score on such matters, you have to count this village—the present one, the village of The Outsider's visit—as Kaktovik IV.

During his brief visit at Kaktovik IV, The Outsider discovered that some of The People he wanted to see were out of town on business, their business being subsistence, while others—how else to say it?—were not in the mood to be seen. Unfortunately, The Outsider had been preceded (and would be followed) by a stream of other journalists and communicators of one sort or another, all desirous of knowing in twenty-five panik words or less what it was like to be an Eskimo in Kaktovik in the Age of Oil. The Outsider understood The People's lack of mood; after all, he has trouble with twenty-five words or less himself.

Moreover, The Outsider could already guess how most of The People felt about oil. He had seen this cityslick booklet put out by Arctic Slope Consulting Engineers of Anchorage, which is a subsidiary of the Arctic Slope Regional Corporation, the Inupiat-owned enterprise established pursuant to the Alaska Native Claims Settlement Act of 1971. The regional corporation holds title to subsurface rights underlying 92,000 acres of land owned by Kaktovik Inupiat Corporation, the village enterprise. In the cityslick booklet, the Eskimo Jacob Adams, president of the regional corporation, explains that it is the considered view of all of the experts that the corporation's subsurface estate and the adjacent 1.5 million acres of coastal plain lying within the Arctic National Wildlife Refuge represent "the most promising and prospective area for commercial oil and gas development in the United States today." Jacob Adams further states that one of the primary legal obligations of his corporation is to maximize economic benefits to its shareholders, the primary economic resource being oil and gas. Then Jacob Adams sums it all up:

> The Inupiat Eskimo people are subsistence hunters and users of the North Slope's fish and wildlife resources . . . It is our judgment that we can have balanced and carefully regulated oil development on our lands . . . and in the coastal plain which will preserve the environment and the wildlife resources of the Arctic National Wildlife Refuge and still benefit our people and the Nation.

The Outsider had digested this message and decided that for all of his own lack of brevity, he could have told the same tale in fewer words. Because, the way The Outsider had it figured, this is what Jacob Adams is really saying: *You can have your cake and eat it, too.*

At Kaktovik IV, The Outsider first called on Herman and Mildred Rexford. Mildred is of the Akootchook clan, and a niece of that keeper of the first Iglukpaluk, Tom Gordon. Herman was a Kaveseklook until the missionaries took that name away from him and christened him Rexford. The Rexfords are among the village's oldest residents. They have resided here through Kaktoviks I, II, and III, and while they are much intrigued with the prospect of oil revenues improving Kaktovik IV, they have much concern about the attendant impacts, both of a social kind in the village, and of a subsistence kind, out in that garden that runs up the Jago and Hulahula to the Brooks Range.

Next, The Outsider went to see Loren Ahlers, who is the

mayor of Kaktovik. Ahlers once upon a time was an outsider himself, come to Alaska to work for DEW in the 1960s. Ahlers married an Eskimo woman and settled down at Kaktovik, and by and by was elected its mayor. Ahlers told The Outsider that Kaktovik was much obliged to oil. Revenues accruing from development at Prudhoe Bay had filtered down into something called CIP, the Capital Improvement Program. CIP had given to Kaktovik a large school, new housing, street lights, water delivery, honey-bucket pickup and disposal. You name it, they got it. "Everything here before CIP was do-it-yourself," Mayor Ahlers told The Outsider. "Now life is easier and safer."

The mayor conceded that The People had questions about drilling for new oil closer to home. And some of the questions—about impacts on caribou, char, bowheads, you-name-it—did not yet have absolute answers. Still, Ahlers was confident, just like Jacob Adams, that The People could have their cake and eat it, too. And Ahlers said to The Outsider: "You can't move the oil somewhere else. It's there, and this country is going to get it sooner or later. I believe we can get it in a way that will not cause significant damage. If we do not get it, we will never have the same opportunity that other people in America have to enrich their lives."

The Outsider said good-bye and Godspeed to Loren Ahlers and went down to the DEW runway that had buried Kaktovik I and got in an airplane with a pilot and some other outsiders and flew south, over the garden of subsistence, toward the Brooks Range. This was in early June. The braided rivers were running free, but patches of snow remained here and there on the tundra. Looking down on it all from the airplane, The Outsider tried to imagine a garden, but what he saw instead was a piece of cake—with icing on it. The Outsider knew damn well that no one can have his cake and eat it, too. The Admiralty English had learned that lesson long ago. The panik Americans were beyond learning. They were hopeless. They would never learn. But the Eskimos?

O Jane, the Eskimos.

A MAN CALLED BIRD

It was a good aerie for an old man in a wheelchair. From any one of the front windows he could look out across East 15th Street to the park, with its littleleaf linden trees lime-green in the springtime and tall, slender scarlet oaks shimmering incandescently in the fall. Summers of those housebound years, the sounds of gaming children drifted through the open windows of the townhouse, no doubt imparting some measure of pain with the pleasure of it, for children of his very own had been denied him. Winters, all the trees stripped bare and the shut-in rooms silent, he could look down the long, empty oval of paving stones to the statue of Peter Stuyvesant at the north end of the park, or across the corner of Rutherford Place to the old red-bricked Friends' Meeting House, or to the edge of the farthest rooftops, beyond which he could only imagine the silhouettes of all those strange new skyscrapers rising above the streets and avenues of his city.

Almost from the beginning, New York had been his city, his anchorage, ready to take him back from the far country, to shake the sagebrush out of his cuffs, put some starch in the detachable collar, shelter him from the uncouth tempests of life afield. Not that he ever forgot who it was *he* was born to be, or how blue his blood; though once, as a young man, he had thought it might be fun to say good-bye to the city and spend the rest of his days hunting and trapping and scouting up Indians across the Big Sky West. Yet even then it was almost too late. Too soon the buffalo were gone, the Plains barb-wired, the Indians under house arrest on their parched reservations. So he would have to spend his middle years remembering what he had seen of the West when it was still wild, and put those memories down on paper. And then, himself arrested in a wheelchair at a window on East 15th Street, his wide-open spaces reduced to a littleleaf linden park, he would await the overdue end trying to remember if there was anything left to remember.

As a matter of fact, there was plenty to remember. His aerie was filled with remembrances. Letters. Notes. Accounts. Lists. Manuscripts. Books. Journals. Clippings. Pictures. Specimens. Fossils. Skulls. He had written of the buffalo skulls long ago in *Scribner's Magazine*. He had found them on the prairie and brought them home to New York as mementos of the great herds that were no more. Two skulls, a bull and a cow. White and weathered, cracked and bleached, they sat on the floor on either side of the fireplace. From his chair late at night he stared at them and dreamed of the old days. He saw again the huge blue arch of the sky. Dark dots moving upon the rolling yellow hills. The herd coming down to water. Long lines shuffling past. Dust powdering the westering sun. Mounted men coming now. Naked Indians. Feathered shafts. Meat. Wolves. Snow. Bones.

He would remember what they had called him. Birdie. It was Birdie to the sporting bluebloods. Bug Hunter to the bluejacket soldiers. White Wolf to the Pawnees. Fisher Hat to the Blackfeet. Gray Clothes to the Gros Ventres. *Wikis* to the Cheyenne; in translation, Bird. It had nothing to do with his true middle name. That had come to him from his father's cousin. The Cheyenne knew nothing of Christian cousins. They only knew that *Wikis* was like most of the other birds of the plains. He arrived and departed with the seasons.

And sometimes, in pseudonymous self-effacement, he had a

special name in type for himself. Yo. The Spanish prependicular pronoun.

He would remember the overlapping stages of his life. The boy. He would remember the boy at Audubon Park. In a sense, he would remain the boy long after he had left Audubon Park in his sixtieth year. He would remember the scientist riding through the Black Hills, the hunter of elk in the Judith Mountains, the editor of *Forest & Stream* on Park Row, the defender of Yellowstone, the protector of the Adirondack Forest, the fanciful admirer of sea serpents, the stuffer of specimen birds, the founding father of the first Audubon Society, the publisher of the first *Audubon Magazine*. THE *Audubon Magazine*, he had called it, employing the definite article as though it were some kind of scent mark, an assertion of territoriality. Volume I, Number 1, February 1887. Published by the Forest and Stream Publishing Company in the interests of THE Audubon Society for the Protection of Birds. The society, the company, the magazine. The territory of George Bird Grinnell.

Somewhere in a desk or cabinet he had tucked away a kind of unfinished sketch map of that territory, a typescript of four pages, a "History of George Bird Grinnell's Life." A draft outline of a history, as it turned out. Short entries, heavily edited in the author's unmistakable hand, running from 1870 to 1911. The last eight of those years—now what did *this* mean, since he was to live until 1938?—are blanks.

These are his words:

1870. Graduated as A.B. from Yale University in June and went west with O. C. Marsh's first expedition to collect vertebrate fossils. Major Frank North and some Pawnee Indians accompanied outfit to Loup Fork River, Neb. Returned in Nov. and entered my father's office as clerk.

1871. Clerk in New York with G. B. G. & Co., 36 Broad Street.

1872. Worked in N.Y. business office. During vacation in summer, hunted buffalo on Republican River with Pawnee Indians and L. H. North.

1873. Still working in Broad Street, N.Y. While on vacation, hunted elk on Cedar River, Nebr. with L. H. North.

There are two entries for 1874. These are his words:

In March, left business in New York and went to New Haven to work there on vertebrate paleontology in the Peabody Museum. I had rooms at No. 6 Library Street . . . Met Hon. Jas. K. Blaine and Gen. G. A. Custer at old Fifth Avenue Hotel (in New York) and at General Custer's invitation accompanied his expedition in June to the Black Hills.

Custer.

The old man at the window on East 15th Street folded his hands in his lap and closed his eyes to shut out the city. Back again. Going back. Going.

Yo.

1. THE SCIENTIST IN THE BLACK HILLS

It is the season for exploring the West, this summer of 1874. The geologist Clarence King is afoot somewhere between the Rocky Mountains and the High Sierra. Ferdinand V. Hayden is poking into the physiographic secrets of Colorado. John Wesley Powell is working the red rock country down Utah way. And George Bird Grinnell is riding out from Fort Abraham Lincoln with George Armstrong Custer, bound for the Black Hills of the Teton Sioux.

This truly is a spectacle, out here beyond the gates of the fort. Here is Custer astride his rosewood bay, in buckskin shirt and gray felt hat, the red kerchief around his throat, staghounds trotting jauntily beside their master's jingling spurs. Here is young Grinnell with the scouts and the headquarters unit, and the sixteen brass-band musicians—all on white horses—playing "Garry Owen," and the rows of cavalrymen with their guidon pennants snapping in the dry Dakota breeze, and the four long columns of canvas-topped wagons, and the Rodman cannon and the Gatling guns, and the close-ranked foot soldiers powdered chalk-white in a billowing plume of alkali dust. Twelve hundred men and one woman. She is hiding back there behind the infantry, eating dust in a lice-ridden suit of men's clothes. They call her Calamity Jane. Custer's orderly will note that the men avoid Jane. It is said that she smells disagreeably.

Except for Custer's staghounds, the full brass band, and Calamity Jane, all the discrete elements of this expedition have been made possible by one man, namely Lieutenant General Philip H. Sheridan, Department of the Missouri, commanding. Little Phil, as they call him, is duty-bound to enforce the Treaty of 1868 with the Northern Plains tribes. The treaty has given the tribes a vast reservation, including the Black Hills, on the west side of the Missouri River in the Department of the Dakota (Major General Alfred Terry, commanding). Unfortunately, Little Phil is the same Sheridan who has coined that epigram about the only good Indian being a dead Indian. And it appears that for some time now, the bad Teton Sioux have been using the Black Hills as a sanctuary from which to launch strikes against the sodbusters of Nebraska, not to mention occasional coup-counting raids upon Union Pacific and wagon-train folks.

The official purpose of the expedition, of course, is not to make good Sioux of bad ones, for that might violate the treaty. The official purpose is to conduct a reconnaissance of unknown country. Toward that end, Little Phil had arranged to invite, among other scientists, his old friend Professor Othniel C. Marsh to accompany the expedition. Marsh, however, is too busy in New Haven at Yale's Peabody Museum, but offers his top assistant, Grinnell, in his stead. So here is Grinnell, having earlier passed Custer muster at the old Fifth Avenue Hotel, serving the expedition as zoologist and paleontologist. And here, too, are the geologist Newton Winchell and the botanist A. B. Donaldson and the Army engineer Colonel William Ludlow. These are the overt reconnaissance players, riding with headquarters. The covert ones are a couple of prospectors, William McKay and Horatio Nelson Ross. McKay and Ross are to carry out Sheridan's and Custer's secret mission. No one is saying much about it, but the real purpose of the expedition is not to goad the tribes or to fill in some blanks on the map. The mission is to discover gold in the Black Hills.

As the entourage proceeds southwest toward Wyoming Territory, it becomes apparent to each scientist that there is to be insufficient time for the conduct of serious work in the field. Each day brings compelling need to press on to the next abundant source of water and grass. Reveille is at 4:00 A.M. Breakfast, at 4:30. Wagons packed and rolling by 5:00. Because of possible hostiles skulking nearby, orders are issued that no one is to stray from the column. Evenings, sciencing is confined to the fringes of camp. The jaunty Chicago journalist William Eleroy Curtis, one of the expedition's three visiting scriveners, is greatly amused. The scientists, he reports, "have been wandering about with bags and hammers for nearly a week, and not yet have they found one [fossil] of importance. It seems that nothing ever died in this region."

Nine days out from Fort Abe Lincoln, the Indian scout Goose leads Custer and the bug hunters to a cave in a sandstone ridge. Goose has excited Custer with tales of how the cave extends for miles and sometimes echoes with the groans of dread spirits. Goose is stretching it some. The silent cave ends after four hundred feet. Artifacts are duly noted: a Canadian penny, a flintlock pistol, a human skull with three perforations in the forehead. The regimental surgeon surmises that it is the skull of a white man. The perforations in the skull are thought to be bullet holes. But the Arikara scouts shake their heads, no. This is the Place Where the Man Was Killed by a Bull. Well, at least *something* has died. Besides, one could hardly ride a half-day in any direction without coming upon the bleached bones of bison. In the Black Hills, Grinnell encounters a remarkable collection of bison skulls. Apparently some Indians have painted the skulls red and blue and arranged them ceremonially in five parallel rows of twelve each. Each of the skulls faces east. What does it mean?

It is August. The column has penetrated deeply into the Black Hills. Grinnell is writing in a little black notebook. He is employing the narrative style of a storyteller. Four men are seated around a campfire: Grinnell, the mustachioed scout Charley Reynolds, Luther North (riding this time out as Grinnell's assistant), and the prospector Horatio Nelson Ross. These are Grinnell's words, though Reynolds is speaking:

" 'No,' said Charley, 'this is a right pretty place and the hills here are a nice country. Lots of wood and water and grass.' "

Grinnell concurs: " 'I don't wonder the Indians hate to have the white man come in, for of course if anyone should come in here and settle, the game would all be driven off pretty quick and like enough the hills burnt off too.' "

Ross: " 'I reckon the white people are coming all right. Shall I show 'em that little bottle of mine, Charley?' he said, as he felt in his pocket.

" 'Of course,' said Charley.

" 'Well now, boys,' said Ross, addressing North and myself, 'don't say anything about this, but look here,' and he drew from his pocket a little vial which he passed over to me and which we both examined.

" 'It was full of small grains of yellow metal which we of course knew must be gold dust . . .

" 'That's gold I suppose,' said North as he handed it back to the miner.

" 'Yes,' said Ross, 'that's gold . . . Of course, I'll have to report it to the General, but he'll keep it quiet until we get out of the Hills . . . There'll be lots of men in here this winter, I guess.' "

Grinnell: " 'Well, that will mean an Indian war I expect, for the Sioux and Cheyenne won't give up this country without a fight.' "

On the column's return toward the fort, there are rumors of large bands of hostiles looking for trouble on the banks of the Little Missouri. But when they reach the river, the Indians are gone. Grinnell will write later of that evening in front of Custer's tent:

"North remarked that perhaps it was just as well the Indians had gone before the expedition got there, as there were a great many of them. Custer commented, 'I could whip all the Indians in the Northwest with the Seventh Cavalry.' "

Perhaps as much as missing anything else of the Old West, the man at the window truly missed the clouds. Oh, there were little puffballs scudding over the park now and then, wetting the sidewalks or piling snow at the feet of Peter Stuyvesant. But nevermore the great banks of summer cloud that laid up like electric mountains upon the western sky, and spit not a drop. Sometimes, still, he dreamed of those clouds as he had long ago in that summer of his sickness. Seventy-seven, was it? Seventy-eight? He was coming in from Bill Cody's ranch, a long ride shivering in the saddle, and the last things he clearly remembered were passing a roundup wagon and getting on the train, east, at North Platte Station. Half-delirious after four or five days on the rails, he tottered into his father's arms and was packed off to bed in the family's summer place at Milford, Connecticut. Nights, he was out of his head. In his delirium, he saw himself riding the edge of a herd of cattle. And then those fantastic clouds would come up in the west with thunder and lightning, and the cattle would break away, and he would be riding after them hell-for-leather.

The old leatherstrappers were all gone now. Cody was gone long ago. Charley Reynolds, even longer, sixty years ago on the Little Bighorn, with Custer. And now his friend Lute North was gone, too, just the other day. Or year. It wasn't easy to be the last one. Sure, you had to be thankful for the lucky times. You stepped around a corner and suddenly here was the short life staring you right in the face and you didn't even know it. You just walked on through. That's how you got to be the last one.

He had stepped around the tightest corner in the spring of 1876. Having spent the previous summer as naturalist on Colonel Bill Ludlow's survey of the Yellowstone park, Grinnell was getting to be known as the fair-haired boy of all the Army's bluecoat bug hunters. Now in May, seventy-six, there was a telegram from Custer. It was an invitation. Custer wanted Grinnell to be his guest on an expedition up the Yellowstone to the Big Horn Mountains. Grinnell begged leave to go. He was eager to be in the West again. But Othniel Marsh of Yale's Peabody Museum shook his head, no. There was too much work in New Haven.

Besides, Custer's was strictly a military expedition. There would be no chance for the collection of fossils. It seemed best, therefore, that Grinnell should telegraph his regrets.

Possibly he was wondering what sort of adventure Fate had denied him that day in early July when the news from the Little Big Horn reached Connecticut. He had been dividing his time between the museum in New Haven and his father's summer place at Milford, where there was good and lawful summer shooting of woodcock in the woods beyond the great front porch. Perhaps he was standing there when they brought him the newspaper. All those men, gone. Custer, surrounded by all those gone men on the open hillside. Charley Reynolds, cut down in midstream as he tried to cover Reno's retreat. Yes, he would have been riding with one of them, had Marsh let him go. Custer or Reynolds, and the short life.

Years later, pursuing his ethnological studies of the Plains tribes, Grinnell would hear this story from an old leatherstrap Cheyenne. It was recalled as occurring the year after the killings on the Washita, which was long before the fight at the Bighorn. The Cheyenne were camped on a fork of the Red River, minding their own business. Then in rode Yellow Hair, that Custer Man, with his bloody troopers. The Cheyenne took Yellow Hair into a lodge to pass the pipe. Medicine Arrow said to Yellow Hair: You are a treacherous man. If you come again with a bad purpose, as you did at the Washita, we will kill you with all of your men. As Yellow Hair listened, a Cheyenne took a stick and loosened the ashes in the pipe they had been smoking and sprinkled the ashes on the toe of Yellow Hair's boot. It was a Cheyenne custom. The ash was to bring the blue-eyed visitor bad luck.

Now, after all these years, the man at the window preferred to remember Custer without his faults of ego and judgment. And he remembered, too, the Little Bighorn fight as crass Bill Cody had depicted it in his Wild West show at Madison Square Garden in the winter of 1887. Grinnell had not liked what Cody had done to the memory of Custer. He did not approve of Cody in an auburn wig, playing the lead role. In a front-page commentary in *Forest & Stream* Grinnell would characterize Cody's little drama as "an outrage on decency." These are his words:

> The death of the gallant Custer, ten years ago, has not yet become an incident of history so remote as legitimately to be made the subject of a circus show . . . From the uproarious mimicries of the deaths of our Generals killed in battle by Indians, it will be an easy transition to realistic plays having for their subject the assassinations of our Presidents. The depraved taste which applauds the one would relish the other.

A few days after writing that scathing notice, Grinnell dashed off a letter to his friend in Nebraska, Lute North. Cody's mimicry of Custer, said Grinnell, was "disgusting," and let it go at that. There was other news. He had been working constantly, he wrote. There had been money troubles, presumably at *Forest & Stream*. He did not elaborate. And then—surprising for so private a person—this confidence: "I have lost the girl that I loved better, I think, than I did my life."

The girl that he loved. *Who?* What was her name? It is not in the letter. If mention of this woman appears anywhere else, no one has found it. Or no one is saying. Bachelor Grinnell was thirty-seven at the time of his letter to North. He would not marry for another fifteen years. So who was *this*? And where had he known her? Milford? Park Row? Audubon Park?

The old man in the wheelchair remembered the name, the face, the place. But he wasn't saying either. He was looking, now, away from the window, across the room, at the Eagle and the Lamb.

2. THE BOY AT AUDUBON PARK

There is ice on the river. The Hudson appears to be frozen solid. Eagles and crows are seen walking about on the ice. They are feeding on the carcasses of small animals. The crows roost in cedars beyond the Harlem River, near Highbridge in the Bronx. In the mornings, they fly low through the treetops to the ice in the river and eagles come to perch and quarrel in hemlocks not far from the Grinnell house. This is one of the many scenes he will remember of Audubon Park.

Once, he had looked upon the frozen river from the other side, from their previous place in Weehawken, New Jersey. The house stood at the lip of the Palisades. The view of Manhattan was superb. The air was cold enough to snap between your fingers. Young George was six or seven that winter. One morning he stood at the edge of the cliff and watched his father walk out upon the ice until he was a mere speck. It was believed that George's father walked all the way across the ice and went to work at his office in Manhattan. People did the unexpected, those days. Life was short.

It was on New Year's Day, 1857, that they moved from Weehawken to Audubon Park. These are his words, years later, as he remembered it:

> George Blake Grinnell [his father] set out from Weehawken early in the day alone, and a little later Mrs. Grinnell, with Hannah, the black nurse, carrying the baby, and the three boys, drove to the Hoboken Ferry and up north on New York Island. Amos, the coachman, drove the two bay horses, Selim and Emperor, to a closed carriage . . . Snow was falling, and the Bloomingdale Road was deep in mud and slush.

Let there be no mistake about this place they have come to. It is not a real park. It is what is left of the estate of John James Audubon, who has been dead now for six years. It was from here that Audubon set forth on his last hurrah to the wild Missouri. This place he called Minniesland; in the colloquial Scot tongue, meaning mother's land. Though not his mother. His children's mother, Lucy. In 1857 the widow Lucy resides in one of the Audubon houses with the eldest son, Victor, who is bedridden. The other son lives nearby. He is John Woodhouse Audubon. John has subdivided lots and built several other fine houses upon the property, for sale or for rent, in order to alleviate the family's substantial burden of debt. It is into one of these that the Grinnells have just moved.

The park is bounded more or less by what will later be known as West 155th Street, Amsterdam Avenue (then, the Bloomingdale Road), and West 158th Street, and all of it lying up against the Hudson River. A little brook tumbles down the hillside to the river. George Bird Grinnell will remember the wildness of the place. He will remember thickets of young hemlocks on the hillside and stands of giant white pine along the river, and scattered deciduous species such as oak and chestnut and tulip and hickory. He will remember the tight board fence along the northern boundary, and the white gate that was closed every night, and how New York City was still seven miles away, its outliers at 14th Street, and how of an evening John Woodhouse Audubon, who would become a close friend of his father's, might stand before his own house, a hundred yards distant, calling the elder Grinnell's name and shouting: "If you have nothing to do, I'll come up and play you a game of billiards."

Audubons young and old are much in his life, here on the shores of the Hudson River, yet Madam Lucy remains the most memorable. He enters the great house where she presides. It is a country sort of house, not yet a quarter-century old but already worn from the tramping of visitors and the play of children. Antlers of elk and deer hang in the hallway, and there are muzzle-loaders and shot pouches and powder flasks, and in the dining room is that painting by John Woodhouse, the portrait of Papa John James with his faithful dog. Young George Bird Grinnell climbs the stairs. Here is her bedroom, at the southwest corner of the second floor, facing the river. He knocks, and enters. It is perfectly all right. This is her schoolroom, too. Here she conducts classes in reading and writing for her grandchildren and their neighbor peers. Even young George calls her Grandma. What a lady: tall, slender, erect, never without her spectacles, always in black, her face framed by a white snood, loved and admired and feared a little by the smaller children. And there on the wall of her bedroom is her husband's painting of the Eagle and the Lamb. For a long time, young Grinnell cannot take his eyes from it.

There is much to enjoy in the out-of-doors, here at Audubon Park. There is fishing for killies and crabbing, and skating in the winter. And inevitably, the hunt. He remembers the first hunt. His words:

> There occurred one autumn a tremendous flight of migrating robins. The ground was almost covered with them. The birds were so many that it appeared impossible to throw a stone or shoot an arrow without killing one or more, and I armed myself with a hickory bow—purchased from the Indians at Saratoga and given me by Cousin George Bird—and two or three arrows, and started out to kill robins. Either there were fewer birds than I supposed or I was not a good bowman, for I secured not one.

Life is so short, a boy must have his gun at an early age. George is twelve, maybe thirteen. There are rabbits and grouse in the Blind Asylum Woods (later Fort Washington Park), shorebirds in the Dyckman marshes, quail up at Bronson's (Van Cortlandt Park, in the Bronx), and muskrats along the Harlem River. In the fall migrant flocks of passenger pigeons pass over Audubon Park. Boys stand on the roof of the Grinnell house and fire away. Several pigeons are killed in a day, with much waste of ammunition. Jack Audubon, the eldest grandson, is privileged to carry his grandfather's gun. One day Jack shoots a blue-winged teal on the Hudson River. Fifty years later, George Bird Grinnell will write: "My present impression is that the little boys of Audubon Park—all of them—ought to have been sent to some reform school."

Perhaps, though Lucy Audubon finds them tolerable enough the way they are. Grinnell will remember her favor to him. His words, written in 1920 for *The Auk:* "The picture of the eagle and the lamb always possessed a fascination for me. I greatly admired it and often talked about it to Grandma Audubon, and on one occasion she told me that after her death the picture should be mine . . . It now hangs in my house."

The surprising thing was that he accomplished so much in the short life, yet left so much unfinished in the long one. The "History of George Bird Grinnell's Life," four pages and incomplete. "Memoirs," dated November 26, 1915, ninety-seven pages, typewritten, ending in the middle of a sentence pertaining to events of the year 1883. It was as if a great yawn had opened suddenly behind the keyboard of his typewriter and swallowed him.

For the amusement of his nieces and nephews, the Memoirs began, he was setting down some recollections of New York as he used to know it, and of certain events which he had seen. This much he gave them for background:

The year of his birth was 1849; the month, September, exactly nine months after the marriage of George Blake Grinnell and Helen A. Lansing. The newlyweds boarded on Dean Street, in Brooklyn. Helen was a pastor's daughter, Knickerbocker Dutch. George Blake—a clerk, then, for George Bird & Company, wholesale dry goods merchants, New York, New York— was a congressman's son, Burgundy Huguenot by ancestral way of 17th Century Rhode Island, 18th Century Connecticut, and the Shelburne Hills near Greenfield, Massachusetts. The congressman remembered how *his* father had settled in the hills at a time when one could see wolves circling a sheepfold on a moonlit night. The congressman and his wife had seven children in addition to George Blake. Of these, clearly the most memorable was the one called Thomas. According to the Memoirs of George Bird Grinnell:

> Uncle Tom, who at that time must have been about twenty years of age, greatly impressed my youthful imagination by the stories that he told of hunting and fishing adventures, and by the pictures that he drew of birds. In his younger days he had made a large collection of mounted birds and mammals, which were in his father's house in Greenfield. Among these were what was said to be the last wild turkey killed on Mount Tom in Massachusetts in 1849, a raven killed in the same place, a deer killed near Greenfield, and a great number of birds large and small . . . I had no more pleasant hours, when at Greenfield, than those spent among Uncle Tom's birds in what was called the bird room.

It would interest the nieces and nephews of George Bird Grinnell to know further that, as a young man, he had never shown much interest in a conventional career. True, he had toyed with the idea of trying medicine. It was an idea whose time never came. His father wanted him in the family investment business. Things had been looking up for George Blake Grinnell & Company of Broad Street. The disaster of the Civil War was behind them now. The war had caught G. B. trading textiles. Most of his suppliers were southern planters, and the losses had almost finished him. But he recovered, bounced back, traded in stocks, paid debts, recouped, became the principal agent on Wall Street for Commodore Cornelius Vanderbilt. Things had been looking so good, in fact, that G. B. decided to retire and turn the business over to his eldest son. This was on September 1, 1873. On the 18th, the banking house of Jay Cooke collapsed, precipitating the panic of seventy-three.

The nieces and nephews would *not* be interested to know the details of how G. B., with his money and influence and savvy, helped his son out of the subsequent fiscal crisis. Suffice it to say, as the Memoir writer did, that father brought son "safely out of the woods" and retired once more to the armchair at Audubon Park. Meanwhile, to take his mind off the pressures of business, the son had begun to write for *Forest & Stream*. His first piece, recounting an elk hunt with Lute North in Nebraska, appeared in October of 1873. The following spring, much to his father's chagrin, Grinnell dissolved the investment house and moved to New Haven to work with Othniel Marsh at the Peabody Museum.

Through the remainder of the seventies, Grinnell at Yale also worked toward a doctorate in osteology and paleontology. His dissertation: "The Osteology of *Geococcyx californianus*." Otherwise known as the roadrunner. And he continued to write for *Forest & Stream* and, with his father, to purchase shares of stock in that company until (according to the Memoirs) for all intents and purposes they had control. Charles Hallock, founding editor and president of the publishing company, was said to be deep in hot water with other stockholders. It was said that Hallock had been neglecting his duties. Hallock was told he would not be reelected president at the company's next annual meeting, in 1880. But if not Hallock as president, then who?

This is one of those Brown Decades that Lewis Mumford will write about in the century after—brown for the mood of America, for its fashions in residential façades and walnut furniture, its spreading industrial dinginess, its antebellum traditions falling away like autumn leaves. It is the decade in which yet another President, James Garfield, is shot; the Brooklyn Bridge is opened; Governor "Chinese" Gordon of the Sudan is slain at Khartoum; Geronimo, the Bronco Apache, surrenders to General Nelson Miles in Arizona; the Hwang-ho flood in China kills 900,000; the Johnstown Flood in Pennsylvania kills 2,200; and the Universal Exhibition, opening in Paris in the last year of the decade, unveils to the public, for the very first time, a carriage that moves without benefit of livestock or rails. They call this an internal-combustion machine. The trade name is Benz.

This is the decade of the rise of the American newspaper. Joseph Pulitzer has come East from St. Louis to make a daily sensation of Jay Gould's *New York World*. For newspapering, New York *is* the world. There is Charles Gordon Bennett's *Herald* and Charles Anderson Dana's *Sun* and Whitelaw Reid's *Tribune* and George Jones's *Times*. The *Times* and several of the others are situated here on Park Row, opposite City Hall Park. On an upper floor of the *Times* Building are the offices of George Bird Grinnell's *Forest & Stream*.

This is the decade of the first flowering of America's hook-and-bullet press. The seventies were only for starters—*American Sportsman* in 1871, *Forest & Stream* in 1873, *Field & Stream* in 1874. Now, in the eighties, it is time for everyone to settle down to the serious business of building good circulations among the devotees of sportsmanship and fair play afield.

Grinnell's is an office filled with competent people. As managing editor there is Charles B. Reynolds (not to be confused with that other Reynolds, long-gone Lonesome Charley of Black Hills and Big Horn fame). There is Fred Mather for angling and C. P. Kunhardt for yachting and Franklin Satterthwaite for the kennel and Josiah Whitley on rifles. And there is Grinnell, president and editor-in-chief, still writing the kind of

natural-history pieces and front-page editorials that he had contributed as a free-lancer in Hallock's day. He has no intention of
spoiling a good thing. His predecessor's business failings aside,
Grinnell is determined to perpetuate Hallock's editorial philos-
ophy. Under Grinnell, the weekly will continue to expose and
castigate the fish hog and the pothunter, pandering to no de-
praved tastes, perverting (as Hallock had put it) none of the legitimate sports of land and water to those base uses which tend
to make them unpopular with the virtuous and good.

Hear now the editor-in-chief himself, from the composing
room of his mind, February 12, 1880, under the heading *The
Corruption of Sport:*

> America, our college professors tell us, is in her money-mak-
> ing stage; and it takes a less astute individual than the ordinary
> university professor of Political Economy to see that the average
> American citizen is . . . "on the make" . . . Possibly this generaliz-
> ation may sufficiently account for the mercenary element of so
> many forms of alleged sport . . . We have in mind more than one
> shooting club whose weekly meetings are only so many gam-
> bling schemes among a clique for the gathering in of purses and
> entrance fees . . . True devotees of sport for the sport's sake need
> not be warned against implicating themselves even in the appear-
> ance of evil. Our popular pastimes are too important in their hy-
> gienic influences alone to be cast into a disrepute which will bar
> gentlemen from engaging in them and reaping their benefits.

Or this, datelined April 20, 1882, lest anyone suspect that
Grinnell might be some kind of sporting snob: "There are pothunters and pothunters." One is the brute who kills brooding
birds for market. The other, who shoots for his own pot,

> would creep through the sedges with all the stealth of a deer-
> stalker and get a shot at a flock of sitting ducks, and pick up his
> half-dozen, and go home satisfied . . . In all his wanderings in
> woods and fields and by waters he was blessed with a deep but
> unexpressed love of nature . . . Yet he was a pothunter. But if our
> old friend had killed a hundred ducks on the wing and left half of

them to rot in the marshes, he would have been a "true sportsman" . . . Verily, there be distinctions which are too nice for the ordinary mind to comprehend.

Or this, under date of May 11, 1882:

The prospectus of the "Yellowstone Valley Hunting Club," which lies before us, offers very exceptional advantages to the tyro who desires to have some basis of fact on which to found the boasts that he will make on his return to the East. The object of this club is to systematize game slaughter in the Yellowstone Valley "for the benefit of tourists and the world at large." It proposes to arrange matters so that the intending hunters can "at once proceed to the field, the habitation of that particular class of game as best suits their tastes and convenience; whereupon they can best enjoy themselves, and gain the object of their visit without dissatisfaction or delay."

And how much do our readers suppose is the initiation fee to this prince of "sportsmen's clubs?" Only $2. Anyone may become a member by sending this trifling amount to the secretary, and this payment will entitle him to all benefits "arising therefrom," whatever that means.

If the game should last more than one season we presume that the philanthropic Yellowstone humanitarians, having reaped a goodly harvest of crisp $2 bills, will be in a financial condition to add some very desirable latest improvements to their self-denying scheme for the amelioration of the sportsman's lot and the benefit of tourists and the world at large. For instance, by an adoption of the burglar alarm system—with which they are presumably familiar—they might intersect all the ravines, plateaus and hills in the Yellowstone Valley with wires, all converging to the "club room," so that every time a brute stirred anywhere in the territory covered by the club an alarm would be given, and the whereabouts of the game shown by the indicator in the club room . . . Or the animal might be roped and tied to a post and then slaughtered by proxy. In this case the "sportsman" could advance and, without soiling his kid gloves or disarranging his necktie, touch the rifle which is held, aimed, and fired by an active member, thus sparing our tenderfoot friend the shock of the recoil. Thus the "sportsman" could kill his game on the same principle as that by which the Prince of Wales, when he lays a cornerstone, touches the block with a silver trowel.

In fact the brain reels as it contemplates all the advantages which this club offers. There is only one thing against it, and this is that its life will be so short. The game will last just about one year.

There was a Theodore Roosevelt bookshelf somewhere in the house on East 15th Street—another reminder to the old man in the wheelchair that he was just about the only one left in the ranks. Roosevelt was so long gone that now only his books could bring the old man back to their times together on the near side of the other century. Theodore's books. And *their* books with the Boone and Crockett imprint. And Volume I of the National Edition of the Collected TR, with Grinnell's own introduction to TR's *Hunting Trips of a Ranchman*. That was the title that had brought them together, in 1885. You couldn't forget that one, could you, old buzzard?

He had reviewed the book in a July number of *Forest & Stream*. The notice was of a sort known in the trade as mixed. Mr. Roosevelt, wrote Grinnell, was a person of exceptional intellect. Mr. Roosevelt had accomplished excellent work as a state legislator at Albany. Mr. Roosevelt's accounts of life on a ranch in Dakota were absolutely delightful. But Mr. Roosevelt's experience afield, his range of western travel—well, these were somewhat wanting. Besides, Mr. Roosevelt was not well known as a sportsman. The reviewer was sorry to see that a number of hunting myths were given as fact.

Apparently, the reviewer did not understand that it was a bad time to be trifling with the pride and passion of Theodore Roosevelt. Just the previous year, death had snatched away Roosevelt's wife and mother. On top of that came a political miscalculation that had cost him the favor of his own party. For the time being, he was *out*, an exile, a man without a constituency. Bereaved and humiliated, Roosevelt retired to his ranch in the

West. He had his book to look after. He had the horses and the hunt. Finally, he had the reviews. Here was a notice from *Forest & Stream*. *What*? What was *this*? Who did this Grinnell fellow think he was? There was only one way to find out, and Roosevelt did it. Back in New York, person to person, face to face in an office above Park Row, Roosevelt demanded of Grinnell an explanation of his patronizing account. And Grinnell gave it. As to the outcome, we have only Grinnell's version to go by, according to which Roosevelt "at once" saw Grinnell's point of view. It seems an astonishing claim. How out of character for both of them. The brash bearer of the big stick at once caving in to the self-effacing editor? No matter. Whatever the score, it was a bully match—and the beginning of a long personal association that would reap big public benefits in the future management of America's natural resources.

Later, in his introduction to Volume I of the Collected TR, Grinnell would recall that Roosevelt called often at his office "to discuss the broad country that we both loved." They had much in common: the patrician blood, Teddy's Harvard and Birdie's Yale, the fascination with natural history, the fervor for the hunt, the absentee ownership of western ranches. This was the decade of the cowpoke and the cattle drive, and neither New Yorker would have missed it for anything. Both had purchased their spreads in eighty-three—Grinnell, in the Shirley Basin country of southeastern Wyoming; Roosevelt, in the Little Missouri grasslands of Dakota, which Grinnell had passed through almost a decade earlier with Custer, on their way home from the Black Hills. And always at the center of these discussions, like a storm cloud riven to the arch of the sky, was their darkest fear that the large wild critters of the West—the elk, the mountain sheep, the deer, and the antelope—were heading for trouble on the tumbledown trail. For this was also the decade of the hide hunters, who, having polished off the bison, were now intent on exploiting new markets that would clearly assure the end of the game.

If Roosevelt at first had any doubts about the extent of the slaughter, no one was better suited to dispel them than Grinnell.

As early as 1875 the Bug Hunter had complained to Colonel William Ludlow of the "terrible destruction" of game in the Yellowstone country, of thousands of animals killed just for their hides. "It is certain," Grinnell wrote in his report to Ludlow, "that, unless in some way the destruction of these animals can be checked, the large game still so abundant in some localities will ere long be exterminated."

Ere long, Grinnell and Roosevelt were offering more than talk to put a stop to it. They had formed a national organization. It was Grinnell's idea. Roosevelt contributed the Manhattan dinner party that brought the founding patricians together. Collectively they would call themselves the Boone and Crockett Club. They would work to promote manly sport with the rifle and exploration in the wild and unknown. They would work for the preservation of large game and the enactment of laws to perpetuate the species. They would pledge themselves to the code of the sportsman and the rules of fair chase. They would eschew the taking of large predators in traps, the shooting of game from a boat, and the use of torches in hunting at night. They would lobby vigorously to outlaw the brutal practice of using dog packs to run down deer. They would follow the lead of Grinnell's *Forest & Stream* to speak in defense of the Adirondack forest and the Yellowstone park. And they would publish books and monographs under their own club imprimatur, lest their ideas perish for all the patricians talking only to themselves.

Grinnell and Roosevelt collaborated in the editing of three of the club's books in the 1890s. These were *American Big-Game Hunting, Hunting in Many Lands,* and *Trail and Camp-fire.* In one or another of these volumes can be found the seeds of several forward-looking conservation concepts. Here was good potting soil for the advancement of new national parks and wildlife refuges and forest reserves. Such splendid notions might never have sprouted in Edwardian America if one of the coeditors had not moved on to that White House on Pennsylvania Avenue, while the other coeditor remained at his post, sowing seeds from a window on Park Row.

There is a forest to seed. Almost everywhere that trees grow in the northeastern United States of America there is a forest to seed in these final decades of the 19th Century. That is another reason the period is perceived to be brown. Brown for the eroded hillsides and the silted streams; brown for the slash piles in the clearcuts and the burnt-over lands and the cookstoves rusting in the ruins of the lumber camps, and the sawyers moving on—from the Maine woods to the White Mountains, from the shores of Champlain to the ridgetops of the Adirondacks. The man on Park Row is brooding. The spectacle of disappearing forests troubles him no less than the specter of diminishing game. He attaches much sentiment to trees. They nourish his soul. They lighten his step. He would save the forests just for the artistry of them. But sentiment and artistry do not nourish most men nowadays. Nowadays, most men demand *value*. He must show them the attainable value of sparing the trees. He sits at his desk in the office of *Forest & Stream*. Outside the window, the trees of City Hall Park are coming into new leaf. It is April of 1882. He writes:

> No law can be enacted that will oblige landowners to spare the trees which shade their ledges and swamps, but it is possible that they can be made to see that it is to their interest to do so. The thin soil of a rocky hill, when deprived of its shelter of branches, will be burned by the summer sun out of all power to help the germination of any worthy seed, or to nurture so noble a plant as a tree through the tender days of its infancy . . . Some swamps may be, at great expense, brought into tillage and meadow, but nine times out of ten, when cleared of the lusty growth of the woods, they bear nothing but wild grasses, and the streams that trickled from them all the summer long in their days of wildness show in August only the parched trail of the spring course.
>
> It is strange that the Yankee, with his proverbial thriftiness and forecast, should, when it comes to the proper and sensible management of woodlands, entirely lose these gifts. Why can he

not understand that it is more profitable to keep a lean or thin soil that will grow nothing well but wood, growing wood instead of worthless weeds? The crop is one which is slow in coming to harvest, but it is a sure one, and is every year becoming a more paying one. Furthermore, it breaks the fierceness of the winds, and keeps the springs from drying up, and is a comfort to the eye, whether in the greenness of the leaf or the bareness of the bough. Under its protective arms live and breed the grouse, the quail, and the hare, and in its shadowed rills swim the trout. If we would have these we must keep the woods a-growing. No woods, no game; no woods, no water, and no water, no fish.

Now *there* is some value to ponder. No woods, no water. It is a theme he will exploit again and again as he lobbies on page one for creation of an Adirondack forest preserve. The seasons pass. He looks from his window above Park Row. The branches of the trees of City Hall Park are winter-bare. He writes:

The reasons why the forests should be preserved are not sentimental, but very practical. If the Adirondacks are cleared the Hudson River will dry up; in fact, with the gradual cutting away of timber lands, it has been gradually drying up for years. This means that navigation will be interrupted; commerce will suffer; the city, the State, the nation will be involved in such a calamity.

He writes:

A land without woods is no country for the farmer. At once it lacks water, for this runs off as soon as it falls. It will soon lack soil, for the spring torrents carry this away and deposit it in the rivers, where it still further blocks up the ever shoaling channels.

We cannot think that the time will be long before some steps are taken in the right direction. The matter is one which touches, or soon will touch, the pockets of merchants, manufacturers, shipowners, and farmers, and the pocket, among the well-to-do, is a very sensitive organ.

Forestry is much on his mind and in the pages of *Forest & Stream*. He is appalled at the wasteful methods. To remove one felled tree from the woods, the skidders are also taking the fifty saplings that stand in their way. It is a false economy to transport timber from the coastal to the central states; let each state grow a portion of its own needs. One does not sustain a forest by barring the sawyer altogether; one hires the sawyer to thin the stand and thereby raises the yield to the highest capacity of the soil, as the Europeans have been doing.

This is his idea for the Adirondacks: Not forever wild, forever *productive*. Save the forest by any and all means, but don't lock it up. Take this wrecked mountain woodland and make of it a showcase of modern forestry. Encourage government to acquire the land and render the region what it should be—"a well-clothed, economically administered timber reserve [he writes], an important source of revenue to the State, a scene of beauty for the tourist, of healthy, pleasurable excitement for the sportsman, and of pride to the people who possess it."

Years later, someone will have a name for what George Bird Grinnell is describing here. Someone will call it "multiple use" and attribute the concept to a younger man named Gifford Pinchot.

In his own time, Gifford Pinchot will not be as self-effacing as George Bird Grinnell.

To the consternation of both, forever wild will prevail over productivity in the Adirondack Forest Preserve.

The city did not seem to have the birds it once had. If it were not for the great Central Park of Manhattan, possibly there would have been no birds to speak of at all, except for the unwild pigeon. Things had been settling up here too fast for the birds. All the woods and meadows that used to separate the edge of the city from the gates of Audubon Park were gone, now. Audubon Park was gone, now. Huge structures of stone and brick had replaced the pines and hemlocks where eagles once roosted. And the *wild* pigeons that had flown in flocks above the river were gone, too—from here, from everywhere, forever. And those newfangled skyscrapers, uptown in the Forties and Fifties. What were *they* doing to disrupt the ancient flight patterns of migrant birds? Still, he could be thankful to see now and then a transient perched on a branch in this small park on East 15th Street. From his own aerie, he could watch flickers and phoebes and finches and grackles, and sometimes with luck an indigo bunting or a ruby-crowned kinglet. He knew them all, knew them inside out. And knowing, he remembered.

He remembered the account books. There were two of them, tucked away somewhere in the townhouse. There was the big one with the faded cover: CLOTH ORDERS 1861. On the inside of the cover was the name of the book's manufacturer, W. H. Arthur and Co. at 39 Nassau Street, and a number of inked doodles in the hand of George Bird Grinnell. Already, the indigo ink had aged on the paper to a soft brown, as in the color of dried blood. Blood brown for the birds. Brown for the names of the dead men doodled in ink on the inside front cover. Brown for Audubon, Alexander Wilson, and Nuttall—one, two, three, just like that, all in a row. Brown for

$$\begin{array}{ccc} \text{SIX} & \text{IX} & \text{XL} \\ \underline{\text{IX}} & \underline{\text{X}} & \underline{\text{L}} \\ \text{S} & \text{I} & \text{X} \end{array}$$

But what did it mean?

And brown, in his faded hand, for the narrative descriptions of the crow, the bluebird, the catbird, the robin, the meadowlark. A young man's own field guide to the birds.

The other book was somewhat smaller. It was the record book that George Bird Grinnell and his brother Mort had kept of their specimens. A young men's book of the dead. The first entry: November 1869. The specimen: a bird of a kind identified only in the taxonomic Latin, and undecipherable. Shot at Washington Heights. Length, 19 inches. Entry No. 10: "Passenger Pigeon. Adult Male in full plumage. March 1870." No further details. Page after page, and many blanks. What entries there were list specimens shot at Bronson's and at Milford, Connecticut, or secured, by proxy, from the racks of game- and songbirds then commonly displayed for sale in the markets of New York City. He would explain in his unfinished memoirs that a man named Wallace, who made the rounds of these markets, kept him supplied with unusual specimens, which Grinnell then took home to stuff and mount in his workshop at Audubon Park.

Some of the specimens were indeed unusual. Reference, for example, that record-book entry numbered 1371. *Cupidonia cupido* (in taxonomy now obsolete). Otherwise known as the heath hen. In fact, there were two *cupido* secured from the New York markets and mounted by George Bird Grinnell in the winter of 1873. He had the mounts still, in perfect condition. A beautiful bird, the heath hen. but the specimens troubled him. The specimens only reminded him that the heath hen, as a species, was no more.

How often he had written of the hen in *Forest & Stream*, tracing its struggle for survival in the brushlands of Martha's Vineyard. It had been reduced to that in his own lifetime—a hundred or so birds on one tight little island, and then there were none. Visitors to the Vineyard, under the guise of hunting rabbits, had taken a terrible toll of the hen at the turn of the century. And then came the foxes. For the purpose of amusing themselves in the chase, some Vineyard fools had introduced the fox where nature did not want the fox to be. And this vermin—yes, that's exactly what he had called it—this vermin had preyed upon the hen all the more successfully because the birds had not inherited from their ancestors the ability to protect themselves from it. Ah, but why blame the fox for the final coup? He had put his finger on the real culprit long ago. "When one comes to study the history of the heath hen in America," he had written in an editorial, "no fact presents itself more distinctly and irrefutably than this, that the bird was exterminated from its old-time ranges by no other agency than market hunting."

The markets! Good grief, what terrible things to behold in the Brown Decades. Everywhere birds for sale. Birds to eat, birds to wear. Gamebirds, shorebirds, songbirds. It made no difference, then. If it had feathers, the bird butchers would not fail to find a use for it. Even the breasts and wings of sparrows could decorate a lady's hat. In the window of a millinery shop, one could behold fifty stuffed skins of the Baltimore oriole, at seventy-five cents apiece. A taxidermist known to the editor of *Forest & Stream* trafficked in upwards of 30,000 skins in a single year. Unholy work, he had called it. A vast army of men and women, waging a campaign of destruction with a—how did he put it?—a diabolical perfection of system.

And there was no counter-system. Legislation of itself seemed to have no effect upon the barbarous practices of the bird slayers. The American Ornithologists' Union in 1884 had appointed a committee for the protection of birds, and G. B. Grinnell was among the six gentlemen selected to constitute that august panel. Yet a year later, the committee reported that adverse circumstances had prevented it from advancing a systematic plan of work. One adverse circumstance, left unmentioned in most accounts, was the unfortunate fact that august gentlemen often tend to talk only to themselves. Grinnell knew this, Grinnell was growing impatient with this. Yes, the efforts of committees and individuals might have an impact, over time. But there *wasn't* time. Something more than this was needed. Something new. Something now.

5 . THE BIRDMAN OF AMERICA

Though the Society is his idea, he will attribute its founding to the Forest and Stream Publishing Company. It makes no difference. The editor *is* the company. He will have to go it alone. Not that he hasn't tried. He has tried repeatedly to secure financial backing from some of the warmest friends of the bird-protection movement, but, alas, they shrink from committing themselves to any share of the responsibility. What was it about the pocket? Ah yes, a sensitive organ. On with the effort. These galleys here, the editorial for February 11, 1886. The lead: "Very slowly the public are awakening to see that the fashion of wearing the feathers and skins of birds is abominable." Now, quickly, to the pocket rationale: "The time has passed for showing that the fashion is an outrageous one, and that it results very disastrously to the largest and most important class of our population—the farmers. These are injured in two ways; by the destruction of the birds whose food consists chiefly of insects

injurious to the growing crops, and of that scarcely less important group, the Rapaces, which prey upon the small rodents
which devour the crop after it has matured." And now, this:
"How can we best go to work to combat this great and growing
evil?" And this:

> In the first half of this century there lived a man who did more
> to teach Americans about birds of their own land than any other
> who ever lived. His beautiful and spirited paintings and his
> charming and tender accounts of the habits of his favorites have
> made him immortal, and have inspired his countrymen with an
> ardent love for the birds. The land which produced the painter-
> naturalist John James Audubon will not willingly see the beauti-
> ful forms he loved so well exterminated.
>
> We propose the formation of an association for the protection
> of wild birds and their eggs, which shall be called The Audubon
> Society. Its membership is to be free to everyone who is willing
> to lend a helping hand in forwarding the objects for which it is
> formed. These objects shall be to prevent, so far as possible, (1)
> the killing of any wild birds not used for food, (2) the destruction
> of nests or eggs of any wild bird, and (3) the wearing of feathers
> as ornaments or trimming for dress.
>
> To bring this matter properly before the public at large, we
> shall employ every means in our power to diffuse information on
> the subject over the whole country. Those who are willing to aid
> us in our labors are urged to establish local societies for work in
> their own neighborhood. To such branch societies we will send
> without charge circulars and printed information for distribu-
> tion among their neighbors. A little effort in this direction will
> do much good.

A bold idea ballooned upon the printed page is not unlike a
drama unfolding behind the footlights of a stage. You never
know how well it sails until the notices are in. In the case of this
Audubon Society of George Bird Grinnell's, the response is
overwhelming. Here is the Honorable Oliver Wendell Holmes
writing to deplore "the waste of these beautiful, happy, innocent
and useful lives on which we depend for a large share of our nat-

ural enjoyment." Hear now the Reverend Henry Ward Beecher, who writes to say:

> If there were no purchasers there would be no demand, and no reason for slaughtering these winged gems. But as only women create a demand, it rests upon them to stay this wanton destruction. I am sure it is only necessary to bring before American women the cruelty of this "slaughter of the innocents" that fashion is carrying on to secure a renunciation of this ornament and the salvation of birds.

The poet John Greenleaf Whittier writes from Danvers, Massachusetts:

> I heartily approve of the proposed Audubon Society. We are in a way to destroy both our forests and our birds. A Society for the preservation of the latter has long been needed, and I hope it is not too late for the accomplishment of its objects. I could almost wish that the shooters of the birds, the taxidermists who prepare their skins, and the fashionable wearers of their feathers might share the penalty which was visited upon the Ancient Mariner who shot the Albatross.

And from Charles Dudley Warner, long removed from his collaboration with Mark Twain on the novel *The Glided Age*, this ungilded observation: "A dead bird does not help the appearance of an ugly woman."

The notices keep pouring in. By June there are 10,000 members. It is necessary to incorporate. Among the incorporators are George Bird Grinnell and his managing editor, Charles B. Reynolds. Grinnell is elected president *pro tem*. Now, at year's end, there are 17,000 members in thirty-nine states and territories (including the one called Indian Territory) and the Dominion of Canada. Actually, the head count is closer to 20,000, for a certain Mrs. Bacon of Grand Rapids, Michigan, has by systematic canvas of the schools enlisted some 3,000 new members not yet officially registered. Moreover, as the president *pro tem* will note, the society numbers in its ranks "a few stragglers from far and wide, who describe themselves as residents of England,

Wales, France, Russia, Burmah, Japan, with one red Indian to round off the list."

It is time, mid-January of 1887, for another editorial. It must be said that letters and circulars have proven inadequate to keep pace with the growth of the movement, and that now the society is to have its own special medium in the world of journalism. Starting in February, *The Audubon Magazine*, "devoted to extending and building up song-bird protection," is to be published in the interests of the society by the Forest and Stream Publishing Company. He writes:

> The special purpose of the new monthly will be to advance the work already so well under way, give stability and permanence to that work, and broaden the sphere of effort in such directions as may with reason suggest themselves. Ornithology, discussed in a popular way, will, as a matter of course, take precedence over subjects of natural history, to which the pages of the new magazine will be largely devoted, but it will treat of outdoor life and animated nature in many forms. The price has been made merely nominal, fifty cents per year.

And here it is. Hot off the press, here it *is*! Volume I, Number 1. The cameo likeness of Audubon on the cover. The first installment of a series of articles on Audubon's life and times. Audubon's Baltimore Oriole, a delightful rendering. Grinnell's statement of editorial purpose: "With inspiration drawn from the great book of nature, how can its pages have other than variety, freshness, and charm?" Mrs. Celia Thaxter's essay on woman's heartlessness: "One lady said to me, 'I think there is a great deal of sentiment wasted on the birds. There are so many of them, they will never be missed, any more than mosquitoes!' . . . and she went her way, a charnel house of beaks and claws and bones and feathers and glass eyes upon her fatuous head." It is a splendid debut, is it not? But there is so much to do, and so little help with which to do it. Now *this*, and *Forest & Stream*, too?

By May it is time for an appraisal. There have been four issues of the new magazine. Membership in the society exceeds 30,000.

It must be said once more that the expenses of this movement have been borne by the Forest and Stream Publishing Company without any assistance from outside persons. Sportsmen, take note if you are reading this in *Forest & Stream*. George Bird Grinnell is asking for your help.

But help sufficient to keep the magazine—and the society—alive is not forthcoming. The year 1888 is not a good one for bird protection. Yes, the membership keeps growing, getting on toward 50,000. But the public press seems inattentive. As is so often the case, the public press has a short attention span; it has lost interest in the cause of the birds, it has moved on to other things. In November there is a dark and brooding editorial on page one of *Forest & Stream*:

> Essays have been written to demonstrate the foolishness of small-bird destruction, laws have been passed to protect the useful species, societies have been organized and tens of thousands of members pledged against the fatuous fashion of wearing bird skins as dress . . . and what is the outcome of it all? Fashion decrees feathers; and feathers it is.

With the December 1888 issue of *The Audubon Magazine*, Grinnell is obliged to throw in the towel. Defeated by the resourcefulness of his adversaries in the feather trade? Not by a long shot. He is done in at last by the success of his own numbers. He cannot keep up. These tens of thousands of members, these myriad subscriptions, are too much for him, too much for his limited Park Row staff. If he should continue with the magazine, the quality of *Forest & Stream* might well be in jeopardy. This double life is killing the publishing company. This physical labor and the personal expense are killing Grinnell. So, after two years and two dozen issues, the name of Audubon retires from the world of journalism. And without its magazine, the defunct society, as a national movement, ceases to exist.

But wait, now. You know better, don't you, old buzzard? What's this we see on the front page of *Forest & Stream*, in the edition of May 2, 1896?

The Audubon Society movement projected and carried on by this journal some years ago has ceased to be an active force in itself, but its influence is still shown in the several societies here and there springing up first in one quarter and then in another and assuming the name of the original institution. We recorded in our issue of April 18 the formation of an Audubon Society in Boston . . . We extend our good wishes to those who are promoting the work.

Yes, he knows. By 1900 there will be Audubon societies in nineteen states. By 1900 the bimonthly magazine *Bird-Lore* (lineal precursor of National Audubon Society's *Audubon* magazine) will be filling the niche carved by Grinnell's short-lived journal. And by the end of 1904, Grinnell in his chair at *Forest & Stream* will be writing yet another installment of the Audubon saga. It is proposed, he notes, to incorporate a National Association of Audubon Societies whose membership shall cover the whole country. A splendid idea. But the time has come to extend the work so as to make it cover more than the protection of birds. More emphasis, he writes, should be given to the economic importance of the work while the sentimental side should have less prominence.

"If the management of the National Association of Audubon Societies should share this view," Grinnell goes on, "the new association would have as a part of its work the protection of birds, the protection of mammals, the protection of forests, and generally, so far as possible, the protection of the natural things of the land."

Foul heresy! some birders say. Some say it still.

The years seemed to have him fooled, the way he made ancient history of them even before they had passed him by. It was as if—somewhere along the way, sometime after the turn of the century—he had lost count, and all his years were yesteryears. Perhaps he suffered a misplaced sense of guilt for having survived some fallen friends. And perhaps the guilt might be expiated if he could view himself as being over the hill when in fact he was still striding toward the top. To a younger friend he wrote of having fallen "into the sere and yellow leaf," his "hold on the twig of life" already loosening. At the time of that dour confession, he was all of sixty-one and vigorous. His life was not to be as short as either he or the actuaries had supposed.

No doubt his summer activities in the West helped to keep him ticking. There was ranching in Wyoming, hunting in Montana, canoeing the rainforest coast of British Columbia. There was the Yellowstone to revisit again and again, if only to fuel the fire of his crusading editorials. In the summer of 1885 and for many summers after, he went into the country of the Blackfeet, the high mountain lake country, the place of the glacier someone later would name for Grinnell. So far as anyone knew (or knows), no white man before Grinnell had ever laid eyes on this ice-sheet. To celebrate the discovery, Grinnell shot and killed a bighorn ram upon the glacier and, with his companions, feasted on its chops by light of campfire that night.

Summer of 1899, he was off to Alaska with the E. H. Harriman expedition. The august New York financier—owner of the Union Pacific Railroad, among other blue-chip holdings—coveted the trophy of an Alaskan brown bear, but brought along a contingent of bug hunters and tree huggers to dignify the journey, which was coastal and therefore by ship. John Burroughs was among the guests, but, being a landlubber, detested the occasional prospect of open sea. Grinnell apparently saw more of the other full-bearded John—that shy Scotsman with the faraway eyes, the one who was said to commune with rocks and to celebrate cyclonic winds with his arms and legs wrapped round the top of a redwood tree. Muir. A curious fellow, that one. Grinnell had seen his work in the *Century* and *Scribner's Magazine*. Muir wanted to save the mountains and the trees, but it seemed to Grinnell that Muir's arguments did not give sufficient emphasis to the economic importance of forests. Muir spoke from the—how else could you call it?—the sentimental point of view, and did not appear to have a great store of knowledge about birds. Muir had started that club of his in San Francisco.

What did they call it? It was some sort of Spanish name, was it not?

On the 21st day of August, in the year 1902, George Bird Grinnell married the Boston widow Elizabeth Kirby Curtis. He was fifty-three. She was somewhat younger. She did not fully share his overreaching enthusiasm for the out-of-doors, though she followed him into it from time to time and eventually took up the practice of photographing many of his western subjects, notably the Plains Indians.

By traditional count 1909 should have been the year of his— or her—seven-year itch. Whatever the sensation, they scratched it by taking leave of Audubon Park and moving downtown to East 15th Street. For more than half a century he had lived at the old place on the Hudson. Leaving was a wrench. "I was pulled up by the roots," he wrote a friend, "and transplanted. The change would have been misery if I had permitted myself to think about and lament it." That was his style, of course. To step around a corner and walk on through. Conquering difficulties was one of the chief joys of life. Or so he said.

In 1911 he sold his interest in the Field and Stream Publishing Company and retired to devote more time to his own writing. After thirty-one years, taking leave of the editor's chair was a wrench, too. He walked on through.

There was his "Jack" series to continue, or complete. He had taken to writing books for boys at the turn of the century. "Jack" was the rugged hero of his tales. Jack the Young Ranchman. Jack among the Indians. Jack in the Rockies. Jack the Young Canoeman. Jack the Young Trapper. Jack the Young Explorer. Jack the Young Cowboy. Good *young* Jack! No doubt Jack helped Grinnell's sere hand keep a hold on the twig of life.

He walked on to and through his multitudinous clubs, trusteeships, and affiliations. The Union Club. The University Club. The Century. The Authors. The Explorers. The Cosmos. The New York Zoological Society. The American Association for the Advancement of Science. The Hispanic Society of America. The American Museum of Natural History. The Ornithologists' Union. The Society of Mammalogists. The Archeological Institute. The National Park Association, wherein he succeeded Herbert Hoover as president in 1925.

He walked on through the woods and fields of the family retreat at Milford, Connecticut. Half the land was good for grouse, the other half for bobwhite quail. They hunted with dogs well bred to the point and the set.

He walked on through to the writing table by the window at East 15th Street. He was using a typewriter now. He was using a typewriter to help him remember a short history of George Bird Grinnell's life. His words:

> 1887. Learned of bad treatment of Blackfeet by the agent M. D. Baldwin, and attacked him for his misdoings at the Indian Office in Washington. No result because of his political influence.
>
> 1889. With Pawnees to get ethnological material. Baldwin, the Blackfeet agent, at last removed.
>
> 1890. At Missouri River with Rees, with Pawnees at Fort Reno . . . was at Ghost Dance.
>
> 1897. Blackfeet Reservation. Saw Medicine Lodge and climbed Mount Jackson with Jack Monroe. Then Northern Cheyennes with phonograph.
>
> 1898. Cheyennes.
>
> 1899. Harriman Alaska Expedition. Cheyennes.
>
> 1900. Cheyennes.
>
> 1902. Sent out to Standing Rock by T. Roosevelt to investigate complaints against the Indian agent there.

For the year 1903 there was mention of association with White Bull, White Hawk, White Shield, Brave Wolf, American Horse, and Two Moons. There was mention of Blackfeet, Piegan, and Cheyenne.

In 1904 the blanks began.

6. WIKIS IN THE WEST

It is good to know this. The Cheyenne will gladly eat badger and skunk, but not magpie. The magpie they do not eat because it won the race for them. They tell *Wikis* of long ago when the magpie won the race to see whether the buffalo should eat the people, or the people should eat the buffalo. This is good to remember, now that the badger has replaced the buffalo in the people's belly. *Wikis* will make this circumstance last forever. He will put the racing magpie down in one of his books.

It is good to know, too, that *Wikis* has the American Indian to keep his mind and ticker clicking through the yellow-leaf years. Not that he has lost touch with, or interest in, ornithology, forestry, hunting, flood control, waterfowl legislation, Yellowstone National Park, Glacier National Park (his idea, 1891; TR's action, 1910), sightings of sea serpents (the unsmiling world needs monsters, does it not?), and assorted other topics relating to the natural and unnatural history of the United States of America. Still, each prior phase of his variegated career has had its focus. This yellow-leaf phase is focused on ethnology and the American Indian of the western High Plains.

As it turns out, he will be remembered for this more than for anything else. Encyclopedias will barely allude to his conservation achievements in order that there might be space to list his books and monographs on the American Indian. The first is *Pawnee Hero Stories and Folk-Tales* (1889). Then *Blackfoot Lodge Tales* (1892), *The Story of the Indian* (1895), *The Indians of Today* (1911), *The Fighting Cheyennes* (1915), *The Cheyenne Indians* (1923), and *By Cheyenne Campfires* (1926), among other titles. It is important to remember that the first of these books appears a full year before the frozen hearts of the massacred Hunkpapa Sioux are buried at Wounded Knee; and that, to most white Americans of the period, Grinnell is espousing foul heresy even to suggest that Indians "are human like ourselves; that they are fathers and mothers, husbands and wives, brothers and sisters, men and women with emotions and passions like our own."

He has much kinship with the tribes. For helping the Blackfeet through their winter of starvation, for using his pen to oust the rascal agent Baldwin, he is honored to be named one of their chiefs. The Pawnees, too, regard him as chief. He is big medicine among the Cheyenne. Each summer now, like a migrating bird, *Wikis* comes to perch among the reservation lodges of the Cheyenne. "Of all the tribes he knew," the anthropologist Ruth Bunzel will write of Grinnell decades later, "it was the Cheyenne he loved best . . . Of all the books written about Indians, none comes closer to their everyday life than Grinnell's classic monograph on the Cheyenne. Reading it, one can smell the buffalo grass and the wood fires, feel the heavy morning dew on the prairie."

He remembers it all clearly, the wet grass and the smoke rising above the lodgepoles. He remembers the exploits of Crooked Neck and Big Head and Tangle Hair and Winter Man and Dives Backward, and the saga of the one named Mouse's Road, whom the Comanches believed to be the bravest ever because it had taken hundreds of them to bring him down. He remembers how the old ones used to call themselves Tsistsistas, The People, and how they explained the ancient migration out of the East, by force and numbers and competitiveness pushing the Kiowa south into the shortgrass and the Crows westward to the mountains; and how the first white man ever came out of Mexico in a coat of mail—an iron shirt—and lost it to an Arapaho who lost it to a Cheyenne, and how the shirt came down through the generations until Alights On The Cloud, who was wearing it, got skewered in a fight with the Pawnees in 1852, and how the Pawnees rode away with the shirt and destroyed it. And how the Gros Ventre taught The People how to steal horses from the southern tribes, who stole them from the Mexicans. And how a man became a Contrary through fearing the thunder, and carried a lance with the skin of a bird tied to one end. And how the warrior who had been there still could not understand why Yellow Hair had stopped on the hillside above the Little Big Horn. The warrior told *Wikis* that if Yellow Hair and his soldiers had continued their charge and forded the river and galloped straight into the Indian camp, the Indians would have scattered and fled and Yellow Hair might have carried the day.

Going way back, he remembers his first meeting with the Cheyenne in the summer of his first buffalo hunt, 1872. The hunters are riding down a wide, dry valley near the Republican River one afternoon when a party of hostiles streams out of the hills. The hunters' horses are unfit to run, and there is no place to fort up, so Lute North orders the men to dismount and bring their horses into a kind of triangle, and Lute tells them to stand inside this triangle with their rifles pointed outward, over the saddles. The Cheyennes start riding around them in a circle. There are maybe fifteen Indians, but only two or three have guns. Grinnell can see dust puffs where the bullets fall short of their mark. There is a commotion in his mind (as he describes it in his memoirs), and he supposes this is the same as having one's heart in one's throat. No matter. The shooting is desultory. Lute wings one of the Cheyenne ponies. The hostiles do not seem to have much heart for this fight, and presently they move off. So do the hunters. And who would have guessed that of all the white-eyes in the world, one of these hunters, in little more than a quarter-century, would be the Cheyenne's best friend?

Still, going back. Going back now to 1870 and the Othniel Marsh expedition. He remembers his first *dead* Indian, or what Phil Sheridan then would have called a good Indian. He is following a creek, jump-hunting ducks for the evening meal. Suddenly he beholds this funeral scaffold made of willows, the corpse elevated on a litter. It is the custom of the Sioux to bury their warriors in the sky. This warrior could not be long dead, for there is no rust on the scalping knife beside him. The long black hair on the skull appears shiny and fresh. And what is *this!* A barn swallow? Two barn swallows skimming the sky to dive beneath the scaffold's litter. The swallows are building a nest. The swallows are robbing the warrior's grave to build their nest. It is a terrible thing to look so closely, but what else can he do? The swallows are *scalping* this fallen warrior. They are lining their nest with the warrior's hair.

Tuesday, April 12, 1938. The weather "ear" in the upper-right-hand corner of *The New York Times* front page that morning forecast a day that would be mostly cloudy. Below the ear, in the lead story, Franklin Delano Roosevelt was promising to take his relief and recovery program to the people in a fireside chat. The ocean liner *Queen Mary*, on an inside page, was reported back on course after a nasty storm. Passengers had been thrown against the walls of their cabins. There were several broken arms. The French opera star, Lily Pons, had raised her lilting voice against the gale. On the editorial page, the commentary was unremarkable, as was so often the case with the *Times* those days. Opposite Editorials was Obituaries. The English novelist Edgar Jepson was dead. The Reverend Eddy Horace Greeley, missionary to Africa and cousin of the famed editor who had told a generation of Americans to go West, was dead. George Bird Grinnell was dead. Died early yesterday at his home on East 15th Street, in his eighty-ninth year. He had long been in failing health. Author, naturalist, explorer, founder of the first Audubon Society, often called "the father of American conservation," the *Times* said. The man had gone West more times than a person could count. He was survived by his widow. Burial was to be in Woodlawn Cemetery. Including the picture, the *Times* had found Grinnell worthy of one column and a half.

On the following Sunday, *The New York Herald-Tribune* lionized the fallen Grinnell with a glowing editorial. An unsigned piece, it has since been attributed to Robert Cushman Murphy. It began:

> The passing of Dr. Grinnell cuts a strong strand in the remnants of the thinning cable that still links America with the age of its frontier." It ended: "Aside from Grinnell's prophetic vision, his forthrightness, his scholarship . . . and the drive that empowered him to carry so many causes to successful conclusion, his outstanding personal characteristic was that of never-failing dignity, which was doubtless parcel of all the rest. To meet his eye, feel his iron handclasp, or hear his calm and thrifty words— even when he was a man in his ninth decade—was to conclude that here was the noblest Roman of them all.

Curiously, the New York press appeared to be more enchanted with the accomplishments of Grinnell's life—and more sorrowed by his death—than much of the conservation community. *The Auk* ("A Quarterly Journal of Ornithology") would run a thoughtful and comprehensive sketch by Albert Kenrick Fisher in its January 1939 number. But *Bird-Lore*, the journal of the National Association of Audubon Societies, would note Grinnell's passing in its July–August 1938 issue with the scantest of send-offs—154 words, to be exact, not even two for every year of his life. "Because he was relatively inactive during recent years," *Bird-Lore* explained, "few people of this generation have any appreciation of Dr. Grinnell's services in behalf of America's outdoors." Even then there was a saying to the effect that if you are not part of the solution, you are part of the problem. *Bird-Lore* similarly neglected to take appropriate note in 1936 of the fiftieth anniversary of Grinnell's founding of the first Audubon Society, or of the magazine anniversary a year later. Though he was fading during the two years that preceded his death, one can hardly escape concluding that the old man in the wheelchair must have taken some sad or aggrieved measure of the oversights.

It was a slow fading. The heart, at first—a coronary attack on a summer weekend in Connecticut in 1929. He rallied. As late as 1932 he was still sufficiently mobile to make the Milford journey. By 1935, it appears, the journeys—however short—were finished. He could not attend to his own correspondence. He sat by the windows above the littleleaf linden park and faded—and fading, remembered.

He never adequately summed it all up. Perhaps the closest he ever came was in a letter to a friend just a few years before his heart attack. "I have had barrels of fun," said Grinnell of his multiple careers in the out-of-doors. "In fact, I suspect that there is no one living who ever had so good a time during his life." That was so typical of the old buzzard, not to mention anything but the good times.

7. EPILOGUE

Time marching on through the war and the postwar might have wiped his name from the slate altogether. To be sure, there was a mention of Grinnell here and there in the literature. Seeing the name, some people associated it with the founder of a corn-country college, thereby confusing George Bird with Josiah Bushnell Grinnell, the abolitionist-agitator who inspired, or provoked, Horace Greeley's classic directive (but who followed it only as far as Iowa). Besides, what difference did it make *who* the father of the conservation movement might have been? Fathers were no longer fashionable. The movement did not want to hear about ancient history. Especially it did not want to hear about ancients who shot bighorn sheep one day and saved national parks the next. That sort of thing just wasn't done.

And so, as baby boomers and flower children prepared to save the planet with recycled cans and Clivus Multrum toilets, the image of Grinnell as founding father remained largely a secret known only to a few over-the-hill birders and to the house historians of Grinnell's old clubs. The Boone and Crockett Club made much of Grinnell in its own history book, *Crusade for Wildlife*, by James B. Trefethen. But much wasn't much enough for the young Ph.D. candidate John F. Reiger, who alone was destined to give Grinnell his place in history at last. Grinnell would become the subject of Reiger's doctoral thesis in American History at Northwestern University and of his book *The Passing of the Great West: Selected Papers of George Bird Grinnell* (Scribners 1972). A second book, *American Sportsmen and the Origins of Conservation* (Winchester Press 1975), would position Grinnell, rather than Gifford Pinchot, as the real "originator and synthesizer" of many of Theodore Roosevelt's conservation ideas. (Both books have recently been reissued, in paper editions, by the University of Oklahoma Press.)

And then there are the unselected papers of George Bird Grinnell, which occupy forty-one linear feet of shelf in the Manuscripts & Archives repository of Sterling Memorial Library at Yale. That they are there at all is a bit of luck, for Grinnell did not bequeath them to his alma mater. In his will, Grinnell passed most of his ethnographic field notes on to the Southwest Museum Library in Los Angeles, California. The bulk of his papers he bequeathed to John Holman of Fairfield, Connecticut, at one time an editor at *Forest & Stream* and later president of the Connecticut Audubon Society. In the fade-away yellow-leaf years on East 15th Street, Holman apparently had enriched a long association with Grinnell by dropping by the invalid's townhouse to pass the time reading aloud from some of Grinnell's works. According to Reiger, what the invalid most liked to hear were passages out of the "Jack" books. Holman told Reiger that Grinnell became so absorbed in the Jack stories that he would sometimes forget altogether that he had written them. "That's right!" Grinnell would exclaim at the end of a passage. "The fellow who wrote that knew what he was talking about."

In Holman's possession, the Grinnell papers were consigned to a small frame building known to members of the Connecticut Audubon Society as the Birdcraft Museum. And it was there that Reiger discovered them in the course of researching his doctoral thesis, and later arranged to have them transferred to Yale. Letterbooks. Notebooks and account books. Lists and manuscripts. Rough drafts and unfinished memoirs. The indigo ink, blood brown. The paper brittle, flaking at the edges. The shards of a very private public life.

Who *was* that girl Grinnell had loved more than his own life, I asked Reiger, for only he had run an eye, page by page, sheet by sheet, across the full forty-one linear feet? Who was that girl, lost in the 1887 letter to Lute North only weeks before Grinnell had published Volume I, Number 1 of *The Audubon Magazine*? Reiger shook his head, no. Nowhere was there another mention of her, as far as he knew. It was as if a great abyss had opened, and then swallowed her. And why *Yo*? Why had the Bird selected *Yo* as his pen-name for the more fanciful pieces, usually about the West, in *Forest & Stream*? Reiger shook his head, to indicate he did not know the answer to that one either. Perhaps it was because Grinnell did not even want to be credited for a turn of phrase.

That was surely an enduring quality of the man, apart from his noblest Roman accomplishments. "Grinnell's gentlemanly desire to remain in the shadows," wrote Reiger in a footnote to his *American Sportsmen*, "is one major reason why his true importance in the conservation movement has so long been obscured . . . As he wrote a friend in 1897, 'Of course, I would rather keep in the background in this matter so far as the public is concerned.' "

So far as the public is concerned, Grinnell's obscurity prevails yet. On the premises of what long ago ceased to be Audubon Park, the only tribute to his times there is a nine-story apartment building at the corner of Riverside Drive and 158th Street. The building is named The Grinnell. Given his gentlemanly wish to remain in the shadows, I suspect the Bird would be pleased to know that hardly one in a hundred of the tenants therein will ever inquire for whom The Grinnell is named. (In fact, it is named for Grinnell's land-owning father.) And at Milford, Connecticut, a developer has turned the old Grinnell country estate into fifty units of condominia. The developer calls the spread Audubon Manor. "Why Audubon?" he was asked point-blank by John Reiger. "Audubon never had ties here. This was Grinnell's place."

"So? said the developer. "So who ever heard of Grinnell?"

ONE GOLDEN ISLE

I t is said that the Timucuan Indians called this island Tacatacuru, but that was long before the Spanish, who called
it San Pedro, or the Englishman Oglethorpe, who renamed it The Highlands without batting an eye. Someone must
have taken the good man aside, explaining that the island lay too
low in the water to be worthy of such a name, for presently
Oglethorpe renamed it again to honor a bonny duke. And this
time the name stuck. So far, anyway. We still call it Cumberland.

For perspective it is best, if you can, to see the island first from
the air, each piece of it snugged in its proper place—the salt
marshes, the forest, the sweetwater sloughs, the dunes, the wide
and lonely beach fused to the edge of the sea. Sometimes the jets
to Jacksonville come south this way, down Georgia's littoral
aisle, its Golden Isles, over Wassaw and Ossabaw and St. Cath-
erines, over Sapelo and Jekyll. And Cumberland. But don't bat
an eye. It passes too quickly. Had Oglethorpe possessed the advantage of high-flying wings, he might have looked down on
this last and southernmost of the Golden Isles and, for naming
it, honored the shark. There is some scant schematic resem-
blance: the tail at the mouth of St. Marys River, the long white

underbelly of the beach, the snaggly mouth at Christmas Creek, the snout of Little Cumberland, the dorsal-fin marshes almost scraping the skin off mainland Georgia. A formidable island, this Cumberland—eighteen miles long if you throw in its little sister, five across at its widest if you measure sound-side marsh at low tide. Thirty years ago, the National Park Service sent its people up and down the Atlantic Coast searching for seashore treasures. Go find the Crown Jewels, they were told. The scouts did that. They discovered this gem at the end of the golden necklace. They reported that it was second only to Cape Cod in natural and recreational values. Someone should have taken the scouts aside to explain the difference between apples and oranges, for Cumberland Island in truth is second to none.

Elsewhere along southeastern shores, other barrier islands are hitched to the mainland by asphalt. But there is something about a treasured island that does not like a causeway. So Cumberland floats free. You come down from the sky to a dock in St. Marys, Georgia, or Fernandina Beach, Florida, and you book passage on a ferryboat and leave the asphalt behind. Now you see the island from another perspective. You see that it is made of mud and sand and leaf litter, sawgrass and tussock sedge, bamboo brier and buttonbush, black gum, palmetto, live oak, loblolly. Across the island, in the foredunes, the sand is like powder, and of a whiteness that is almost blinding at noon of a cloudless day. Pelicans glide low over offshore waters. Terns and skimmers dance down the tide line. A whisper of wind comes from the jade-blue sea. You are second to none now. There is no one else on the beach. The mind and the eyes are free to wander. Is this how the Timucuan saw it? No doubt the birds are the same. Cockles and whelks still leave the same kinds of shells on the beach. But wait. Here in the sand is the spoor of a beast unknown to the Timucuan. The Four-Wheel-Drive. And here in the drift zone, half-buried, a jug of white plastic, a milk carton, a tatter of sun-bleached cloth. What the sea brings forth, the sea at last must take away. It is the law of the edge. Here today, gone tomorrow. And no exceptions. So good-bye to the milk carton and the tracks in the sand. And good-bye, too, to Cumberland Island, though not yet. By a long shot, not yet.

Of all the substantial stewards of Cumberland Island over the years, I do believe I am most grateful to the one whose tenure was shorter than any other recorded before or since. I refer to the bonny duke of Sea Pines Plantation, one Charles Fraser, who came here in 1968 and acquired some 3,000 acres in order to develop a salt-air community much like his modular village on Hilton Head Island, off South Carolina. There was to have been a significant difference, however. There would be no causeway to Cumberland Island. Fraser would string an aerial tramway above Cumberland Sound, and folks would arrive in gondolas. At Sea Camp, near the southern end of the island, Fraser built a house to serve as his headquarters while development plans were a-brewing. He did not get on well with his neighbors. They were barely a handful but all of a family, with Cumberland roots running back past the turn of the century. They liked the island the way it was, without gondolas—and the way it had been, without Fraser.

As things turned out, neither Fraser nor his neighbors got what they wanted. But the National Parks Service got what *it* wanted, for it had not forgotten that Cumberland Island was second only to Cape Cod. In 1972, harassed less by insular critics than by a mainland army of eco-beachniks, the developer pulled up his own shallow roots, sold his land to a parks foundation, and fled home to Hilton Head. Thus did Charles Fraser fulfill his destiny—serving, as the writer John McPhee then described it, as "the catalyst that converted Cumberland Island from a private enclave to a national reserve."

Officially and statutorily, Cumberland Island is a national seashore. As authorized, it embraces some 36,000 acres, of which the Park Service currently owns about half. The rest of the park includes submerged lands and tidal marshes owned by the State of Georgia, a few private in-holdings whose owners have life estate for themselves and their children, and Little Cumberland Island—the snout of the shark—which is to be maintained as a natural and scenic preserve by its private owners. Eight thousand acres on the main island were designated wilderness in 1982. Eleven thousand more are to be so designated when all reserved rights and uses have expired. Fraser the Catalyst did well. And so did the Park Service.

To be sure, there was a rush at first to go in the other direction, away from the wilderness idea. After all, Cumberland had been touched, and not so lightly, by the human hand. There were relics of passage behind every oak tree. Under the forest litter, the bones of loggers and cotton pickers lay a-moldering in their graves. And then there was this beach—this great white magnificent beach that had hardly been touched at all, that could stand a lot of handling. Why, you could put 10,000 people a day on this beach (said one Park Service director). You could have extensive facilities for visitors. A conference center, perhaps. Marinas. Jitneys to save on shoe leather. Concessioned hotels. Why not? If Cape Cod could be Number One for all of its own residual glitter, shouldn't Second Only be likewise appointed? So the Park Service invited public comment. And what did the public want? It wanted its apples and oranges in separate baskets. It wanted less development and fewer visitors. It wanted Cumberland as *Cumberland*, a place apart. Back to the drawing boards went the planners. Out went most of the jitneys and the glitter. Down came the "visitation ceiling" to 1,460 persons a day. Once more the Park Service invited comment—and got it, more than 4,000 letters and uncounted phone calls, most saying *phooey*. It was still all too much.

Now there is a new general management plan, and it is the last word on the matter for at least the next five to ten years. Now you have to stoop to get under the ceiling, which is fixed not at 1,460 persons a day but at 300. Two boatloads daily from St. Marys. And on the island, two stops only—one at the place called Dungeness, for the history buffs and the day-trip beachcombers; the other, a mile north at Sea Camp, the trailhead for hikers and backpackers heading up-island for the backcountry, the uppercase Wilderness, the gators in the sweetwater lakes, the ghost forest near Duck House, the old-growth tupelos at Red

Bridge, the Spanish moss and epiphytic ferns festooning the oaks of Yankee Paradise.

At Sea Camp, a Park Service ranger stands on the porch of the visitor center, assigning campsites to backpackers newly arrived from the mainland. There are questions. A visitor wants to know about diamondback rattlesnakes. He is advised to keep to the trails and watch where he puts his feet. Another wants to know where to find relief from pestiferous insects. She is advised to seek refuge on the beach. The visitors shoulder their packs and move out.

The center's architecture is tropical-rustic and low-slung. I like it. It does not look like government-issue. "Nice place," I say to the ranger on the porch. "It blends."

"Sure does," says the ranger. "You might even call it a case of adaptive restoration."

"This building?"

"This house," says the ranger. "It used to be Charlie Fraser's place."

Adaptive restoration of one kind or another has been the cultural leitmotif of Cumberland Island for a very long time. Before backpackers, before Fraser, before Oglethorpe and the Spanish, even before the Timucuan, men and women now called Archaic—for want of historic imagination—hunkered along Cumberland's backshore to dine on mussels and oysters and whatever else the sea brought forth. And each successive clan or generation adaptively restored the middens of its predecessors by adding to them, shell upon castaway shell. The Archaic people had deep roots on Cumberland Island. Some scholars say they roasted oysters here for 3,000 years.

The Timucuans were the last of the ancient line. They were here when the first white sails slipped out of the sunrise. In 1562, the Frenchman Jean Ribault tacked north from Florida along the Golden Isles. Having never seen Cape Cod, he decreed these southern lands to be "the fairest, fruitfullest, and pleasantest in all the world." And he declared them to be French, which angered the Spanish. So the Spanish built a fort on Cumberland Island, or San Pedro as they called it, and imported some friars to begin a new process of adaptive restoration—in this case, of the Timucuan soul. How well or poorly the priests fared in this endeavor is not a clear matter of record. In any event, the Tims were not long for this mortal world. In the seventeenth century, Guale Indians from the Carolinas, fed up with the English, came south to Cumberland and pushed the poor Tims into the sea. And on the heels of the Guales came the blue-eyed English, building forts at either end of the island and, for Oglethorpe and his subalterns, a hunting lodge they would call Dungeness.

For all the fort-building, Cumberland's isolation did not lend itself to great events. Some Redcoats staged up here on their way to seize Savannah for King George III. But most of the eighteenth-century shooting was strictly for meat. There were deer and birds galore, and succulent pigs gone wild from Spanish days. A Georgian outcast could cross the sound and live off the fat of the land, and more than a few did that. Then someone discovered an adaptive use for the great live oaks—as naval timbers. Cut and hewn, the oaks of Cumberland went down to the sea in ships. Now the sun beat down on clearings in the forest, and the clearings were restored into fields of Sea Island cotton and oranges and figs.

Of notables, the island has surely embraced more than its proportionate share. In 1783, General Nathanael Greene, the bluecoat hero of the Carolinas, acquired a stake in the island and proceeded to dabble in lumber and cotton and molasses. Somewhere near Oglethorpe's hunting lodge, Greene decided to build a Dungeness that one could really write home about. Four stories high it would be, and all of tabby, a kind of cement made of sand, lime, and oyster shells. Now this was adaptive restoration of a second or third kind, for rather than simply restoring old Oglethorpe's deer camp, here was Greene adaptively reusing shells from the ancient middens. Unfortunately, the general died in his forty-fourth year while the great manor was still a-building. Whereupon his widow, Catherine, married the plantation manager, one Phineas Miller, and together these two completed the project.

There is no record of claim that George Washington ever

slept at Dungeness, but Eli Whitney, the cotton ginner, did (thus, Lake Whitney at the island's north end), not to mention Light-Horse Harry Lee of Revolutionary fame. In fact, Lee died at Dungeness and was buried in the Greene-Miller cemetery until almost a century later, when someone decided the remains of old Light-Horse would rest more comfortably in Virginia, next to the grave of his son, Robert E. Lee. Meantime, Robert Stafford came to Cumberland to grow cotton. (Hikers trudging north from Sea Camp can still see the great fields where Stafford's slaves toiled under the hot Georgia sun.) But the cotton era was not long for this mortal world. One day Stafford's people looked out across the fields and saw a line of Union soldiers tramping up the oyster-shell road. And that was the end of it. The slaves were liberated and carried away to Amelia Island, Florida. The plantation—gone with the wind. Dungeness—in ruins, gutted by fire.

Carnegie would be the next great name to grace the island's roster. Not Andrew, the man of steel, but his brother Thomas, who purchased a spread here in 1881 and three years later laid the cornerstone of yet another Dungeness, and right on the ruins of the old one. Here began the Gilded Age of Cumberland, as Park Service historians like to call it, much to the disdain of surviving Carnegie heirs. But gilded it was. The huge Victorian manor house, with its turrets and massive chimneys. The forty other structures scattered roundabout: carriage house and greenhouse and smokehouse and icehouse, and a playhouse with swimming pool and squash court and billiard room and beauty parlor and barber shop. It took upwards of a hundred and fifty groundsmen and domestics—"The Hands," they were called—just to keep the place going. There were horses to ride, and carriages. There was "Squaw Town," where Carnegie ladies and friends dressed up as Indians and had a good time. There was Duck House for the shotgunners, way off in the dunes near the sweetwater lakes. There was music and laughter and lantern light. And sometimes a haunting notion of *déjà vu*, for Thomas Carnegie, like Nat Greene before him, would miss the best times. The Dungeness mansion was hardly finished when Carnegie died, leaving his widow and nine children. He was only forty-two.

As the children grew older, Lucy Carnegie acquired lands north of Dungeness and built satellite mansions at Greyfield and Plum Orchard and Stafford's old place. It was a lot to keep up. After Lucy's death, the windows of Dungeness were locked and shuttered and sheets were draped over sofas and wing chairs. Briefly in 1936 the big house was reopened for a family wedding; then once again shuttered and sheeted. *Déjà vu.* One night in 1959 there was a red glow in the sky over Cumberland Island, and in the morning Dungeness lay in ruins. Most folks blamed the fire on poachers from the mainland; but others, citing history, laid it to a curse.

Now, under National Park Service stewardship, the ruins of Dungeness—stone and mortar and brick, jagged façade and massive chimneys—remain much as they might have appeared when the smoke cleared away. After all, there are limits. One can adaptively restore only so many times at the same site. Let us call this, instead, a case of creative preservation.

It is a melancholy thing, to be here fresh and early in the morning before other visitors arrive. Behind the ruins, on the great lawn that once stretched a hundred yards to the flagstone edge of formal gardens, you can hear the wind in the palmetto, stroking the fronds—*tacata tacata tacatacuru.* The sky this morning is the color of slate. It seems to have no depth or dimension. The remnant chimneys are pasted upon it like cutouts. Like make-believe. But there is real life here, too. A large bird is perched atop one of the chimneys. A buzzard, it is. A turkey vulture. Suddenly the wings of the bird unfold and it soars above the lawn, looks me over, discerns that I am not ready yet for the morning's breakfast, circles higher, finds a thermal, and at last glides away toward the edge of the place where the day begins.

Greyfield overlooks Cumberland Sound about a mile north of the Sea Camp visitor center. It is an imposing white structure with a full front veranda and a red tin roof, and it sits well back from the oyster-shell road in a grove of girthy, contorted, moss-spangled oaks. Built at the turn of the century for a daughter of Thomas and Lucy Carnegie, Greyfield at the time of my visits remained a private enclave within Cumberland Island National Seashore. It had passed from one generation to the next, mother to daughter, Margaret Carnegie Ricketson to Lucy Ricketson Ferguson, who after 1968, first with her son and later her grandchildren, had managed the place as a country inn. No matter that the building is far less spacious and elegant than Dungeness might have been. Given its setting, its remoteness, its charms and southern comforts, Greyfield—as country inns go—was second to none.

The living room is at the end of the hall. It is paneled in dark wood and filled with heavy furniture and shelves of books with faded covers. The skull of a loggerhead turtle stares at you from a window sill. John James Audubon's American eagle perches in its frame over the fireplace. There is a portrait on the wall, an oil painting. The subject, a young woman in an aquamarine dress with a red scarf tied about her head. The face is thoroughbred classic, fair skin, dark eyes, high cheekbones. There are diamonds at the throat, just a small touch of class. It is a picture of a woman of beauty and privilege. And yet there are elements of the unexpected. There is a folded deerskin in the foreground. The bracelet is of braided elephant hair. And from the belt around the woman's waist hangs a hunting knife in a leather sheath. Who *is* this lovely lady? Is she some holdover Timucuan princess in Carnegie clothing, or some Carnegie princess in "Squaw Town" disguise?

"That's Grandma," said Gogo Ferguson, who was running the inn that year. I had just checked in. I was getting the tour. "She's Grandma to us, and to everyone else, Miss Lucy."

"When was it done?"

"In the twenties," said Gogo. "Must have been. Her age runs with the century. She's eighty-three."

"And lives . . ."

"Up near Stafford, You'll meet her."

"I'd like to," I said. "Why did she carry the knife? Or did the artist just put it there?"

"She skinned her own deer," said Gogo. "There's a story that Grandma believed you should never go anywhere on Cumberland Island without your knife."

"I don't have one."

"You don't need one," said Gogo Ferguson. "Not with Grandma around."

In the morning I went up the road to Miss Lucy's, past the oaks overreaching and the cottonless fields of Stafford. The house sat in a clearing. Dark wood siding and red tin roof, turn-of-the-century. Some of The Hands had lived here in earlier years. Now it was Grandma's place. I went through the gate and knocked at the door. And there was Miss Lucy, thoroughbred classic, three-score years off the Greyfield wall. "Come in," she said, "and I'll show you around."

We began with the photographs of yesteryear. Ladies with parasols, gentlemen in straw boaters and spats. There was a story to go with almost every frame on the wall. She remembered her great uncle Andrew, of Pittsburgh steel. He had come but rarely to Cumberland, never stayed long, and sat at the head of the dining room table. She remembered him there with his eyes closed. "And I didn't like that," said Miss Lucy, "because you know what he did? He always peeked out at us children from under his eyelids." Once, on a visit to Pittsburgh, an old man had told her: "Don't underestimate your grandfather. When there was a contract, a word was all you needed from Thomas Carnegie. Andrew had to sign on the dotted line."

Here in the next room is a picture of a nanny holding Miss Lucy's youngest daughter. "That woman was a hundred years old the day this picture was taken," Miss Lucy said. "She was very proud of her mother and father. They were on the last ship-load of slaves up the St. Johns River. Comesee Comodo—now don't try to spell it—that was her name. She never got used to glass. I used to take her with me in the truck. When she spit, it hit the windshield. She was wonderful." And perhaps there was another wonderful person among The Hands, somewhat earlier, because for several years Miss Lucy thought she might like to be a laundress when she grew up. Instead, she went away to boarding school and lived in Washington, D.C., and traveled abroad and married a Yankee. No doubt there was straight-and-narrow familial advice about the dubious wisdom of going home again to Cumberland Island. No doubt Miss Lucy listened, ladylike, and took it all with a scratchy grain of salt.

The photographs she had to show me were numerous, though not so numerous as the bones and skins and shells of animals that had been her friends and enemies over the years. There were alligator skulls and armadillo shells and snakeskins. They appeared to compete for display space with the parasoled ladies and the gentlemen in spats. As we passed among the relics, Miss Lucy paused to run her hand lightly over the skin of a long-gone diamondback rattlesnake. "This is my best one," she said. "It's seven feet long. It would have been longer, but I lost some when I had to cut off its head. *Had* to. It was eating my turkey eggs."

Apart from rattlers and coons, which likewise eat eggs of one kind or another, Miss Lucy appeared inordinately fond of all creatures great and small. Her Cumberland menagerie from time to time included kangaroos (imported from the Washington, D.C., zoo), a tapir, Sicilian burros, indigo snakes, and an assortment of birds, both exotic and native. Until recently, Miss Lucy had been at war with the National Park Service because it did not share her benevolent view of the island's free-ranging feral hogs and wild horses. That issue seemed to have been resolved—though more to the Park Service's satisfaction than to Miss Lucy's—by the final management plan. Under the plan, the hogs must go (through live trapping and removal to the mainland), but some of the horses may stay (if they behave themselves). "That Smokey Bear," said Miss Lucy, referring to her uniformed adversary, the Park Service. "When they first came out here, they wanted to get *all* the feral animals off the island. The horses, the burros, the hogs. And me. As far as Smokey was concerned, there wasn't much difference."

I saw Miss Lucy several times after that, over the course of separate visits to the island. Encountered at the wheel of her jeep somewhere along the oyster-shell road, or tending to affairs of family business in the kitchen at Greyfield, she always had some fresh and pungent observation to report—about making peace with Smokey Bear, about her plans to "go forward again" with the raising of indigo snakes, about the island. Always, about the island.

My last time out that way, she told me she was worried that beetles might be killing the pines of Cumberland, that the live oaks appeared under stress from accumulated drought. She said, "It's slow, but the island is changing."

"Well," I said, "don't let it."

And she said, "That's a good idea."

In the Summer of 1981, mid-July, lightning flickered over Cumberland Island and struck deep into pine-oak duff at the north end. It had been a dry year. The sweetwater sloughs had gone sour. Lake Whitney had sunk to a thin algal pool. In the forest, the fire spread fast through decades of accumulated leaf litter. Pushed along by forty-mile winds, it jumped the oyster-shell road. It raced into the canopies of longleaf and loblolly pine. It lunged toward the little community of homes at Halfmoon Bluff. Right away, someone got on a radio-telephone and rang up Carol Ruckdeschel in Atlanta. Ruckdeschel has a place at Halfmoon, out between Terrapin Point and Christmas Creek, and the caller told her she'd better get down to the island in a powerful hurry. She got in a car and drove all night. The fire lurched and swerved, then lit out in a different direction. The houses were spared, but the fire burned for two weeks—and over 1,600 acres. Folks unaccustomed to fires of this sort said that the north end would be a desert for years to come. Carol Ruckdeschel figured that was stretching it some.

She had been living at the north end, off and on, for about ten years when I first met her. She had worked as caretaker for the Candler family (the major north-end landowner, before the Park Service bought in), and later, with a background in amphibian biology, as a field naturalist under contract with the Smithsonian Institution to collect and analyze the ossified remains of sea turtles washed up on the beach. And, when I met her, she had just completed a follow-up study of the north end's recovery from the big burn of 1981. The study had found that the process of adaptive restoration is not necessarily confined to historic buildings and oyster middens.

For a year after the fire, Ruckdeschel and another researcher, H. B. Jordan, had monitored the recovery of seven distinct plant communities, visiting each at three-month intervals to see how well or poorly various species were bouncing back. They started in an area of pine-oak scrub where the fire had burned hottest. The pines here had suffered hugely, and many were goners. But by late fall, barely four months after the burn, sumac was sprouting out of the ashes, and palmetto a meter high had, as they described it, "changed the appearance of the area from one of devastation—black—to one of life—green." Devastation and rebirth. The sequence was much the same elsewhere, in other plant associations. Sawgrass—totally incinerated in July, two meters high by the following spring. Black gum sprouting, pawpaw in flower. And the best news of all came out of the sweetwater sloughs. The fire, burning organic muck, had lowered their bottoms, dredged them out, cleaned them up. The next generation of gators would be grateful for that. Of course, here and there were some long-term losses. A few pines here, a few oaks there. No matter. Something else would take their place. Something else always did.

One day I walked with Carol Ruckdeschel through the burned-over land at the north end. But for a few charred snags above the palmetto, you would never have known what had passed this way barely two years before. We followed a jeep trail past blueberry bushes ready to pop, and palmetto and wax myrtle and flowering lyonia so fragrant that Ruckdeschel declared she found the air intoxicating; and so did I. She pointed to a towering snag and said that an osprey had nested on it the year after the fire. The nest was still there, and so was the osprey. She poked into rainwater pools, searching for salamanders. And she said it was all coming back. As it always had.

Was there a lesson here? Yes, said Carol Ruckdeschel. When the lightning comes, let it burn. The land was meant to burn. It *had* to burn. If it did not burn, if Smokey raced north with his pumper to save the wilderness from itself, then the land would change, sooner than later, in ways Mother Nature never intended. Sure, get the people out. Protect the inholdings. But let it burn. The fire would put itself out, as it had before. And the gators would be grateful for it, and the ospreys, too. But wouldn't that fly in the face of conventional management? Carol Ruckdeschel thought about that for a moment and said, "I don't want to see them manage anything in the wilderness. I want to see this *one* island left alone."

In the late afternoon, I left Carol Ruckdeschel at the north end and went down the shell road past Plum Orchard to the fields at Stafford. Back in the oaks there, in sun-dappled shadow beyond the edge of the fields, were the remnants of Robert Stafford's slave quarters—seventeen sagging chimneys of tabby brick. Legend has it that Stafford, in a pique, burned the cabins to the ground to show the world what he thought of the black man's emancipation. Doubtless legend is unkind to the planter's memory, for archeologists have found no evidence that those cabins were ever put to anyone's torch. Rather, it is supposed that during or after the Civil War the structures were cannibalized for lumber, in order that their boards might elsewhere be adaptively restored as siding or fuel.

The day was getting on toward sundown. I left the slave-quarter ruins and crossed through the dunes to the beach. The tide had just turned around, sweeping its litter across the sand to the endless sea. A remarkable thing, the tide; a thing of accretion and depletion, of devastation and rebirth. In cosmic time—and that is the best time to go by when you are alone on a beach as long and wide as this one—nothing was likely to outlast the tide. Tabby chimneys could tumble and Cumberland crumble, but there would still be the tide. And with it a whisper of wind off the jade-blue sea.

REFUGES

Once there was a system, and it worked remarkably well. There was a time and a place for everything. There was water, there was land. The rains came. Rivers carved canyons to the sea. Grasses flowered on the savannas, sedges in the swamps. Trees shot up from the ferns and the mosses to challenge the lightning. The wind sowed pollen and seeds. Life moved. Life seemed to be everywhere. Fish and reptiles and birds and mammals, each in its own place. *Smilodon*'s cousin begat the jaguar. The silvertip bear stalked out to hunt elk on the short-grass plains. Bison moved through a forest where dawn shimmered fresh from the edge of the eastern sea. There were auks and heath hens and parakeets, kit foxes and key deer. And the only threat to these creatures was time, for the clock was running. No matter that cunning two-legged predators were moving across the land from the arctic gateway. No matter that these pennyskin people had a dreadful capacity to kill. They were too few to count. Even with firebrands and precipice stampedes thrown into the bargain, the system still worked; the ancient ones were a part of it. But the clock was running against the system where the dawn shimmered fresh at the edge of the eastern sea. In a tick or a tock—pale sails in the sunrise, pale skins on the beach. Then westward the star of empire as the system rolled back, yielding beaver hats and buffalo robes and pigeon breasts. And homesites.

Now there is a new system. It is called the National Wildlife Refuge System. It is one of the last resorts, a kind of monument to human repentance, a quitclaim to the bestial quick and the dead. For what we have left of wildlife in America—and for ourselves—this fractional, fragmented system, too, could work. If only we would let it.

Fractional it may be, but in aggregate the National Wildlife Refuge System is one large piece of the federal estate—more territory here, in fact, than is contained within that other great system, the National Parks. The refuges embrace nearly 140,000 square miles. In Alaska alone, they could just about swallow a spread the size of New Mexico; in Hawaii and the lower forty-eight, they could gird the likes of Vermont and New Hampshire with room to spare. There are, altogether, 772 separate units (counting waterfowl-production areas and lands managed cooperatively with state wildlife agencies). There are potholes and prairies, dismal swamps and tundra plains. If a person had the time and patience to see them all, he would encounter behind the sign of the flying goose—the refuge symbol—a range of land and life forms more diverse even than those so proudly hailed by the sign of the Park Service eagle or of Smokey, the foresters' bear. As systems go, in these post-Columbian times, there is nothing quite like this one anywhere else in the world.

Between the arctic range of the caribou and the palmetto retreat of the tiny key deer, from Moosehorn of Maine to Hanalei of Kauai, the refuges supply essential habitat to more than 800 species of birds and mammals, some 63 of which are considered endangered. To help sustain the whooping crane, there is Aransas in Texas; for the trumpeter swan, Montana's Red Rock Lakes. To succor the desert bighorn sheep, there is Kofa in Arizona; for the Everglade kite, Loxahatchee in Florida. Many of the refuges, sprinkled down the great migratory flyways of the continent, cater chiefly to waterfowl; others are managed for moose or elk, for pronghorns or bison. The largest refuge is Arctic National Wildlife Refuge, 18 million acres of wilderness in northeastern Alaska, summer range of the Porcupine caribou herd, home of the polar bear and the grizzly and the wolf, of lynx and marten and wolverine, of plovers and phalaropes and red-throated loons. And all the lesser places, though only in measure of size: Buffalo Lake and Bosque Del Apache, Chincoteague and Choctaw, Monomoy, Montezuma, and Muscatatuck, Kodiak and Quivira, Seedskadee and Salt Plains, Santee and Salton Sea. Links in a chain, jewels on a necklace.

Still, for all its superlatives, the refuge system endures a kind of identity crisis, such that many Americans do not even know the system exists. One outdoor traveler of my acquaintance—a person familiar with the scenic wonders of our most popular national parks, an aficionado of hot springs and alpine summits and storybook waterfalls—confesses that he is yet to set foot in a national wildlife refuge. Never got around to it, he says. For the record, I asked him to name a few of the refuges he might like to visit, when he got around to it. He could not name *one*.

Part of his problem, and ours, is imposed from within the system itself. The U.S. Fish and Wildlife Service, which administers the refuges, seems content to compete with the Bureau of Land Management for the distinction of holding the lowest profile of any resource agency in the federal government. There is a peculiar inattention to image and panache. Cecil Andrus, former secretary of the Department of the Interior, called it, with regret, "a commitment to anonymity." It is a sorry state of affairs, to be without substantial constituents.

Part of the problem lies beyond the control of the refuge custodians. This part is rooted in the way we look at wild places and wild things. The unfortunate fact of the matter is that most of us, like my friend, are collectors of waterfalls. We lean toward the bold and romantic. We expect Grand Tetons from the Black Hills, Acadia from Aransas. On our way to the purpled peaks, we pass unmindful of the duckweed potholes. In the presence of wetlands, we stifle the yawn, yearning for turquoise lakes. Beneath our abiding admiration for wildlife lurks a subconscious twinge of regret at the critters' indifference to any sense of human aesthetics. Why do so many of the most admirable beasts so often prefer the blandest or scratchiest settings on earth? For that matter, why can't a refuge look more like a park?

It takes time from a running clock to sort out the answers. The scratchiness has to grow on you.

For my own part, I was a late arrival to the National Wildlife Refuge System. The goose and I for years had been flying in opposite directions. I cannot begin to count the times I breezed past Brigantine, on the Jersey Shore, always heading for some other place; or sneaked past Seney, on Michigan's Upper Peninsula. I suppose I had collected a dozen waterfalls before I crashed the gates of my first refuge—Great Swamp, near Morristown, New Jersey—and then, only because it occurred to me that I might never again have the chance. Big thinkers were talking at the time of turning Great Swamp into an international jetport. It was thought to be a place better suited to airplanes than birds. As it turned out, the birds had more friends than the big thinkers ever imagined. And Great Swamp went on to become one of the first additions to the National Wilderness Preservation System. (As it also turned out, the jetport was not needed. New ones usually are not.)

My respect for the system grew after that, as well as my curiosity. I thought: If there could be such a splendid place as Great Swamp prevailing practically in the morning shadows of the towers of Manhattan, then what might the larger refuges be like farther afield? And one day, about as far afield as I could get, I sat beside the pilot of a bush plane flying northwest out of Bethel, Alaska, and for close to an hour looked down over one of the most unusual land forms in the world—the great deltaic flats athwart the Yukon and Kuskokwim rivers, 2.9 million acres of it within the boundaries of Clarence Rhode NWR. (Under the Alaska National Interest Lands Conservation Act, Clarence Rhode has since been incorporated into the much larger Yukon Delta NWR.)

Three thousand feet below us, the flats spread out like a great golden tarp splattered with water—sloughs and ponds and lakes and lagoons speckling the tundra plain. An in-over-your-head kind of place. Parachute down into that maze and you would likely need a lifetime to find your way out. Only the birds know how to do it faster. It was springtime in the delta. The birds were at their nests. Tens of millions of them. Shorebirds and passerines and waterfowl. Birds from Antarctica and Asia, from Central and South America. Trumpeter swans and emperor geese. Sandhill cranes and golden plovers. Terns and gulls, oldsquaws and brants and spectacled eiders. Nowhere else in the world, a Fish and Wildlife Service person had told me in Bethel, was there an area of similar size so critical to so many avian species. How many species altogether? And the birdman had said, in a slow cadenced count, "One . . . seven . . . seven." I did not ask about waterfalls, of which there are none.

Possibly my closest encounter with the true spirit of the flying goose came on another spring morning, though not so far afield, as I was driving through the cross-timbered grasslands of the Wichita Mountains NWR in Comanche County, Oklahoma. It was just after dawn. A rosy sheen gilded the rimrock. Patches of red cedar stood close on one side of the road, post oak sentinels faraway on the other. And grass—grass the way it must have been before cows and barbed wire. In the corner of my eye, then, an image shifted, as though one of the scrubbier oaks, far out, had picked itself up and moved. Then one more followed, and a third. I pulled the car onto the shoulder of the road and waited, watching, while the roselight tumbled out of the rimrock into the grass. Sure enough, now, and Birnam Wood was coming to Dunsinane right here in Comanche County, Oklahoma. The timber had feet. And as the light improved, I could see that the timber had other curious qualities. It had a big shaggy head and a hump over the shoulders. It had horn, and the horn glinted now under the rising sun. Bison. I could see ten, maybe twenty bison, far out and heads to the grass. A herd of bison come home to the grama and bluestem; not all the way home to the way it was before wire and railroads and wagons and wrathy pale riders with big-bore rifles, but home at least to where the old system had more or less ended, and the new had begun.

Someone was saying, and probably just the other day, that absence makes the heart grow fonder. It is a universal sentiment, though here in America we seem to have turned it into an art form of public policy. The negative action breeds the positive response. Pack the country folks into the cities, then render them parks to replace their lost fields. Clearcut the groves of Dunsinane, then call the second growth Birnam Wood National Forest. Slaughter the beasts, then (if you can) bring 'em back alive. Shoot first and ask questions later. The National Wildlife Refuge System evolved out of such a response. After 200 years of relentless shooting (and cutting and filling and fencing and plowing), folks of the fonder heart saw fit to ask questions.

In the beginning, at the buckskin beachheads, there was not time for questions; nor much inclination either, for there seemed to be this incredible abundance, this inexhaustible, movable feast of fish and flesh and fowl. Early sailcloth rovers saw it all through spyglasses from their poop decks and announced that they had arrived at the shores of plenty. And when the shores dried up, there was game to be had beyond the far ridge. In 1769, footloose Daniel Boone quit his pastoral piedmont and wandered out of North Carolina into "the wilderness of America." Across the Appalachians, in Kentucky, he encountered "everywhere abundance of wild beasts of all sorts" and buffalo "more frequent than I have seen cattle in the settlements." Yet barely forty years later, returning to the bluegrass from his new home in Missouri, Boone would wonder where it all had gone. "A few *signs* of deer were to be seen," he noted. But "as to the deer itself, I saw none."

It went fast. By 1820, the succulent heath hen was virtually gone from New England. The great auk—the "wobble," they called it, "such an admirable instrument for the sustentation [*sic*] of man" and once so plentiful that Atlantic seamen could sweep the birds into their longboats with boards—was gone forever by 1844. The Carolina parakeet, a nuisance in the orchards of the

Southeast, and the passenger pigeon, a dinner-table delight (whose peak time upon the national menu unfortunately coincided with the invention of refrigerators)—both birds scarce by the 1890s, both extinct by 1914. The sea mink of Maine and the Maritime Provinces—gone. The long-eared kit fox—gone. The Badlands bighorn sheep—gone. The jaguar—"el tigre," the continent's largest cat and once an established species as far north as the Red River of Arkansas—gone from its North American range. The timber wolf, bountied and loathed perhaps more than any other predator—gone from the East. The cougar—also gone from the East (though reports persist that a few have skulked back into remnant wilds). The grizzly—gone from the plains. All gone by 1914. On September 1, 1914, the last passenger pigeon in the world fell from its perch in a Cincinnati bird-cage and died of old age, or loneliness, perhaps. The obituary was brief, for the newspapers were filled those days with accounts of the Great War getting started in Europe. The other war that year—the one some pundit would later call the "bucolic holy war" against wildlife in North America—was beginning to wind down, if only because the weaker side had been suffering heavy casualties. And because people at last were asking questions.

Of all the biological battlefields, few, if any, raised quite so many pertinent questions—or garnered such positive responses—as the grassy ones of the West where, by the 1880s, the number of wild American bison had dwindled from historic tens of millions down to a precious few. To be sure, public reaction against the slaughter of birds for the plume trade was not inconsequential in turning the national head toward wildlife conservation. But that development came a bit later. The first jolt was felt on the plains in the 1880s, when folks heading west on the newfangled railroads gazed out through their parlor-car windows into a blinding whiteness of buffalo bones.

About thirty years was all it took to make the boneyards. First came the old beaver men down from the mountains, put out of plews by their own excess and the silk hat, now trading in buffalo robes. Next came the overland wagons; folks had to eat. And railroads with the likes of William F. Cody, who was said to have bagged 4,300 bison in eighteen months, just to keep the Kansas-Pacific road gangs in meat. In 1872, some enterprising chap discovered a way to tan bison hide into serviceable leather. Soon Dodge City was "the wickedest town in America"—not because of its mythic gunslingers, but because two-thirds of its 4,000 residents were engaged in the hide trade. The hides piled up at Fort Worth. Auctions moved as many as 200,000 a day. The hunter, Orlando Bond, boasted of having killed 300 "bluffers" in a single day—and there were hundreds like him. Bond was deaf. He had listened too much to his Sharps rifle. The Sharps, in a fifty caliber, could drop a buff at 1,000 yards. Among the Indians, it was known as the gun that "shoots today, kills tomorrow." The Indians were astutely correct. In more ways than one. Plucky Phil Sheridan, the bluecoat commander of the West, addressed the Texas legislature in 1875. Sheridan said that the hide hunters in two years had done more to settle the vexed Indian question than the entire regular army had done in the past thirty years. Sheridan said that the hidesmen were destroying the Indian's commissary. "Let them kill, skin, and sell," said Sheridan, "until the buffalo are exterminated. Then your prairies can be covered with speckled cattle and the festive cowboy, who follows the hunter as the second forerunner of an advanced civilization." Sheridan got his way. By 1903, the zoologist William T. Hornaday could count fewer than 1,000 bison remaining in the coterminous United States, and most of these were hand-fed relics, behind wire fences.

In time, a fence was erected in Comanche County, Oklahoma. This occurred shortly after President Theodore Roosevelt decreed that the Wichita Forest Preserve should also preserve game. In 1903, Roosevelt had already set aside three-acre Pelican Island, in Florida, as a sanctuary for colonial nesting birds. Then, in 1905, the Wichita unit would become the first refuge for four-footed creatures, and big ones at that. In fact, Bill Hornaday himself was to pick out fifteen feisty critters from his herd at the New York Zoological Park and, in 1907, ship them by rail to the Wichita Mountains. Comanche came on horseback to the depot to watch as the animals were unloaded. Some of the Indians were not even old enough to remember bison, much less recognize a living one.

The new system took a while finding its feet, somewhat in the fashion of a Bronx buffalo, seven days in a boxcar and suddenly loose in the Wichita bluestem. Presidents and Congresses were compelled to move cautiously in replicating the Pelican Island and Oklahoma precedents, especially when so many of their constituents clung to the utilitarian precepts of the passing frontier. Some folks, then, still believed in the gospel according to Cotton Mather: *What is not useful is vicious, amen.*

On the other hand, times and thinking processes were undergoing radical change at the turn of the century. There was a new preacher, albeit in spirit only, for he was dead now some twenty years. His name was Darwin. Natural science suddenly meant more than a split hair with a Latin name appended to it. Animals assumed an importance beyond their capacity to contribute to the "sustentation" of man. Among the urban gentry, a new breed was heading for the great outdoors. They called themselves "sportsmen." They believed in the gospel of Teddy Roosevelt and in the principles of fair chase. They lobbied for laws to put the game hogs and the poachers and the market gunners out of business.

But laws protecting fish and wildlife—even such a law as the Lacey Act, enacted in 1900 to prohibit the interstate traffic in birds or animals killed in violation of state statutes—were clearly not sufficient by themselves to restore some balance out there in the forests, fields, and streams of America. There had to be some kind of land base as well. There had to be habitat. There had to be refuges.

There *would* be refuges. With one foot on little Pelican Island and the other in the Wichita Mountains, the system stepped out. To the National Bison Range in Montana, in 1908. To the National Elk Refuge in Wyoming, in 1913. To the Upper Mississippi River Wild Life and Fish Refuge, in 1924. By 1925, there were refuges in twenty-four states. Here was a system of more than 4 million acres, and growing, where the concept of multiple use for a time would not prevail. It was the pleasure of Congress, and of the people, too, that the dominant use be for and by wildlife.

If the first two decades of the system's expansion seemed to foster a certain bias toward protecting such large wild ruminants as the elk and the bison, the third and fourth tipped decidedly toward the protection of migratory waterfowl. By the late 1920s, some species appeared to be following the long-gone Labrador duck into the great black hole of extinction. In the East, for example, the colorful wood duck was in heavy trouble, less the victim of wanton killing than of beaver extirpation: take away the beaver, no beaver dams; no dams, no backwater flooding; no flooding, no root-drowned snag trees; no snags, no nesting sites; no nests, no ducks. So it goes, and so it nearly went. But hunting, too, had its impact, and not just on wood ducks. Even with regulated bag limits, the rules at first played too liberally with marginal waterfowl species. And the blood sports were getting popular. A duck blind in the backyard and two canvasbacks in every pot. And one need not belong to the tweedbag elite in order to own a shotgun. Mass production had made the shotgun democratic. Then even the weather turned against the ducks. A great drought fell across the glaciated grasslands of the northern plains, and the sloughs and potholes that had not already been filled and plowed over for cropland began to dry up.

Negative action, positive response. In 1934, Congress passed the Migratory Bird Hunting Stamp Act, imposing on waterfowl hunters a one-dollar tax to finance the acquisition and management of wetlands for waterfowl habitat. The first federal legislation to create a special fund exclusively for wildlife conservation, the so-called duck stamp program got off to a shaky start. Large portions of the fund somehow got siphoned into the administration bureaucracy instead of wetland and refuge acquisitions. Understandably, the hunting fraternity raised a howl; and though it took quite a number of years for the howl to sink in, Congress at last, in 1958, earmarked the fund entirely for acquisition.

On the subject of hunting, one is tempted to overemphasize the excesses while undervaluing the very large contributions, both to the system itself and to the wildlife-conservation movement, that were made over the years by gentlemen of the hook-and-bullet persuasion. I resist. Heaven only knows how the early battles on behalf of wildlife might have gone had it not been for the help—in many cases, the leadership—of individuals who cherished the smell of gunsmoke and the taste of wild meat. Hornaday was a hunter, albeit an apostate one in his later gadfly years. George Bird Grinnell, editor of the influential nineteenth-century sporting magazine *Forest & Stream*, is often remembered as one of the founding fathers of that tweed-bag hunting fraternity, the Boone and Crockett Club, in 1887. Nonconsumptive types nowadays tend to forget that in 1886 Grinnell had also provided the inspiration for the first Audubon Society (whence an association later known as the National Audubon Society), and would go on to give Roosevelt a big push toward creation of the refuge on Pelican Island. Will H. Dilg, a Chicago publicist and evangelical outdoorsman, first conceived the idea of a big refuge athwart the Upper Mississippi, and later founded and led the Izaak Walton League in a crusade against a new fangled destroyer of the wildlife resource. This was in the 1920s, and folks then could hardly pronounce the name of what it was that worried the man. Dilg called it pollution. And then there was J. N. "Ding" Darling, a duck hunter and scattergun editorial cartoonist whose drawings were syndicated to 300 morning newspapers. His feverish editorializing for the protection of wildlife got him appointed head of the U.S. Biological Survey in 1934, from which eminence he established an additional 840,000 acres of refuges and helped engineer passage of the Duck Stamp Act.

If some contemporary people want to say, and they do: "All right, but the sports only did it in their own self-interest, to perpetuate the game"—fair enough, so long as the rest of us benefit. And we *do*. Same as the sedentary duck-blind sport benefits each time a footloose backpacker casts a vote for Wilderness, in order that he may leave his footprints on the ferns.

Does it matter? How important is wildlife anyway, if you still can have waterfalls? After all, you do not see the critters a whole lot of the time. I do not think I have ever seen a trumpeter swan, or an uncaged cougar in the West, and probably never will. But they are out there, somewhere. Maybe that is what matters. Maybe what matters is knowing that so long as there is wildlife somewhere—and I do not mean garbage-can raccoons and sub-urban whitetails—then somewhere there is wildness. There is wilderness.

The historian Roderick Nash once dissected the etymology of wilderness. He began with the word *willd*, meaning uncon-trollable in the Old Style Norse and Teutonic tongues. Then, from Old English, Nash extracted *dēor*, meaning animal or beast. Putting those two words together, after dropping an *l* and a *d*, he came up with *wildēor*, which appears in *Beowulf* "in refer-ence to fantastic, monstrous creatures that live in a dark slimy pool in the forest." Whereupon Nash felt that the derivation was about as clear as it could be. *Wildēor* contracted to *wilder*, then prefixed to *ness*, meaning quality, thus yielded *wilderness*—the quality of being a place of wild beasts. By the logic of etymology, therefore, wildlife refuges should be foremost in the fonder hearts of those who appreciate wilderness. And if there must be waterfalls, too, and I hope there always will be, then let there be something fantastic lurking in the pool at the foot of the cas-cade.

True wilderness folks understand this connection. Aldo Leopold defined it best while describing the autumn landscape of the North Woods, and how it all added up to "the land, plus a red maple, plus a ruffed grouse." In terms of physics, he figured that the grouse represents but one-millionth of either the energy or the mass of an acre. "Yet subtract the grouse," wrote Leopold, "and the whole thing is dead."

THE NEEDLE OF THE EYE

Mile Zero and we're heading south, all buckled up in a brown sedan. Fahrenheit Zero, too, just in case I might try to forget where it is that I am. I am in Michigan, way up in cul-de-sac Michigan with my tailpipe to the Soo. It is a bit past noon. Thin clouds overhead and patches of ice on the highway. The mileage under the speedometer reads zero-seven-nine-one-four. The maps show forty-two miles to the Mackinac Bridge, eighteen hundred to Miami. Pit stops upcoming in or around Saginaw, Detroit, Toledo, Cincinnati, Lexington, Knoxville, Chattanooga, Atlanta, Macon, Tampa, Fort Myers. The Dixie Highway, they called some part of this road in flivver days. Now it's Eye-Seven-Five, though most folks bat the Eye and call it up by the numbers. 75. It's faster that way, it's aerodynamic, it's undifferentiated Interstate modern. Two digits and you're done with it, just like that.

"And you'll be returning it when?" asked the clerk at the rental car check-out.

"Friday," I said. "In Miami, Florida."

"I don't think we've ever had a drop in Miami," she said. "From here, people fly."

"But you can't see the country that way."

"This time of year, why bother?" she said. "You know what I mean?"

Sure, I knew what she meant. But how could I possibly explain what I meant by driving eighteen hundred miles from Sault Ste. Marie to Miami, in the dead of winter, to commemorate the thirtieth anniversary of the Interstate Highway System, to kick it around a little, and to see to what extent it was showing its age? So I said, having just arrived by winged craft, "I have a fear of flying."

"Good for you," she said. "Do you take the liability, or just the collision?"

It is a fine road up here, straight-out and flat-out across the farmland of Chippewa County. The best of it, in season, produces hay. Racehorses grow taut and saucy on Chippewa hay, and I-75 is a handy conduit for getting that golden fiber into the thoroughbred bluegrass country around Lexington, Kentucky. A heavy-footed hay-trucker could start his day up here with an Upper Peninsula pasty pie for breakfast, and end it with grits for dinner in Dixie. Could, that is, if he got beyond the sanitized fast-food emporiums hugging the cloverleafs. Life, someone once observed of expressway travel, begins at the exit ramp.

And what a dull life it would be if we didn't have these Interstates to blame for a lot of lingering grief in the domestic affairs of the nation. For my own part, I am glad enough to have these highways for convenience, for efficiency of movement, and—even at 55 miles per hour—for husbandry of time. They get you there, and without too much pain. Shots of linear Novocain, that's what they are. Lifesavers, too. Still, putting convenience and safety aside. I can think of a hundred and one reasons to rue the Interstates—the mountains scarred, the plains puckered, the waterfronts riprapped, the wetlands filled, the streams rechanneled, the sanctuaries breached, the farms gerrymandered, the suburbs trashed, the city centers skewered, the towns passed by, the railroads abandoned, the subways not built, the flavors of human differentness flattened under standardized panache, and the franchise a run-amok monster. More than any other phenomenon of our time, the Interstate Highway System has irrevocably altered the way America must see itself. Some folks don't much like what they see. Others do. Me, I figure it's time for another look.

So why must I-75 take flak for the System's faults? After all, it's only one of dozens of federal expressways, and reflects but five percent of the System's overall miles. I suppose I could have picked one of the long coast-to-coast highways—say, I-80—in order to pay my grudging respects to Dwight Eisenhower's *Autobahnen*. But that would have been too much Novocain. No, I-75 should be just about right. Apart from its systemic flaws, it has almost everything. It has the North Woods up here (or will, as soon as I get out of these snow-covered hayfields). It has the Appalachians. The big rivers—the Ohio and the Cumberland and the Tennessee; and the smaller ones—the Au Sable, the Rockcastle, the Chattahoochee, the Suwannee. The great wetlands—the Big Cypress and the Everglades, what's left of them. And it has all of these Class A industrial cities in between, the Rust Belt hitched to the Sun Belt by this thread of concrete. Matter of fact, I-75 was the very first "border-to-border" highway completed in the Interstate Highway System. That was in 1977, before the highwaymen decided to push I-75 beyond Tampa. Then, the last segment to be opened was near Marietta, Georgia. President Jimmy Carter telephoned the celebrants from Plains, saying with unabashed provincialism that this very road was "the most important Interstate route in the nation."

I suppose it is, to some people. It is to me, though not for any practical, conventional reason. I don't live within five hundred miles of I-75, and never have. But once upon a time, before there even was an I-75, I lived about five miles from a Cincinnati creekbottom the highway would follow on its way to the big river. So it was the *corridor* I knew, then. It was U.S. 25, the original twisty, two-lane Dixie Highway, that I remember. It crossed the Ohio on John Roebling's great suspension bridge and then lit out for bluegrass and Dan Boone country, on the same track more or less that the Interstate takes today, and as soon as you got over the first hill south you could smell horses and fresh hay all the way into Lexington. Going the other direction, north, it was old U.S. 127 I remember, a bit to the west of the Dixie Highway. That one took off for the paper-birch, pine-scented woods of Michigan, where my folks had a summer place in the thirties. We seemed to be oriented in those two directions, in those motorcar days. A black motorcar, I recall, with a gleaming silver ram's head poised front and center on the fold-up hood, and my father at the wheel, going on at length (and apocryphally) about the great events and heroes of the country we were passing through. That limestone ledge up there? Now that's where Boone got away from the Shawnees. That crooked pine tree, edge of the bluff above the lake? Well that's the famous *L'Arbre Croche*, landmark for the *voyageurs* our of Michilimackinac. Incredible. That one could learn so much, however skewed, and imagine so much, on a trip down a two-lane road. North or south, this was the corridor that hatched my incubating interest in the out-of-doors, the axis on which I spun my earliest impressions of history's landscape, the center stripe on my sense of place.

And now, this. The old gray meridian, she ain't what she used to be.

For this, we can thank The Sumerians. If the Sumerians had not invented the wheel, the Romans, much later, would never have lifted a finger to build the world's first system of engineered roads. The Romans gave the wheel a big boost in the fight against friction; they discovered how to make a rough way smooth with stone blocks, and flint gravel for topdressing. Then they invented the divided highway. The *Via Appia*—the "queen's road" that reached from Rome toward the East—had one-way lanes down the outside, stone curbs for dividers, and a fast lane, the *cursus rapidi*, straight down the middle. The Romans were high rollers when it came to roads, just as we are. You don't build an Appian Way and leave it at that. You build a Cassian Way and a Valerian Way and a Postumian Way and an Aurelian Way, and before you know it you have an interprovincial system of paved Ways stretching out across 53,000 miles, which, by rough linear measure, would beat our own Interstate Highway System by the length of five and one-half I-75s. Some of those ancient roads are still around. Come the Year 4000, will ours be?

Come the next decade, will ours be? That's what some people are wondering. The Interstate Pothole System, they call it. And out come the deadly statistics to score the point: 40 percent of the infrastructure already over the hill, and not yet thirty years old; bridges crumbling, pavements heaving, the cost of maintenance doubling every ten years, outstripping infusions of new and higher gasoline-tax revenues; purveyors of shock absorbers and front-end alignments laughing all the way to the bank.

Up here in the Frost Belt, things could be a lot worse. Sure, I feel a surficial crack now and then, enough to remind me that there is something about ice that never meant to let concrete last forever. But I haven't come all this way to do pothole patrol. I have better things to chase, such as Chippewa farmland giving way to Mackinac forest, the jagged boreal skyline, spruce and cedar and tamarack and aspen, the scratchy look of the North Woods, the Straits coming up, the long bridge, a giddy acrophobic feeling so high above the water, Lake Huron to the left of me, Lake Michigan to the right. And now the memory of old familiar summer places, the Shore Drive and Seven Mile Point off there to the west at the edge of the great blue lake, the cabin, the path going down the side of the bluff to the dunes, the icehouse under the sugar maples, and the watercress swamp way back in the endless woods on the other side of the gravel road. There is a temptation to have a peek, to make a detour down memory lane. No. Not this time. I have promises to keep. And miles to go for a franchised sleep.

This is good country, northern Michigan. The unfortunate fact of the matter is that it may be too good, for people who used to define goodness in proportion to their own proximity to spas on the Atlantic or snow slopes in the West are now—thanks to

I-75 and a handful of puddle-jump airports—elbowing the regional gentry aside in their haste to replace an old-style Kennebunk or Vail with a newfangled Petoskey or Nubs Nob. Things are crowding up, changing fast. One lonely reach of golden lakefront that stretched two miles south from our old place, and with nary a shack or castle on it, is now cluttered with cottages in the dunes. Summer subdivisions are sprouting in the second-growth woods. Harbor Springs, once home port to a fleet of flaky gray fishing boats with windchapped men in faded overalls and black rubber boots, has become a place of chic boutiques and fern bars filled with Yuppies in Lands' End twills. Not that I-75 should take the full rap. Fern bars would have found their way up here sooner or later, even without an Interstate Highway System. As for the end of the old lake trout flotilla, we must address the lamprey eel and decades of overfishing, not bulldozers and concrete. And I suspect that what happened within the right-of-way may turn out, when all the votes are in, to be the least of it.

The thought occurs in the gathering dusk of this Michigan evening that I should be much obliged to the much-maligned Interstate Highway System, for it helped to make a card-carrying conservationist of me. And I am not alone in owing such a debt of negative gratitude. I know a dozen ecofreaks who honed their eyeteeth on the barricades of the highway wars, *Ante Terra Dies*. Before Earth Day. Consider my perspective on it.

It is the turbulent decade of the 1960s. The Interstate Highway System—or, rather, the National System of Interstate and Defense Highways, as it is called in the generic legislation—is already sufficiently rich, thanks to the Highway Trust Fund, to be putting down horizontal concrete in almost every state of the Republic. And there is something about horizontal concrete that was never meant to make most people like it, especially if the concrete is being poured, or there are plans to have it poured, into a person's much-beloved neighborhood, cornpatch, or park. It is not like air or water pollution. You don't need a Ph.D. in chemistry to understand and fear the trickle-down effects of horizontal concrete in your backyard or back forty. To be sure, there are a few uncomplicated glamour issues waiting to be championed by folks of the environmental persuasion. You like trees, you can get excited about those redwood clearcuts in California. You like red rocks and roaring rivers, you've got the Grand Canyon to keep undammed. You live in New York and revere the Hudson Highlands, or in San Francisco with affection for the wilder Sonoman shores, okay—you can get madder than hell at the power brokers' schemes to dig holes at Storm King and Bodega Head. But what about all these other folks whose personal bias runs toward natural things, who do not have Storm King or Bodega or a Ph.D. in chemistry, who perhaps have been frustrated in their pursuit of political causes, such as bringing civil rights to the South or peace to Vietnam, who are asking not what their country can do for them but what they can do for their country, and who are practically dying to lock horns with an adversary just as loathsome as a redneck sheriff or a redwood logger? You've got it! *They've* got it. The Highwayman.

The Highwayman seemed to be everywhere in the 1960s-turning-1970s. He was a tiger at the gates of Franconia Notch in New Hampshire's White Mountains and of Overton Park in Memphis, Tennessee. He had scuttled the Schuylkill at Philadelphia and the Brandywine at Wilmington. He had folks up in arms in Cleveland and Chicago and Denver, in Milwaukee and Seattle and New Orleans. He wanted to fill in the blanks on the maps. He wanted the Sunken Forest at Fire Island and the alpine meadows of Mineral King. He wanted to open the roadless backcountry. It wasn't enough that this 42,500-mile Interstate Highway System was abuilding. That one wasn't half-built before the U.S. Commerce Department was talking about *another* system—100,000 miles of scenic roads and parkways, and a quarter of the projected mileage through places never before serenaded by the tappets of internal combustion. Driving for pleasure was America's No. 1 outdoor recreation, said Commerce. It was time for the birdwatchers to get off the backs of the road-builders, opined *Engineering News-Record*, official mouthpiece of the pavement industry. Anyone with a slide-rule sense of esthetics knew that roads didn't destroy natural beauty. They took people to it, and sometimes even *created* it.

Much as I hate to admit it, I had to agree with part of that—the getting-to-it part, not the creation part—for hadn't I been taken to the natural beauty of the North Woods and Bluegrass Dixie by roads? Smaller roads, true; but roads nonetheless. Yet because of that experience, here I was, 1960s-turning-1970s, locking horns with the Highwayman over a patch of wooded hills and hollows in my adopted community's backyard. Highwayman wanted to skewer *my* woods with a road called the Richmond Parkway. It wasn't a full-blown Interstate, but rather an intraurban connector between I-95 and I-278, a four-lane shortcut from New Jersey to Long Island, using my burgh, Staten Island, as linkage. Its architect: none other than the Grand Dragon of Highwaymen, the Master Builder and Power Broker himself, Robert Moses. With the help of the New York State Department of Transportation, the Federal Highway Administration, and a handful of troglodytic pols, Moses was determined to create natural beauty on Staten Island by pouring concrete across a de facto greenbelt that happened to embrace one big undeveloped city park, a nature center, two summer camps, and the top of a hill said to be the highest point on the Atlantic Coast between Maine and Carolina, as well as such salubrious secret places as Bloodroot Valley, Buck's Hollow, and Hourglass Pond. This clearly was a case where what happened within the right-of-way would *not* have been the least of it.

Many, many years ago that was, when the fight began, and I am long gone from that place, too. But the greenbelt isn't. The greenbelt lives. We were but a handful of conservation bush leaguers in the beginning, but we and our successors at the barricades stopped Moses's parkway in its unpoured tracks, dug in, and held fast while the cost of war in Vietnam, inflation, recession, oil embargoes, shifting priorities, increasing levels of environmental literacy, and massive defections from the troglodyte camp slowly eroded any reasonable chance that a four-lane divided highway would ever threaten the heart of the Staten Island greenbelt again.

I do not gloat. To gloat might bring bad luck to the greenbelt, and I would never want that. Right now, all I want is a warm and safe haven for the night, franchised or disenfranchised, a loaf of bread, and a jug of wine to toast the Highwayman. As follows:

Saludos, Old Bean. And many thanks. Not for what you did or didn't do to land or life-styles. We'll come back to that later. I mean thanks for giving us a bumper crop of bona fide *Ante Terra Dies* tree-huggers. And that includes me, for certain.

Day II and an inch of new snow, falling still. A whiteout in the wake of every passing truck. Whoops. Take it slow now. There's plenty of time. We're out of the North Country. The pitch and toss of timberland has given way to a supine calm. Big barns stand braced against the sky at the corner of every quarter-section. We have entered the region known contemptuously to northerners as Down Below. Checkoff Standish, Pinconning, Bay City, Saginaw, Frankenmuth, and Clio. Here now the outskirts of Flint. Wouldn't you really rather have a Buick? No, I would rather have a cardboard cup of coffee, or a cup of cardboard coffee, whichever comes sooner. Off at the Pierson Road exit and cruising. Here's Muffler Man Hardee's Double D Market Dambros Rental Center Sarah's Buffet Goodyear Union 76 K Mart Friendly Food McDonald's Best Western Burger King Wendy's. Each in its own corporate shell. Corporal, line these imposter architects up against that wall. No final words, no last cigarettes, no blindfolds. Let them see what they have wrought.

City of Pontiac coming up, city of Pontiac going by. And now Detroit, home of King Car, the city that pretty much started it all. Here's Chrysler Freeway. Here's the Reuther Freeway and the Ford Freeway and the Fisher Freeway, each memorializing a leading figure in the 20th-Century crusade to put a car within reach of every red-blooded American. Not that they ever quite succeeded. But they sure worked hard to come close.

If I had to pick a date and a place and say, Here began the ascent of King Car up the long road to the throne room, without hesitation I'd pick the first day of August 1903, New York City. On that day in that city a gentleman in a dirty, white, calf-length duster stepped out of a horseless carriage and informed a cluster of newsmen there assembled that he had just driven his strange-looking machine all the way from San Francisco. How long did it take? someone asked, knowing that a train took four days (but not knowing what Orville and Wilbur Wright were up to down at Kitty Hawk, because *that* wouldn't happen for another five months). The man in the duster puffed up his chest a bit, stared out across the heads of his audience as though he were about to reveal the fate of mankind and the destiny of the Western World, and then, finally, said: Sixty-nine days! The crowd cheered. Before the year was out, before Orville could fly, another gentleman put on a duster and drove *his* flivver across the country. In only *fifty-three* days.

It was a miracle that a machine could make it across at all. Not that there weren't roads enough. Good heavens, there were plenty of roads. The Office of Public Road Inquiries of the United States Department of Agriculture took a census the very next year (1904) and announced that, apart from city streets, America had a bit more than 2,150,000 miles of rural roads. Trouble was, only the 150,000 were what you might called "improved." The remaining 2,000,000 were plain old dirt—sand, some places; mud, most other places months at a time. Of the so-called improved roads, maybe two-thirds had topdressings of gravel. Most of the rest of it, improved, was oystershell or crushed rock or clay. And a hundred miles or so were paved solid. Brick, mostly. There wouldn't be a single unincorporated rural mile of two-lane Portland cement for another four years. But then who—apart from a travelin' man looking to get his head and feat into the book of records—who really cared that much that America wasn't making its rough ways smooth? In 1904, in the entire nation, there were only 55,000 registered motor vehicles. Of course most folks thought that was a lot. In 1899 there had been fewer than 5,000.

Possibly the first great American highway visionary of the au-

tomotive age was Carl Graham Fisher of Indianapolis (no rela-
tion to the "Body" Fisher of Detroit). Old C. G. was a man of
much energy, and he applied it vigorously over the years to such
endeavors as manufacturing automobile batteries, co-founding
the Indianapolis Speedway, and investing speculatively in a
mangrove swamp soon to be known as Miami Beach. But
Fisher's true passion, his mission in life, was to pick America up
by its axles and pull it out of the mud. Toward that end, in 1911,
he issued a rousing call for construction of a "hard rock" highway from coast to coast, from New York to San Francisco—
"one magnificent highway," he would write later, to "stimulate
as nothing else could the building of enduring highways everywhere." He turned to his peers and colleagues and asked for
help. The president of Goodyear Tire and Rubber Company
gave Fisher $300,000 and promised more. The president of
Lehigh Portland Cement Company said his industry might contribute three million barrels of cement. Soon Thomas A. Edison
took an interest in the project, and H. B. Joy of the Packard Motor Car Company, and young Edsel Ford (Papa Henry abstain-
ing). There weren't any state highway departments to speak of
in those days, and no one really expected the federal government
to help. So do-it-yourself was the only way to go. To capture the
public's attention, Fisher and his friends invoked the name of
Abraham Lincoln. Their road would be known as the Lincoln
Highway. It would light out from Philadelphia on the Old Plank
Road left over from Dutch Colonial days. It would follow the
Lancaster Turnpike of frock coat times. Across the Ohio, Indian
trails would take it west toward Chicago. Beyond the Missouri,
it would pick up the Oregon Trail in the Valley of the Platte. Beyond the hardrock mountains it would aim for Great Salt Lake
and the Overland Stage route to California.

But do-it-yourself just couldn't get it done. A bit was completed here and there, even long stretches where folks weren't
too anesthetized by county politics. Progressive Iowa, for example, completed its share of the Lincoln Highway wall to wall.
Eventually, after passage of the first Federal Aid Road Act in
1916 and subsequent acts, Fisher's dream came true. U.S. 30

defines the way from Philadelphia to Chicago. Beyond that it's nonstop Interstate all the way. Forgive us, Mr. Lincoln, but we call it *80*. Two digits and you're done with it, just like that.

South of Toledo, down the western side of the Buckeye State almost to Dayton, the land tries to trick you into thinking you are somewhere else. Maybe Indiana or Illinois, for all the corn stubble above a veneer of snow, and wide-open fields, each side, reaching to a faraway line of winter-bare trees. There was a time, and not so long ago at that, when I held this kind of country in contempt. Born a hill person, spoiled by a few boreal lakeside summers and briefly exposed to other exotica, such as hard-rock mountains, I had allowed myself—when contemplating agricultural flatlands—to embrace the predictable response of an effete, card-carrying physiographic snob. I found flats like these, in a word, flat. They were a dreadful inconvenience, taking up valuable space between wherever I happened to live and wherever it was in exotica I was aiming to visit. And they took so *long* to cross. It was enough to make one pray for a four-lane divided highway, and no speed limit, just to get it all behind you in a hurry. Wouldn't you know. About the time my landscape values took a turn for the better, a deviant prayer got answered. Here was I, at last savoring the intrinsic beauty of good flat food-producing land set among shimmering deciduous shelterbelts, and there was Highwayman, pouring concrete through the amber waves of grain. So it goes. The most I can be thankful for is that some Arabs put the lid on our speed limit.

Here we are past Lima already, past Bluffton and Beaverdam and the road west to Delphos. And how about *that*? It's U.S. 30, the old Lincoln Highway. Coming up on Wapakoneta, home of the first man to walk on the moon, the Neil Armstrong Air and Space Museum right beside the exit here, the parking lot empty, closed until March 1. Too bad to miss a good thing, for this is an Ohio Historical Society museum, and those folks do it right. One of the very best historical museums I have ever seen is another society showcase halfway across the state near Zanesville, and, curiously enough, hard by the boyhood home of yet another pioneer astronaut, John Glenn. That museum eschews the aerospace motif and concentrates instead on two Earthbound themes—the life and times of the hometown hero and western wordslinger, Zane Grey, and the story of the National Road, which was the very first federal road ever, long before anyone dreamed of Portland cement and automobiles, or even the steam locomotives for that matter. Pretty soon now, once we get down past Sidney and Piqua and Troy, we'll be intersecting the corridor of that ancient and historic byway, too. That's Ohio for you. More first-time astronauts and classic crossroads than any other state in the Union.

It has been said that North America's pioneer road-builder was the buffalo. In the forested East, where its range once extended to the Appalachian piedmont, the buffalo traced paths of least resistance, making its way from water to grass, from stamping ground to salt lick. Wherever the wild hoof went, there in time the moccasin followed. And after the moccasin came the boot and the wheel. Old-timers, pressed to explain how a certain road came to be where it was, had the answer down pat. "It was the Buff'ler, the Injun, and the Injuneer," they'd say. "And the one just plain followed the other." So it was with the beginning of the National Road.

The beginning was in Maryland, at the confluence of Wills Creek and the Potomac. The city of Cumberland sits there now; then, 1752, an outpost of the Ohio Company of Virginia. At that point, barely eighty miles separate the Potomac from the Monongahela—not counting vertical distance getting over the mountains. And the Virginians had a powerful urge to get over the mountains to trade with the Indians of the western waters. So they hired the Delaware chief Nemacolin to blaze a path for them. Young George Washington followed Nemacolin's trail in order that he might instruct the French to cease and desist in the Ohio Valley. He was not successful. Neither was General Edward Braddock, who, heading west, employed five hundred axmen to make the path wide enough for his wagons and artillery. On the hasty return trip, the Redcoats were obliged to bury their general in the roadbed, so that the ruts of retreat might obscure the grave from the eyes of desecrating pursuers. (A few years later, British General John Forbes did succeed in ousting the French from the forks of the Ohio. Forbes marched to victory along a path occupied today by the Pennsylvania Turnpike, otherwise known as I-76.)

That so tainted a way as Braddock's road-to-ruin should become the initial entry in a national transportation system was largely the doing of G. Washington of Virginia. In 1784 Washington perceived a second nation of transmontane settlers "groaning" under the "inconveniences of a long land transportation." He saw them standing on a pivot—the touch of a feather, he said, capable of inclining them, commercially or politically, toward the bayou Spanish or the Michilimackinac Brits. America, said Washington, must "open a wide door and make a smooth way" that the produce of Kentucky and western Pennsylvania might find its way back across the mountains to friendlier markets.

The wide door was a long time opening. Treasury Secretary Albert Gallatin got his toe in the crack in 1802 by suggesting that a portion of the proceeds from sale of public lands in the Northwest Territory be used for the construction of roads to and through the states-to-be. The enabling act admitting Ohio to the Union the following year was contingent on such a provision. Inevitably, there was much interstate haggling as to where, other than at Cumberland, a road to Ohio might begin; and much constitutional debate as to how far, if at all, the federal government might go in helping the states with their internal improvements. It was 1811 before construction of what was then called the Cumberland Road began; 1818 before the road reached the Ohio River at Wheeling. Meanwhile, Ohio was clamoring for extension of the road on its side of the big river. Its cause was soon championed by the great expansionist himself, Henry Clay of Kentucky, who had visions of a manifestly destined republic bound together by an overland road. In 1825 the road took off across Ohio, overland for sundown.

The road was thirty feet wide and paved with interlocking pieces of limestone. Macadam, folks called this newfangled pavement, after John Loudon McAdam, its Scottish inventor. By 1833 the road had reached Columbus. And on it went, across the state line to Indianapolis and Terre Haute. Soon there was talk of taking it across the Mississippi into Missouri, or maybe even to the hard-rock shining mountains of the wagon-train West. But even as the road proceeded in that direction, the federals discovered that maintaining the existing roadbed was too expensive. So they handed the highway back to the various states through which it passed and said, You do it. The states tried to do it with tolls. In the East, the cracks in the road grew wider. West, the road scudded to a halt halfway across Illinois. Something was up. Something new was on the wind. It was steam—overland steam and the hoofs of an Iron Horse clanging the rails.

And here it comes. Not the Horse, obviously. Alas, for serious transportation, we have been forced to abandon both Old Horse and Iron Horse. I mean here comes the corridor of the first overland road to the West. Here comes U.S. 40, the successor of the National Road, and, just beyond and paralleling it, I-70, up there on the overpass, flicking its shadow across the hood of my car as I skedaddle for Dayton. Sun's getting low, foot's getting heavy. Good-bye, I-70 and U.S. 40. Goodbye, Old National, Old Toll Pike. And Good-bye, Dayton. I'm hell-for-leather for the ancestral seven hills of a riverside city crowned Queen of the West when the West was East. Porkopolis, the burghers called their town when it was hog butcher of the world. Now it's just *Sin-sin-naughty*.

When Interstate comes, can anything once familiar ever be the same? The names of streets and neighborhoods remain, but the perspective from the highway is as strange as a journey across the landscape of a dream. I have been here many times over the years, yet I do not recognize a single landmark. It might be Detroit or Dayton, though that's not true. The time and license plates give it all away. At 5 o'clock of a workday afternoon, with every other southbound car bearing Kentucky tags, where else north of the Ohio River could I possibly be?

Just in case, though, I am going to make sure. One exit shy of Mitchell Avenue I turn into the Norwood Lateral to get a bit closer to the precincts of youth. A detour, I confess; a deliberate break from my self-imposed plan to follow only the mainline of I-75. The Lateral takes me east through cut-and-fill toward I-71. I know of these places the signposts say I'm passing. I remember them, but not like this. Paddock Road, yes. But where are the paddocks? This boulevard called Montgomery—where now the overhead trolley wires? Streets I once traveled no longer connect. Chain-link fences interdict them along the highwalls. I am traveling through the sub-cellars of eminent domain. Where did all the people go? Before the cut and the fill blew them away, did we ever meet? Just once did I bat an eye at one of them from the window of a passing car? That one there, sitting in my imagination in his summer undershirt, on the front stoop. What was his name? How long had he lived here when they broke the news to him—a map on page one of the *Post*, the dotted line impaling his neighborhood? Then the knock at the door and the talk of appraisal. Not *this* house! he said. He had lived here all his life and they would have to bury him with their bulldozers. But in the end, he moved. Hundreds moved. Across the country, through three decades of right-of-way acquisition, *hundreds of thousands* moved. It was all for the greater good, there were told. It was for America. Ask not what you can do for your country, just get out of our way.

Bound for the big river now on I-71, Edwards Road coming up, Dana Avenue, what used to be Duck Creek winding off on the left. A hillside with little frame houses. Then a steep wooded hollow running off to the south. That was *our* hollow, once. It was ours without owning it because we played there. Sticks and stones and puppydog bones, in that hollow. Furtive Indians and shadowy figures in fringed buckskins, rifles snugged in the crooks of their arms. And tin hats and BB guns and once or twice, shamelessly, a lucky shot at a lovely bird. I am surprised that Highwayman did not choose our hollow to save a mile getting I-71 down toward the river and its rendezvous with 75. I know nothing of engineering such a thing. Probably it was not feasible.

Still, for practically a full mile, there wasn't—and likely still isn't—a whole lot in the way except for sycamore trees and sumac thickets. So just suppose Highwayman *had* decided to come this way, down through the hollow, and I had been kicking around here then, looking for trouble. To defend these hallowed grounds would I have rushed to the barricades, proclaiming the hollow a natural area blessed with biological diversity and urging an alternate route, perhaps the route now taken, the one trailing memories of little frame houses with stoop-sitters in summer undershirts? Would I have argued that you can relocate people but not sycamore trees? Disturbing questions, and I have no answers for them. I *want* no answers for them. It is all settled. The people have been relocated, and the hollow has been left to its own free pasturing. So I-71 carries me down through Cincinnati to an Interstate merger with I-75 just west of where that big white flying saucer has landed—the one called Riverfront Stadium—and together the two Eyes cross as one over the River Ohio into Covington, Kentucky, and from here on out it's finger-lickin' Dixieland all the way.

Red sky in the morning, the sailor takes warning. But not the motorist. This motorist is absolutely delighted with the red sky at dawn, Day III on the road. Besides, the radio weatherman is full of ebullient good news. He says that the barometer is holding steady under an eastering high. If he's right, we'll be halfway between Mile Zero and Miami long before noon.

Last night I stood at the darkened window of my franchised motel room and watched the passing pinpricks of light out here on the fast lane. I thought how incredible it is that this continental tangle of interurban links could ever have been put together. Not all together, to be sure, for some 1,000 of the authorized 42,500 miles remain to be built. And many of the gaps may never be built. That, too, is astonishing. For despite the system's near-completion, how does one fully explain the remarkable record of victories scored by folks at the barricades, against Highwayman? Little victories, to be sure, if one counts them only by miles unbuilt or rerouted. Not so little if one takes pride in the park, or sits on the stoop, that was spared. Among the not-so-little victories that come to mind:

— The Embarcadero Freeway in San Francisco. One of the first to be halted in its tracks, full stop. An elevated structure, it ends abruptly in midair. There is talk of tearing it down.

— I-93 at Franconia Notch in New Hampshire, held to a two-lane road in scale with the topography.

— Boston's so-called Inner Belt, which would have paralleled the already substantial Route 28 corridor and savaged a score of lower-income communities.

— I-410 in New Orleans. A Moses concoction, which would have skewered the historic *Vieux Carré* district.

— I-494, Chicago's long-contested, hotly politicized Crosstown Expressway.

— New York City's hotly politicized Lower Manhattan Expressway.

— I-478, alias Westway, a depressed highway proposed for Manhattan's west side—depressed in everything but cost. (It would have been the costliest ever.)

— The Hudson River Expressway—a sort of Westway North from an earlier era, running along the river's east shore from Tarrytown north to Beacon, New York. One segment eventually did get built.

— The District of Columbia's Outer Beltway, the Potomac Freeway, the Inner Loop, and the North Central Freeway, which by underpass would have rattled the subcellars of the Mall and the Lincoln Memorial. This not-so-little victory, coinciding with a successful national effort to pry open the Highway Trust Fund for nonhighway transportation projects, allowed the District to trade in $2.5 billion of Interstate dollars for construction of its subway system.

Yes, but let us not natter on about victories. A few may not be as permanent as we would like.

Red sky turning Kodacolor blue, winter bluegrass tawny in the sunlight. Strangers to this country are often perplexed to find that even in the summer the name of this grass is a color-blind deception, though it is said that under certain light the anthers of bluegrass blossoms in May do take on a steel-blue tint. No matter. We've barely scratched the edge of the bluegrass's native range. The real stuff lies ahead on that rolling, phosphoric limestone plateau centered around Lexington. There the turf is said to be so rich and resilient, Derby contenders graze it every month of the year.

Lexington was a not uncommon destination in my early Buckeye days. My mother had kin there, and I remember the long drive down the Dixie Highway through all the little slow-down towns we've been zipping past this morning—Dry Ridge and Hilltop and Corinth and Stonewall. Those towns stretched the ninety miles out a bit. So did gasoline rationing during the war years, when Lexington was about as far as a patriotic Cincinnatian could go without appearing subversive. The old man, normally an aggressive driver, let up some on the accelerator during the war. And coasted wherever he could, cutting off the ignition over the crest of a hill and then starting her up on compression as the car was about to roll dead at the toe of the next hill. Those days, I'd guess we spent more than three hours covering the ninety miles between the big river and Lexington. Now, I-75 puts it all away in a shade over an hour and a quarter, if you cheat a little on the speed limit.

How the miles fly, for beside the highway already are the long plank fences of the horse farms east of Lexington, the broad velvet downs, the widely spaced shade trees of oak and maple, the faraway stables gleaming white in the morning sun. One solitary horse, muzzle to the bluegrass, stands in the center of a pasture as big as an Interstate cloverleaf. And suddenly I am remembering the names of the great Kentucky thoroughbreds folks talked about in those days—Seabiscuit and Gallant Fox and Man o' War. Once, from mother-kin's place, we went out to visit Man o' War in his retirement. He had topped world records in his time, was clocked at forty-three miles per hour in a workout, was said to have a twenty-five-foot stride, and had sired such other big winners as War Admiral and Mars. I'd have given anyone twenty-to-one odds Man o' War could have beaten my old man's Dodge back to Roebling's bridge by fifty lengths. But only so long as gasoline rationing was in effect.

The old man was extraordinarily fond of horses. A Kentuckian himself, he had grown up with horses aplenty under his butt in the motorless century before, had played a bit of polo in college, helped organize a troop of cavalry in the Ohio National Guard, and went with that troop to Texas in 1916 to ride Pancho patrol on the Rio Grande. Throughout his life, he seemed never to have understood fully that the automobile was not designed to respond, as a horse will, to tactile commands. I can almost see him now, wintertime on an uphill grade, the wheels of the car spinning on ice, the old man rocking back and forth in the driver's seat—or is it the saddle?—as though his own forward momentum might somehow encourage the vehicle—the nag?—to overcome the physics of traction. There had been a riding crop among the military and equestrian artifacts that lingered in his closet over the years, and I suppose I would not have been greatly surprised if he had taken it out to flail the flanks of the family Dodge on one of those icy occasions. He was a horse soldier in theory, if not in practice, to the end of his days.

Dwight D. Eisenhower, General of the Army and White House patron of the Interstate Highway System, was *not* a horse soldier. Had he been one, I am thinking as I-75 takes me south from the bluegrass into the hardscrabble Kentucky Knobs, there is no conceivable way he could have lost Kentucky to Adlai Stevenson in 1952.

In fact, it was the kind of soldiering Eisenhower did pursue that got him thinking early about roads. Originally assigned to an infantry outfit after graduating from West Point, Ike in time found himself transferred to Camp Meade, Maryland, to help organize and train Tank Corps units for overseas duty during World War I. He was hoping to head in that direction himself when the war ended abruptly in the autumn of 1918. The following summer the War Department came up with a novel plan to keep some of its peacetime officers busy. There would be a

The Needle of the Eye 311

convoy "Through Darkest America with Truck and Tank," as Ike titled a chapter of his memoir *At Ease: Stories I Tell to Friends*. "The trip," wrote Ike, "would dramatize the need for better main highways. The use of Army vehicles of almost all types would offer an opportunity for comparative tests. And many Americans would be able to see samples of equipment used in the war just concluded; even a small Renault tank was to be carried along."

The convoy, with Lieutenant Colonel D. D. Eisenhower aboard, left Washington under fair skies on the 7th of July, with orders to proceed westward to San Francisco along the general route of the far-from-finished Lincoln Highway. From the beginning, Ike would note, the horseless soldiers "were well supplied with trouble." Unsafe bridges, detours, disabled magnetos, ignition problems, bad valves, broken fanbelts, the heavy trucks up to their axles in mud. Some days, ten hours on the road would reward the convoy with all of sixty miles covered. Two months out, the convoy sputtered into Oakland amidst blowing whistles and fluttering flags. "The trip had been difficult, tiring, and fun," Ike would write. "I think that every officer on the convoy had recommended in his report that efforts should be made to get our people interested in producing better roads. A third of a century later, after seeing the autobahns of modern Germany and knowing the asset those highways were to the Germans, I decided, as President, to put an emphasis on this kind of road building."

A good bit of transportation history goes by the board in Ike's quantum leap from the ruts of the Lincoln Highway to the fast lanes of Hitler's autobahns. For example, there was the Federal Highway Act of 1921, which did something no previous roads bill had ever seriously attempted. It provided big money ($75 million for 1922 alone) to help the states begin paving over some of their mudholes. Then, long before the Germans got to it, the Italians in the 1920s took a crack at limited-access highways and called their results *autostrade*. In the United States, young Robert Moses and his contemporaries would soon be stitching the Westchester County and Long Island suburbs of

New York City with their landscaped parkways. The Bronx River Parkway, first ever, in 1923. The Hutchison in 1928. The Saw Mill in the year of The Crash. The Depression slowed things up a bit, but by 1940 the first 160 miles of the Pennsylvania Turnpike were open and the City of Los Angeles, with state and federal assistance, had begun construction of the Arroyo Seco, soon to be known as the Pasadena Freeway.

Some historians trace the primary origin of our Interstate Highway System to a report by the Bureau of Public Roads to the U.S. Congress in 1939. Titled "Toll Roads and Free Roads," the report proposed construction of a 26,700-mile network of toll-free superhighways, for which the federal government would pay more than its traditional 50-percent share. President Franklin D. Roosevelt pursued this idea in 1941 by appointing an Interregional Highway Committee to sketch out the routes, but by year's end the nation was plunged into another war and FDR was obliged to halt all the pending construction. Even after the war there were very few roadbuilding starts. Steel and lumber were scarce. Rights-of-way were not only costly—how and where could the government relocate rights-of-way folk in the midst of a housing shortage? There was no shortage of gasoline, however. With all of that hill-coasting over and done with, motorists were out on the roads again, pounding the tired pavements to dust. So by the time Adlai of Illinois managed to steal Kentucky from the horseless general, the highways of America were anything but super. They were overcrowded. They were dangerous. They were a mess.

South of Berea now, we're coming through the Knobs toward the Cumberland Mountains, hot on the trail of Dan Boone and his Wilderness Trace. Eye-catching, rough-and-tumble hound-dog country, it is; all garnished with bowers of pine and thickets of oak and eroded outcrops of ocher rock. The Rockcastle River carves its green way through narrow gorges not far from here, as does the great Cumberland, farther along; and maps of the region are sprinkled with earthy place names bestowed on the country by the descendants of footloose buckskinners who followed Boone's path over the mountains in flintlock days. O, to break the no-detour pledge just once more and mosey off the Eye along backroads to Bark Camp, Julip, Salt Gum and Gum Sulphur, Black Snake, Bluehole, Burning Springs, Wild Cat, Dog Walk, Bee Lick, and Thousandsticks. All back yonder beyond the timbered ridges, beyond the reach, one hopes, of eminent domain.

There is much myth about Boone and his overland path. Some schoolroom accounts have the old scout discovering that wind gap in the Cumberland Mountains all by himself, which does a great injustice to the pennyskin warriors who had long trod the gap in passage between Shawnee lands, north, and the precincts of the Cherokee Nation (before the tribes were relocated from the right-of-way of Manifest Destiny). And almost two decades before Boone would cross the gap to gaze upon the wilds of Caintuck, one Thomas Walker had been there, first white man ever. None of this, however, should take from Boone the credit for turning Cumberland Gap into one of the first great portals through which pioneering folk passed on to purple sunsets and fruited plains. In 1775 the Carolinian Judge Richard Henderson, who had just acquired from the Cherokee some big acreage north of the Cumberland, dispatched Boone and thirty wood-choppers to clear a packhorse trail from the Holston Valley (at what is now Kingsport, Tennessee) over the ridges, down through the Knobs, and across the bluegrass to a site, at the confluence of Otter Creek and the Kentucky, that would soon be known as Fort Boonesborough.

Boone's Trace wasn't the only trail into this western appendage of Old Virginia. Right behind Boone came Benjamin Logan, chopping a path westward from Boone's at the Rockcastle River, up past Crab Orchard and on to the Falls of the Ohio (soon to be known as Louisville). And before too long there would be a well-worn trail linking Simon Kenton's Limestone on the Ohio River (Maysville) with the interior settlements and stockades. The Ohio River itself, at least as far downstream as Maysville, would become a major trail to Kentucky once the Shawnees cooled down enough to suspend their naval operations against passing flatboats. But for the most part it was the narrow track through Cumberland Gap that accounted for the burst of emigration to Kentucky in the years between 1775 and 1790. By 1800 Kentucky contained as many inhabitants as Connecticut, more than a half as many as Massachusetts, and legions more than either New Jersey or Georgia.

At mid-century, Henry Clay is said to have ridden from his home near Lexington into these mountains to address the highlanders. On the cusp of the Gap, Clay halted with a hand cupped to his ear. "What is it?" someone asked. "What do you hear?"

"I am listening," said Clay, "to the tread of the coming millions."

But by 1850 the millions had already passed through, cached their kin behind the ridgetops, and moseyed on across the Mississippi. A few were already beyond the far terrestrial passes, in Oregon and California, shaking their fists at the gapless ocean. So Henry Clay must have been listening to something else, like the whistle of a locomotive coming out of the future, shuttling factory goods to the bark-cabin folks and Cumberland coal to the big-river barges. Or maybe he could hear the faraway song of the eight-axle tractor-trailer, pulling the long grade up Jellico Mountain on Eye-Seven-Five.

Coming down a long grade now in Tennessee. Big sign by the roadside. Big sign says Tennessee has "the world's largest underground lake." Now that's really something, seeing as how the day before yesterday I was in spitting distance of the world's—now just forget about the Caspian Sea—largest overground lake. Goodness how we Americans love our quantitative superlatives. Why, back at Indian River, Michigan, just this side of the Straits, there was a sign for the world's largest crucifix.

Tell me, Son, of all the wonders of the world, which is it you most want to see?

Well, sir, I'll tell you, sir. When I grow up, I want to see the world's largest crucifix and underground lake.

And then?

And then I want to see the Great American Interstate Highway System.

The Needle of the Eye 315

You do?

Yes I do, sir. It is the greatest engineering marvel in the world. It is bigger than the Pyramids. Bigger than the Panama Canal.

That's not very big, Son.

Then think of it this way, sir. If you took all the sand, gravel, and stone that has gone into the System, and stretched it all out, you know what you'd have? You'd have a wall around the world fifty feet wide and ten feet tall.

Okay, Son. That's big.

It is Friday, June 29, 1956. The place: the President's room at Walter Reed Army Medical Center in Washington, D.C. And you are there. This is the President's twenty-first day at the hospital after abdominal surgery, on the 9th, to relieve the painful effects of a sudden attack of ileitis. The President has successfully concluded the first phase of his recovery. Tomorrow morning he will be discharged from the hospital and transported to his farm at Gettysburg, Pennsylvania, for an additional period of recuperation. For the most part, the trip will be over two-lane highways, and linear progress may be slow, given the strong call of the open road this time of year as well as a destination attractive to rubbernecking Saturday drivers.

Though today is to be his last in the hospital, it is actually the first in which the President shall be allowed to conduct the affairs of office. There are bills to be signed, twenty-seven of them, in point of fact. The signing will be conducted in three separate sessions throughout the day, so as to reduce the possibility of the patient's becoming overly tired. Particular caution shall be taken that the President is not overwhelmed by visitors. One visitor will be granted an audience of fifteen minutes, in order that he may brief the President regarding the visitor's upcoming trip to South Vietnam and the Philippines. The visitor is the Vice-President, Richard M. Nixon.

Moreover, certain events have transpired throughout the world this week which may demand the President's attention. For example, there is still this impossible business in Poland. Just yesterday there was rioting again in Poznan, dozens killed, streetcars overturned, Soviet tanks sputtering about the city square. And the Red Chinese—good grief! Up to their old trick again, the Reds were reported to be razing the holy monasteries of Tibet. Relatively all quiet on the home front, however. Adlai of Illinois is scurrying about the Empire State, trying to steal convention delegates from New York Governor Averell Harriman (and Adlai will get some, but will lose once again to the horseless general in November, and this time in Kentucky, too).

There is other news in the making today, apart from what the President may do. A writer for *The New York Times* is preparing a piece that will appear on page one of tomorrow's editions. This story will announce that "the largest ship in the world" (what else?) will be "built in this country" (where else?) for Aristotle Socrates Onassis (who else?). A supertanker, it is going to be. One hundred thousand tons, deadweight. Elsewhere, a sportswriter sits in the pressbox counting the Brooklyn Dodgers down and out in the ninth inning. And why not, since the Philadelphia Phillies have a socko lead. But hold on now. Look who's coming up to bat for Dem Bums, back to back. It's Duke Snider, Randy Jackson, and Gil Hodges. Pow. Pow. Pow. Back-to-back homers, just like that. Dodgers 6, Phillies 5. It's never over until it's over.

A newsbreak even bigger than Dem Bums' is about to occur later today at the Westchester County Courthouse in White Plains, New York. An indictment? No. A verdict? Not quite. A marriage. The marriage of the playwright Arthur Miller and the actress Marilyn Monroe. It is to be noted by the press that he is forty and twice-married; she, thirty and thrice-married. It is to be noted further that, for the ceremony, the bride is attired in a sweater and skirt but no hat, and that the groom is wearing a blue suit and white shirt but no tie. It is a brief ceremony, not even five minutes. One reporter will note the precise time: 7:21 P.M. Whereupon the newlyweds will be seen getting into their sports car and driving off into—what? The sunset? Seclusion? The future? How do you call it, Mr. Reporter? "Into the traffic."

The President sits now by the window of his room at Walter

Reed hospital and takes up his pen. Here is the bill—the two bills, in fact—that he has been waiting for, that those unresponsive Democrats of the 84th Congress had denied him in one form or another the previous year. He had pleaded with Congress to get the nation moving again. The nation had been going nowhere except into the traffic. Accidents were killing tens of thousands of motorists every year (including the *Paris-Match* reporter who, while following the Miller-Monroe sports car to Roxbury, Connecticut, collided in her own vehicle with a tree). Unrepaired potholes and the like were boosting the cost of operating motor vehicles at the rate of $5 billion a year. Something had to be done, and at last something had been done. The Senate-House conferees had pulled it off on the 25th, and the following day both houses approved the measure overwhelmingly.

All right, now. Here we have Title I, the Federal-Aid Highway Act of 1956. This is the program. The authorized miles. The guidelines for adoption of standards. The commitment of $25 billion as the federal share of construction over the period 1957–69. And here is Title II, the Highway Revenue Act of 1956, which sets up a Highway Trust Fund and assigns to it certain user taxes for the payment of highway construction costs.

The President's pen is poised above the documents. He is ready to sign it all into law. There. Done. Now what was it that Secretary of Commerce Sinclair Weeks just said? How did Weeks describe this magnificent highway system? *The greatest public works program in the history of the world.* That's good, though in his own writings the President will qualify Weeks's appraisal by adding the word *peacetime*. It is the greatest peacetime construction program ever undertaken anywhere in the world. Yes, but how about the peacetime constructions of the military-industrial complex the President will be telling us about at the end of his next term? Ike, of all people, is going to caution America against letting its military-industrial complex get out of control. Okay, Ike. "Peacetime" may have been a legitimate qualifier in 1956, but it doesn't quite cut it now, not with all these peacetime warheads and missiles and silos and ships and submarines abuilding to keep America Number One. Pow. So let's just call the National System of Interstate and Defense Highways the greatest *nonmilitary* construction program ever undertaken anywhere in the world, and let it go at that.

Coming on through down-under Appalachia now, Oak Ridge off somewhere to the right, Knoxville and the Great Smoky Mountains to the left. For a while it is two Interstates for the price of one, 75 piggybacking 40, then pulling away for a slant-shot at Chattanooga. And that puts us over the wide waters of the Tennessee River just downstream from Loudon, the Tellico Dam, and snail darter country. Remember the snail darter, the little fish that brought such righteous utilitarian wrath down on the Endangered Species Act a few years back? Well, this is where that one played, and without much final damage to either the dam or the darter, as things turned out. Things do take curious turns in Tennessee. I can't think of a single state with a profile as quietly sweet 'n' low as Tennessee's. Forgot about Nashville, of course. Nashville makes all those strange, loud noises to which tone-deaf folks like to stomp their feet. The rest of the state stays out of people's lives, and pretty much out of the headlines. Not that Tennessee or Tennesseans lean toward being in the least bit soft or retiring. Not when you can count among the state's notables such fiercely hard and heroic men as Andrew Jackson, Davy Crockett, Sam Houston, Admiral Farragut, and Alvin York. Not when you measure the bloodstains of Civil War at Chickamauga and Missionary Ridge. Not when the secret gets out—in a mushroom cloud over Hiroshima—that all those silent men working up in the hills at Oak Ridge through the war years had been making the bomb to end all bombs. Not when you recall that Clarence Darrow and W. Jennings Bryan squared off in a trial that had a profound effect on how clearly or distortedly Americans were to view the nature of life. And just as surely not when you take note that two of the most fiercely contested environmental battles of our time were fought right here on Tennessee soil. Snail darter was one of them. The other, involving Highwayman, occurred across the state in Memphis, at a place called Overton Park. That was a big one, Overton. I'm going to get a stretch farther along the highway here, and then pause to see what I can remember of it.

Meantime, there is this wide Tennessee River to behold. This *lake* is more like it. One great big lake stretching from Knoxville, down the Moccasin Bend at Chattanooga, down a lazy loop through Alabama, back again, back clear through Kentucky to the Ohio River at Paducah. With all these Tennessee Valley Authority dams holding things up and spreading the water every which way, who ever would guess that this low-profile river is the nation's eighth largest (as measured in average cfs, cubic feet per second, of flow) and, if you throw in the French Broad headwaters, at nine hundred miles the ninth longest? Some Tennesseans like to say in all modesty that if it wasn't for *their* river, the Ohio wouldn't have enough water to float itself on to the Mississippi.

Meantime, too, there are these billboards to behold. I had almost forgotten about the billboards. Somehow, I had imagined them all done away with long ago by Ladybird Johnson or Edward Abbey's monkey-wrench gang. I see I was mistaken. I see I forgot to take into account the power of advertising. Highway beautification acts and activities to the contrary, the billboard lives—and all the more so in direct proportion to Interstate latitudes south. O, for the good old days of barnside Mail Pouch Tobacco and bumper-size Burma Shave, right there beside the highway where you needed them for diversion before the car radio became standard equipment. I remember the huge yellow Mail Pouch lettering on what must have been every other barn in sight. It was comforting to have these landmark messages, simple and direct and identical, greeting me then from the rural roadsides of the Dixie Highway. As for the Burma Shave jingles, I'm not quite sure what happened. Perhaps there was a generational decline in the national aptitude for, and appreciation of, doggerel. Perhaps too many men, *Ante Terra Dies* men, decided to grow beards. Whatever happened, I find it distressing that the quiet, low-key poesy of yesteryear is now usurped by uninspired institutional prose. Cracker Barrel This Exit. Crazy Ed's. Fireworks Restaurant. The Scottish Inn 11 Miles Exit 49. Snuffy's.

Best Western. Holiday Inn. See Ruby Falls. I'll be damned if I will.

Billboards make strange bedfellows. For example, one of the most articulate critics of roadside clutter over the years was none other than our old nemesis from the greenbelt barricades, Master Builder Robert Moses. In a piece for *Harper's* magazine just a few months after Ike signed the Interstates into law, Moses warned of flaws in the new program that would turn the superhighways into "gasoline gullies" bracketed by "continuous rows of offensive advertising." Moses wanted nothing less than a holy war against the "Billboard Barons" and a mandatory 500-foot setback written into the law. But hardly anyone listened. It would be almost ten years before passage of the Highway Beautification Act of 1965, and we all know how effective *that* loopholed law has been in protecting our eyes from roadside blight. As the writer Ruth Norris once noted, there are fourteen billboards for every ten miles of U.S. highway—"more than twice as many as there were when the law was passed." Here and now on I-75, I just passed those fourteen billboards. In fourteen hundred feet.

Part of the problem is that people nowadays don't seem to care much what they see through the windshields of their cars. They don't have time to care. Their minds are already at the other end of the journey. The destination is everything. The getting-there is nothing (where it used to be half the fun). Just put all systems on automatic, shove a cassette into the tape deck or turn up the Nashville, and go. Like these travelers out here, with their Ohio and Michigan license plates, all heading for the golden sunshine of Florida.

This afternoon I feel like a dwarf in my mid-size sedan. If it isn't the eight-axle trucker putting me down, it's some Ohioan or Michigander in his oversize camper. Every other noncommercial vehicle in the southbound lanes this afternoon appears to be a self-contained living unit. It makes me wonder about the economic future of all these basic-necessity establishments clamoring for our patronage beyond the billboards. I mean, as long as Car is King, the motel will continue to provide the royal bed-chamber. But if *Camper* is King?

O, for the good old days of the wayside inn. True, that was a bit before my time, but I like to imagine those ancient hostels, hugging the side of the rutted track, the smell of woodsmoke and manure, the hounds at ease upon the porch, the signposts—the billboards—with their picturesque names. The Black Bass Inn. The Ten Mile House. The Sign of the Orange Tree. The Bull's Head. The Sheep's Ear. The White Swan. The Golden Lamb. There was music in those names, and romance. And I'm enough of a romantic to say I'm sorry I never got to know those places. Instead I arrived into a motorized world just in time to hear the last hurrahs of the tourist cabin and the small-town hotel.

The tourist cabin—a relict few remain—was America's answer to the overnight housing shortage that prevailed along the nation's highways in the years between the two World Wars. It was the bridge, if you will, between the wayside inn and the modern motel. Most of the early models were crude: a roof, a door, a window, a bed, and the communal two-holer out back behind the forsythia bushes. Indoor plumbing arrived in the 1930s. Tourist cabins were operated for the most part as family businesses, built and furnished by family labor and serviced by same. Diversity flourished. No one, then, would have dreamed of saying (as one might say today of the standard motel room), "When you've seen one cabin, you've seen 'em all." And there were some stretches of highway where you didn't see them *at* all. For the best surviving evidence of just how few and far between the cabins must have been even in their heyday, I refer to those marvelous compendiums of folklore and geography, the *American Guides*, put together in the late 1930s by the Federal Writers' Project of the Works Progress Administration. Open almost any one of the state guidebooks that arrange material according to motorcar tour routes (many do), and you will find a common refrain at the start of each tour: "Accommodations chiefly in towns; limited elsewhere."

In towns, then, accommodations meant the Main Street hotel. That three-story brick edifice on the corner there with the tall glass doors with brass handles and the wicker furniture in the lobby. Almost every town big enough to have a dog warden had its hotel. Nothing fancy, mind you. Just a place where you would almost always find a clean room and fresh linen and maybe a passable menu in the dining room or a little sit-down watering hole off to the side with the stuffing just starting to pop through cracks in the seats of the leather barstools. And no Nashville. Always, it was the in-town hotel that my parents sought when they took me on the road with them after the gas-rationed war. Tourist cabins were at their peak of rustic elegance, and those newfangled motor courts were making a modest appearance on the city fringe. But with the exception of one big new motel near Zanesville, Ohio, which had somehow earned my parents' favor on a trip to the East, we regularly passed these places by—these "drive-ins," my father called them—in order to sample the conservative hospitality of the Main Street hotel.

And these, too, shall pass—for the most part *have* passed. Here and there in mid-size, out-of-the-way towns, a few of the old downtowners hang on through successive rehabilitations, largely supported by the patronage of romantic old fogeys and traveling salesmen on no-disco-action expense accounts. These are the exceptions. More than likely, the downtowners where I once stayed have gone the way of the rule—converted into welfare housing units or senior centers, or boarded up, or torn down to make space for a vacant lot. Does it matter? After all, I am not following I-75 to get downtown. I am following I-75 to get to the end of I-75. That is my destination. Still, night must fall twice more before I get there. So what'll it be? Ho-Jo's or the Holiday Inn?

Take away Memphis, the I-40 city where it all happened (beyond the range of our present itinerary), and Lake Allatoona, right here on I-75, is going to be as good a place as any for remembering Overton Park. If it had not been for Overton Park and I-40 over in west Tennessee, Lake Allatoona—and it *is* a lake, albeit an artificial one—would surely have been run through by I-75 here in north Georgia. The way Highwayman had figured it, I-75 was to have come out of Chattanooga on a slant shot straight for the heart of downtown Atlanta. And there wasn't a whole lot in its way, except for Lake Allatoona and its 25,000 acres of surrounding woodland. The skewering script called for five bridges across the lake and its appended inlets. But then something happened. Something happened to I-75 on its way to Atlanta. Look to the map and see for yourself. There is no straight-arrow slant shot into Atlanta. There is this bulge, this bend in the highway that is taking us right now around the edge of Lake Allatoona. And what happened to make it this way, so contrary to the best judgment of Highwayman? What happened was Section 4(f) of the Federal-Aid Highway Act of 1966, as applied by the people of Memphis at the barricades of Overton Park.

It is an uncommon park, Overton, though I must go on what others have said of it, for I have never been there myself. Some 340 acres, it is, practically smack dab in the middle of the city, embracing a nine-hole golf course, the Memphis Academy of Arts and the Brooks Memorial Art Gallery, athletic fields, playgrounds, picnic areas, the Memphis Zoo, and the *pièce de résistance*—an old-growth oak-hickory forest with a stream winding through. The park honors the name of one of Memphis's founding fathers, Judge John Overton, and by all accounts it does him proud.

So there, in Year One of the Interstate Highway System, was this magnificent cultural park and urban natural area; and here, on the planning map of Memphis, were these dotted lines projecting the possible paths of I-40 on its way from the Carolina piedmont to the parched outback of southern California. Highwayman looked down upon the map and saw that only one of the lines truly pleased him. It was the line that ran straight east and west through Judge John Overton's honor. Highwayman's finger traced a ballistic parabola over the map and came down with a thud smack dab in the middle of the old-growth forest. And Highwayman, seeing that it was good, said: I'll take this one.

As word got around town in the early 1960s that I-40 was indeed for real, folks started choosing up sides. Highwayman already had the state roads crowd. Now he had the governor, the mayor, and a whole slew of civic-boosting panjandrums dedicated to the proposition that a straight line is the shortest distance between two points, and shorter still when it runs through a park. On the other side of the barricades were a number of residents who called themselves Citizens to Preserve Overton Park. The highway commissioner called those citizens "little old ladies in tennis shoes" and predicted that their squeaks would sooner or later be squelched. But the commissioner hadn't figured on something. In predicting a crushing defeat of his foe, it had never occurred to the commissioner that the little old ladies would show up in court with Section 4(f) of the Federal-Aid Highway Act of 1966.

In a world in which there was not yet a National Environmental Policy Act or a Clean Air Act or an Endangered Species Act, Section 4(f) of a *highway act*, of all things, was a breath of fresh air. In effect, it proclaimed for the very first time that the needs of transportation must be placed in balance with the necessity of preserving environmental values. It declared that special efforts must be made "to preserve the natural beauty of countryside and public park and recreation lands, wildlife and waterfowl refuges, and historic sites," and it specifically prohibited the use of parklands for federally funded highways in cases where the U.S. Secretary of Transportation finds that a state has failed to show that there is no "feasible and prudent" alternative.

Armed with 4(f), Citizens to Preserve Overton Park marched into court, where arguments rattled back and forth and then straight up through the federal judiciary to the highest court in the land. On March 2, 1971, the U.S. Supreme Court rendered a unanimous decision in the matter of *Citizens v.* [Transportation Secretary John] *Volpe.* Section 4(f), the court ruled, constitutes a "plain and explicit bar to the use of federal funds for construction of highways through parks—only the most unusual situations are exempted." Congress had spoken clearly, the court said, and if "the statutes are to have any meaning, the Secretary cannot approve the destruction of parkland unless he finds that alternative routes present unique problems."

For almost two years following that decision, Transportation Secretary Volpe studied the factual record developed during the litigation, and then he weighed in with his own ruling: "I find that an Interstate highway as proposed by the state through Overton Park cannot be approved." Among Volpe's reasons for denying federal funds was the state's own admission that I-40 passing through Overton Park would violate federal noise and air pollution standards—in the case of air, by as much as 500 percent.

One would think that would have ended it. But in the highway wars, that kind of thinking tends to be dangerous. If there is one thing Highwayman isn't, it is a quitter. Highwayman hangs in there stubbornly right to the end and beyond. In the Overton Park case, Highwayman simply waited for Secretary Volpe to be replaced by Secretary Claude Brinegar. But Secretary Brinegar also said: No road through Overton Park. So Highwayman waited for Brinegar to be replaced by William T. Coleman, Jr. And Secretary Coleman said: No road through Overton Park as proposed, but we might consider an enclosed tunnel *under* the park. That wasn't even half a loaf for Highwayman, so he simply waited for the next Secretary of Transportation and took the old dog-eared, grade-level plan to him. And guess what Secretary Brock Adams said. No road through Overton Park.

A churlish legislative effort to ram I-40 straight through the park was made in 1978, by none other than Senator Howard Baker of damn-the-snail-darter fame. Senator Baker thought it would be a splendid thing if I-40 in Memphis were simply grandfathered right out from under the restrictions of Section 4 (f). To the further credit of Citizens to Preserve Overton Park (as well as its allies, including the Sierra Club, the National Wildlife Federation, and the National Audubon Society), Senator Baker's effort got exactly what it deserved. *No road through Overton Park.*

So now the Interstate traffic flows peripherally around the center of Memphis on what originally was to have been the northern loop of I-240. It is merely a matter of a few miles more, a few minutes more. And Judge John Overton's old-growth honor stands intact, though you can be sure that Highwayman would like to change that—and will, if he ever gets the chance. Be that as it may, the message from Memphis went out in every direction to the other barricades of the highway wars. We heard it—and used it—in our fight for the Staten Island greenbelt. And Georgians used it right here on I-75, to make this bend around Lake Allatoona. "Overton Park is a historic place," said William Futrell, a Georgian himself and, at the time of the Baker affair in 1978, president of the Sierra Club. It is "a battle site like Gettysburg and Yorktown. It is the first place where individual citizens used the law to stop the state and federal highway-builders and all the money and power behind them. That had never been done before anywhere in the United States."

Across the Chattahoochee and into the towers of Atlanta. What a mistake it was to do it this way, at afternoon rush hour, when I could just as well have gone around the city on I-285. All the big cities like Memphis and Atlanta have these peripherals. I had always thought that the peripherals were a good idea to keep things moving. I mean, I-240 certainly helped to bail Memphis out of that Overton mess, and I-285—if I had only been paying attention—could have bailed me out of this mess. But somehow, subconsciously perhaps, I think I must have soured on these peripherals after I read what Francis Turner once said about them in a magazine interview. I forget the magazine, but I can't forget Turner. Turner, for many years, was a top man at the old Bureau of Public Roads, and it is said that his hand was much in evidence in the crucial planning for an Interstate Highway System. Whatever the case, I recall that Turner told his interviewer on this particular occasion why the big cities had these peripherals. The concept, said Turner, was that every major city had to have not only a road that penetrated but a road around. And the reason for that was The Bomb. If The Bomb came down in the middle of a city and created a mess—as at Hiroshima—well, the military would need a way to get around the rubble and on with its business. So, unless Turner was stretching it some with that interviewer, the peripherals were actually conceived as conveniences for the horseless soldiers on Armageddon Day.

The farther we creep along in this downtown rush-hour traffic, the more I am convinced that The Bomb has already fallen. It is one horrendous mess here in the heart of this great Sun Belt capital city. It is one big extruded construction site. The highway is not quite finished, or it is being improved. Overpasses, interchanges, ramps—all rubble and fresh concrete and the exposed ends of reinforcing rods. Suddenly we have six lanes pinched into three. Stop and creep. Stop and creep. Is this familiar? Have I been here before, or was it New York City? Or Hartford? Or Boston? Always I find these people in hard hats who are fixing things up, and always at rush hour. I suspect that generations will come and go and still they'll be fixing things up. And when at last the needed improvements are complete, they'll already be obsolete, as useless as peripherals for horseless soldiers on Armageddon Day. They'll have to be excised, demolished, in order that generations yet unborn may have something new to build and fix up and tear down. I suppose it was this way in the beginning and ever shall be.

Hospital Next Right, the sign says. *Trauma Center*. Don't give me that stuff. I know about trauma. Just look at us out here in the slow lanes. Just look at that face behind the wheel of the car in the next lane over. A pathological killer sits behind the wheel of that car. See the lines of rage radiating from the corners of his eyes, his mouth contorted in a primal scream. Quickly I roll up the window to keep that scream from reaching me. And now we stop. And now we creep.

Perhaps it is peevish to complain of improvements. After all, this is truly our first jam in a thousand miles, and that's a pretty good score for this day and age. And until just a few years ago, as a matter of fact, there wasn't much money for highway improvements. Twenty years of new Interstate construction went by before Congress voted a single penny earmarked specifically for repairing the System. Trouble was, and is, that the states are obligated to maintain that other system of highways, the U.S. Primaries, and there are a quarter of a million miles of *them*, and most of those miles are twice as old as the Interstate miles. Trouble was, and is (as one state transportation chief told *Time* magazine), politicians don't cut ribbons over fixed potholes. One Washington-based research organization estimates that nearly two-thirds of America's paved-road network is substandard and in need of rebuilding. Each year the repair crews are falling farther and farther behind. And each year there are more and more motor vehicles. "More highways only bring more cars," former Transportation Secretary John Volpe once said, "which bring more congestion, which brings more highways."

Years ago, in the First Decade Interstate, a great newspaper that is no longer with us (*The New York Herald Tribune*) assigned a great chronicler of the human condition (Tom "The Right Stuff" Wolfe) to stage, across the full length of Manhattan's bustling 42nd Street, a rush-hour race involving one pedestrian, one bicyclist, one horse and rider, and one taxicab. I forget which of the contenders came in first. The cyclist, I think. But I do remember which came in last, for that was the whole point of the story. You guessed it: The taxicab.

Day IV on the road, Macon to Fort Myers, scooting south without a glance at by-passed Cordele, Tifton, and Valdosta, Georgia; at Lake City, Gainesville, Ocala, Tampa, and Sarasota, Florida. It has been a day in another country, in a foreign land. I have felt unconnected. The South does that to me. Beyond Chattanooga, coming this way, the soils start to redden up a bit, and the hardwoods fall behind, and the conifers I see beside the highway are not the ones with names I know from memory of the North Country. For me, the Southland presents a social and physiographic puzzlement I encounter nowhere else in America. I suspect there is some regional bias at work here, though not of a flag-waving kind. I mean I am not now, have never been, and never will be a *professional* Yankee. I mean there have been times in my life when some of my best friends were southerners. A few might still be friends if I had taken the time over the years to keep up with them, visit a spell now and then instead of always marching through places like Georgia in airplanes or, as was the case today, with a heavy foot on the accelerator and a watchful eye for speed traps. See, that's what I mean. I have the South all wrapped up in a stereotype, and one essential part of the fiction is this uniformed redneck under a trooper's hat, just waiting to haul me up for big bucks before some 'bacca-spittin' justice of the peace.

Not that Yankee-trapping never did take place down here in deep-fry Dixie. In olden motorcar days, before the Interstate Highway System put most of the region's vehicular law enforcement under the jurisdiction of state police departments (which tend to be more—how do you call it?—accountable about such things), some burghs along the byways to sunny Florida were able to keep the lid on local taxes simply by snagging out-of-state speeders and making them post outrageous cash bonds. Consider, for example, the case of the little peachtree city of Ludowici, Georgia, situated about twenty miles off I-95 southwest of Savannah and, more conveniently, at a strategic dogleg in U.S. 301, a major tourist route to Florida in pre-Interstate days.

Four different Georgia governors over the years tried to find cause for corruption indictments at Ludowici, and failed. Governor Lester Maddox, frustrated by a lack of clearcut evidence, erected billboards on the city limits. "Beware," the signs said. "You are in Long County and approaching Ludowici, Georgia. Do not get fleeced in a clip joint. Do not get caught in a speed trap." Governor Jimmy Carter came to the conclusion in 1972 that most of the real wrongdoers in Ludowici were already in their graves, and let it go at that. I-95 no doubt siphoned off most of Ludowici's potential customers. But as recently as 1983, the Associated Press reported that Ludowici appeared to be up to its old tricks. An investigation by the state police, the AP said, found that revenue from forfeited traffic bonds increased from $7,502 in the first five months of 1982 to $32,965 in the same period of 1983. State investigators reportedly challenged every one of the 1,553 traffic violations issued by Ludowici over a twenty-month period, and noted that out-of-staters, who are more likely to forfeit bonds than local offenders, accounted for three-quarters of the arrests.

Can't say I'm sorry I never got to Ludowici. If my luck holds out, I never will. In any event, Day IV from Macon to Fort Myers, I haven't had even one close call with the radar guns. In fact, the conspicuous absence of constabulary control over my driving habits, combined with the flat-out grade of the straight-away road, the sawmill pinelands and the slaughterhouse pastures, dashboard Nashville, FM preachers, rosy sundown, salty fragrance off the Gulf Coast sea—all these are beginning to wear down my watchfulness. Time to turn off and turn in. Tomorrow it's but half a day—and half an Eye—to the end of the road.

Tomorrow has arrived. Counting south from the Soo, we are at Milepost One-Seven-Three-Four and turning east into the sun. It is warm in the car with the windows down, maybe Fahrenheit Seventy already, just in case I forget where it is that I am on this January morning. I am at Golden Gate, Florida, with my tail-pipe to Naples. I have come to the end of the Compleat Eye-Seven-Five. Here, on my map, ends the blue line of the free, limited-access Interstate highway, and here begins the green line of the two-lane, toll-taking, limited-access Everglades Parkway, otherwise known as Alligator Alley but shortly to be known as I-75, as soon as the hard hats get those additional lanes built, not to mention the contested underpasses to accommodate the distribution of Big Cypress water and Florida panthers, of which there are said to be thirty left.

We check the fuel gauge; a sign says that there are no services for ninety-two miles. We pay the toll-taker seventy-five cents. We note a second sign, black on yellow: *Entering Panther Habitat*. We spot a wood stork sliding overhead. And we are on our way into the scraggly outback of Collier County, the sunshine boonies, the homestretch.

It is a place of barricades, too, this cypress-running-on-into-glades country. In fact, I can't think of any other place in America that has witnessed such a continuing profusion of environmental traumas, alarms, showdowns, shootouts, most having one thing or another to do with the overland movement of water into Everglades National Park. First it was the flood-control districts, pinching off the flow over in Broward and Dade counties. Then it was the mail-order real estate developers over here with their draglines and tree-crushers, building, as they called it, "new worlds for a better tomorrow." Then came the promoters of an Everglades jetport and a city-in-the-wilderness, saying it was the responsibility of decent folk to exercise dominion over the land, sea, and air above as the higher order of man intends. Etcetera, etcetera, etcetera. And as soon as conservation-minded people at the barricades modified or deflected one of these threats to the south Florida ecosystem, another threat would flare up somewhere else along the line. Yet until recent years, the decibels of public debate over Alligator Alley never reached the high levels generated in conflicts over other issues. Perhaps the parkway was too far removed from the park. Perhaps at the time of its construction, environmental folks were all tied up on other fronts. Whatever the cause or the reason, the Alley at last is getting the kind of attention it always deserved. And for that we must thank I-75—for better or worse—and the Florida panther.

Panther Crossing Next 9 Miles, the sign says. Old *Felis concolor coryi*. A little guy or gal compared with the hard-rock puma, lean-flanked for slinking between the cypress knees, tight-bellied to get by on short rations of red meat. And only thirty left, the sign says. The most rare of the endangered, the most endangered of the rare. But how do they come up with a number like thirty? Obviously the swamp gentry are somewhat skeptical about that figure, because they have all but obliterated it with graffiti—a sign to me that, given the opportunity, they would as soon obliterate the panther as well. By swamp gentry, I don't necessarily mean the resident outbackers here, though not a few of them may still poach a deer or a gator or two when the spirit moves them—their spirits being, almost to a man, utilitarian. But there is not much use to killing a panther, unless you are looking to puff yourself up with barstool brag and swagger. No, by gentry I mean the weekend potshots from Miami and other urban places who come out here in their swamp buggies and ORVs to play *guns*. Miami seems to have a corner on these fellows. They are known to shoot at almost anything, including each other.

Entering Fakahatchee Strand State Preserve, the sign says. Fifty thousand acres running off to our right all the way down to the Tamiami Trail. A wet wilderness of sloughs and hammocks festooned with garlands of Spanish moss. Prime panther habitat. Prime bald cypress habitat, too. Now there's a southern conifer—albeit a deciduous conifer—that breaks down my allegiance to all things boreal. *Taxodium distichum*, the swamp giant. Once, the Fakahatchee probably held the greatest strands of old-growth bald cypress in North America. But that was before loggers found a market eager to turn the tree's light, durable, rot-resistant wood into gutters and coffins and the hulls of torpedo boats. A few of the big cypress linger on, but for the most part the Fakahatchee is now a place of mixed tropical hardwoods and epiphytic orchids—still wild, though, and not to be sneezed at. I'm told that between the U.S. Fish and Wildlife Service and the State of Florida, there's another hundred thousand acres in and around the Fakahatchee that is targeted for acquisition. And that will be good news for the panther, if the feds ever get around to uncorking the necessary funds.

Even with the safety net spread wider, there is still this problem that wild animals have with roads, and especially that nocturnal predators have with headlights coming down the fast lane of a limited-access highway. Since 1979, road kills of the big cat have averaged almost one a year, which is a dreadful lot when total living numbers are fewer than fifty. Two of the most recent kills occurred near here, on Alligator Alley. The cats were bowled over within a marked "panther crossing" area, not far from the point where Florida wildlife officials have projected the need for one of some thirty-six underpasses to make the coming of I-75 a bit more compatible with the natural circulation of both water and wild cats. Safer passage for the panther has long been a sore point between Florida and the Federal Highway Administration. The feds have obdurately insisted that if a dozen underpasses were good enough for Florida in 1973, when the initial I-75 studies were under way, they ought to be good enough today. Anything more than that, said the feds' man in Tallahassee, would be a "boondoggle." (Can you imagine? Some popinjay in the Reagan Administration talking about *boondoggles*?) And besides, said the federal highwayman, I-75 would have "no adverse impact" on the panther in any event. Well, we shall see about that.

Sun getting high now as we roll down Alligator Alley into Broward County, leaving the scratchy cypress behind us and getting on with the sawgrass Glades. The River of Grass, wrote Marjory Stoneman Douglas just about a year before a scant part of the Everglades was tucked away in a national park. Harry Truman was President at the time. He didn't know the Everglades as Marjory Douglas knew them. In dedicating the park, she would never have been so naive as to state that the Glades would now be safe forevermore.

Not that I'm faulting Harry Truman. I wouldn't want to do that any more than I'd fault Dwight Eisenhower for predicting that his *Autobahnen*, this Interstate Highway System, would be all wrapped up and finished by 1969—and at a cost of only $30 billion or so. So we'll be lucky—or unlucky, as the case may be— if Ike was only off by twenty years and maybe $100 billion. I mean this final stretch of I-75 won't be completed until 1990, and who in Ike's day would ever have dreamt that part of the segment's cost override would have to be written off on panthers. Of all things. And that gives me a good feeling. Because after all that I have seen and felt and remembered over these past few days along the needle of the Eye, I need to believe that there is still a niche in America for the unexpected, the impractical, the indeterminate, the individualized, the incalculable. And the lost cause.

Only a few more miles down the Alley to the end of the road. Then I'll skedaddle for Miami International Airport, turn in the car, and hightail it for the first flight home. I'd better hurry. The highway is getting to me. It is going away like a three-dimensional rendering of infinity. Infinity with a broken yellow stripe down its diminishing center. And suddenly I am imagining the Alley as Interstate, four lanes coming and going, and the apex of my vision tunneling out through the Glades toward the golden sands of Fort Lauderdale. At the end of the road someone is standing in the surf at the edge of the beach. It is our friend and nemesis, the old gray Highwayman. And you know what he's doing? He's shaking his fist at the unbridgeable ocean. Because it finally stopped him.

BACK TO

THE BEAVERKILL

Barnhart's Pool holds a slick stretch of water about a mile downstream from the place where the big river begins. It is not so famous a fishing hole as that other place, the Junction Pool where the upper Beaverkill scoops up Willowemoc Creek; but it is surely among the big river's better pools, for the water runs deep, and trout seem to know they are better off here than elsewhere. Now, I don't expect the fish understand too much about regulations—no-kill, catch 'n' release, and that sort of thing. They probably just know abut fishermen, and how some are too lazy to park their cars on the shoulder of Old Twisty, old Highway 17, and then walk a long quarter-mile in waders across the floodplain flats to the east bank, which is the only bank one can diligently wade out from in order to cast a fly into Barnhart's Pool.

We had scouted the pool in the morning, flicked a muddler minnow or two at the edge of the glide. No hits, no runs, a few errors. The fish ran it up on us. And so did the water. It was running high for late May. There had been cloudbursts in the mountains a week earlier. Coming down across the edge of Barnhart's Flats, we had noticed signs of the flood's passage—

driftwood tangled in the underbrush, windrows of sediment piled high above the level of the river. The flats looked to be fine farmland, once upon a time, though Squire Barnhart and various successors to the land no doubt had problems. Time to time. Flood to flood. New corn, had it been seeded here the week before, would likely be down past Phillipsburg on the Delaware by now, or beyond Philadelphia. That's the way it has to be with a river. If you want to hold on to anything, you'd better keep it out of a river's way. The fifty-year flood never waits on half-centuries.

"Got pictures of it with the river running through," Art Lee was saying. Lee is a field editor for *Fly Fisherman* magazine and lives upriver in Roscoe. We were walking from the pool toward Old Twisty, and Lee solemnly waved his flyrod over the stubbled flats and said, "After the rains last week, the water here was up to your knees. Can you believe it? This is where they want to put the Titan sewage plant. Right here on the flats. One good flood and you can say good-bye to the river."

To hear some anglers tell it, the events of Creation followed a logical sequence. God created the Catskill Mountains of New York on the first day, the Beaverkill River on the second, the caddis and mayfly on the third, the brook trout on the fourth, the rainbow trout on the fifth, and the brown trout on the sixth. On the seventh, instead of resting, God waded into Junction Pool—or Barnhart's, for that matter—with a rod of Tonkin bamboo cane, a reel from Hardy's of London, a floating line (weight-forward, for longer casts), a tapered leader (7X), and possibly a Light Cahill or Hendrickson or Ausable Wulff or Rat-faced McDougal. Thus equipped, God is said to have run it up on the trout. And probably with little mercy, for this was long before God created the notion of bag limits or the practice of no-kill, catch 'n' release.

Over the years of recorded time, piscatorial agnostics and riparian heathens have renounced this version of the genesis. I have a few doubts about it myself. After all, the Delaware Indians knew nothing of tapered leaders. And the Dutch patroons probably went fishing with nets and clubs. Matter of fact, until quite recently, most folk didn't have much time for the Catskill rivers, except to use them as conduits to carry away the mountains' wealth. And the mountainfolk's waste. Along the Beaverkill, pines were felled and rafted to the shipbuilders of Philadelphia. Acid factories sprang up, producing acetate for dyes and nitrous cellulose for explosives, and poison for the rivers. Tanlords moved into the valleys of the Schoharie and the Bataviakill and stripped the hemlocks of their bark, for tanning leather. The rivers ran red.

Yet in some streams the brook trout prevailed. A lunker or two may have been skulking in Barnhart's Pool about the time the factories moved west and the mountainfolk reverted to greener pastures and agrarian ways. And surely trout in goodly numbers were coursing the Beaverkill when, at the turn of the last century, one Theodore Gordon of Pennsylvania—the patron saint of flyfishing in America—anointed the first dry fly in the holy waters of Junction Pool. No record has yet been found to prove that Gordon fared poorer with trout than God did.

Those were the days of the tight lines for certain. There were private clubs at Balsam Lake, in the Beaverkill headwaters; at Turnwood, and Debruce on the Willowemoc. There were legendary names to match the rivers, too—George LaBranche and Ed Hewitt and Sparse Grey Hackle, and later the likes of Art Flick and Lee Wulff and Harry Darbee. Soon, disciples of the great ones were flocking not only to the Beamoc, as the big river has come to be known, but to the Neversink and Esopus, and the East and West branches of the Delaware. Now, by the grace of the State of New York, there were rainbows and German browns to supplement the native brookies in Catskill waters, and mile after mile of streamside easements to make the trout accessible to those whose tackle—or pedigrees—might not pass muster among tweedier types at the clubs.

In time, of course, there would be a number of defectors from the ranks of the Catskill flyfishers. Some would bolt from Barnhart's Pool to the Adirondacks, to the AuSable of Michigan, to the Firehole or Madison out yonder in the shining mountains of

Montana. Yet no matter how far afield they might wander, they would each share a kind of lingering reverence for this place where God or Gordon started it all. And sooner or later, most would come back for another cast. "To celebrate Opening Day on the Beaverkill," wrote the dean of American sportswriters, Red Smith, "is a little like observing Christmas in Bethlehem."

At noon, Art Lee sneaked off to a secret pool of his on the Delaware, and I headed back into Roscoe with Pat Smith, the television writer. The two of us have this bad habit of showing up on the Beaverkill whenever there's trouble. Like a couple of buzzards. Obit scriveners, somebody called us in the spring of 1965, when our respective newspapers dispatched us to Roscoe to chronicle apocalypse for the fabled stream. Then, the villain of the piece had been a superhighway, the Quickway that would retire Old Twisty by stitching a dozen bridges into the Beamoc along one six-mile stretch. Yet for all of our dire predictions, the concrete pylons of the bridges inflicted no fatal wounds. Scars, yes. And here and there a dreadful rearrangement of the riverbed. But for the most part, the riverine habitat of caddis and mayfly survived, and so did the trout, thanks in good measure to a program of heavy stocking and the setting aside of some two river-miles for no-kill, catch 'n' release.

"And now, this," said Smith, looking from our car as we passed the flats where treated waste would be pumped to the river. "I wonder how Harry Darbee feels about their turning his stream into a sewer."

"Let's go find out," I said. Since there was time to kill before the evening hatch at Barnhart's Pool—because, more importantly, Harry Darbee was one of the great ones—these two old buzzards flapped on down Old Twisty, and did just that.

Titan Group, Inc., is a corporation with headquarters in Paramus, New Jersey. It owns some nine hundred acres a few miles southwest of Junction Pool. Up Abe Wood Brook and over the height of land and there you are, on the shores of Tennanah Lake. Titan has plans here for one of the largest private developments to come the Catskills' way in a generation. It is titanic stuff. Hookups and facilities for a thousand recreational vehicles. And should casino gambling be legalized in New York State, Titan holds the option to construct a 1,000-unit casino hotel on the same tract. Fill up every rec-vehicle slot, and all the hotel rooms, and what you'd have is a transient population double, maybe triple, that of the town of Rockland, which embraces the village of Roscoe, where the Tennanah sewage would flow by pipeline for treatment, before it is dumped into the conduit of the Beaverkill River. More than 300,000 gallons of sewage a day, for openers. As time goes by, not doubt, more to come.

On paper, the game plan for sewage disposal has been played by the rules. After all, the effluent would be treated. It would meet standards for a stretch of water that the state has classified as C(T), meaning good enough for trout, but not for two-legged swimmers. And not for drinking. For certain. The New York State Department of Environmental Conservation is not overly enthusiastic about the idea of dumping more treated sewage into waters it stocks with trout. I mean, how much can a river take? The department doesn't know. It can only cross its fingers and go on stocking—heavily, just in case.

To be sure, the situation is conditional. *If* casino gambling is legalized. *If* Titan in the meantime doesn't overextend itself. *If* federal funds can be pried loose from an $8 billion backlog of water-quality projects already authorized, and no new spending in sight, at least for the duration of the Reagan presidency. *If* . . .

"Oh, the hell with 'if,' " said Harry Darbee. "The river can't take it at low water. That's all there is to it."

Darbee's farmhouse sits by the side of Old Twisty on a hillside that rolls gently down to the Willowemoc. In the old days, he could walk out his back door and down a path through the fields to the river; or he could sit out back and just watch it flash and sparkle along, and know that the big trout weren't about to go anywhere until he got good and ready to move them with the barb of a home-tied fly. But now, he doesn't look in that direction as often as he used to, for his view of the river, his access to the river, his presence *with* the river are gone. Something concrete came between Harry Darbee and the Willowemoc about fifteen years ago. Folks round-about call it the Quickway.

We found the old fisherman inside, tidying up a clutter of feathers and threads in his fly-shop study. He was through tying flies, he said. The eyes were going. "No one ever said a man could tie flies for a hundred years," he said. "I'm no exception." We sat in the study, then, and talked about the rivers and the fish. There were things in frames on the walls, salmon flies and Catskill scenes. Above the roll-top desk in the corner hung a large watercolor of the old covered bridge on the upper Beaverkill, and Darbee said he had caught his first trout right there, when he was eight. "Used a hickory pole with the bark peeled off, except on the handle," he said.

"Worm, or fly?"

"Neither," he said. "Used a grasshopper."

"What'd you get?"

"Seventeen-and-a-half incher," he said. "The half-inch was important. That made for a fair-size fish, those days. Not a *big* fish, but big enough."

Darbee didn't have much time for fishing in the early sixties. He was too busy fighting the highwaymen, trying to get the Quickway shelved across the hills instead of riveted to the streambed. Darbee was the lightning rod then; pulled in fifteen thousand signatures on petitions, took them to the governor's office in Albany, and was turned away at the governor's door. An aide to the state's chief executive said at the time that "one good highway is more important than any river in America." Darbee still believed that the Quickway hurt the Beamoc badly. "It silted up the deeper pools," he said. "The fish don't have a chance to grow the way they used to." And now, this.

The way Darbee saw it, the proposed Titan sewage plant would be just one more insult added to the river's injury. Water quality, and water temperature in periods of low flow, were already up against the thin edge, at least for living trout. "It's not just Titan," he said. "It's all the holding tanks and septic systems along the river. No one knows what's getting into the water.

There's a threshold for nutrients, but where's it at? Sure, you can treat the sewage. But is treatment *enough*?"

We asked him about Art Lee's concern—the threat of a flood flushing the whole Titan sewage works into the river. Darbee said, "Sure it could happen. What worries me, though, isn't flood. It's the other extreme. It's low water. Late summer, you can *walk* across some pools. The river can't take it." Lee had mentioned this, too; had told us that effluent in summer would be pouring into the river at temperatures of eighty to ninety degrees—and this when the normal water temperature was already within a couple of points of rolling most trout belly-up in the current.

On that dour note we concluded the interview and Darbee ushered us to the door, where another visitor was waiting to see him. As we turned from the door, Darbee called, "Where you fishin'?" We told him. He smiled. "A good spot," he said, and then seemed about to qualify that judgment. But didn't.

We stopped at the Antrim Lodge, in Roscoe, before returning to Barnhart's Pool. The Antrim is a venerable establishment, a favorite among hunters and fishermen, each in their season. Downstairs in the restaurant there are things in frames on the walls—stuffed fish, and photographs yellowing with age, and, beside the great stone fireplace, a bronze plaque proclaiming Roscoe to be Trout Town, U.S.A. Roscoe, and the Antrim, too, owe a great deal to trout, and to the men and women who come from afar to pursue them.

Doug Bury, the Antrim's proprietor, was standing out front of the inn under a row of tall spruce trees. He is a friendly man, a gracious host, and active in the community. Unlike Darbee, fifteen years ago, Bury was warmly in favor of riveting the Quickway to the streambed of the Beamoc. And now he is much in favor of allowing the Titan Group to pump 300,000 gallons of treated sewage into the Beamoc from Barnhart's Flats. Still, some of Doug Bury's best friends are fishermen.

He was standing, hands on hips, watching an army of forest tent caterpillars devour his spruce. And I felt true sorrow for him, for only a day earlier I had been standing in southern Connecticut watching an army of gypsy moth caterpillars devour my oaks. Bury said nothing, pursed lips. His spokesman appeared to be this angry young man with the red face, who, likewise with hands on hips, continued to pace round and round the most noticeably defoliated spruce, shouting: "Goddamn environmentalists!"

"But just hold on, now," I said. "Those aren't environmentalists. Those are forest tent caterpillars."

The young man swore again, and said, "No! It's those *environmentalists*. They won't let you spray. I hope the goddamn trees fall down on their heads."

Doug Bury just stood there, shaking his own head, saying nothing.

A bar of amber light fell across the river before sunset, and a hatch of shadflies came out of it like a flurry of driven snow. Waist deep in the water, I felt the Beamoc's pull and tug at my waders, saw the cobbled bottom dropping away under the glide, heard the purl and slap of the big one rolling on toward Horse Brook Run and Cairn's and Wagon Tracks Pool and Painter's Bend and Horton Bridge and Chiloway and Fish Eddy, hellbent for the bigger Delaware, and for the sea. The flyrod in my hand moved from ten o'clock to two o'clock, two o'clock, ten o'clock, feeding the line out, getting a reach for the leader to uncurl as though it had floated out of God's heaven with a wisp of a fly for the waiting trout's dinner. Well, not quite, though Smith could put out a line like that, and was doing it now, downstream. Still, the score was the same: no hits, no runs, a few errors.

The score seemed no great matter. Not to me, anyway. Although now I found myself hoping that Art Lee might have been mistaken when he told me that morning that the ritual of fly fishing is a metaphor for life. If Lee wasn't full of beans on that one, then I was in big trouble, for the trout had been running it up on me of late more often than I on them. An interesting idea, nevertheless. Perhaps the trout was a metaphor, too, in its own right. For freedom, possibly. For beauty. For wildness.

For tenacity. It was a creature of the Ice Age, this fish; a thing conditioned to inorganic glacial waters, and here it was, hanging on against a flood of phosphates and nitrates and perilous temperatures. Besides, what would this river be without you, fish? What would any river be, where springs well out of mountains over mossy ledge, and brooks somersault under hemlock and spruce, and creeks thunder down to the valleys of the big ones hellbent for the sea? Without trout? They would be dead.

On the surface of this river, now, the bar of amber light drew inward on itself like a line reeled up from the water. I reeled up, too, and waded back to the east bank and sat down against the butt of a willow to watch for the rise of feeding fish. Presently, Pat Smith came around a bend in the river. He said, "They're not rising."

I said, "The hell they aren't. I had a good one on. Must have been a rainbow, 'cause he jumped three times."

"Get outa here."

"Seventeen-and-a-half inches."

"Is," said Smith, "the measure of your longest cast."

We walked back across the flats to the car. After a while Smith said, "How are you going to call it, this time around? Like the Quickway? Apocalypse now?"

I told the old buzzard that wasn't such a bad idea. It would give us both an excuse to come back to the Beaverkill to check the accuracy of the prognosis.

"You hot-damn environmentalists," said Smith. "Who needs excuses?"

NOTES ON COSPII8

There is a gold autumnal light upon the marsh this morning. It augurs first frost and geese passing through, and before too long the old white oak—the leaner—will cast its last leaf for an early winter. Let 'er come, I say. Bring on the final browning of the sedge, the crackle of the ice. It's time for a change.

I view the marsh this morning, as I do most every morning, through the doorway of the room where I work. The inverted funnel of vision reaches out across the clutter, past the stacked books, the fishing rods, the wood stove, a second doorway made of glass, a patch of crabgrass, a border of fern and poison ivy, blackberry and tulip poplar, tussock sedge and buttonbush, a sparkle of open water, a cluster of crooked snags at the edge of the woods on the other side. Summertime, the funnel gets clogged with cutin and cellulose, as though a green curtain had been drawn across the place. Claustrophobia sets in by September, but then the leaves begin to fall. First from the poplars and maples; next, the red oaks and white ash—until only the leaner hangs on, grudging the change of season. Me, I welcome it, the better to see into Lonetown Marsh.

A city friend walked with me to the edge of the marsh one afternoon and asked what we were likely to see. I said we were more than likely to see redwing blackbirds and kingfishers, and possibly the great blue heron that had just checked in, or a red-shouldered hawk, if we were in luck. And we might see a muskrat or two, the pesky garbage-can coon, or the resident snapping turtle—the one that scoops holes in our garden in order to lay her eggs. How long does it take for the eggs to hatch, my friend inquired. They don't, I said. The coon has too good a nose. And sometimes in the fall, I said, an osprey might fly up from tidewater just to vary its diet. With feral goldfish, I explained. Low-sodium carp grown fat and juicy in yonder spring-hole; pound-and-a-halfers not uncommon. The idea of goldfish gone wild in the waters of the marsh puzzled the visitor. He said, How did they get here? I said, Maybe the same way gators came to inherit the sewers of New York; they got too big for someone's bathtub. Though I couldn't be sure of that. Whatever the circumstance, it happened before my time at Lonetown Marsh.

Almost all of it happened before my time at the marsh. I mean the developers and their scheme for a shopping plaza right out there in the buttonbush—right on *top* of the buttonbush. I mean Sam Hill and *his* scheme, and one town's dauntless dream that—through open-space planning and preservation—it just might pull into the homestretch of the twentieth century a length or two ahead of the towns around it. "A town is saved," wrote Thoreau of Concord, "not more by the righteous men in it than by the woods and swamps that surround it." A good thought from a good man, and no doubt about the wisdom of it, but better yet the town that saves itself with swamps from within. As this town did. And it all began right here, beyond the glass doors, about twenty years ago. Murphy's Swamp, they called it then. Soon to be known by the folks up in Hartford as COSP (Connecticut Open Space Project) 118.

Open space. One fears the term may soon be lost to common usage. Not that it ever tripped lightly off the American tongue, for it lacks a certain magic—the specificity of "park," the poetic cachet of "wilderness." To speak of open space in some quarters is to invite a furrowed brow, a drooping eyelid. What is it, after all, but vacant land, an empty quarter, the smallest of blanks on the map? Has anyone ever heard of a National Open Space? Of course not. Only villagers speak of open space, and city planners grown long in the tooth; and when they do, it is likely to be with a fair measure of nostalgia for the good old days—nineteen sixties turning seventies—when the successful pursuit of open space was a political phenomenon out of all proportion to the numbers of players in the game. On that score, I'd be the last to complain. Had it been otherwise, the neighboring turf here might have become a shopping mall instead of the sanctuary it did become under COSP 118.

It has been said that open space was begat by the American Dream, in the golden fantasy that the good life could be had with a home in the suburbs and a patch of lawn (with herbicides to hold down the crabgrass). Almost since the end of World War II, Americans by the millions had been flocking to suburban and exurban places: Marblehead and McLean, Pepper Pike and Pleasant Prairie, Tiburon and Torrance. They came first to the burghs at the city's edge, and filled them up, and then moved on to fill the next tier of shade-tree towns down the glimmering highway. Why not? It was a cinch, then. The GI Bill and five percent interest on the mortgage. Down came the shade trees, up went the houses. And in came the *city*. Folks said, It can't happen here. Those folks were wrong. Suddenly they were looking at this great big crack in the picture window of their American Dream.

A sense of what had been lost to the dream, not to mention the prospect of bulldozers scalping the village commons, brought forth reactions. Among the first and most effective was a report issued in 1960 by the Regional Plan Association of New York City: *The Race for Open Space*. Conceived by the visionary planner Stanley Tankel, the study showed that at its current rate of growth, the twenty-two-county New York metropolitan region was likely to lose as much land to urbanization in one generation as had been settled and built upon over the preceding two hundred years. To a great extent, *The Race for Open Space* was a seminal document in the landsaving effort that would follow, as were Ann Louise Strong's *Open Space for Urban America* (for the U.S. Department of Housing and Urban Development) and the writings of William H. Whyte (for the Outdoor Recreation Resources Review Commission, among other sponsors). Meanwhile, the idea of open space was attracting a constituency—in the town-government communities of New England, in the suburbs of Chicago, in the San Francisco Bay area. And in New York City, Richard H. Pough was putting together the Open Space Action Committee, with the writer Charles E. Little at its helm to dispense the procedural information. The word spread fast. By 1965 open-space preservation had become the environmental leitmotif of the region. It wasn't all rhetoric, either. In that same year, Congress for the first time offered to municipalities, through their state resource agencies, a share in the growing largess of the Land and Water Conservation Fund. And none too soon, for in this particular municipality, Murphy's Swamp was ready to slip through that crack in the American Dream.

When it all began in 1965 there were two maps on the table, and the marsh figured centrally on both of them. One was a plan of development prepared at the behest of the gentleman who owned the marsh and its adjacent uplands. His name was Murphy. The other was a draft open-space plan prepared at the behest of the chairman of the town's conservation commission. And his name was Samuel E. Hill.

In fairness to Murphy, I should explain that the shopping plaza was somebody else's idea. It had appeared on yet another map, somewhat earlier, at a time when town planners could look at a wetland such as Murphy's Swamp and see no value in it. According to the prevailing wisdom of those days, wetlands were wastelands. They were uliginous mosquito factories. So someone suggested that Murphy's mosquito factory might make a capital site for a shopping center, a kind of development then much in vogue. To what extent the idea may have been kept alive by Murphy's own plan is unclear, for the first map on the table in 1965 showed only nine building lots, though Lot #2, at five acres, looked just about right for that mall.

Sam Hill's map, of course, was altogether different. It proposed that Murphy's Swamp be acquired by the town as dedicated open space. And not only Murphy's Swamp, but the valley of the Little River, and the Dayton Tract down south by Devil's Den, and the deep woods around the falls of the Saugatuck River. And even more. Why, if you took a closer look at Sam Hill's open-space map you would have seen his magic marker squiggled around—good grief!—not twenty, not two hundred, but two thousand unacquired acres of rough-and-tumble land.

It took Sam Hill about a year to get his plan adopted as a town policy goal; some folks thought it a mite ambitious. As for acquiring Murphy's Swamp—well, there were still a few townspeople around who felt that this was sheer nonsense. Dangerous, too. It was said, for example, that Murphy's "muck hole" contained certain treacherous areas of "bottomless quicksand." It was said that unsuspecting schoolchildren would be swallowed in the ooze. And then there were the Murphys to contend with, and long negotiations over price. Yet Hill prevailed. In November 1966 the conservation chairman brought his first acquisition proposal to a special town meeting. The question: Would the town appropriate $14,000 to buy a 7.5-acre swamp? The answer, without a murmur of opposition: Yes indeed.

The schoolchildren. Like the great blue heron, they come in season to Lonetown Marsh. They troop up the trail through the woods on the other side, straggle Indian-file along a short boardwalk through sedge, and finally emerge upon a small and rustic observation platform which constitutes the sanctuary's only concession to recreational development. Or, rather, call it a concession to the children's education, for they come from our school across the road not to play but to see how wild things work out there in the real world. An "outdoor classroom," some people like to call it—though I suppose one could conduct a class in a shopping plaza and call *that* the outdoors, too.

This morning, the children on the platform across the marsh appear to be very young. Seven-year-olds, maybe. Eight, nine . . . it's hard to read a person's age through binoculars at two hundred yards. I watch the class in session. I wonder what their teacher is telling them about the real world. What these children hear and see today, out *there*—it could make a difference. Who knows? Twenty years from now it could help them to patch and protect the American Dream.

As dedicated open space, the marsh was ten years old, a mere stripling, when I moved here, up from the precincts of New York City, up from sewer-gator country. But that's no proper way to read a wetland's age. Better to think of the place as a venerable ancient, hunkering under the southern slope of a glacial drumlin, the left-behind ice grinding a shallow hole for itself, then rotting, the water pooling, and now a pond slowly filling with its own organic decay, and now a sedgy marsh with a stream cutting through. No doubt at one time or another the water level has been such that one could not properly call it a marsh—the snag trees attest to that. Possibly a swamping occurred when a small wooden gate was placed at the marsh's outlet to facilitate improvements to State Highway 107, locally known as Lonetown Road. Swamp or marsh, it is all the same to the blackbirds and kingfishers; though for anthropocentric druthers I suppose that Lonetown Marsh strikes a richer chord than Murphy's Swamp. (Sure, and only a Murphy could disagree.)

The place we bought into here predates Murphy's plan, or Hill's plan; goes back, in fact, to a time when no one planned anything because they didn't have to. Goes back to a time when, if you owned the land, whether wet or dry, you could dig it up or fill it up or—if you'll pardon the English—screw it up. They knew how to screw it up good back then. To make the place we bought into, they trucked in fill to bury a slice of Lonetown

Marsh. What's done is done. No blood on *our* hands. We, the beneficiaries.

Down past the realigned edge of the marsh, under the leaf-shedding maples and trespassing over a property line into neighboring private turf, I come to a sanctum sanctorum—the girthy relict stub of a fallen tree. Only the heartwood remains, sun-bleached and wrinkled and deeply grooved, as though it had passed through some kind of time warp, through the lost horizon of a sylvan Shangri-la. I touch it. I ask, Are you oak or chestnut? The wood does not answer. I suspect it is chestnut. Surely it is old enough to have been living here before the blight, and what a huge specimen it must have been, larger even than my leaning oak. I'll bet it dominated the whole near side of the marsh—who can say otherwise?—for a hundred years. I'll bet it was a climbing tree for boys in high starched collars and buckle shoes. They probably went up it like monkeys, up to the highest branches overlooking the marsh. Truants and mischief-makers, probably; playing hooky and robbing birds' nests. And getting educated to the way wild things work out there in the real world. I am sure there were blackbirds and kingfishers then, and coons, and otters, too, maybe; but no goldfish. And no gardens nearby for the snappers to lay their eggs in. Without gardens, doubtless the snappers had better luck. Or maybe the coons had better luck. Without garbage cans.

Looking into Lonetown Marsh, I sometimes find the mind wandering off to other open spaces in our town—such salubrious places as the Rock Lot and Grouse Run and the Noose and Fall's Hole and Bogus Brook, and that pool in the Little River where the peripatetic (or, as his doubters would have it, the mythic) Trapper Henderson fell from a swinging grapevine and almost drowned (only sprained his ankle, say those familiar with the Little River). Preserved—each one of these places and many more, as permanent natural areas. Snatched right off the top of the auction block. And largely because of the foresight and feisty perseverance of Samuel E. Hill, who started it all right here at Lonetown Marsh.

The name of the game in those days was grantsmanship, and Hill was a master of it. Having cajoled the town into appropriating and spending $14,000 to secure the marsh, he then proceeded to recoup three-quarters of that sum by filing an application—COSP 118—for state and federal assistance through the Land and Water Conservation Fund. Bingo! He got it. And then went after more. Again the community, by unanimous town-meeting vote, committed itself to an appropriation—this time, of $1.3 million. Again Hill fired off the applications to Hartford and Washington. And scored almost every time, not only with the state resource agency and the U.S. Interior Department (which administers the Fund), but with the Department of Housing and Urban Development's open-space grants program, as well. By 1975 Hill's aggressiveness as a landsaver had secured for the town nearly a thousand acres of open space. He was, said First Selectman Mary Anne Guitar on the fifteenth anniversary of the Lonetown acquisition, "a prophet with honor in his home town."

In the business of landsaving, there is a saying that you can win the battles but never the war. A place cannot truly be saved forever, for folks or forces of one kind or another will always be wanting to carry it off in little pieces, until nothing is left. And so it is beyond the glass doors.

Not that anyone still speaks of drainage and building lots. Or shopping centers. I do believe we're past all that. Nowadays the threats are subtle and oblique, and come packaged in the guise of zealous management or cloaked within the concept of "multiple use." And sometimes, too, old Mother Nature shows her remorseless, impartial hand, reaching out to set the clocks a little faster—the alarms a little louder—than we might otherwise like or expect them to be. Consider the phragmites, for example. Those incursive reeds have been doing what comes naturally ever since the state highway folks started improving the shoulders of Lonetown Road. Today there is a wall of phragmites along much of the highway-side of the marsh, and some aficionados of wetland ecology are raising alarms to the effect that phragmites may soon take over the entire marsh. I doubt it. But I do not doubt that the reeds bear watching. As well the purple loosestrife there. Take it off, some swampers say. Take if all off. I say, Let's wait and see. And of what's there, Just let it be.

The current disdain for reed and loosestrife reflects, to my way of thinking, a commitment to zealous management. Let's not kid ourselves. Within almost every paleolithic sneakerface preservationist beats the heart of a weed-hating neolithic gardener. Bad habits are hard to shake. Now a few zealous manager types are raising alarms about the goldfish. The way they tell it, the damn fish, like sharks in a feeding frenzy, are nibbling away the roots of the tussock sedge. No matter that the fish in turn feed the herons and the kingfishers. Save the sedge! How? Poison the fish! Turn the whole marsh over, clean sweep. I ask, But what about the snappers and the frogs, and the bullheads, too? No answer. But that's all right. The frogs have friends.

In fact, the frogs and their friends figured prominently in the latest rhubarb over Lonetown Marsh. And so did our volunteer firemen. It happened like this. The firemen wanted to improve the marsh as a source of water for fire-fighting purposes. They said that the school across Lonetown Road might burn right to the ground if the conservation commission did not promptly give them a permit to dig a hole at the edge of the marsh—a hole from which their pumpers might draft a sure flow of water. From the firemen's point of view, the consy commissioners were anything but prompt. The consies wanted to know if there were not alternatives to a hole in the marsh. The consies wanted to know what sort of environmental impacts might be involved. And all of this took time. There were harsh words and letters to the editor. The consies, said the assistant fire chief, were only interested in one thing: "Save the frogs and let the school burn down." People took sides, mostly the side of the firemen. After all, who but a consy could love frogs more than schoolchildren? Ultimately the matter was resolved by First Selectman Guitar (a former consy commissioner herself), who came up with an engineering solution calculated to reduce the impacts to an acceptable level. So, after all the fuss, the firemen got their hole in the marsh, but only a little one and with attached conditions restricting its use. And what did the frogs get, besides a gigging in the press? Sometimes it's hard to tell about frogs. They were awful quiet last summer.

The business of landsaving, Lonetown style, has fallen of late on hard times. There are, to be sure, a number of organizations across the country—the Nature Conservancy, the Trust for Public Land, to name just two—that are still very much in the race for space. And so are a few of the states. But at the municipal level, and especially the small-town municipal level, all the old sound and fury of landsaving has been largely reduced to a muffled croak. I am reminded by Arthur Davis, director of resource policy at the Western Pennsylvania Conservancy, that "people generally scratch where they itch." Nowadays, he says, "it's pretty hard to persuade people they need a bond issue for a park when the town's just laid off its road crew."

Even in the best of times, few towns could afford to go it alone. Like ours, most municipalities look to the federal government for assistance. Now the sources of that assistance are either shut off altogether, as in the case of Housing and Urban Development's open-space grants program, or cranked down to a trickle, as in the case of Interior's Land and Water Conservation Fund.

The day's winding down, now. Beyond the glass doors a softer light has fallen across the marsh. Sundown, soon, and only the treetops a-glitter as she goes. I'll want to catch that, down the path under the maples, down past the antique stub of the climbing tree at the edge of the marsh.

The edge of this marsh is a good place to live, if you like frogs and mosquitoes (though never enough frogs, and never too many mosquitoes). This *town* is a good place to live. If you like open space. Twenty thousand acres, seven thousand people. And only sixty-five miles from sewer-gator country. Abutting towns of Ridgefield, Danbury, Bethel, Newtown, Easton, Weston, and Wilton. General Israel Putnam bivouacked his brigades here in the winter of 1779; the Noose, in the Gallows Hill Natural Area, is shamelessly named to commemorate the hanging nearby of two Redcoat spies. Charles Ives, the music man, lived here once upon a time. As did Edward Steichen, the photographer. And Samuel Clemens, the creator of Huckleberry Finn. Matter of fact, Sam Hill's last bingo COSP—numbered 329—secured 160 acres of the former Clemens estate. The old curmudgeon—that's Clemens I'm referring to—called the place Stormfield. Buzzards roost there now, on a high ledge above the Saugatuck River.

Once upon my own time, I felt a measure of guilt for living here. Not because my city friends got to calling me "Squire"— pshaw, I preside over barely three acres of land (not counting the marsh, which belongs to everyone). But guilty because, with so much open space here and so little of it almost everywhere else, it struck me as inequitable. O, the ratiocinations of the parlor liberal. I am the wiser now, guiltless. And full of reasons why this town needs every acre of open space it can get. To preserve its country atmosphere. To maintain natural diversity. To protect our water resources—as an aquifer for ourselves, as a reservoir for the region. O, the platitudes of the paleolithic sneakerface. Who needs *reasons*? As my open-space mentor Charles Little used to say, "It is well to remember, sometimes, that the fern fiddleheads do not ask to be justified."

Enough. In a moment or two, I am going to make myself a martini and carry it down the path to the time-warped stub of the climbing tree. I am going to place one hand upon the wrinkled heartwood and, with the other, raise my glass in a toast. To the long-gone open-space grants program of the Department of Housing and Urban Development—may it rest in peace. To the Land and Water Conservation Fund—may it rise from the almost-dead under the auspices of better times, and may it disburse its land-acquisition funds to the towns that missed out the first time around. To my predecessors on the battlefronts, my benefactors. To Sam Hill and those who succeeded him as chairman of the conservation commission. To Clois Ensor, our open-space trail boss—may his twenty-five miles of hiking paths stretch out to fifty. To Mary Anne Guitar, co-founder of our local land trust, the conservationist "mayor"—may the example of her leadership prevail until the marsh fills up with phragmites and goldfish scat. To our autumn visitor, the heron. To the coon and the snapper. To the treetops. To the last light.

INDEX

357